Europe since 1945

Europe since 1945 is an exciting new survey of the history of Europe since the end of the Second World War. In the second half of the twentieth century Western Europe has known a period of peace and stability unprecedented in its history and virtually unparalleled in the rest of the world. *Europe since 1945* explains the reasons for this state of affairs. Thought-provoking and wide-ranging, the book discusses political, economic, social and cultural change in modern Europe. Covering both Western and Eastern Europe comprehensively and featuring extensive analysis of the 1990s, this book includes examination of:

- the Cold War
- war at the edges – Northern Ireland and Yugoslavia
- the European Union
- the issues of Nationalism
- the end of the dictatorships
- economic prosperity, the EEC and the Euro
- the break-up of the European Empires and the consequences.

Europe since 1945 is an important introduction to modern European history from the end of the Second World War to the new millennium.

Philip Thody was Emeritus Professor at Leeds University and the author of *An Historical Introduction to the European Union* (Routledge, 1997) and *The Fifth French Republic* (Routledge, 1998).

To the memory of Alan Milne, 1922–1998

'Of manhood the man, of courage the brave, of wisdom the wise. I saw no flaw in him.'

King Faisal of Iraq on T.E. Lawrence, adapted.

Contents

Foreword

Philip Thody was a phenomenon. A distinguished academic and teacher, he ranged across discipline and period with an ease, skill and panache which astonished peers, colleagues, readers and students.

I was fortunate enough to work with Philip on three books, including *Europe since 1945*. He was a model of professionalism with all his publications. The most wonderful company, he was as at home with Wodehouse's Blandings as with Sartre, and spread jewels of insight and kindness around him.

We would like to thank Professor Edward Spiers for undertaking so carefully all the editorial queries associated with the book.

Heather McCallum
Senior Editor, Routledge

Acknowledgements

Fred Bridgham, Bill Johnson and Tony Verity read through long sections of this book and made invaluable suggestions for its improvement. All mistakes are my own.

Europe since 1945 should be read in parallel with David Childs's admirable *Great Britain since 1945: a political history* (Routledge, 1997). Professor Childs's approach is broadly sympathetic to the left. Since there is no such thing as neutral discourse, readers should make allowance for the fact that my views are more conservative.

Philip Thody
Leeds 1999

Part 1 *Peace at the centre and war at the edges*

Prelude

Peace in Europe – exceptions and explanations

DEFINITIONS

In the autumn of 1939, less than 21 years after the signature of the armistice of November 11, 1918 which put an end to the fighting in the First World War, Great Britain and France were once again at war with Germany. Twenty-one years after the end of the Second World War, in May 1966, the only dispute dividing France and Germany was a technical question of finance in what was then known as the European Economic Community (EEC). Should part of the customs duties levied on agricultural produce entering the Community be allocated centrally by the authorities in Brussels, the arrangement preferred by the Belgians, the Germans and the Dutch? Or should all the money remain under the exclusive authority of the Community's six member states, the idea inspiring French policy at the time?

The adoption of the first solution would have constituted the first step towards the unification of Europe on a federal basis. The decision to keep the money under the control of the individual nation states would have meant something different: a Europe organised on the much more traditional lines which de Gaulle defined as 'l'Europe des Patries', a co-operation between sovereign states still in full possession of their traditional powers.

Great Britain was not involved in this particular quarrel. It was still smarting under the humiliation of having had its application to join the European Community vetoed by Charles de Gaulle on January 14, 1963. It was nevertheless preparing, this time under a Labour administration, to make a second application for membership, only to see it once again rejected by de Gaulle, on November 27, 1967. Both vetoes were to give rise to some sharp exchanges between France and its five partners in the EEC. There was also, in the autumn of 1967, still some lingering resentment in Belgium, Holland, Italy, Luxembourg and West Germany at the way France had used the 'empty chair' policy between June 30, 1965 and January 1, 1966, in order to assert the principle of 'l'Europe des

Patries' over that of a federal Europe, preferred by the Germans, Dutch and Belgians.

The idea that these arguments might give rise to anything but some sharp words over a conference table, or to a series of acerbic comments in the newspapers or on the radio, was nevertheless unthinkable. Twenty-one years after the ending, on May 8, 1945, of the war which had begun in Europe on September 1, 1939 with the German invasion of Poland, and gone on to involve virtually every country in the world and to cause some 38 million deaths, the countries of Western Europe seemed finally to have put away the habit of going to war against one another.

So, too, though for different reasons, had the countries of Eastern Europe. Charles de Gaulle always spoke of Europe as that part of the world which went, as he put it, 'from the Atlantic to the Urals', and there is an anecdote in Eric Newby's 1978 travel book, *The Big Red Train Ride* which suggests that his definition is less eccentric than some of his later policies. 'Finally', writes Newby:

> at kilometre mark 1777 (1110 miles) from Moscow and a measly height of 1345 ft above the sea, we had a fleeting vision of a white obelisk to the right of the line with EUROPE on one side and ASIA on the other (in Cyrillic).[1]

Geographers and historians both agree with what the obelisk says. For all the cultural as well as political problems which it raises, the narrative as well as the analysis in this book is based on the idea that Europe includes western Russia.

Politically this inclusion can be justified by the fact that between November 1917 and December 1991 the Russia which dominated the former Union of Soviet Socialist Republics spent 76 years trying to put into practice a set of economic theories developed by the quintessentially European Karl Marx (1818–1883), an exiled German Jew whose best-known work, *The Communist Manifesto* (1848) was first published in Paris. Even the Cold War, the event which dominated not only European but also world history between 1945 and 1989 can be seen as an essentially European event. From the point of view of the ideas involved, it was primarily a struggle between two essentially European views of society. It was only incidentally a contest between geographical entities such as Russia and America.

It is true that Edmund Burke (1729–1797) had given some hint of a purely Russian threat to Europe when he commented on first partition of Poland, in 1772, 'Catherine has breakfasted in Poland. Where will she dine?'. But there was no question of Catherine the Great (1729–1796) imposing a different social system on any of the territories falling within the influence of the Russian empire. In the Cold War, what was at stake was precisely the ideology in whose name Europe should be governed: that of Karl Marx, or that of the thinkers who had inspired the idea of parliamentary democracy found in the United Kingdom or the United States.

Communism also had European origins, having been based on Marx's analysis of what had happened to the British working class during the Industrial Revolution of the late eighteenth and early nineteenth centuries. The first volume of Marx's most important book, *Das Kapital* (*Capital*), was published in London in 1867 and based in large part on research carried out in the reading room of the British Museum. When Marx died in 1883 and was buried in Highgate cemetery, one of his most famous statements, the eighth of his *Theses on Feuerbach* (1845), was engraved on his tombstone. It read 'Philosophers in the past have sought only to understand the world. Our task is to change it.'

It is this idea which made the philosophy adopted by the leaders of the Soviet Union so thoroughly European. The tyranny they exercised over their subjects may have been Asiatic, but their wish to change society was European. It was as far removed as could be imagined from oriental fatalism, or the acceptance of a pre-ordained divine will.

What is now more frequently referred to as free-market economics also had its intellectual roots in Western Europe, where it had inspired the English Revolution of the seventeenth century, the American Revolution of 1776 and the French Revolution of 1789. When Emerson (1813–1882) said that 'Europe ends at the Alleghenies; America lies beyond',[2] he was talking of a period when much of the West was still uncharted territory with its own distinctive culture. Since the end of the nineteenth century, this has changed. In almost every respect it is in the United States of America that European culture has found its ultimate and logical expression.

Thus the view of society inspiring the creation of the United States of America was based on the ideas of Englishmen such as John Locke (1632–1704), Scotsmen such as David Hume (1711–1776) and Adam Smith (1723–1790), and French philosophers cast in the mould of Montesquieu (1689–1755) and Voltaire (1694–1778). The contrast between the kind of society stemming from Locke and Voltaire and the one inspired by Marx and Lenin (Vladimir Ilych Ulyanov) is reflected in the difference between the way in which peace was maintained after the end of the Second World War in the countries east of the Elbe and the way in which it has prevailed since 1945 in Western Europe.

Thus while the countries of Western Europe, which had been liberated in 1944 and 1945 by the armies of the English-speaking democracies, gave every appearance of having quite freely chosen to put earlier quarrels behind them, those dominated by the Soviet Union were given no other option. Not only were these countries required, under the threat of force, to abandon their earlier quarrels, and thus to enjoy a particular kind of peace; they were also left little choice as to the way they organised their economic and political life. If they tried to alter the order imposed upon them, either the use or the threat of military force made them change their minds.

In the nineteenth century, the fact that the German-speaking area of Pomerania and Silesia had been taken from Germany by the peace settlement of 1945 and given to Poland would have almost certainly led the Germans to mount an invasion to recover the lost territories, and this is what Churchill thought would happen. 'One day,' he wrote in 1954, 'the Germans will want their territory back, and the Poles will be unable to stop them'.[3] It was, for once, an inaccurate prediction. Until the ending of the Cold War in 1989, the eastern part of Germany was firmly under the control of the Soviet Union, while in the west, the Federal Republic of Germany was far too busy integrating itself into the new Europe represented by the European Economic Community to have any thoughts of trying to win back lost territory.

EXCEPTIONS

The account of the Cold War in Chapters 1, 2 and 3 suggests some reasons why neither the hostility between Marxism and capitalism, nor the enmity between Russia and America, nor the opposition between Europe and Asia, gave birth to open warfare. Chief among these, of course, is the existence of nuclear weapons, which kept the peace in a way which their inventors had neither intended nor predicted. Where there was no possibility of their being used, as in the former Yugoslavia, the peace which prevailed was of an unusual and less satisfactory kind. There was fighting between different groups, and the horrors of war were there in all their cruelty and terrifying reality. But there was no organised warfare between states.

Thus even in the former Yugoslavia, where from 1991 onwards Serbs, Bosnians, Kosovan Albanians and Croats fought one another with great ferocity for the control of territory, they did so primarily as ethnic groups. Although there was state terrorism, especially from Serbia, there was no formal declaration of war. While units of the Serbian army wore uniforms, most of those whom they were fighting did not. And at no point did any of the sides involved make an official statement of its war aims. The fighting was thus of a different type from that which had led either to the dynastic wars of the past, or to the combination of religious passion and political ambition which, in the Thirty Years War of 1618–1648, had led to the loss of one-third of the population in the German-speaking area of Western Europe. It was also different from the wars of the French Revolution and Napoleonic empire, or from the conflicts which had caused the bloodshed of the two World Wars of 1914–1918 and 1939–1945.

As in Northern Ireland, the violence reflected religious differences as well as ethnic hatreds. Christians from the Greek Orthodox Church fought Roman Catholics, both attacked Muslims, and Muslims attacked both. This fighting came to a partial end with the Dayton agreements of 1995, after air strikes by planes from the North Atlantic Treaty Organisation (NATO) had compelled the Serbian government to moderate its behaviour, only to flare up again in an even more violent and tragic form in early 1999 in Kosovo. But there was, again, no formal declaration of war, any more than there was when the British army used force against both the mainly Catholic-inspired Irish Republican Army and Protestant-based organisations such as the Ulster Volunteer Force. It did so in support of the civilian authorities, and acted more as an auxiliary police force than as a formal fighting unit.

When, in April 1999, aircraft from the NATO alliance attacked targets in Serbia, they did so without a formal declaration of war. The countries which sent them, principally the United States, Great Britain and France, did so for motives absent from almost all military conflicts of the past. They were not seeking to defend either their own territory or that of one of their allies. They had not been directly challenged by Serbia, and there was no conceivable gain that any of them could make by way of either treasure or territory. They were, perhaps for the first time in history, making war for totally humanitarian motives. Their desire to protect the Kosovan Albanians was also inspired by another feeling, which had been absent from the reasons inspiring countries going to war before 1945: that of guilt. Although the violence which they were seeking to prevent came from a country over which they had no control, and in whose initial establishment they had played no part, they still felt responsible for crimes which its forces were committing. This feeling was constantly reinforced by the media, which insisted that the conflict taking place in the Balkans was either 'at the heart of Europe' or at 'Europe's back door'.

In both the former Yugoslavia and in Northern Ireland, the situation was thus quite different from the one which led to the wars of 1948–1949, 1967 and 1973 in the Middle East. Then it was the official armies from the Arab states which were trying to destroy Israel, and were doing so for the motive inspiring most of the wars of the past: that of acquiring territory. In Bosnia-Hercegovina and Kosovo the fighting was also different from the 1980–1988 war between the two Muslim states of Iran and Iraq. There, as in the armed clashes between India and China in October 1962, organised armies confronted one another along internationally recognised frontiers. When J.M. Roberts remarked, commenting on the accession of Ghana to independence in 1957, 'in the next 27 years, twelve wars were fought in Africa and thirteen heads of state were assassinated'[4], he was again talking about wars of a traditional type, undertaken for the defence of territory already acquired or with the desire to expand one's frontiers. Compared to what has been happening elsewhere, and with the exception of what has been happening in the Balkans since the early 1990s, the Europe born of the Second World War has known a period of peace and stability unprecedented in history, and for which the only contemporary parallel has been the states of Central and South America.

Why, since it is obvious from the behaviour of human beings in other parts of the world that violence still remains the dominant way of settling national and political differences, has most of Europe been so peculiarly blessed?

EXPLANATIONS

THE COLD WAR

The first and most obvious reason for the long European peace which followed the ending of the Second World War is the existence of a threat from the East. On March 6, 1946 an openly political description of this threat was given by Winston Churchill, when, in a speech at Fulton, Missouri, he described how:

> From Stettin in the Baltic to Trieste in the Adriatic, an iron curtain has descended upon the continent

and added that behind it there lay the majority of the ancient capitals of Eastern Europe. All of them, as he put it, were

> subject, in one form or another, not only to Soviet influence but to a very high and increasing measure of control from Moscow.

What the Soviet Union wanted, as he put it, was 'not war but the fruits of war, the indefinite expansion of their power and doctrines', and the events which followed his speech seemed to confirm his analysis of the USSR as an aggressive and predatory state which would seek to extend its power by every means except the firing of guns. If the countries of Western Europe have refrained from violence against one another since 1945, it was because between 1945 and 1989 almost all of them were involved on the same side in the Cold War against the Soviet Union. Once the Soviet Union had exploded its first atomic bomb, on or about September 22, 1949, there was the constant danger that, if the Cold War went hot, it would almost immediately become nuclear. This gave rise to a salutary awareness, on both sides, of how fatal it would be to the existence not only of civilisation but of human life itself if any crisis were to be allowed to escalate into open warfare.

It would be idle to pretend, at least in the immediate post-war period, that the French felt very keen on linking their fortunes to those of the Germans or the Italians. The Belgians were unenthusiastic about having very much to do with the country which had already invaded them twice, while the Dutch found it hard to forgive the brutality with which the German invasion of 1940 had destroyed the neutrality they had enjoyed between 1914 and 1918. In August 1974 Turkey sent a large military force to protect the Turkish-speaking inhabitants of Cyprus against what it alleged was an imminent attack from their Greek-speaking neighbours. In earlier days such an action might well have given rise to prolonged fighting involving other powers. However, since Greece and Turkey were both members of the North Atlantic Treaty Organisation – the alliance set up on April 4, 1949 to protect Europe against any possible incursion from the Soviet Union – no exchange of fire disturbed an admittedly uneasy peace.

Needs must when the devil drives, and by 1950 the countries of Western Europe had come together in a series of alliances unparalleled in the history of the continent. The most important of these were the military ones: the Treaty of Dunkirk, signed on March 4, 1947, the Treaty of Brussels, signed on March 17, 1948, and the treaty establishing the North Atlantic Treaty Organisation, signed on April 4, 1949. By the 1990s the countries of Europe were members of so many different military, political and economic organisations that the most convenient way of summing up their relationship with one another was to make a list of acronyms: WEU, NATO, ECSC, EEC, EFTA, EC, Euratom, EU, EMU, and CSCE (Western European Union, North Atlantic Treaty Organisation, European Coal and Steel Community, European Economic Community, European Free Trade Area, the European Community, the European Association for the Development of Atomic Energy, the European Union, the European Monetary Union and the Council for Security and Co-operation in Europe).

The existence of the most important of these military alliances, the North Atlantic Treaty Organisation, emphasises another aspect of the history of Western Europe since 1945: its virtually total dependence for its defence on the United States of America. The treaty establishing NATO marked a fundamental change in American foreign policy. In 1945 America was giving every sign of reverting to the isolationism which had characterised its foreign policy throughout the nineteenth century and which had led Congress, on January 20, 1920, to refuse to join the League of Nations. Indeed, at the Yalta conference in February 1945, President Roosevelt had spoken openly of his intention of removing all American soldiers from Europe within two years. Now the United States was committing itself in advance to the defence of Western Europe.

It was doing so, however, on the understanding implicit in the establishment of the North Atlantic Treaty Organisation: that there would be an end to the quarrels which had divided the continent of Europe in the past. There was, it is true, a political price to pay, though one which proved very small in comparison with the price which might have been exacted if the countries of Western Europe had been required instead to accept the help of the Soviet Union. In 1919, in the immediate aftermath of the First World War, the French poet and essayist Paul Valéry had already commented that Europe would be punished for its political behaviour, 'deprived of wine, beer, and other things', and his prophecy had become even more tragically true for the people who were dying of hunger in Europe in 1945. But, at the same time, the prediction implied by Valéry's remark that 'Europe clearly longs to be governed by an American commission' had also come true; and it is part of the good luck which has marked the history of Western Europe since 1945 that we should have been compelled to behave ourselves by what Valéry calls 'those happy people who will impose their good fortune on us'.[5]

Thus the North Atlantic Treaty Organisation was complemented by the Marshall Plan, which from 1947 onwards provided the money for the economic revival of Western Europe. The twin existence of these organisations meant that Europe ceased to be the continent where wars began and were then exported to the rest of the globe. It became, instead, the prize in the contest between two superpowers, which then seemed destined to share the world between them. The last time a European politician made a decision which changed the course of history was when Hitler, on December 11, 1941, declared war on the United States. It was, from every point of view except his own, the most fortunate mistake ever made. Not only did it lead President Roosevelt to give priority to the need to liberate Western Europe over the need to defeat Japan. It also ensured, once the Americans had at one and the same time freed Europe from Hitler and saved Western Europe from being liberated by Stalin, that the United States would find itself unable to abandon the countries of Western Europe to the threat of Soviet expansionism.

One of the main reasons for the long European peace of the second half of the twentieth century thus lies in the coming together of two factors: the perceived threat to the independence of Western Europe created by the foreign policy of the Soviet Union; and the readiness of the United States to offer to do the Europeans' fighting for them. The four aims of NATO, real enough if not written down in any official document, were to keep the Americans in, the Russians out, the Germans down and the French quiet.[6] If it has not been entirely successful in the fourth of these aims, the first three have been accomplished with quite admirable efficiency.

The readiness of the Americans to do the Europeans' fighting for them was made necessary, in the 1940s and 1950s, by the fact that the Europeans themselves did not have the resources to do their own fighting. In a number of cases, they also lacked the necessary will or unity of purpose. One acronym not mentioned above, the EDC or European Defence Community, designates an organisation which a vote in the French parliament on August 30, 1954 prevented from coming into existence. It was a vote in which French nationalists, and especially the members of the *Rassemblement du Peuple Français* established by Charles de Gaulle, joined forces with members of the French Communist Party, an organisation which had already indicated that, if a war broke in Europe between the United States and the Soviet Union, it would side with the latter.

It was nevertheless the French government, in which neither the Communists nor the Gaullists were then represented, which had already taken the first step towards the movement towards European unification that offers a second reason why the nations of Europe have stopped going to war with one another. It had done so in collaboration with the government of the Federal Republic of Germany, the régime officially established on May 23, 1949 – and whose democratic nature clearly distinguished it from the two régimes whose armies had invaded France in August 1914 and May 1940.

From 1951 onwards, it was the movement of positive reconciliation between the two countries whose rivalries had been the root cause of so many European wars from the sixteenth century onwards which helped to lay the foundations for the long European peace of the second half of the twentieth century. The Treaty of Versailles, which had put an end to the First World War in 1919, deprived Germany of its colonies, required it to recognise that it alone had been responsible for the outbreak of the war in 1919, and required it to pay reparations for the damage inflicted by its armies on Belgium and France. No attempt was made to help Germany recover from the damage which the war had inflicted on society, and it was the punishment inflicted on it as a pariah nation which helped lay the seeds for Hitler's rise to power.

For a variety of reasons, one of which was the need to ensure a common defence against the Soviet Union, the same treatment was not inflicted on the Germany of 1945. Instead, it was given every help to recover, both through the Marshall Plan and by the readiness of French politicians to put an end to the centuries-old enmity between the two countries. Germany's guilt for the 1939–1945 war was so obvious that it did not need to be underlined by any article in a treaty. What was seen as essential was the need for it to be put back on its feet again as quickly as possible, both to avoid the growth of more resentment and to remove the danger of a power vacuum in central Europe which the Soviet Union might quickly occupy.

THE MOVEMENT TOWARDS EUROPEAN UNITY

On April 18, 1951 France and Germany signed the Treaty of Paris establishing the European Coal and Steel Community (ECSC), and were joined by Italy, Belgium and the Netherlands. This was followed, on March 25, 1957 by the Treaty of Rome establishing the European Economic Community (EEC). Originally, this existed by the side of the ECSC and Euratom, the organisation for the peaceful development of atomic energy. Then, on July 1, 1967 the executive bodies of these three organisations merged to transform themselves into the European Community (EC). On December 1, 1991, by the signature of the Maastricht Treaty, this became the European Union (EU), which on January 4, 1994 effectively absorbed the rival organisation, the European Free Trade Association (EFTA), established at the initiative of the United Kingdom on January 4, 1960.

The aim of the ECSC, acknowledged at the time, was to make war between France and Germany impossible by giving control of what were then the essential industries of coal and steel to a supranational body. Its transformation into the European Economic Community, and then into the European Union, has certainly played a central role in enabling the countries of Western Europe not only to live together in peace but also to work together in a number of specific economic contexts. It is nevertheless best seen as a result of the absence of warfare between the states of Western Europe rather than as a major cause of it. It is hard to imagine it happening, at least in its initial stages, outside the context of the Cold War, and it is unlikely to have worked in the absence of the other major reason why the states of Western Europe have remained at peace with one another since 1945: none of them has either wanted to dominate the others or has had the military means to do so.

EXHAUSTION AND GUILT

Thus Germany, the country which had defeated France in the war of 1870 and whose aggressive policies had given rise to the wars of 1914–1918 and 1939–1945, had undergone the most comprehensive defeat ever inflicted on a modern state. Its industry had been destroyed, over five million of its population had been killed, and its principal towns lay in ruins. It had been divided by its conquerors into four zones, none of which enjoyed any genuine political autonomy. It was also about to be required to recognise, in all their horrifying detail, the reality of the policies which had led to the murder of six million Jews, as well as to the atrocities carried out by its soldiers on the civilian populations of all the countries they had occupied.

In 1919 the German General Staff's skilful presentation of the defeats inflicted on the armies of the Second Reich in the closing months of the

1914–1918 war had created the myth of the 'stab in the back', the belief that only the treachery of the civilian politicians had led to Germany failing to win the war and thus to its being required to sue for an armistice in 1918. Just as the French, after their disastrous defeat by the Prussians in 1870, had longed for 'la revanche', the opportunity to right the wrong done to them by the loss of Alsace–Lorraine to the newly united Germany, so the Germans of the 1920s and 1930s came to be inspired by the desire to recover the dominant position which, in their view, they ought never to have lost.

It had therefore been possible, in the 1920s and 1930s, for German nationalists to present the death in battle of 1,700,000 soldiers between 1914 and 1918 not as a tragic waste incurred as the result of the pursuit of a fundamentally misguided policy, but as a blatant injustice crying out for vengeance. There had been, after 1918, no trials for war guilt or for crimes against humanity, and no readiness on the part of the Germans themselves to accept that what had happened was their own fault, and not that of a small number of treacherous politicians. In 1945, in contrast, for the first time in the history of Europe, the citizens of what had been a sovereign state were tried and punished by its conquerors. Through their behaviour between 1939 and 1945, the Germans had lost everything, including the right to the possession of a legal system whereby they could pass sentence on the crimes committed by their own citizens. It was only later, after the establishment of the Federal Republic of Germany on May 23, 1949, that the Germans themselves took over the task of punishing those of their fellow citizens who had committed the worst of the atrocities of the Nazi era. By 1970, German courts had prosecuted 12,900 persons suspected of offences and imprisoned 5,200 of them, 76 being given life sentences.[7]

It is a sign of the extent to which both the Christian and the humanist tradition had penetrated the German mind that there was, at the time, no serious attempt in Germany itself to protest against this ultimate deprivation of sovereignty, or to call into question the judgement of the Nuremberg tribunal. The doubts expressed about this came from Winston Churchill, who commented to one of his colleagues that they had better make sure they won the next war. Whereas the Japanese, whose war crimes both against civilians and against prisoners of war inspired the same justifiable horror, never acknowledged their guilt, the Germans did. It was only later, on December 7, 1970 when Willy Brandt knelt in front of the Warsaw Ghetto Memorial to express remorse for the crimes committed by the soldiers of the Third Reich, that 48 per cent of those questioned in an opinion poll sponsored by Der Spiegel thought that his gesture was 'overdone'.[8]

The readiness of Europeans to acknowledge guilt for their political behaviour marked a new step in history, and one which has profoundly altered the attitudes to the use of violence adopted by the politicians and religious leaders of both Eastern and Western Europe. When, in Northern Ireland, civilians are murdered by either the IRA (Irish Republican Army) or the UVF (Ulster Volunteer Force), churchmen from both the Catholic and the Protestant communities express contrition as well as condemnation. It is impossible to imagine Martin Luther (1483–1546), who in his 1525 pamphlet *Against the thieving and murderous hordes of the peasants* urged the German princes to show no mercy in repressing the revolt of their subjects, ever thinking that he was not quite preaching the central message of the Gospel. It is equally difficult to think of the Duke of Alva (1508–1582), who from 1567 onwards tried to drown the revolt of the Protestants in the Low Countries in blood, feeling regret or guilt for actions of the Spanish forces under his command, much less giving voice to it.

The basic reason why Japan has issued no apology for the behaviour of its forces between 1935 and 1945 is that the Shintoism which still forms the basis of Japanese culture is based not on the concept of guilt but on that of face. To say that you are sorry means the loss of face, and this is something which you are not prepared to endure. For all the dramatic changes which have taken place in Chinese society since the Communist victory of 1949, it still remains imbued with the Confucianism which has dominated it from before the time of Christ. Like Shintoism, this is an essentially worldly philosophy, whose principal concerns are the respect due to one's ancestors and observance of correct social behaviour. Since this eschews the fundamentally European concept of guilt, there has been no expression of regret for the violence and state-inspired terrorism which – inspired by the teachings of, and organised by, Mao Zedong – caused some twenty million deaths in China during the Cultural Revolution of the late 1960s.

When, in the Middle East or elsewhere, atrocities are committed by groups claiming allegiance to Islam, any criticism or apology emanating from Muslim leaders, whether of the Shi'a or Sunni persuasion, never seems to reach the world press. They may express it, but they find little success in making it known in the West or in influencing the behaviour of their more enthusiastic followers. Since there is no single spiritual head entitled to issue formal statements of belief on behalf of Islam, there is also no possibility of an equivalent to the document about to emerge from Rome, in which, as the London *Daily Telegraph* put it on September 25, 1998, the Vatican asks for

> pardon for the 'sins' committed over the last 2000 years including the outrages committed in God's name during the Crusades.

The almost automatic condemnation of violence by religious leaders has, until now, been a phenomenon peculiar to the culture of Western Europe and to the civilisation of North America, which Europe has directly or indirectly inspired. This new attitude on the part of the religious leaders of the West may have been a minor factor in the disappearance of organised warfare from Western Europe. But, since 1945 it has become one of the most widespread attitudes officially adopted not only towards violence by the leaders of virtually every state in Europe, but also towards all forms of religious or racial persecution.

When, on March 31, 1994 King Juan Carlos of Spain knelt by the side of President Chaim Herzog of Israel in a Madrid synagogue to express regret and remorse for the expulsion of the Jews from Spain five centuries previously, it was a gesture which paralleled the action of Willy Brandt, the former Mayor of West Berlin and Chancellor of the Federal German Republic, when he had knelt in contrition before the memorial in the Warsaw ghetto. In neither case had the man concerned been personally involved in any of the atrocities. Indeed, Willy Brandt had frequently been criticised in Germany itself for having fought on the side of the Norwegian resistance movement in the Second World War. But both men spoke on behalf of the majority of their fellow citizens.

If it is possible to define Europe other than in purely geographical terms, it is this readiness to admit responsibility for the crimes and errors of the past which is one of its most attractive, as well as one of its more recent, characteristics. It lies deep in European culture, and the fact that Mr Yeltsin should have been reported in the *Daily Telegraph* on September 19, 1998 as being about to apologise for the Soviet invasion of Czechoslovakia in 1968 came as no surprise to anyone who had read the novels of Dostoevsky. The characters in his novels are forever telling everyone how sorry they are for what they have done. The Slavonic soul may have not have a gift for the intellectual analysis that has distinguished the European mind since it first came to birth in the Athens of the fifth century before Christ, but the passion for repentance is one of the features which marks out the Russian mind, and Russian culture, as being as thoroughly European as the most fervent admirer of traditional Christianity could possibly wish.

The disappearance of organised warfare from the continent of Europe since 1945 is thus the result of a combination of factors: the impact of the Cold War, the rise of the movement for European unification, the lack of desire by any country of Western Europe to dominate its neighbours, and the fact that the major European powers were too exhausted to go to war with one another. These factors have combined with the relatively new, and peculiarly European, habit of feeling guilty for political crimes, and this has been coupled with the lack of fervour in religious matters which has come to characterise most Europeans. This has meant that the kind of organised warfare pursued by Catholics and Protestants against one another in the seventeenth century is as outdated as the weapons used at the time. Even in Northern Ireland, the conflict between Catholic and Protestant has taken the relatively new and characteristically twentieth-century form of urban guerrilla warfare. It has not, as it did in the seventeenth century, received any support from the organised churches.

There has, however, also been another factor: the virtually universal acceptance, even in the countries east of the Elbe, of some form of parliamentary government. This has not always brought with it either the political or the economic benefits which its less experienced admirers originally expected it to produce. But it has borne out the truth of Winston Churchill's observation that democracy is the worst possible form of political organisation except for all the others. It is also a phenomenon which can just as easily be classified either as a consequence or as a cause of the long peace by which the vast majority of Europeans have been blessed in the second half of the twentieth century.

THE DISAPPEARANCE OF DICTATORSHIPS

Compared to what has gone before, the apparently universal appeal of parliamentary democracy is as welcome an achievement and as agreeable a change in Europe as the disappearance of organised warfare. In 1939 two of the major states in Western Europe were dictatorships; Italy had been one since 1922, and Germany since 1933. On April 1, 1939 the victory of General Franco in the civil war which had begun in 1936 marked the abolition of democracy in Spain, whose neighbour Portugal had already become a dictatorship in 1926. Belgium and the Netherlands, it is true, had remained parliamentary democracies, as had France. But the speed with which, on June 18, 1940, the Deputies and Senators of the Third Republic voted by a majority of 569 to 80, to give supreme power to Marshal Pétain and establish the authoritarian Vichy régime, is a reflection of the limited nature of the appeal which parliamentary democracy made to the French in the 1930s and 1940s.

In central and eastern Europe, Austria had been swallowed up in Hitler's Reich by the *Anschluss* of March 12, 1938, while the one state in eastern Europe which did seem to have a viable democratic system, the Czechoslovakia created by Versailles settlement of 1919, was dismembered by the Munich agreement of September 1938 before being invaded and taken over completely by Germany on March 15, 1939. Poland had been a dictatorship since 1926, while in the Soviet Union, any early hopes that the Revolution of 1917 might give rise to a form of democracy recognisable as such in traditional, western terms had been killed off long ago by Stalin's dictatorship.

In 1975 the death of General Franco put an end to the last dictatorship in Western Europe. France, somewhat to the surprise of his detractors, had remained a parliamentary democracy after the return to power of Charles de Gaulle in 1958, while in Portugal the death of Salazar in 1970 was followed in 1974 by the creation of a valid system of democratic government. There had been no problem in restoring parliamentary government to the Benelux countries of Belgium, Holland and Luxembourg, and – although the Italian electoral system produced so many rival parties that by the end of 1998 there had been 57 different coalition governments – this instability had not prevented the country from achieving an unprecedented level of economic prosperity. The ending of the Cold War in 1989 was rapidly followed by the disappearance of the dictatorship of the Communist Party in all the countries east of the previous Iron Curtain except the former Yugoslavia.

There is no necessary link between the two blessings currently enjoyed by the majority of Europeans, the absence of inter-state warfare and the existence of parliamentary government. In spite of the arguments put forward by Immanuel Kant in his *Project for Perpetual Peace* (1795), parliamentary democracies can and do go to war with one another. In August 1914 the socialist deputies in the Reichstag voted for the war credits necessary for Germany to go to war against France. The left-wing members of the *Assemblée Nationale* replied in kind, and there was little dissent at Westminster when Great Britain declared war on Germany on August 4. But parliamentary régimes are much less likely to take the initiative in going to war than are dictatorships. The first moves in the 1914–1918 war came from the Austrian, German and Russian empires, countries in which civilian control over the army was either non-existent or highly theoretical. It was Hitler's dictatorship, aided and abetted by that of Stalin, which caused the Second World War, a conflict which the parliamentary régimes of Great Britain and France had done everything they could to avoid. It was also the defeat of this dictatorship which ushered in the long peace which is one of the main blessings enjoyed by Europe since 1945.

THE IMPACT OF PROSPERITY

Another factor working towards peace in Western Europe, as indeed in other parts of the world, has been the prosperity of the post-war period, and especially of the golden years between 1949 and 1973. In spite of the various crises to have affected the world economy, especially in the late summer and early autumn of 1988, there has so far been no equivalent to the Wall Street crash of October 24, 1929, and consequently nothing like the Great Depression of the 1930s which enabled Hitler to seize power. The prosperity of post-war Europe did indeed suffer what turned out to be a temporary setback brought about in the autumn of 1973 by the sudden increase in oil prices decreed by the Arab-dominated

Organisation of Petroleum Exporting Countries (OPEC). But, unlike the crash of 1929, this setback did not inspire either a movement towards protectionism or the rise of a new hostility between the states affected by the increase in the price of oil.

In the past, and especially if the Marxist theory of international relations had been true, the sudden shortage of as invaluable a source of energy as oil might have been expected to give rise to an intense rivalry, culminating in open warfare. What is most remarkable about the aftermath of the oil shock of 1973, discussed in more detail in Chapter 9, was that nothing comparable happened in Western Europe. It did not increase international tension among the members of the European Communities, and it did not have the effect desired at the time by the Arab countries: that of blackmailing the West into allowing the Palestine Liberation Organisation to fulfil its proclaimed desire of driving all the Israelis into the sea.

During what may yet come to look like a lost paradise, it is this remarkably long period of affluence enjoyed by the Western industrialised world which offers yet another possible reason for the absence of armed conflict on the continent of Europe in the second half of the twentieth century. Like the inhabitants of Australia, North America and countries such as Japan or Malaysia, Western Europeans have become steadily richer. They have also learned to enjoy an increasingly hedonistic life-style, and have consequently no desire to forfeit their wealth, their wine, their foreign holidays, or the increased opportunities for sex afforded by the contraceptive pill, in exchange for the hypothetical advantages of military glory.

As John Keegan commented in his 1998 Reith lectures *War and Our World*, warfare has become primarily an occupation of the poor, and is fought with simple weapons which they can afford. Many of the 800,000 Tutsis killed in Rwanda in 1994 and 1995 were, he points out, 'hacked or bludgeoned to death'. Even when modern technology is involved, it is in the form of what he calls 'the cheap assault rifle'.[9] Perhaps not surprisingly, the readiness, and even eagerness, of the poorer nations of the world to go to war gives them a considerable advantage over the economically satisfied nations, which do so only with reluctance.

Between the beginning of the Vietnam War in 1964 and the withdrawal of Soviet troops from Afghanistan in 1988, the two most powerful countries in the modern world, the United States of America and the Soviet Union, were defeated by volunteer armies from two of the most poverty-stricken countries of the Third World. In the spring of 1999 the most expensive and sophisticated fighter-bombers of the North Atlantic Treaty Organisation took almost two months to stop the ethnic cleansing of the Albanian-speaking inhabitants of Kosovo by Serbian infantry armed with rifles and bayonets. Had the NATO powers been able and ready to use ground troops, they might have succeeded. But the richer a nation becomes, the more reluctant does it become to send its young men to be killed.

The signature of the North Atlantic Treaty on April 4, 1949 had been preceded in 1947 by the offer by the United States of economic aid under what was known, from the Secretary of State who launched the idea, as the Marshall Plan. It was the arrival between 1948 and 1952 of over six billion dollars in aid which provided the basis for the success of the European Economic Community as well as of the economic revival of Western Europe as a whole. The sums of money involved were not particularly large, expressed as a proportion of the Gross Domestic Product both of the donor nation and the recipients. Six billion dollars was less than one per cent of the annual American GDP. The money received by the United Kingdom was under two per cent of its annual GDP, that received by France less than six per cent, Italy five per cent and Germany seven per cent.[10]

The money arriving in Western Europe was nevertheless enough to perform the pump-priming function advocated by Keynesian economics, and the psychological impact was immense. In 1924 the President of the United States, Calvin Coolidge (President from 1923 to 1929) gave a succinct reply to the question of why America was insisting on the repayment of its enormous war debts by the Europe which had just ruined itself by the 1914–1918 war: 'They hired the money, didn't they?'. The contrast with the attitude inspiring the Marshall Plan could not have been greater.

When Francis Fukuyama followed Kant's example by arguing in *The End of History and the Last Man* (1992) that democratic countries do not go to war with one another, he emphasised that this was especially the case in periods of prosperity. When Herbert Hoover, President of the United States between 1929 and 1933, said 'the business of America is business', he was expressing an attitude which has increasingly become that of the Western Europeans. However regrettable this may seem to the moralists who deplore the triumph of what they call purely materialistic values, it bears out the wisdom of Dr Johnson's adage that a man is seldom more innocently employed than when making money.

THE ABSENCE OF MOTIVE

In the eighteenth century, one of the main reasons for the Seven Years War of 1756 to 1763 between France and England was the rivalry over which power should dominate India and North America. The French lost, and avenged themselves for their defeat by successfully supporting the American colonists in the rebellion against England in 1776, and thus helping to bring about the end of the first British Empire. An important side-effect of the British victory over the French in the Napoleonic wars was the confirmation by the Treaty of Vienna, in 1815, of British sovereignty over the Cape of Good Hope, over the country then known as Ceylon (the modern Sri Lanka), over Tobago, Saint Lucia and Mauritius. Although colonial rivalries between the European powers never led to any fighting between them on the continent of Europe after 1815, they were always there as a cause of friction – as when they threatened to bring France and Britain into conflict for control of Egypt at the Nile in the Fashoda incident of September–November 1898. As late as 1942 de Gaulle was so convinced that Great Britain was trying to replace France as the dominant power in the Middle East that it is very difficult, when reading the second volume of his *Mémoires de Guerre*, to remember that he was, at the time, officially at war with Germany.

In March 1905, and again in July 1911, the apparent desire of the Germans to claim authority over Morocco had almost provoked a war, first of all with France and then with Great Britain, and certainly contributed to the tensions which led to the war of 1914–1918. But the Versailles treaty of 1919 deprived Germany of all its colonies, and the only European colonial adventure since 1945, the Suez expedition of October–November 1956, saw France and Britain fighting side by side. They did so with a remarkable lack of success, and Chapter 13 analyses the Suez fiasco against the general background of the failure of all the attempts made by the countries of Western Europe to hang on to their colonies after 1945.

The armies of France and Portugal, and to a lesser extent those of Great Britain, were involved in military activity outside Europe, and Chapters 11 and 12 look in more detail at the conflicts in Algeria, Angola, Cyprus and Indochina, as well as at the impact which the failure of the European powers to win these wars had on political life in Europe itself. But in no case did the Europeans fight one another. The conflicts were between the Europeans on the one hand and their previously subject peoples on the other. There was, consequently, no risk of the fighting spreading to the continent of Europe itself.

THE RECURRENCE OF A PATTERN

It is not essential that a nation should acknowledge its guilt before ceasing to act in an aggressive and predatory manner. In spite of the refusal of its leaders to apologise for the appalling crimes committed by its armed forces between 1937 and 1945, Japan has ceased to offer a military threat to its neighbours. It has been too busy in the equally harmless activity of making money: an area in which, at least until the late 1990s, it proved remarkably successful. At an earlier period in European history, France never said it was sorry for the slaughter caused by the

Napoleonic wars, any more than it did after the failure of its bid for supremacy in Europe under Louis XIV. But after the final defeat of Napoleon at Waterloo on June 18, 1815, France undertook no more wars of conquest.

In this respect, the long period of peace which Western Europe has enjoyed since 1945 is not an entirely new phenomenon. As Graham Evans and Jeffrey Newman point out in their *Penguin Dictionary of International Relations*, the 'Concert System' established after 1815 led to a situation where there were no wars between the Great Powers for over forty years. Between 1815 and 1859, the only fighting on the continent of Europe was in the Crimean war of 1854–1856, in which the armies of France and Great Britain finally defeated those of the Russian empire in a campaign to prevent it from assuming the right to protect the Christians in the Turkish empire. Evans and Newman also refer to the statistics put forward by the American scholar Quentin Wright in 1964 in *A Study of War*, to show that there has been, as they put it, 'a decline in frequency in Europe from the sixteenth and seventeenth centuries to the nineteenth and twentieth', resulting in the fact that 'whereas in the early period European states were more often at war than not, by the twentieth they spent less than one-fifth of their time at war'.[11]

If one thus relies on the actual number of wars fought, rather than on the casualties inflicted, the wars of 1914–1918 and 1939–1945 can be seen less as the culmination of an increasingly disastrous tendency than as a pair of aberrations interrupting the development of a general pattern. This pattern is also reflected both in the small number of the wars fought between 1815 and 1914 and in the limited nature of their objectives. The Crimean war of 1854–1856 was successful in its immediate aims, and was followed by an equally brief war of France against Austria in 1859. This, too, was successful, in that the battle of Solferino, on June 20, 1859, ensured that Austria would no longer hinder the process of Italian unification. But in neither case, unlike the campaigns of Hitler or Napoleon I, were they wars of conquest. Once the immediate objective had been attained, the fighting stopped.

Bismarck also completed the process of German unification by three short wars, the first against Denmark in 1864, the second against Austria in 1866 and the third against France in 1870. But these were all wars which remained under control, in the sense that they were fought for a specific and limited purpose. There was no attempt to impose a new political system on the defeated adversary, as there was when Nazi Germany invaded the other countries of Western and Eastern Europe in the 1930s and 1940s, and as there would almost certainly have been in Western Europe if the Soviet Union had won the Cold War. Between 1871 and 1914 Europe enjoyed almost as long a period of peace as it has been given us to savour since 1945, and it is tempting, in this context, to agree with the thesis put forward by A.J.P. Taylor when he argued in his 1963 study, *The First World War*, that it was the result of a series of accidents rather than of a deep-laid plot on either side.

It is in the context of what happened after the defeat of France in 1815 that the long peace which has reigned among the nations of Western Europe since 1945 fits into another general pattern. Only after the defeat of a power seeking to dominate Europe has the continent been able to enjoy a period of relatively prolonged peace. Only after the Austrian Habsburgs had seen their bid for domination defeated by France in the Thirty Years War of 1618–1648 did Spain and Austria cease to threaten the peace of Europe. Only after the armies of Louis XIV and Napoleon I had lost their power to threaten their neighbours did France become a country whose foreign policy was essentially defensive. And only after the defeat of Hitler's armies had completed the job left unfinished in 1919 could both Eastern and Western Europe finally begin to live in peace.

Happy peoples have no history. Unhappy ones endure events which require a lengthier narrative and more detailed explanation. The study of the two areas in Europe which did not share in the long peace which followed 1945, Northern Ireland and the former Yugoslavia, brings out by contrast some of the reasons which so many of the inhabitants of Western Europe have to count their blessings. These blessings have not, however, been brought about merely by a combination of happy accidents. They are the result of a mixture of shrewd judgements and considerable political courage, especially on the part of President Truman, of President Eisenhower, of President Kennedy and of President Reagan. Without the decisions which they took, and the risks they chose to run in order to protect the inhabitants of Western Europe during the long years of the Cold War, the continent now celebrating the progress to unity embodied in the arrival of a single currency could have been one where no-one was left alive to weep over the unity of a smouldering heap of radioactive ruins.

1 The contest for Western Europe (1)

The Berlin crises of 1948–1949 and 1958–1962

PRELIMINARIES

When, in 1921, Lenin said that, 'Whoever holds Berlin, holds Germany. Whoever holds Germany, holds Europe',[1] he provided in advance the central key for an understanding of the form which the Cold War took in Europe. This may indeed have begun, as Caroline Kennedy-Pipes argued in 1995, with the Bolshevik Revolution of October 1917.[2] It was not until after 1945 that it became a central issue in world politics, and did so primarily in the form of struggle for the domination of Western Europe.

Although this struggle continued, in an attenuated form, until the fall of the Berlin Wall on November 9, 1989 marked the beginning of the rapid end of the Cold War, the main issue was virtually decided by 1962. The most important consequence of the success of President Kennedy in forcing the Soviet Union to remove its nuclear missiles from Cuba in October 1962 was the ending of the attempt by Mr Khrushchev to compel Great Britain, the United States and France to remove their forces from West Berlin. After 1962, as far as Western Europe was concerned, the Cold War took a different form: that of a confrontation about the level of intermediate-range nuclear weapons that each side should be allowed to keep in the part of Europe which it dominated.

Outside Europe, where not a single shot was exchanged between the two main contestants, the Cold War was a struggle which involved actual fighting. 'South America and sub-Saharan Africa', writes Martin Walker:

> continents which had been largely spared the earlier struggles, were sucked into its maw. Turks fought in Korea, Algerians fought in Vietnam, Cubans fought in Angola, and American and Russian schoolchildren, whose lessons had been interrupted by nuclear air-raid drills, grew up to die in Saigon and Kabul.[3]

There was also another difference between the form which the Cold War took within Europe and the way it was fought in the rest of the world. In Western Europe, with the possible exception of Italy in the late 1940s, when the CIA intervened to make sure that the Communist Party did not win the Italian election of April 1948,[4] the United States defended governments which enjoyed genuine democratic legitimacy. In South Korea or South Vietnam there were serious doubts about the support which the population gave to their government. This did not apply in Western Europe, and especially not in West Berlin.

BACKGROUND

The Berlin crisis of 1948–1949, like the later crises of 1958–1960 and 1961, arose because of two factors: the arrangements made for the future of Germany at the conference held between the United States, the Soviet Union and Great Britain at Yalta, in the Crimea, between February 4 and 11, 1945; and the fact that between 1944 and 1945 the Soviet Union had acquired mastery over a swathe of territory in Eastern Europe which was larger than Spain and Portugal, and gave no sign of being prepared to give it up. Had Stalin waited a year or so, until the effect of his behaviour in Eastern Europe immediately after 1945 had worn off, his actions might not have evoked so immediate or so effective a response. But in 1948 memories were still vividly alive of how the Soviet Union had used force, fraud and threats to install satellite régimes in all the countries occupied by its armies after 1945.

One of the advantages which Stalin derived from the Nazi–Soviet pact of August 23, 1939 had been the clause whereby Germany and Russia were to share Poland between them. Even after the German invasion of Russia on June 21, 1941 had theoretically made the Poles and the Russians into allies fighting on the same side, Soviet policy towards Poland remained essentially that of an enemy to a conquered foe. Already, between March and April, 1941, 4,143 Polish officers had been killed by the Russians in Katyn, and in August 1945, when the Polish resistance rose in rebellion against the Germans in Warsaw, the Red Army deliberately held up its advance in order that the Germans could more easily defeat the uprising and save them the trouble of killing more Poles on their own account.

Once the Second World War was over, the Soviet Union consistently refused to allow free elections in the countries which it had occupied, and insisted on installing puppet régimes in Bulgaria, Poland, Hungary and East Germany. If the dissident Yugoslav leader Milovan Djilas is to be believed, Stalin had no illusions as to the lack of genuine popular support for these régimes. 'This war,' he said in a conversation taking place in the spring of 1945:

is not like the wars of the past; whoever occupies a territory also imposes on it his own social system. Everyone imposes his own social system as far as his army has power to do so. It cannot be otherwise.

Later in his book, talking about conversations which he had with them early in 1946, Djilas reports Stalin and the other Soviet leaders as having told him that all Germany should be theirs, that is to say, governed according to the precepts of Soviet Communism. Djilas attributes this to their being 'caught up by the flush of military victories and by their hopes for the economic and political dissolution of Western Europe'.[5]

The governments of Eastern Europe were not allowed to accept the help offered by the Marshall Plan, which was presented by the Soviet Union as a device whereby American economic imperialism was seeking not only to dominate Europe but to subject European interests entirely to those of the United States. It was this argument which was used on July 10, 1947 to justify its refusal by the Czech authorities.

This refusal, taken under strong Soviet pressure, heightened the unpopularity which was already threatening the survival of the coalition government established in Czechoslovakia after the 1946 elections, and it was that unpopularity which led to the *coup d'état* whereby Czechoslovakia ceased to be the last country in the Soviet bloc with a semblance of democratic legitimacy. On February 25, 1948 the Communists seized power in Prague, and on March 10 the Foreign Minister, Jan Masaryk, was found dead beneath the window of his office. Officially, it was suicide. But it made people wonder about what might happen in West Berlin if the Soviet Union were allowed to behave there as it had done in Czechoslovakia.

CIRCUMSTANCES

In themselves, the arrangements for administering Germany seemed eminently sensible. The Third Reich had lost all moral authority and all effective power. Since Germany was visibly unable to govern itself, it seemed reasonable that it should be divided into separate areas, each of which was administered by a member of the victorious alliance. With some twenty million soldiers and civilians killed by the Germans, the Soviet Union had endured the heaviest casualties. Therefore, in other people's eyes as well as its own, it had acquired the right both to occupy that part of Germany invaded by its armies, and to have a major voice in determining policy towards the country whose soldiers had caused it so much suffering.

The United States had sustained only 291,557 fatal casualties on all the fronts in which its forces were committed during the Second World War. But sixty per cent of these had been in Europe, and the United States had provided the lion's share of the decisive military hardware. It therefore had a right to its share. Without the refusal to surrender of the United Kingdom after the fall of France in June 1940, there would have been no possibility of mounting a liberating invasion of Europe from the West. Great Britain therefore also deserved an occupation zone, hard though it was for it to take on the financial and other burdens which this involved. In 1948, these included the introduction of bread rationing – a measure never found necessary between 1939 and 1945.

Although France had officially been out of the war since the signature of the armistice on June 22, 1940, Churchill successfully insisted on it receiving a zone to administer as well. Whatever problems he may have had in his relationship with Charles de Gaulle, encapsulated in his remark that the heaviest cross he had to bear in the Second World War was the Cross of Lorraine, he recognised the moral and political authority which de Gaulle had acquired by insisting, from June 18, 1940 onwards, that the real France had not given up the struggle. France therefore received not only a zone to administer in the part of Germany occupied by the Western allies, but also one of the four sectors into which the city of Berlin had been divided by its conquerors.

The Soviet Union never really needed to share the administration of the former capital of the Third Reich with anyone. The Yalta agreements stipulated that Berlin should be divided into four zones, each occupied by one of the four main allied powers, but with the whole city under joint allied military control. But, even before the Yalta conference of February 1945, it was perfectly obvious that Soviet troops alone were going to take Berlin, and could therefore do more or less what they liked with it. General Eisenhower had insisted throughout the campaign to liberate Western Europe that the troops under his command would advance on a broad front. In his view, a push to be first in Berlin could have cost up to 100,000 American lives, and he refused to take such a risk for essentially political motives. 'Why', he asked, bearing in mind the agreements already reached with the Soviet Union at the Yalta conference of February 1945, should the Western allies:

> endanger the life of a single American or British soldier to capture areas we shall soon be handing to the Russians?[6]

This meant that the Russians, and the Russians alone, entered Berlin on April 30, 1945. Had they then wished to insist on principle that what they had, they held, there was nothing that the Western allies could have done about it, short of beginning the Third World War before the second one had even finished.

Moreover, the Soviet Union was in a strong position to apply pressure on West Berlin. No formal and legally binding agreement had ever been made whereby the British, French and Americans would have permanent and authorised access to the city by land. Although there were three land corridors carrying traffic by road, rail and barge between Berlin and the West, the use of them was not governed by anything comparable to the very strict rules governing the administration of the four sectors into which the city had been divided. There, even (and perhaps especially) when tension was at its highest, the French, British and Americans exercised their right to have their sectors patrolled by their soldiers, and never failed to reassert the four-power responsibility for the city by each sending a daily jeep into the Soviet sector. But although the symbolic power of armed men in uniform was such as to dissuade the Soviets from any thought of trying to extend their version of what they called 'people's democracy' into the Western sectors, the allies were in a highly vulnerable position. The Soviet Union could, at any time, interrupt land traffic between West Germany and West Berlin. And, between July 24, 1948 and May 12, this was what it proceeded to do.

CHALLENGE AND RESPONSE

By March 1948 the economy of the three Western zones had revived to the point where the Western powers were able to introduce a new, unified currency. The Soviets interpreted this as an unjustified, unilateral decision, and riposted by cutting all the land links between West Germany and West Berlin. In their view, the only currency which should be allowed to circulate in the city was the one which they issued.[7]

Tactically, the Western powers were in a very weak position. To defy the Soviet blockade by sending through a convoy preceded by tanks was difficult and dangerous. In February 1948 the Western allies had only 6,500 combat troops in Berlin, and they were opposed by 18,000 Soviet troops in Berlin itself and 300,000 in East Germany. Any attempt at military intervention thus had more than the disadvantage of being doomed to failure in advance. It would also, in all probability, set off a full-scale war which the West would be unlikely to win without the use of atomic weapons, and even these were not yet sufficiently numerous to be decisive. The Soviet Union always had enough ground forces to counter-attack, and thus transform any land war for Berlin into a full-scale invasion of West Germany.

But if the Cold War did not become hot in Europe in the summer of 1948, it was not because the United States and its allies were ready to back down – as France and Britain had backed down at the Munich conference of September 1938, when they handed over a third of the territory of Czechoslovakia to Hitler. It was because neither side was prepared to fire the first shot, and because the allies had the technological superiority which enabled them to supply West Berlin by air.

Between June 24 and May 12, 1949 the United States Air Force, assisted by the RAF, flew enough supplies into the three western-administered zones of Berlin not only to keep their own garrisons fed, clothed and provided with ammunition, but also to provide food, warmth and industrial supplies for the two-and-a-half million inhabitants of West Berlin, none of whom showed any sign of wishing to exchange their life-style for that of their fellow citizens in the eastern sector.

In all, the American and British air forces mounted a total of 200,000 flights, bringing 2,325,808 tons of supplies which its inhabitants could not get from the Russian-occupied zone surrounding Berlin, and which the blockade prevented from arriving by land. The Soviets could not shoot at the planes, which were using agreed air corridors, for fear of setting off the hot war which both sides were equally anxious to avoid. When, on May 12, 1949, the Russians finally lifted the blockade, it was the first victory of the West in the Cold War, and in many ways the most important. It had shown that the West possessed not only the political will to resist but also the technical ability to do so. On May 23 the country popularly referred to as West Germany officially became the Federal Republic of Germany. The process whereby, as Bertel Heurlin put it in 1996, Germany 'became the real winner of the Cold War',[8] had begun.

THE BERLIN CRISIS OF 1958–1962

PREMONITIONS

In August 1957 the Soviet Union announced that it had successfully tested the first intercontinental missile. If this claim was correct, it could now, in less than half an hour, send nuclear bombs to explode over New York. There would be no need for its planes to penetrate the American air-defence system. A series of rockets would be enough; and any retaliatory strike by the Americans would have to be made by manned bombers vulnerable to Soviet fighters and anti-aircraft fire. Almost overnight it looked as though the Russians had effectively neutralised the American nuclear deterrent which had, for the more pessimistic of the analysts of the Cold War, been the only force restraining them from doing as they wished in Western Europe or elsewhere. On October 6, 1957 scepticism about the Russians' claim to have rockets capable of delivering a payload more or less where they wanted was dispelled by the news, verified by every radio telescope in the world, that the USSR had launched the first man-made satellite, the Sputnik.

Enthusiasm for this extraordinary achievement was tempered by the frequency with which Nikita Khrushchev (who had come to power in 1955, two years after Stalin's death on March 5, 1953) began to remind everybody of the ease with which Soviet rockets could destroy aggressors anywhere in the world. Just as Stalin's actions in Eastern Europe had placed the first Berlin crisis in the general context of what the West saw as Soviet expansionism, so Mr Khrushchev's rhetoric in the summer and autumn of 1958 pointed to the apparent adoption of an aggressive policy which set out deliberately to challenge the West.

American troops were not involved in any fighting in the Lebanon crisis of July 1958, and it was not until October 1973 that there was a serious confrontation between the USA and the USSR in the Middle East. The tendency of Mr Khrushchev to rattle more than the occasional rocket in the summer and autumn of 1958 nevertheless suggested that brinkmanship had ceased to be an exclusively American habit. In late August 1958 the Chinese Communists began a systematic bombardment of the offshore islands of Quemoy and Matsu, still held by the Chinese nationalist army under Chiang Kai-shek, who had retreated to the much larger and more distant island of Taiwan after his defeat by Mao Zedong and the establishment on October 1, 1949 of the Chinese People's Republic.

On August 31 Mr Khrushchev made the alarming announcement that any help given by the United States to the Chinese Nationalists in the event of a liberating invasion of these islands by Communist forces would cause the Soviet Union to come to the fraternal help of their Chinese comrades. Threats and counter-threats between Washington and Moscow led to a mood which the left-wing *New Statesman*, which had by then become the principal organ for the Committee for Unilateral Nuclear Disarmament, described on Friday, September 18 as 'the rim of hell'. In the long crisis which began over Berlin in late Autumn 1958, the ability of the Soviet Union to punish aggressors was mentioned with increasing frequency.

CIRCUMSTANCES

The first Berlin crisis had ended in a series of defeats for the Soviet Union. Not only had Stalin failed to make the United States, France and Great Britain evacuate their forces from West Berlin. He had succeeded, in under three years, in enabling the inhabitants of West Berlin to present themselves to the world as the heroes of freedom. Thanks to Stalin's policy, Germany was no longer the pariah state which it had been in 1945. The main event of post-war European history, the revival of Germany and its renewed preponderance in Western Europe, had begun. It was, in the context of the politics of Western Europe, a highly ironic outcome to a process which had begun in 1870 and 1871 with the defeat of France and the establishment of a united Germany under Prussian leadership. Between 1914 and 1918, and again between 1939 and 1945, France and Britain had fought two World Wars, and lost over two million lives, in order to prevent Germany from dominating Europe. From 1948 onwards, thanks to the policy of a Marxist dictator who had never visited any country outside the confines of the Soviet Union, they found themselves required to co-operate in the process whereby their former enemy became not only their partner and ally, but the country whose need for protection was to be the main preoccupation of their foreign policy.

The Germany created after 1945 by the efforts of the Western allies, and above all by those of the United States of America, was nevertheless a different country from the Second Reich of Wilhelm II, and it differed even more sharply from the Third Reich of Adolf Hitler. Together with Italy, the other country of Western Europe defeated in the Second World War, from 1945 onwards West Germany enjoyed an unprecedented economic revival. But it had also benefited, as one of the fruits of this revival, from the development of a form of democratic government that gave it great attraction in the eyes of the countries of Eastern Europe which it had earlier sought to dominate by force of arms.

This improvement in the image and reputation of West Germany was not the only result of Stalin's attempt to force the Western allies to abandon Berlin in 1948 and 1949. The fears provoked by the Soviet blockade of Berlin, together with the skill and determination with which it was defeated, led to the first decline in the Communist vote in France and Italy since the war. And, perhaps more importantly, it confirmed the fundamental change in the foreign policy of the United States of America, symbolised by the proclamation of the Truman Doctrine in March 1947 and the adoption of the Marshall Plan in June of the same year, and culminating in the signature of the North Atlantic Treaty in April 1949. The collective security whose absence had helped to encourage Hitler's aggression in the 1930s was there, in force, to discourage Stalin's.

The speed with which the United States intervened on June 24, 1950, when troops from the Communist north invaded South Korea, was another sign that Stalin had miscalculated when he agreed to allow the North Koreans to try to unify their country by force. The failure of Soviet foreign policy was ultimately less obvious in Korea than it had been over Berlin. The fact remained that Korea was not unified under a Communist régime, and, as far as Western Europe was concerned, the principal effect of the war was, again, to heighten the suspicion and hostility with which the Soviet Union was increasingly regarded. Although there is little evidence for the widespread belief that, if the United States had not intervened in Korea, Soviet forces would then have attacked Western Europe, the frequency with which it occurred in the continental and even the British press in the summer of 1950 showed how thoroughly any tendency to trust the Soviet Union had disappeared.

PRELUDE BY DIPLOMACY

The inheritance which Stalin left to his successors was thus one in which it was very difficult for them, even if they had wanted to do so, to create a climate in which what they had begun to call 'peaceful coexistence' could become a reality. The phrase was first used in the summer of 1953, during the brief thaw which followed Stalin's death on March 5, 1953, and found practical expression in the signature on May 15, 1955 of the peace treaty which put an end to the four-power occupation of Austria But, while the United States, Great Britain and France had no objection to Austria becoming a neutral country, and thus being forbidden to ally itself either to the Western powers or to the Soviet Union, the same was not true of Germany.

Between January 21 and February 18, 1954 a four-power conference was held in Berlin to try to decide the future of Germany, but reached no agreement. On May 23, 1949, six days before the ending of the Berlin blockade, the three Western zones had officially merged as the Federal Republic of Germany, and on October 7 the Russian-occupied zone, otherwise known as East Germany, had become the German Democratic Republic. The two states were organised on entirely different principles, with capitalism in the West and socialism in the East, and were also, in 1954, on the point of being linked to different alliances. On May 9, 1955 the Federal Republic of Germany became a member of NATO, and on May 14, 1955 the German Democratic Republic became a founder member of the Warsaw Pact, the alliance formed in response to what the Soviet Union always described as the threat of the North Atlantic Treaty alliance.

German unification also seemed a very distant prospect in the 1950s, and indeed for several decades afterwards. On March 10, 1952 a Soviet note to France, Great Britain and the United States of America had made such an offer, but only on the condition that unification should be accompanied by political neutrality. Given that the Federal Republic of Germany had been part of the European Coal and Steel Community, since the signature of the Treaty of Paris on April 18, 1951, this was not an acceptable condition. Although the main political aim of the ECSC was to abolish the possibility of any future war between France and Germany, it was also a treaty which linked the Federal Republic very clearly and very firmly to the Western, capitalist world. This was why the ECSC, like the European Economic Community to which it gave rise in 1958, was so constantly denounced in the Communist press of the time as a 'cold war manoeuvre', a clear indication that a Germany united on Soviet terms would not be able to remain a member either of the ECSC or of the EEC. This is born out by the fact that it was only when Austria agreed to be neutral that Soviet troops began to leave the country in May 1955, and even more so by the fact that it was only in 1995, five years after the end of the Cold War, that Austria became able to join the European Union.

PROPOSALS

The note sent by the Soviet Union to France, Great Britain and the United States on November 27, 1958 was the first ultimatum in the Cold War. It was also (apart from the American insistence in October 1962 that Mr Khrushchev should remove the nuclear missiles which he had secretly installed in Cuba) the only one during the whole period for which the conflict lasted. Other threats in the Cold War always took the form of telling one's adversary that a certain course of action would have serious consequences. No power other than the Soviet Union ever set a deadline for its demands to be met.

The Soviet note gave the Western powers six months to sign a peace treaty with the German Democratic Republic, and to accept the transformation of West Berlin into a 'Free City'. If France, Great Britain and the United States did not agree to the new arrangements by that date, the note added, the Soviet Union would sign a separate peace treaty with East Germany. This would have the effect of putting an end to the right of the allied powers to station troops in West Berlin, as well as to the obligation of the Soviet Union to guarantee access to the city along the three land and air corridors. Any renewal of access rights, the note continued, would have to be negotiated with the German Democratic Republic, declared a sovereign state by the Soviet Union in September 1955.

However, the note also added, the Soviet Union still had treaty obligations to this state, and troops on its territory. Any attempt by the West, after 28 May 1959, to send convoys through to West Berlin would therefore be resisted by force. The implication was that it would be unwise of the Americans, British and French to risk a conflict with a Soviet Union whose rockets could now, as Mr Khrushchev was in the habit of reminding the West, deliver nuclear warheads wherever it chose.

The ultimatum sent to the Western Powers also came at a time when events in central and eastern Europe had once again shown the Soviet Union in a peculiarly unattractive light. On November 4, 1956, less than two years before Mr Khrushchev's ultimatum, Soviet troops had intervened to prevent Hungary from leaving the Warsaw Pact and developing its own version of socialism. It was an action which gave a very clear idea of just how free the 'Free City' of West Berlin would be without the protection of the Western garrison which the Soviet Union seemed so anxious to remove.

It was not, however, solely in this context that the Soviet note of November 27, 1958 took on its full significance. Thanks to Marshall Aid, but more particularly to the enterprise and industry of its own citizens, the Federal Republic of Germany was now the richest country in Europe. In 1955 it had become a member of NATO, and thus had the traditional right of an ally to have its interests protected. While recognising that West Berlin had a separate status and was not technically part of the territory of Federal Germany, the West Germans looked forward to the day – which finally came in October 1990 – when their country would be reunited. When the NATO alliance talked of an attack on one of its members, the initial idea had been that such an attack would be a military one. But a unilateral change in the status of West Berlin, whose inhabitants rejected such a change with virtual unanimity, would have been a moral and political defeat whose effects would have been just as fatal as the loss of a battle.

In the light of what happened, the United States, Great Britain and France acted throughout the Berlin crisis with exactly the right degree of tact and firmness. In spite of hints from the left – *The New Statesman* – that Berlin was not worth the risk of a world war, and from the right – *The Daily Express* – that British lives ought not to be sacrificed to protect the inhabitants of the former capital of the Third Reich, there was no capitulation to the threats, and the inhabitants of West Berlin were not handed over to a régime which they disliked. There was no fighting, and allied troops stayed in Berlin until Germany was reunified. But they did so only after a series of events which, like the blockade of 1948, showed the Soviet Union in an increasingly threatening light, and which emphasised how completely Western Europe depended for its defence on the United States of America.

THE SEARCH FOR A SOLUTION

In February 1959 the British Conservative Prime Minister, Harold Macmillan, went to Moscow and succeeded, with some difficulty, in persuading the Soviets to withdraw their ultimatum. Once this had been done, the West agreed to negotiate.

Talks began in Geneva in June 1959 and dragged on inconclusively throughout the summer. The West would yield nothing of substance, and the Russians had placed themselves in a position where they could not lose face by withdrawing a demand to which they had attached so much importance. Both sides were let off the hook by Mr Khrushchev's acceptance of an invitation – for which he had been angling for some time – to visit the United States. It had been obvious since 1956 that it was he who took the decisions in Moscow, and that the 'collective leadership' which had theoretically followed Stalin's death no longer existed.

Although Khrushchev, in a public debate with Richard Nixon in May 1959 in the model kitchen of an exhibition of Soviet domestic equipment, had promised to 'bury' capitalism and told his hosts that their grandchildren would live under socialism, the idea of visiting the United States obviously pleased him enormously. The visit proved fairly tumultuous, with Mr Khrushchev being very rude on occasion and expressing great indignation at the immorality of the West when attending a rehearsal for the film *Can-Can* in Hollywood. It nevertheless ended in a second withdrawal of any idea of an ultimatum on Berlin and an agreement to hold a summit conference in Paris on May 16, 1960.

ANTICIPATION AND ANTI-CLIMAX

Mr Khrushchev had been wanting a summit conference for some time. His critics in the West, who were fairly numerous, said that this ambition was inspired by what had happened at the wartime conferences of Moscow, Teheran, Yalta and Potsdam, and especially Yalta. The Western statesmen at those conferences, unable to go home without an agreement, had not seriously contested the right of the Soviet Union to hold on to the territory occupied by the Red Army. Mr Khrushchev clearly thought that, if he once got the top statesmen of the world round a conference table, Western public opinion would make it impossible for them not to agree to some of his demands.

As May 16, 1960 approached, however, any solution to the Berlin crisis seemed less and less likely, partly because President Eisenhower had come to realise that any change in the status of West Berlin likely to please the Russians could only be to the disadvantage of the West, but more particularly because of the increasingly close relationship between the French President, Charles de Gaulle, and the Chancellor of the Federal Republic, Konrad Adenauer. The countries always referred to by de Gaulle as 'Les Anglo-Saxons' might be willing to accept a compromise. But no agreement could be reached without France. And France, West Germany's newest and most enthusiastic ally, was not likely to miss the opportunity of annoying the United States by objecting to any settlement which damaged what de Gaulle and Adenauer saw as the interests of Germany and of Europe. Fortunately, what might have become a dangerous public squabble transformed itself in the second week of May 1960 into a harmless, if occasionally frightening, farce.

On May 5, 1960 the Soviets announced that one of their anti-aircraft rockets had brought down a high-flying American reconnaissance plane, a U-2. Since the launching of the Sputnik on October 6, 1957 the United States had been obsessed by the idea that a surprise attack by Soviet missiles might destroy enough of its Strategic Air Command's aircraft to make the American nuclear deterrent ineffective. Memories of December 7, 1941, when the United States had lost a third of its Pacific fleet when the Japanese had attacked Pearl Harbor without any formal declaration of war, were still very much alive, and there was little in Mr

Khrushchev's public behaviour at the time to distinguish him from the dictators of the 1930s and 1940s.

The B-52s of Strategic Air Command were considered in the 1950s and early 1960s as the West's only defence against the overwhelming superiority which the USSR possessed in conventional forces. But the Soviet Union was, at the time, a closed society, and the only way to find out what its armed forces might be planning to do was by spying. As it was, the shooting down of the U-2 and the capture of its pilot, Gary Powers, gave Mr Khrushchev exactly the excuse he wanted to break up a conference which he could now see was going to give him nothing, and to place the blame for its failure on the West. He released the facts about the U-2 in such a way as to show the Americans as lying as well as spying, and made great play with Russian proverbs describing what peasants did to foxes when they caught them in a hen coop. However, on Friday, May 20, after five days of histrionics, he left Paris for Moscow and stopped off in East Berlin. There, in a speech which sent the London Stock Exchange index soaring when business was resumed on the following Monday, he announced that there was no urgency about the peace treaty with East Germany, and no need, for the time being, to change the status of West Berlin.

THREATS RENEWED

The Berlin problem, however, had not disappeared. By 1960 President Eisenhower had come to the end of the second four-year term which the American constitution allowed him. His successor, by only a narrow margin over the Republican Richard Nixon, Eisenhower's Vice-President since 1952, was the Democrat John F. Kennedy. Kennedy was the first Catholic to enter the White House and, at 44, also the youngest President to hold office. He had been a lieutenant in the US Navy during the Second World War, his best-known exploit taking place when the motor torpedo boat he commanded was run down and capsized by a Japanese destroyer. During the Second World War Khrushchev had been Political Commissar at Stalingrad, a city of two million inhabitants which had fought a heroic and successful defence against the Germans that was one of the major turning-points in the war.

At a meeting in Vienna on June 3 and 4, 1961 Kennedy failed to impress Khrushchev with his ability or determination to defend West Berlin. The Soviets still seemed to be ahead of the Americans in missile technology, sending Yuri Gagarin on the first manned spaceship to orbit the earth on April 12, 1961: a fact which Mr Khrushchev often mentioned in his speeches as proof of his ability to destroy aggressors wherever they were found and calm down what he insisted on calling the hotheads in the West. The tension was all the greater in that no precise date was given for what was now presented as the increasingly urgent need for a peace treaty with East Germany. A clash might take place at any time, and the Soviet authorities increased the number of spot checks made on convoys travelling through East Germany in such a way as to give the impression that the blockade of 1948 was about to be repeated.

A TEMPORARY RESPITE

What had been officially known since October 1949 as the German Democratic Republic was, like the Soviet Union, a closed society whose citizens could not travel freely abroad. The protected status of West Berlin made it a natural escape route to the West, and the Soviet threat to change this status made a large number of Germans cross into the western zones of the city before it became too late. A flow of two thousand or more refugees a day struck the Soviet authorities as so serious a threat to the economy of the German Democratic Republic that on August, 13, 1961 they allowed the East German leader Walter Ulbricht to do what he had been wanting to do since 1958: close all crossing points between East and West Berlin to all East German citizens.

In spite of vigorous protests against this change in the status of what was still, theoretically, a city under the joint control of the Americans, the British, the French and the Soviet Union, the Soviet and East German authorities began to build a wall separating East from West Berlin. Between August 13, 1961 and November 9, 1989, when it was dismantled, some two hundred East Germans trying to escape to the West were shot and killed by East German border guards. The wall was not a good advertisement for Communism, and contributed only marginally to a relaxation of tension over West Berlin. Admittedly, it reduced the immediate need for the Soviet Union to change the status of West Berlin in order to stop East Germans using the city as an escape route to the West. But Mr Khrushchev kept repeating the need for such a change, backing up his demand by the resumption of nuclear tests. On September 13, 1961 the Soviet Union exploded a device with the equivalent of 56 million tons of TNT, some 2,800 times more powerful than the first atomic bomb dropped on Hiroshima on August 6, 1945.

The Americans also began testing again, after an unofficial moratorium which had begun in 1958, and commentators compared the behaviour of the two superpowers to that of two gorillas confronting each other in the jungle. Each was puffing out his chest, bellowing as loudly as he could and making his hair stand on end, so as to look bigger and intimidate his opponent. Both, however, seemed to have developed the same kind of inhibitory mechanisms which prevent members of species other than man from carrying their aggression to the point where they do serious damage to each other; in a state of nature, it is extremely unusual for wolves, tigers, scorpions or even rattlesnakes to kill members of their own species. In the winter of 1961 tension over Berlin gradually dropped, and the struggle moved to the other side of the world – to the island of Cuba, in the Caribbean. It was there, in the week of October 22–29, that the fate of West Berlin, and with it that of Western Europe, was decided.

CONFRONTATION IN THE CARIBBEAN

Historians who place the blame for the Cold War on the Americans point to their behaviour towards the states in Central and South America, and especially towards Cuba. Like Costa Rica, Panama and Nicaragua, Cuba had been treated as an economic colony in which the threat or use of American military force kept dictatorial régimes in power in order to perpetuate the exploitation of their inhabitants by American-based companies. Until 1959 the United States had supported the corrupt and tyrannical régime of Fulgencio Batista. When he was finally overthrown in early 1959 by Fidel Castro – who waited until his revolution had succeeded before declaring himself a Marxist – all United States property was sequestrated.

On January 1, 1961 the USA broke off diplomatic relations with Cuba, and from April 17 to April 20, 1961 supported a landing by a group of anti-Castro guerrillas at the Bay of Pigs aimed at overthrowing Castro's régime. In August 1961 the Soviet Union warned the United States of the serious consequences which might strike a country that insisted on behaving in the aggressive manner said to be characteristic of all capitalist and imperialist states, and, once again, mentioned the rockets which the Soviet armed forces had at their disposal to help their friends.

Early in October 1962 a high-flying, U-2 reconnaissance aircraft detected on Cuba signs of the construction of a number of launching pads for medium-range missiles. Further flights confirmed that this was happening, and that the Russians were thus breaking a series of undertakings not to install in Cuba rockets which would be capable of hitting targets in the United States. At eight o'clock on the evening of Sunday, October 22, 1962 President Kennedy made a television and radio broadcast to tell the Americans – and the world – what was happening, and what the United States intended to do. This was to use its overwhelming air and naval strength in the Caribbean to blockade Cuba, both as a means of preventing the arrival of any more material for the rockets, and as a sign of its determination to take further action if these were not removed.

Towards 5.00 p.m. on the afternoon of Wednesday, 25 October there was considerable anxiety, in Europe and elsewhere, as the first Soviet ships approached the 200-mile exclusion zone, and a marked sense of relief as the news came that they had changed course and were heading north. A confrontation on the high seas between two relatively junior naval officers was a situation which President Kennedy feared as most likely to develop into an exchange of fire which could not be controlled, and such an escalation might well have taken place had both sides not been so acutely aware of the destructive power of nuclear weapons. But the deterrent deterred, and – after a week-end of tension in which it became known that the Russians were continuing work on the launch pads and on the rockets already in place, and rumours spread that the Americans were preparing to attack the sites with conventional high explosives – news came that the Soviets had agreed to withdraw the rockets. They had ceased, at least in public, to require the Americans immediately to withdraw their rockets from Turkey in exchange, and were satisfied with an American undertaking not to attack Cuba.

As though by accident, the Berlin crisis then disappeared from the world scene. There was no more talk of the overwhelming need for a peace treaty between the Soviet Union and the German Democratic Republic. Except for a series of brief and inexplicable incidents in October 1963, when the Soviet authorities held up a United States military convoy on the autobahn between West Germany and West Berlin, there were no more hints at the possible renewal of the 1948 blockade. In October 1964 Mr Khrushchev was outvoted at a meeting of the Soviet Presidium, and required to resign from the post of First Secretary which had been the basis of his virtually dictatorial power.

The situation then quietly evolved to the point where, in May 1971, both Germanies signed an agreement whereby the Americans, British and French were given permanent occupation rights, endorsed by the Russians, in a West Berlin which was also recognised as having a particular relationship with the Federal Republic of Germany. Both in Western Europe and elsewhere the Cold War took on a different form thereafter, until it finally ended, as it had begun, in the country which had caused the Second World War and which had become the main prize in the rivalry between the United States and the Soviet Union. On November 9, 1989 the Berlin Wall came down; on October 3, 1990 Germany was reunified; and in June 1997 Berlin became the capital of a reunited Germany.

A very different series of events might have taken place if President Kennedy had allowed the Soviet Union to install its missiles in Cuba. There would have been a pause while the Democrats were allowed to win the mid-term Congressional election (a formality to which the Communist Party in the USSR was not at the time subjected), before new proposals were made about the status of West Berlin. Just as the note of November 27, 1958 had been accompanied by reminders of the Soviet superiority in long-range missiles, so these proposals might have referred to the ability of the USSR to deliver nuclear missiles from a much shorter range, reaching as far west as Dallas, Texas, and as far north as Chicago or Washington DC. An American President who had acquiesced in the installation of such dangerous weapons so close to his borders might not have been believed when he refused to accept any change in the status of West Berlin. A power whose surveillance systems had not noticed what was happening might not have been judged capable of offering military support to its friends.

If such a President had done nothing when the peace treaty was signed with East Germany, and accepted that road and rail links between the Federal Republic and West Berlin had to be renegotiated with the German Democratic Republic, he would have had even more difficulty in convincing anyone of his determination to keep his troops in West Berlin. If, on the other hand, the attempt by the Soviet Union and East Germany to change the status of West Berlin turned out to be based on a false view of American weakness, and the USA had tried to keep open the land routes between Berlin and the West by force, this could have led to fighting with conventional arms which rapidly went nuclear. At no point during the Cold War did the NATO powers feel strong enough on the ground to fight a successful war in Europe without using nuclear weapons.[9]

The withdrawal of the Soviet missiles from Cuba led to an improvement in relations between the USA and the USSR which showed itself in the signature on June 28, 1963 of a treaty banning all nuclear tests above ground, as well as the installation of a 'hot line' between Moscow and Washington to prevent any outbreak of war by accident. Both the Americans and the Russians continued to carry out underground tests, and although Great Britain signed the Test Ban Treaty, China and France did not.

Mr Khrushchev's attempt to put the missiles in Cuba suggested that the USSR did not have the superiority in long-range missiles that he had claimed. Had it done so, he would not have needed to provoke his adversary by probing quite so far into what the Americans had always, rightly or wrongly, considered as their sphere of influence. The belief, assiduously propagated since August 1957, that the Soviet Union had an overwhelming lead in missile technology was thus publicly acknowledged to be a myth. Indeed, it was later discovered that in October 1962 the Americans had at least seven operational nuclear missiles for each Soviet rocket.[10]

Why, then, did Mr Khrushchev take the risk of issuing so blatant a challenge in a part of the world which he knew that the United States considered so peculiarly its own. After all, the Monroe doctrine, which stated that the United States would not allow interference by any European power in any country of the American continent, went back to 1823, and there had never been any secret about its existence. Chapter 2 will suggest some possible answers.

2 The Berlin crises and the contest for Western Europe

Explanations ancient and modern

MODERN ATTITUDES

On January 30, 1950 the State Department authorised the distribution to selected members of the United States Foreign Service of what was known as National Security Document 68 (NSC 68), an analysis of how it saw the aims and objectives inspiring the foreign policy of the Soviet Union. It describes the Kremlin's approach to international affairs as 'utterly amoral and opportunistic', and the Soviet Union itself as 'animated by a fanatical faith which seeks to impose its absolute authority over the rest of the world'.[1]

In spite of his description of the document, from a stylistic point of view, as 'the most ponderous expression of elementary ideas', the American Secretary of State Dean Acheson agreed with the general tenor of its findings. Indeed, he went so far as to say that it showed the foreign policy of the Soviet Union to be 'singularly like that which Islam had posed centuries before with its combination of ideological zeal and fighting power'. Forty-nine years later this particular comparison was taken up in an article by the British historian Norman Davies in an article written for the special issue of *Time* magazine published to mark the introduction on January 1, 1999 of the Euro. Before becoming 'the sick man of Europe', Professor Davies wrote:

> the Ottomans were the major force to be reckoned with. Like the Russian empire, which in many parts supplanted them, they lived on depredation. If the King of Poland, Jan Sobieski, had not triumphed before Vienna in 1683 at the head of his winged hussars, the consequences of a Christian defeat are hard to exaggerate. Edward Gibbon once speculated famously about the might-have-beens if the Muslims had not been stopped by Charles Martel a thousand years before on

the Loire. The Christian victory of 1683 on the Danube merits the same sort of reflection. Perhaps, Gibbon wrote 'the pulpits of Oxford might today demonstrate to a circumcised people the sanctity and proof of the revelations of Mohammed'.[2]

The cultural and ideological consequences of a Soviet victory in the Cold War might have been remarkably similar. Literature in Western as well as in Eastern Europe would have been firmly based upon the principles of Socialist Realism. British athletes would have received the same kind of training which used to enable the representatives of the German Democratic Republic to carry all before them; at the Montreal Olympics in 1976 the GDR won more gold medals than any country bar the Soviet Union, and followed this up with a comparable triumph at Seoul in 1988, when its total of 37 was one more than that of the United States.[3] The Khrushchev Professor of Modern History at Cambridge would have expatiated on the Nature of the Dialectic, demonstrating how inevitably the inner contradictions of capitalism had given rise to the Bolshevik Revolution of 1917 and thus to the classless society predicted by Marx. I should have been out of a job.

The idea that a society's cultural life and political system depend for their survival upon its ability and readiness to use force is a very old one. It is encapsulated in the Latin motto 'Gladius legis custos' (the sword is the guardian of the law). But, as the Greek historian Thucydides (460–400 BC) argued in his *History of the Peloponnesian War*, you do not need to see your adversary as an evil power inspired by the ambition to dominate the world in order to realise that you must resist him. What the first analytically minded historian in European culture showed was that the relationship between sovereign states could be treated with the same moral neutrality and objectivity as the relationship between physical bodies in the external universe.

AN ANCIENT PARALLEL

On December 27, 1850 the English utilitarian philosopher Richard Cobden (1804–1895) made a speech at the Manchester Athenaeum in which he reported that he had 'heard it said that one copy of *The Times* contains more useful information than the whole of the historical works of Thucydides'. Most readers would have little instinctive hesitation in endorsing the remark. Indeed, the war between Athens and Sparta, which began in 431 BC and ended with the total defeat of Athens in 404, was so different from the contest for supremacy in Europe waged by the United States and the Soviet Union between 1945 and 1989 that, at first sight, it is almost perverse to suggest that Thucydides' *History of the*

Peloponnesian War offers one of the most intellectually rewarding ways of looking at the Cold War of 1946–1989.

At the height of this conflict, the combined forces of NATO and the Warsaw Pact countries numbered well over four million men and women. In 1980, the USA had 2,022 launchers for 10,608 nuclear warheads, and the Soviet Union 2,545 launchers for 7,545 comparable warheads. Thucydides describes the battle of Mantinea, in 417 BC, as 'the greatest battle that had take place for a very long time among Hellenic states', but the casualty figures he gives suggest that not more than a thousand men were killed on both sides. In 412, in the greatest disaster endured by either side in the Peloponnesian war, 7,000 Athenian soldiers were taken prisoner in the débâcle which ended the Sicilian expedition launched the previous year. Compared to the millions of lives lost in the Korean War of 1950–1953, the 58,000 American soldiers lost in Vietnam between 1959 and 1975, and, even more, with the estimated million or so Vietnamese casualties, it all seems pretty small beer.

It is also difficult, if not impossible, to maintain that even the history of the eastern Mediterranean, let alone that of the rest of the world, would have been very different if Athens and not Sparta had won the Peloponnesian war. Within seventy years of the surrender of Athens to Sparta in 404 BC the whole of the Greek world was taken over by the vastly superior forces of Philip of Macedon (382–226 BC), whose empire then gradually gave way to that of Rome. In contrast, had the Cold War not ended as it did, the history of the whole world would have been totally different. Either the use of atomic weapons would have destroyed not only society as we know it but also quite possibly much of biological life on the planet, or else the triumph of the Soviet Union would have produced over the whole of Western Europe a society with virtually no resemblance to the pluralistic democracy now seeking to establish itself, not only in Eastern Europe but also in Russia itself.

In spite of all these manifest differences, however, there are parallels between the Peloponnesian war and the Cold War which suggest that Thucydides might have got it right when, in the first chapter of his book, he expressed the hope that, since human nature remains the same, his history of the conflict between Athens and Sparta would 'retain its value for all time'. Indeed, the greater and more numerous the initial contrasts between the two conflicts, the more striking is the fact that Thucydides' analysis of power politics in the eastern Mediterranean in the fifth century BC should be so applicable to the contest for supremacy in Europe which took the form, in 1948–1949, and again between 1958 and 1962, of a crisis over the future of West Berlin. It is even possible that it could throw light on the phase of the Cold War characterised by the argument in the 1980s about the installation in Western Europe of the American cruise and *Pershing* missiles.

One of the questions which Thucydides set himself was to ask why, in 416, the Athenians attacked the neutral island of Melos, conquered it, slaughtered all its male inhabitants, sent the women and children into slavery, and despatched 500 colonists of their own to take it over. He did so in what is known as the Melian Dialogue, in Book V of the *History of the Peloponnesian War*, where a group of Athenian envoys explain to the representatives of the island of Melos why it is in their own best interest to give up their neutrality and join the Athenian empire.

As the Athenians point out, it is necessary for the prestige of Athens as a maritime power that islanders such as the Melians should not be seen as able to defy it by remaining neutral. When the Melians object, pointing out that they are not doing anybody any harm, and basing their claim to neutrality on what would nowadays be called the right to self-determination, the Athenians persist. They draw the attention of the Melians to the fact that their forces are there in overwhelming strength, that neither the Gods nor the Spartans are likely to come to the Melians' aid, and finally justify their conduct by the argument that:

> of the Gods we believe, and of men we know, that by a law of their nature wherever they can rule they will.[4]

It is, naturally, hard to imagine Mr Khrushchev expressing himself with quite such endearing candour when he sent the tanks into Budapest in 1956 or threatened to impose a second blockade on Berlin. But, to see how applicable Thucydides' analysis is, it is enough to carry out a series of substitutions. Once a phrase such as 'the situation of the Soviet Union as a major power on the continent of Europe' takes the place of 'the prestige of Athens as a maritime power', the parallel is made. The comparison is even more telling if the Soviet Union is described as 'the natural and predestined defender of the achievements of the Revolution'. As Pericles (490–429 BC) explains in the Funeral Oration in Book II of the *History of the Peloponnesian War*, Athens had long since come to see itself as the model which all other Greek states ought to imitate.

It is equally easy to see how similarly to the Athenian delegates at Melos Mr Khrushchev would have behaved if, in 1959 or in 1961, he had been allowed to expel the allied forces from West Berlin and had succeeded in making it into what he insisted on calling a 'Free City'. Once the obstacle posed by American, British and French troops to the incorporation of the whole of Berlin into East Germany had been removed, Mr Khrushchev would have been able to rule with all the disregard for consequences which characterised the Athenians at Melos. He might not have killed them all physically, but he would certainly have taken away all their freedoms.

If, as it turned out, he was not finally allowed to 'rule wherever he could', and remove what he referred to as the 'bone in the throat of the Soviet Union', it was because the Western leaders, consciously or not, based their own conduct on the principles which Thucydides presented as inseparable, at all times and places, from the political behaviour of all sorts and conditions of men. If you believe that all states are driven by the desire to rule, and wish at the same time to retain your own autonomy, as well as the freedom of your allies, it is a good idea to treat all proposals, however apparently innocuous, as barely disguised threats. Had the Western leaders not done this in the case of Mr Khrushchev's suggestion that West Berlin should become a 'Free City', it is highly improbable that there would have been a West Berlin for the Wall to come down into on the memorable evening of November 9, 1989 which marked the beginning of the end of the Cold War.

The ambition of Thucydides as an historian was nevertheless not limited to the anticipation of parallels, however telling or unexpected they might be, between the major conflict of his day and those which he saw as inevitable in the future. What he sought to do was discover the laws which govern the way men behave politically, and to do so with a neutrality which has not, so far, been an outstanding feature of most histories of the Cold War. It is this ambition which leads him, in the Melian dialogue, to present one of the great war crimes of the fifth century not with the moral indignation which Euripides (484–406) showed when he evoked it by analogy in *The Trojan Women* in 415, but as an illustrative example of why men act as they do in the world of warfare and of politics.

It is, Thucydides argues, because the political groups to which they belong place them in situations where they cannot choose but rule. Since the exercise of power excites in those who are ruled a constant desire for rebellion and revenge, the rulers cannot give up their power without making themselves vulnerable to the hatred which they have inevitably inspired. They are thus forced, by fear, to behave with a cruelty which no conscious desire to inflict suffering could possibly inspire.

It is in this respect that Thucydides is the father of the realist school of international relations. This is the one which thinks that all nation states are animated by the same desire for power, and are equally ruthless in their efforts to acquire it. In this respect, they are all like the England of which the nineteenth-century statesman Lord Palmerston (1784–1865) once said that it had no permanent friends and no permanent allies, but only permanent interests. Moral considerations and ethical obligations are as irrelevant to the conduct of foreign policy as they would be to the study of a virus or the analysis of the electron.

One of the earliest modern disciples of Thucydides was the English philosopher Thomas Hobbes (1588–1679), who translated the *History of the Peloponnesian War* into English in 1629, and whose later remark in the

Leviathan (1651) struck a very Thucydidean note when he wrote of there being, 'in all mankind':

> a perpetual and restless desire for Power after power, that ceaseth only in Death. And the cause of this is not always that a man hopes for a more intensive delight that he has already attained to, or that he cannot be content with a moderate power; but because he cannot assure the power and means to live well, without acquisition of more.

This is almost a paraphrase of what Thucydides argues in his opening chapter, when he writes that 'what made war inevitable was the growth of Athenian power and the fear which this aroused in Sparta'. In 1960 the Marxist historian Isaac Deutscher argued in very similar terms that Berlin was 'the Achilles' heel' of both the Soviet and the Western bloc. 'From the Soviet standpoint', he wrote:

> the preservation of the *status quo* [i.e. the security of Eastern Europe] requires that the Western enclave be eliminated from Berlin. From the Western viewpoint, this precisely would upset the *status quo*. If Soviet diplomacy seeks to insure the Soviet bloc against the tremors that a turbulent Berlin might yet send through Eastern Europe, the West is afraid that its withdrawal from Berlin would send no less dangerous tremors through NATO and induce the Germans (and others) to begin to reconcile themselves to Soviet supremacy in Europe. None of these fears is just the figment of a frightened imagination; both sides have enough ground to be afraid. The result is a stalemate of fears.[5]

It could be argued that the Soviet Union's main concern throughout the Cold War was not, as NSC 68 alleges, to dominate the world. It was merely to avoid a repetition of the invasions of Russia from the west which had been begun by the Teutonic knights in the thirteenth century, continued by Napoleon I in 1812 and by the Germans in 1914, and had culminated in Hitler's Barbarossa campaign of June 21, 1941. Under Khrushchev, as under Stalin, the Soviet Union's ambition to protect itself from the West took the form of the desire to create a Germany which was politically neutral and militarily impotent. It was this which led to the pressure which both Soviet leaders exercised on West Berlin, and inspired the risks which Mr Khrushchev was prepared to run in order to make the Western powers abandon what he saw as the bridgehead for yet another invasion of Russia from the west.

THUCYDIDES THE EUROPEAN

One of Thucydides' critics, G.E.M. de Ste Croix, speaking of the 'moral bleakness' of his vision, also describes it as his 'unique virtue'.[6] Like that other quintessentially European thinker Niccolò Machiavelli (1469–1527), Thucydides sees no place for morality as a basis either for the way nation states ought to act in their relationship to one another, or as a useful starting point for any analysis of their behaviour. The Athenian delegates at Melos do not present their proposed course of action as in any way unusual. They insist that the law which says that men rule everywhere they can was already in existence before they came to Melos. Indeed, in their view, it has dominated human political conduct since the very beginning of history. It is not a law which they have invented, and they would not be in the least surprised if the Melians acted with the same degree of ruthlessness if it were they, and not the Athenians, who held the upper hand.

When Richard Cobden dismissed Thucydides with such contumely, it was not only because he thought that any account of what had happened so long ago could not possibly have any relevance to the problem of the present day. It was also because he completely disagreed with the moral implications to emerge from the analysis of political behaviour in the *History of the Peloponnesian War*. He was one of the leading intellectual representatives of the opposite tradition in international politics, the one associated in England with William Ewart Gladstone (1809–1898) and in America with Woodrow Wilson (1856–1924). It is a tradition which gives primacy to the importance of trade among the nations, and presupposes that all countries will, if properly enlightened, base their foreign policy upon the twin ideas of co-operation and trust. If they do not, they must be vigorously denounced, as Gladstone denounced the Bulgarian massacres of the Armenians in 1876. But they should also, as Woodrow Wilson tried to do in 1919, be encouraged to behave towards one another with compassion and understanding, and to base their foreign policy on the highest ethical principles.

It is an attitude which Thucydides would certainly have understood, but with which he would not have sympathised. He would have taken the view that, if you behave as Cobden, Gladstone and Wilson recommend, you will rapidly be defeated by the disciples of Machiavelli. He was, in that respect as in others, the archetypal realist. At the same time, however, he was also one of the thinkers who did most to set European thought on to the path which led it to its present dominant position, one where it has few if any international rivals.

When Dr Johnson commented that in Thucydides, more is said than done, he intended it as a criticism, suggesting that he personally could have done with a little more action. There are, indeed, a great many speeches. But the fact that they are so much more interesting than the accounts of the battles points to the great superiority of Thucydides as a historian: his ability to analyse human behaviour, and to say why men act as they do. It is in this respect that he stands at the very beginning of the intellectual tradition which we now see as characteristically and quintessentially European. In Greek, the word *historia*, from which we derive the word 'history', means learning or knowing by enquiry. What Thucydides did was to find out the facts by systematic, empirical enquiry, and to analyse his findings. Once he had done this, Europe, intellectually, had started to come to birth.

ALTERNATIVE POSSIBILITIES

Officially, the USSR always insisted that its sole intention in installing the rockets which President Kennedy succeeded in having removed in October 1962 had been to protect the Cuban régime of Fidel Castro from a repetition of the Bay of Pigs. Since the Americans had made it very clear that they would not allow a Soviet military presence so close to their own shores, it seems a big risk to have taken to protect a new and not very important ally. And since Mr Khrushchev had so frequently described the Americans as 'hotheads', it is also surprising that he should have once again decided to raise the temperature of the Cold War quite so sharply.

This analysis of Soviet tactics in terms of the need to protect Cuba might nevertheless still be correct. Since 1962 Cuba has never been subjected to the same kind of interference from the Americans as Nicaragua, Panama or Honduras. In 1983 American troops overthrew the newly installed Marxist régime in Grenada, and in 1989 they reoccupied the Canal Zone bases in Panama in defiance of the 1977 treaty. On both occasions the USA was condemned for its intervention, both by the Organisation of American States and by the International Court of Justice at the Hague, but did not change its policy. Cuba, in contrast, remained under the control of Fidel Castro.

It could be argued, too, that Mr Khrushchev also fulfilled his original intention as far as Berlin was concerned. His admirers in the West claimed that, as in Cuba, he had successfully applied the opposite tactics to those implied by the French proverb *reculer pour mieux sauter*. He had, in their view, taken a big jump forward in order to place himself in a situation where he could more easily draw back. It was this which enabled him to achieve what all along had been his original, fairly limited objective: that of making sure that the Federal Republic of Germany remained within the limits originally established when the three occupation zones were allocated to the French, the British and the Americans in 1945. The East German régime of Walter Ulbricht survived until 1989, and the Communist régime of Fidel Castro to the present day – something which might not have happened without the initial display of bellicosity implied by the open threat to expel Western troops from Berlin and the more secretive attempt to install the missiles in Cuba.

This was not, however, how Mr Khrushchev's colleagues on the Central Committee of the Soviet Communist Party saw matters. In October 1964 he was outvoted at a meeting of the Presidium, and required to resign from the post of First Secretary, which had been the basis of his virtually dictatorial power. The success of the campaign of deStalinisation, with which he was most closely associated both in the Soviet Union and in the West, was then evident in the fact that he was allowed to retire unharmed and even to write his memoirs.

Although Khrushchev had moved away from Stalin's belief in the ideas of the botanist Lysenko, who maintained that acquired characteristics could be transmitted through inheritance, his agricultural policy of opening up the 'virgin lands' of Siberia also had been a total failure. Nevertheless, the main charge brought against him was that of 'adventurism' in foreign affairs. This certainly fitted the predominant image of him in the West, and made him more frightening than Stalin. At least with Stalin, and even more with his foreign minister Vyacheslav Mikhailovitch Molotov, you knew where you were. The latter could always be relied on to say *niet*, and the former to kill anybody who even looked as if they might stand in his way. It is nevertheless Khrushchev's relationship with Stalin which offers the first clue to the policy which he pursued towards the West, and particularly towards Western Europe. Stalin, after all, had failed to make the West abandon Berlin. In so doing, he had transformed the Soviet Union, in less than three years, from the country universally admired for its victory over the Third Reich in 1945 to a power which differed from the Hitler's Germany only by its greater success in dominating the whole of Eastern Europe. Khrushchev clearly wanted to do better than Stalin, both on the public-relations front and in the results achieved by a more dynamic foreign policy.

He also needed to do so in order to keep his power within the Soviet Union itself. In February 1956, in a secret session of the Soviet Communist Party, he had given a long speech denouncing Stalin, accusing him of crimes against socialist legality; of a 'cult of the personality' which had destroyed the traditions of the Party; of negligence in foreign affairs and defence matters which had almost led to the defeat of the Soviet Union in the first months of the German invasion of June 1941; as well as of the murder, in the purges of 1936–1938, of a large number of totally innocent Soviet politicians, military leaders and ordinary citizens. Although these were not charges with which the West was unfamiliar, it was highly instructive, when reports of Khrushchev's speech began to circulate outside the Soviet Union, to know that they were being confirmed by the acknowledged leader of the Soviet Communist Party.

They immediately led to a situation in which first Poland, then Hungary, tried to assert their independence from the Soviet Union, and had to be restrained. In Poland, this was achieved by the appointment of a more popular and open-minded leader, Wladyslaw Gomulka, to replace the hard-line Stalinist Boleslaw Bierut, who had been in power since 1945. In November 1956 the Red Army intervened in Hungary, at the cost of 20,000 Hungarian and 3,000 Soviet lives, in order to keep the country loyal to Moscow. By an immense sacrifice of popularity, the Soviet Union had succeeded in retaining its power in Eastern Europe. But the events of October–November 1956 were a warning to Khrushchev of how dangerous his policy of deStalinisation could become, and how it could be pursued, both within the Soviet Union and outside, only from a position of strength. It was this strength which Khrushchev was seeking to maintain, both in international affairs and in the context of Soviet internal politics, through his Berlin policy and the even riskier venture of installing the missiles in Cuba. If he could succeed where Stalin had failed, not only would his critics have to acknowledge that he was a leader whose more liberal ideas could make the Soviet Union a better place, they would also have to see him as a better politician than Stalin in terms of *Realpolitik*.

The fact that it is possible, and perhaps even inevitable, to analyse the Berlin crisis of 1958–1962 in terms of the internal politics of the Soviet Union is another reminder of how, after 1945, Western Europe had become an essentially passive player on the world political scene. Berlin, one of the great European capitals before 1939, had become a mere pawn in a struggle between politicians of opposite persuasions in Moscow. In 1848 the French historian Alexis de Tocqueville had predicted that the two powers of Russia and the United States of America would compete for domination of the whole world. It was a prediction which, by 1948, and even more by 1958 and 1962, seemed to have come true, with the fate of the former capital of Germany being decided by the way this rivalry expressed itself in the Caribbean.

For historians of a left-wing persuasion, the struggle for Western Europe was not to be seen as the expression solely of the policy needs of the Soviet Union. It was also the product of the economic needs of the United States. One of the most influential of these historians – who earned themselves the title of 'revisionist' by seeking to reject the conventional idea that the Soviet Union, and the Soviet Union alone, was responsible for the Cold War – was Walter Lafeber. In his view, both the Truman Doctrine and the Marshall Plan had the same origin. Both stemmed from the fact that the American economy could, in 1947, remain buoyant only by exporting sixteen billion dollars worth of goods, and the principal market for the purchase of these goods could only be Western Europe.[7]

For its left-wing critics, the Marshall Plan was an essentially self-interested measure, whereby the United States sought to avoid a repetition of the autarkic tendencies of the 1930s. These had led the countries of Western Europe to put up tariff barriers to protect their industries from American competition, and thus exacerbated the effects of the Great Depression. Implicit in the acceptance of the money provided by the Marshall Plan was the undertaking that the Europeans would not do the same again. Their markets would remain open to American goods, and the world would be made safe for American capitalism, if not for parliamentary democracy.

Another historian of the revisionist school, D.F. Flemming, supports this interpretation by quoting Dean Acheson (Under-Secretary of State 1945–1947, Secretary of State 1949–1953) as saying that 'We cannot have full employment and prosperity without foreign markets', while Fred Halliday, the leading British revisionist historian, expressed the same idea when he wrote of how 'the Marshall Plan proclaimed in 1947 aimed to revive European capitalism under US influence'[8]. Other writers make even more dramatic claims when they argue, as Stephen J. Whitfield does, that in 1961 it was President Kennedy who 'provoked the Soviet Union into matching the massive American military build-up', and not the other way round. He points out that Kennedy's message to Congress in May 1961 asking for increased military spending preceded the meeting in Vienna in June of that year at which Khrushchev renewed his threats on Berlin.[9] Just as Mr Khrushchev needed to keep on the right side of his foreign-policy hawks in order to be able to implement his domestic reforms, so President Kennedy could not neglect the pressure from what President Eisenhower had earlier called 'the military-industrial complex'.

Another feature of the Berlin crises of 1948–1949 and of 1958–1962 is the reminder they offer of how it was not only the politicians of Western Europe who had ceased to take the initiative in world affairs. Even before 1945 no twentieth-century American politician had done anything but react to events elsewhere. Woodrow Wilson did not declare war on Germany on April 7, 1917 until provoked into doing so by the German High Command's decision in 1917 to launch a programme of unrestricted submarine warfare. On December 11, 1941 it was Hitler who declared war on the United States, not the other way round.

One of the main arguments against any interpretation of the Cold War in terms of an American ambition to wield absolute political power is the obvious desire of the United States to pursue an isolationist policy in foreign affairs. In the Cold War of 1946–1989 it was the Soviet Union which issued the challenges, whether directly in Berlin, by proxy in Korea, or by implication in the deloyment of the SS-20s in the 1970s. In the Vietnam war of 1964–1973 the aim of American forces was to protect South Vietnam from a rebellion inspired and helped from the North. In November 1979 it was the Islamic Fundamentalists who invaded the American Embassy in Teheran, and in 1990 the forces of Saddam

Hussein which invaded Kuwait. In 1995 and 1999 it was the Serbian nationalists' policy of ethnic cleansing which led to American-armed intervention in the former Yugoslavia.

It is often argued that the United States is far more guilty than the misleading enumeration of such events might suggest, especially since it has more subtle and effective ways of pursuing a policy of world domination. This analysis is most frequently heard in France, where frequent use of phrases such as 'l'impérialisme économique et culturel américain' draws attention to the idea that it is not only by the consciously adopted policies of its government that a country can conquer the world. It can do so by the assiduous projection of its own economic and cultural model, a projection which need not always be conducted by entirely honest methods. Like a press baron driving rival publications out of business by the ruthlessness of his take-over bids, the tactics of his promotion campaigns and his readiness to follow the dictates of the major publicity agents, a country of the size and wealth of the United States can effectively dominate the economy and destroy the culture of every other country on the globe.

There is nevertheless an alternative explanation for the desire of so many people to eat at MacDonalds, wear jeans, listen to Madonna, watch American films and television programmes, adopt American business methods and try to ape the American way of life. It is that this is a very pleasant way of carrying on. It may be vulnerable to the quip that we must needs love the lowest when we see it. It may involve the adoption of an irresponsible and hedonistic life-style which will eventually destroy itself. But in the meantime, it reflects a genuine choice, something which the model presented to Europeans and others by the former Soviet Union never succeeded in doing. There is also the point, illustrated by the fact that British pop music continues to carry all before it, that European culture can rival that of the United States throughout the world.

Another example of the relative blamelessness of the United States in the major crisis of the Cold War to take place in Europe is the extreme improbability of any American President deliberately choosing to put Berlin, Ohio, at risk in order to defend Berlin, Germany. However, it is also hard to see why Mr Khrushchev should have consciously chosen to put Minsk or Moscow at risk in the atomic war which could so easily have arisen as a result either of the Berlin or the Cuban crisis, so there is a mystery about the Cold War in general, as well as the Berlin crisis, which not even the example of Thucydides can entirely explain. This is even more true of another trial of strength that took place in Europe, the argument between left and right as to whether or not to accept the installation of American cruise and *Pershing* missiles in the countries of the NATO alliance.

3 The contest for Western Europe (2)

Détente and the missiles of the 1980s

THE CONCEPT OF DÉTENTE

Between 1962 and 1979 there was a certain improvement in relations between the NATO powers and the Soviet Union. In a process known as Détente, a series of agreements were signed which seemed to place their relationship on a more permanent and stable footing. Many of these were the fruits of the *Ostpolitik*, or eastern policy, pursued by Willy Brandt, the leader of the German Social Democratic Party (SDP; Sozialdemokratische Partei Deutschlands, SPD), and Chancellor of the Federal Republic of Germany (FRG; Bundesrepublik Deutschland, BRD) from October 1969 to May 1974. Before then, he had been Mayor of West Berlin between 1957 and 1966, and maintained excellent relationships with the Western powers during the whole of the 1958–1962 crisis. In November 1966 he led the SPD into the 'Grand Coalition', in which it governed in alliance with the conservative CDU (Christlich Demokratische Union), in which he became foreign minister.

Brandt's view of the relationship between the Federal Republic of Germany and the German Democratic Republic (GDR; Deutsche Demokratische Republik, DDR) was fundamentally different from that of former CDU leaders. Unlike the founding father of the Federal Republic of Germany, Konrad Adenauer, and his immediate successor, Ludwig Erhard, he did not regard East Germany as a totally evil and unacceptable régime. One of his first acts on becoming Chancellor in October 1969 was to abandon what was known as the Hallstein doctrine – named after Walter Hallstein, the relatively junior minister who had formulated it in 1955. This stated that the Federal Republic of Germany could not have diplomatic relations with any state, apart from the Soviet Union, which afforded diplomatic recognition to the German Democratic Republic.

Brandt's abandonment of this doctrine led to a number of agreements which were praised by his admirers as forming a basis for Détente, and criticised by his opponents for giving permanence to the division between

East and West Germany whose only real basis lay in the presence of Soviet troops on German soil and their readiness to fire on anyone demonstrating against Soviet policy. But there seemed, at the time, to be no other alternative but to accept a state of affairs which offered no possibility of change. The Russians were there to stay, and the only solution was to make the best of it one could. In the 1950s and early 1960s the American Secretary of State John Foster Dulles had talked about 'roll back', and Konrad Adenauer was said to have found it quite attractive. It had now, however, been permanently replaced by what turned out, when the Cold War ended in 1989, to be the less dramatic but more successful policy of containment.

In 1970 a series of agreements were signed which placed the relationship between the Federal Republic of Germany and the German Democratic Republic on an official legal footing. The two governments agreed on arrangements for postal and telephone communications, and on March 19, 1970 Willy Brandt met Willi Stoph, the then Chairman of Ministers in the GDR. On August 12, 1970 the Moscow Treaty was signed, by which the FGR accorded *de facto* recognition to the German territory annexed by the Soviet Union and Poland at the end of the Second World War. On December 7 the Warsaw Treaty was signed, guaranteeing the inviolability of the new frontiers given to Poland in 1945, and thus ensuring that there would in the future be no basis for the accusations levelled against West Germany of being a *revanchard* state plotting to recover its lost territories.

These treaties were followed by an agreement signed on September 3, 1971, the 38th anniversary of the outbreak of the Second World War, which guaranteed free access to West Berlin for French, British and American forces as well as their right to remain stationed in the city. Finally, by the Basic Treaty (*Grundlagenvertrag*) between the Federal Republic of Germany and the German Democratic Republic, each recognised the right of the other to exist. The only proviso written into the treaty was that the FRG looked forward to the eventual self-determination of the whole German people, while the GDR remained quiet on the issue.

The régime led since 1960 by Walter Ulbricht was not in fact in a position to express any such hopes. On the night of 20–21 August 1968 forces from the Warsaw Pact countries (of which the GDR had been a member since its creation in May 1955) moved into Czechoslovakia to suppress the movement known as the 'Prague Spring', the attempt under Alexander Dubček to install what he called 'socialism with a human face'. They did so under the leadership of the Soviet Union, whose tanks and soldiers formed the bulk of the invasion force, and whose then leader, Leonid Brezhnev, then proceeded to formulate the doctrine which took his name. This stated that the Soviet Union had the right to intervene in the affairs of any country in which socialism already existed in order to protect its achievements from internal disorder or external interference.

This doctrine remained in force until 1989, and was accepted in practice by the NATO powers. It did not, unlike the policies pursued by Khrushchev, threaten the stability of either Eastern or Western Europe. It was not a charter for spreading the Russian version of socialism, only for ensuring that it was not overthrown in countries where it already existed. As such, it was implicitly accepted by the Helsinki agreements, or Final Act, of August 1975, which marked the high point of Détente. These agreements were signed after a conference held in the Finnish capital in July and attended by representatives from 34 nations, including the members of NATO and the Warsaw Pact. The 9 states then making up the European Economic Community – Belgium, Denmark, France, Great Britain, Ireland, Italy, Luxembourg, the Netherlands, and West Germany – were also there, represented by the President of the Commission, Roy Jenkins, and thus spoke, on this occasion at any rate, with one voice.

The Final Act dealt with three matters: co-operation in military affairs, especially in attempts to avoid the fear or reality of surprise attacks; economic and political co-operation; and respect for human rights. It also established the Conference on Security and Co-operation in Europe (CSCE), which was later to make a number of efforts to solve the wars of the Yugoslav secession. The 34 participating countries held a series of other meetings, and in that respect the Helsinki Conference can be seen, like the United Nations, as having fulfilled the useful function of keeping communication open between East and West.

But in two other respects – human rights and disarmament – it scarcely justified the high hopes placed in it. It rapidly became obvious that the Soviet Union was not really interested in either, and its indifference encouraged the view that totalitarian systems were not capable of reform from within. They could be changed only by conquest from without, as the Third Reich had been, or by a process of internal collapse. Although it was internal collapse and not the defeat of its forces on the field of battle which finally put an end to the Soviet Union, nobody in the 1970s predicted that it might one day happen.

It was not until 1980 that the Russian dissident Andrei Amalrik published his essay *Will the Soviet Union Survive until 1984?*, and one of the books which it helped to inspire, Donald James's *The Fall of the Russian Empire* (1982), was presented as a piece of science fiction. As Jim Petras and Morris Morley put it in an 1982, in an article published under the auspices of the European Nuclear Disarmament Programme,

> the growth of Soviet Bloc economic and military power is an indisputable fact of the first order in evaluating the prospects of the new confrontational politics of the Reagan administration.[1]

The Soviet Union, it was felt, was here to stay, and there was a widely held view that the Russian people, together with the inhabitants of the other Republics of the Soviet Union, were as firmly attached to the achievements stemming from the Bolshevik Revolution of 1917 as the French were to the conquests brought about by the Revolution of 1789. Nobody could imagine the French abandoning either the ideal of *Liberté, Égalité, Fraternité*, or the seventeen articles of *Les droits de l'homme et du citoyen* (The rights of man), a document still posted up in every police station, or the principle of the 1905 separation of Church and State. Similarly, it was inconceivable that the Russians would ever give up the planned economy, the leading role of the Party, or the ideal of the class-less society.

It was partly for this reason that the Helsinki agreements were welcomed with a certain degree of enthusiasm. Nothing else was available, and in Czechoslovakia the movement calling itself Charter 77 attracted the signature of 243 people, all of whom called upon the government to respect the principle of freedom of speech enshrined in the Helsinki Final Act. However, most found themselves dismissed from work or sent to prison for their pains. It also became apparent, when the Soviet Union began to deploy what were seen by Western analysts as a new and particularly accurate type of medium-range missile, that there were other limitations to Détente apart from the reluctance of the authorities in the Soviet Union and Eastern Europe to respect human rights.

PRELUDE IN AFGHANISTAN

What finally killed off Détente was the Soviet invasion of Afghanistan on December 25 and 26, 1979, especially when it became known in the West that the physicist Andrei Sakharov, who had played a major part in the development of the Soviet hydrogen bomb, had been exiled to Gorki and placed under house arrest for protesting against it. This invasion was an attempt to put an end to the in-fighting and murders which had recently taken place among the leaders of the Marxist régime in Kabul which had been in power since the military *coup d'état* of April 27, 1978 had deposed the President, General Mohammed Daoud and replaced him by the Armed Forces Revolutionary Council. There had always been strong opposition to the régime from the Islamic Fundamentalist rebels known as the *Mujahadeen*, or soldiers of God, and by December 1979 the situation had become so desperate that the Politburo, moved by the argument advanced by the chief ideologue, Mikhail Suslov, that the collapse of the government would imperil Communist régimes everywhere, decided to intervene.

Like the repression of the Hungarian revolt in October 1956 and of the 'Prague Spring' in August 1968, this was an action which the Soviet

Union had to make if it wanted to maintain its power. In that respect, both the indignation which it aroused in the West and the fears to which it gave rise were equally misplaced. It was not followed by an incursion into the Indian Ocean or the Persian Gulf, and did not involve any threat to the oil supplies reaching the West. It was far more of a defensive manoeuvre, to be interpreted in the same terms as those put forward in 1954 by Isaac Deutscher in his comments on the workers' rebellion in East Berlin on June 16 and 17, 1953 (see note 5 to Chapter 2).

Necessary though it may have been, the invasion of Afghanistan turned out to be an intervention which the Soviet Union could not afford to make. Not only was it the geopolitical equivalent of the ambition to take 'a bridge too far' which had led to the allied military disaster at Arnhem in September 1944. As far as the ability of the Soviet Union to project its military power beyond its original frontiers was concerned, it marked the beginning of its defeat in the Cold War. The fact that it led in Afghanistan itself to a civil war calculated to have led to the death of over a million people, and created five million refugees, is a further reminder of how little actual, physical suffering was caused by the Cold War in either Western or Eastern Europe. In 1988, having lost over 50,000 men, the Soviet army withdrew, and the civil war continued.

In the public statements made after the invasion of Afghanistan there were hints that a fairly vigorous debate had gone on in the Kremlin between the hawks and doves of the Politburo as to the right course of action to take. Andrei Gromyko, Foreign Minister of the Soviet Union from 1957 to 1985, said that it had been 'a difficult decision', a coded way of letting the outside world know that not everybody had been entirely in favour of the invasion. The compulsion of fear about what might happen if no action were taken was even stronger than in earlier cases of Hungary and Czechoslovakia. The large Muslim population of the Soviet Union had never been happy with the doctrines of Marxism-Leninism, and to countenance disorder and a possible counter-revolution in so rigorously Muslim a state as Afghanistan would be to invite comparable trouble in the predominantly Muslim republics of Azerbaijan and Kazakhstan.

From this point of view, it was far from obvious that the invasion of Afghanistan showed that the USSR had gone back to being as predatory a state as it had looked when Stalin and Khrushchev were trying to eject the American, French and British garrisons from West Berlin. But the fact that the Brezhnev doctrine was now being applied outside Europe, and in a part of the world where Soviet dominance had not been given the kind of acknowledgement afforded by the Helsinki agreements, was only one symptom of the death of Détente. What looked even more threatening was the intense programme of rearmament, whereby the Soviet

Union was increasing its nuclear capacity in such a way as to give it a clear advantage over the United States of America.

THE MISSILE CONFRONTATION

By a coincidence which was unknown at the time, but which brings out how closely the two final crises of the Cold War were linked together, at least in Western public opinion, the meeting of the Politburo at which the Soviet Union decided to intervene in Afghanistan was held on the same day, December 12, 1979, that the leaders of the North Atlantic Treaty Organisation announced that they would deploy cruise and *Pershing* missiles into Western Europe.[2] The two crises were not connected in any other way, since the Soviet Union's decision to install a new type of missile, the SS-20, went back to 1977, whereas the decision to intervene in Afghanistan was taken under the immediate pressure of a local crisis. But the publicity given to the sudden freeze which came over US–Soviet relations in 1979 created an atmosphere in Western Europe which was as intense as the climate of constant anxiety that had reigned during the Berlin crisis of 1958–1962 and reached its peak during the Cuban missile crisis of October 1962.

For the Soviet Union, the SS-20 missiles which it began installing in late 1977 were not an escalation of the arms race. They were merely the replacement of existing missiles, and therefore not a breach of the Strategic Arms Limitation Agreement (SALT) signed with the United States on May 26, 1972. The United States, however, together with the governments of its NATO allies, saw matters differently. It was no longer necessary, as it had been in 1960, for the United States to send spy planes over the territory of the Soviet Union and the Warsaw Pact countries in order to see what was happening. The satellites now in constant orbit could send back pictures which, the boast went, could enable observers in Washington to read the newspapers being carried by pedestrians in Moscow.

The pictures sent back by these satellites confirmed the view that the SS-20s represented much more than a bringing up to date of the Soviet deterrent. For a start, they were highly mobile and could be fairly easily moved about by giant transporters. They therefore looked to Western analysts like first-strike weapons intended to be used either in a crisis or, on a more long-term basis, as a permanent threat to keep the West Europeans under Soviet control.

They also differed from earlier land-based missiles in being highly accurate. Earlier missiles had been so inaccurate that they could destroy a specific target in Western Europe such as an aerodrome or missile site only if they contained so large a nuclear charge that the fallout, carried by the prevailing west–east winds, would do almost as much damage to the Soviet Union as to the inhabitants of Germany, Italy or Holland. The SS-20s, in contrast, were capable of landing so close to their target that it had become technically possible for the Soviet Union to wipe out all American bases in Western Europe in one surprise attack. This would leave the United States with the choice between abandoning its allies and retaliating by an attack against the Soviet Union's cities, thus bringing about a Soviet counter-strike which would kill most of the population of North America.

But the most important difference between the SS-20s and the other weapons in the Soviet nuclear arsenal was that they were aimed solely at targets in Western Europe. They could not reach the territory of the United States, except Alaska. This explains why, in the political analysis of Soviet intentions put forward in the West, the crucial expression was the new term 'decoupling', first used by the West German Chancellor Helmut Schmidt in a speech in 1977. As at the time of the Berlin crises of 1948–1949 and 1958–1962, the aim of the Soviet Union seemed to be to dominate Western Europe; it was not interested in conquering the United States. As Mr Khrushchev suggested in 1961, when he talked about the two big brothers keeping all the other little brothers in order, it was quite happy to share out the world with Uncle Sam, but it wanted Uncle Sam to go home. The hawks in Western Europe as well as in the United States had no difficulty in seeing what the Soviet Union was trying to do by installing the SS-20s. It wanted to ensure that, once Uncle Sam had departed, there would be no obstacle to the fulfilment of the Leninist aim of obtaining, first of all, mastery over Germany, and then mastery over the rest of Western Europe.

PROTESTS AND ARGUMENTS

Not everyone shared this view of Soviet intentions, and the 1980s were marked, both on the continent of Europe and in the United Kingdom, by more demonstrations against nuclear weapons than had been seen since the time of the crises over Berlin and Cuba. The Campaign for Nuclear Disarmament had been formed in the United Kingdom in 1958, and the annual Easter protest march to the British nuclear research establishment at Aldermaston rapidly became the most popular way for politically conscious people, young and old, to combine their fears of a nuclear holocaust with the expression of a general dissatisfaction with the modern world. In 1958 the philosopher Bertrand Russell, one of the founders of the CND, created the more radical Committee of 100, and in 1961, at the age of 90, was imprisoned for a week as a result of his campaign for civil disobedience.

The movement for unilateral nuclear disarmament, which had declined in popularity after the solution of the Cuban missile crisis, found a new appeal in the protests against the proposed installation of 108 *Pershing* and 96 cruise missiles in West Germany, 106 cruise missiles in Great Britain and 96 in Italy, together with 48 each in the Netherlands and Belgium.[3] France had not been a member of the NATO military command structure since de Gaulle ordered American forces to leave France March 1966, so no missiles were to be sited on French soil. However, France had remained a member of the NATO political alliance, and on January 20, 1983 François Mitterrand, the first socialist to be elected President of the Fifth French Republic, gave a speech to the Bundestag, in the West German capital of Bonn, in which he supported NATO policy by declaring that 'the pacifists are in the West, but the missiles are in the East'.

Other left-wing politicians were more hostile to the installation of the cruise and *Pershing* missiles, and the British Labour Party, under the leadership of Michael Foot, fought the General Election of June 1983 with a programme which recommended, in particular, leaving NATO as well as the European Economic Community, while at the same time giving up Great Britain's independent nuclear deterrent. More significant, however, were the popular and apparently spontaneous movements against what was seen by many on the left as the deliberately provocative policy which the United States and its NATO allies were adopting towards the Soviet Union.

The cruise missiles – whose usefulness from a strategic point of view was that they, too, could be moved about quite easily, and they flew close enough to the ground not to be detected by Soviet radar – were to be sited at Greenham Common in Berkshire. This was to become the site of one of the most widely publicised of the many protests organised in Western Europe and elsewhere against what was seen as a highly dangerous escalation of the arms race for which the West was held to be mainly responsible.

Comparable blame might have been openly placed by the citizens of the Warsaw Pact countries on their governments, if these citizens had possessed a comparable freedom to organise public protests. The European Peace Movement was always vulnerable to the criticism voiced in François Mitterrand's lapidary phrase about the missiles being in the East but the pacifists in the West. It was nevertheless a movement which received a great deal of genuine popular support, and which did not need the financial and other help which the Soviet Union allegedly gave it. It was certainly in the interests of the Soviet Union to do everything possible to weaken Western Europe and separate it from the United States: the example of a Western Europe which was prosperous could have only a deleterious effect on public opinion in the People's Democracies of Czechoslovakia, East Germany, Hungary, Poland and Romania. Insofar as it was the reluctance of these states to accept the kind of economic organisation imposed since 1945 which was eventually a key factor leading to the collapse of the Soviet Union in 1991, it was quite sensible for it to do everything possible to stop Western Europe offering so attractive an alternative. A Soviet observer noted with satisfaction in late 1983 that:

> To the credit of the basic nucleus of the present anti-war movement, it has been able, surmounting its internal weaknesses and rejecting the diversionary prompting of unbidden 'well-wishers', to ascertain the truly decisive element at this stage of the struggle to ensure peace and stability in Europe. This element, as the absolute majority of anti-war organisations acknowledges, is the prevention of the deployment in Western Europe of new American nuclear weapons and the conversion of Europe into a nuclear-free zone.[4]

His analysis reflects the fact that the organisations most active in campaigning against the installation of the cruise and *Pershing* missiles were the World Peace Council, the World Federation of Trade Unions, and the Christian Peace Conference. All were widely known as Soviet front organisations, and the WPC had been expelled from Paris in 1951 and from Vienna in 1957 for subversive activity. *Pravda* reported on May 31, 1982 that Soviet citizens were voluntarily going without pay one day a week in order to donate their wages to a 'peace fund', and it is improbable that the money thus collected was needed for a comparable campaign within the Soviet bloc itself. Although only three to five per cent of the 3,000,000 or so participants in the various peace movements in West Germany were Party members or extreme left-wingers, they made up forty per cent of the co-ordinators and well over fifty per cent of the organisers.

The fact that they received such enthusiastic support from Soviet front organisations as well as from the Soviet Union itself does not mean that the millions of West European citizens who took part in the peace campaigns of the 1980s were insincere. Neither does it mean that they necessarily wanted to install in their home countries an economic and political system modelled upon that of the Soviet Union. Their objective was summed up in the title of the collection of essays edited in 1980 by one of the most eminent intellectuals of the movement, the left-wing historian E.P. Thompson: *Protest and Survive*.[5] For them, the installation of American medium-range missiles could give rise only to an arms race whose inevitable result would be a nuclear war. Since this would be followed by a 'nuclear winter' which would wipe out human life in the whole of Europe, no support for the policy adopted by the NATO powers was justifiable either on intellectual or on moral grounds.

From 1981 onwards, a group of women, some of whom were still there in 1998, long after the missiles were removed and the Cold War was over, kept constant vigil outside the base at Greenham Common. In October 1983, 200,000 people formed a 'Peace Chain' 67 miles long between Stuttgart and Neu-Ulm, while in Bonn, another chain of protest was formed in front of the embassies of the five nuclear powers: Great Britain, China, France, the Soviet Union and the United States. Again in 1983, 200,000 people came to hear Willy Brandt denounce the lack of progress at the disarmament negotiations then being conducted in Geneva, and from which the Soviet delegation walked out on November 23. On two occasions, in 1982 and in 1983, a fault in the computer at Omaha, Nebraska, controlling the operations of the American Strategic Air Command almost triggered a full-scale attack against the Soviet Union, and one of the most popular films screened again and again by student organisations throughout Europe and North America was Stanley Kubrick's *Dr Strangelove, or How I Learned to Stop Worrying and Love The Bomb*, described in 1991 by Stephen J. Whitfield as deserving to be ranked 'among the most important achievements of the movies'.[6]

The brightest and best, both young and old, in Western Europe and in North America, gave the peace movement their unstinting and passionate support. It was, culturally as well as politically, the great cause of the age, akin to the reaction to the horrors of the 1914–1918 war which led in 1919 to the creation of the League of Nations and to the war pacifist movements of the 1920s and 1930s. In 1963 Joan Littlewood had produced, with *Oh, What a Lovely War!*, one of the most successful musicals of post-war England. In 1969, when it was made into an equally successful film, it had an important sub-text: since the useless slaughter of 1914–1918 was the consequence of the stupidity and lust for power of the military men responsible for Passchendaele and the Somme, what possible grounds could there be for trusting their successors, armed as they were with even deadlier weapons and animated by a comparable zeal for conquest?

In this atmosphere, it was both difficult and unusual for the supporters of the policy actually adopted towards the Soviet Union to win much of a hearing. In 1960 Constantine Fitzgibbon's novel *When the Kissing Had to Stop* argued that if a left-wing government took power in Great Britain, a Russian take-over would very rapidly follow. The political climate of the time, dominated as it was by the highly audible rhetoric of Mr Khrushchev and the clearly articulated threats against West Berlin, meant that the book enjoyed a degree of success with the critics and was sufficiently popular with the reading public to go into paperback.

This did not happen to David Fraser's *August 1988*, a novel which put forward in dramatic and exciting form the basic argument in favour of nuclear weapons: that you did not have them in order to use them yourself, but to deter your opponent from using them on you. It describes how a left-wing government in Great Britain, having given up nuclear weapons and left NATO, follows the logic of the idea that 'left can speak to left' by signing a number of commercial and cultural agreements with Romania. This annoys the Soviet Union, which immediately sees the possibility of Romania escaping from its area of influence and joining the more liberal ideas of the West. The Soviet Prime Minister visits London and tells the British Prime Minister that, unless the agreement is immediately rescinded, one SS-20 nuclear missile will land on Scarborough, the town at which the agreement with Romania had been signed. Since the United Kingdom is no longer a member of NATO, it is no longer covered by the US nuclear umbrella, and it has no nuclear weapons of its own with which it can deter the Soviet attack by threatening to respond in kind. There is no solution other than a surrender over the Scarborough agreement, the first step in a process which will make the United Kingdom another Soviet satellite.

When *August 1988* was published in 1985, it was denied the reviews without which a serious work of fiction cannot attract readers, and sank without trace. This may have been because the publishers, Collins, had made the tactical error of revealing that its author was General Sir David Fraser, and putting on the back of the book a photograph of him dressed in full military uniform. The English have always preferred their soldiers to appear in public in civilian clothes, and to abstain, like the Royal Family, from commenting on political issues, even when in retirement. An alternative explanation depends upon the acceptance of the view that there was, in the London literary establishment, an unofficially formulated agreement that views which went against the prevailing climate of opinion should not be given too wide a hearing. After all, since no sensible person saw the Soviet Union as likely to behave in this way, there was no need to give widespread publicity to such hysteria.

Opinions were more sharply divided in the Christian Church than they were in literary circles and universities. While the Church of England, in a pamphlet published in October 10, 1982 entitled *Christianity and the Bomb*, advocated unilateral nuclear disarmament, Cardinal Basil Hume, in a letter published in *The Times* on November 11, 1983, drew attention to the statement by Pope John Paul II to the effect that:

> in current conditions, 'deterrence' based on balance, certainly not as a cure in itself, but as a stage on the way to a progressive disarmament can still be judged morally acceptable.

This was not the view taken by one of the most distinguished of English Catholic intellectuals, Anthony Kenny, in *The Logic of Deterrence*. As a former Jesuit priest, and at the time Master of Balliol College, Kenny had few rivals for the acuity of his philosophical analysis. There was no disputing his contention in his Introduction that 'the existing deterrent policies of both East and West are unacceptable on three grounds: that they are murderous, dangerous and extravagant'.[7] The conclusion which he drew from this was that the NATO powers should formally renounce the use of nuclear weapons. This was not, however, the guideline adopted by the politicians who brought the Cold War to an end.

THE REAGAN SOLUTION

Although the 1980s began with the Cold War already in one of its most critical phases, many on the European left saw the crisis becoming even more serious with the election in 1980 of Ronald Reagan as 40th President of the United States. Unlike his Democratic predecessor Jimmy Carter, Reagan was a hard-line anti-Communist, who regarded Carter's record since his election in 1976 as a total disaster in foreign-policy terms. This led Reagan to be presented throughout Europe as an irresponsible warmonger, a view not shared by Margaret Thatcher, who, with the victory of the Conservative Party in the general election of May 1979, had become the first woman Prime Minister of the United Kingdom.

Like President Reagan, she saw East–West relations as a struggle in which what Reagan called 'the evil empire' of the Soviet Union might well win unless resisted with much more fervour than had been shown by President Carter. She agreed with the hawks in the American foreign-policy and military establishment, who regretted the fact that Carter had yielded to pressure from the peace lobby in April 1978 when he postponed the development of the neutron bomb, described by its critics as the perfect capitalist weapon because it killed people while leaving property intact.

Its value as a tactical weapon was that it could neutralise the considerable superiority which the Soviet Union was said to enjoy in the number of tanks it could deploy against Western Europe. Although the neutron bomb might not have had the military value attributed to it, it had an immense symbolic importance. With the Soviet Union in the apparently aggressive mood suggested by the invasion of Afghanistan and the installation of the SS-20s, it was important not to send out the wrong kind of message. Yielding to the peace lobby was the kind of gesture which could only encourage the Soviet Union in the policies which had already killed off Détente.

Such encouragement never came from Ronald Reagan, and it is improbable that his decision to increase American military spending was merely intended as a gesture. He believed, as the majority of research scientists did not, that it was possible to install a protective screen of laser rays around the airspace covering the United States, so that they could shoot down any missile before it had time to explode. This project, officially known as the Strategic Defence Initiative (SDI), or 'Star Wars', after a recent and highly successful science-fiction film, was announced by Reagan in a speech on March 23, 1983. It was enormously expensive, costing an estimated $US33 billion, and was never in fact completed. Its supporters argued that it did not need to be, since by the mid-1990s it had produced the desired effect of bringing the Soviet Union to the nego- tiating table and making it give up the policies which, in the view of most politicians in the West, had brought about the Cold War.

Nobody seriously contested that the SDI went against both the letter and the spirit of the agreements to reduce the level of nuclear armament reached earlier with the Soviet Union. In particular, it went against the doctrine described by the appropriate acronym of MAD (Mutually Assured Destruction), which had been enshrined in the Anti-Ballistic Missile treaty of 1972. This was that both the United States and the Soviet Union had enough nuclear weapons, and enough means of delivering them even after a surprise attack had destroyed the majority of its forces, to destroy one another completely. If the United States could protect itself in this way against the Soviet Union, it would be able to reply to any Soviet moves, whether against Western Europe or elsewhere, with the reasonable assurance of not being totally destroyed.

The only way in which the Soviet Union could counter this move was by developing a comparable system of its own, and it was said to have tried to do something similar by putting a laser shield round Moscow. But in spite of devoting fifteen per cent of its Gross National Product (GNP) to defence,[8] as against six per cent by the United States, the Soviet Union could match the Strategic Defence Initiative only by putting an unbearable strain on its already faltering economy. It was this, in the view of President Reagan's admirers, which led Mr Gorbachev, on April 7, 1986, to inaugurate a totally new Soviet policy by announcing a mora- torium on the deployment of Soviet missiles. In February 1987 he agreed to the 'zero-option' policy recommended by the West from the beginning of the crisis – the elimination of all Soviet and United States intermediate-range nuclear missiles in Europe – and the last major confrontation of the Cold War had come to an end.

The breaching of the Berlin Wall on November 9, 1989 marked the effective end of the Cold War. On October 3, 1990 Germany became one country again for the first time since the end of the Second World War, and at the Paris summit meeting of the Organisation for Security and Co- operation in Europe, held between November 19 and 21 1990, the members of NATO and the Warsaw Pact signed a Treaty on the Reduction of Conventional Forces in Europe which contained the declaration that they were 'no longer adversaries' and did not 'intend to use force against the territorial integrity or political independence of any state'. On April 1, 1991 the Warsaw Pact itself was formally dissolved, and on November 6,

1991 the Communist Party was temporarily outlawed in the Soviet Union. On December 25, 1991 the USSR broke up into the constituent republics which now form the Commonwealth of Independent States.

METHODS AND EXPLANATIONS

Two main explanations can be offered for the ending of the Cold War. The first, advanced by the admirers of Ronald Reagan and Margaret Thatcher, was that the United States had 'spent the Soviet Union into the ground'. Unable to respond to the challenge of the massive American rearmament programme of the 1980s, the Soviet régime had been left with no choice, as Martin Walker put it in *The Cold War and the Making of the Modern World*, but to plead 'nolo contendere', an expression meaning that they were simply giving up the struggle. In this respect, the Cold War and the collapse of the Soviet Union are intimately connected, the first having directly brought about the second.

The second explanation is that the West won because its economic system was better than that of the Soviet Union and because, on the whole, it enjoyed the support of the majority of its citizens. From this point of view, the Soviet Union collapsed because it was too rigid a society to withstand the reform movement launched by Mr Gorbachev: a movement itself made necessary by the internal economic situation not only in the USSR itself but in its satellite states.

After an account of Northern Ireland and Yugoslavia, the two areas in Europe where peace has not prevailed in the same way as it has between the major states of both East and West, the rise and fall of the economic experiment begun in the Soviet Union in 1917 will be the subject of Part 2 of this book. There the two possible explanations for the ending of the Cold War will be further examined.

4 War at the edges

Northern Ireland and Yugoslavia

COMPARISONS AND CONTRASTS

THE WEIGHT OF HISTORY

In spite of the 1,500 miles between them, Yugoslavia and Northern Ireland share a number of features which help to explain why they should have been the scene of so much violence in an otherwise peaceful Europe. The first and most obvious is that both, for centuries, have been mixed communities in which the struggle of rival groups for dominance over their immediate neighbours has been masked by periods of uneasy truce. In Kosovo, the province where the greatest humanitarian catastrophe in post-war Europe took place in the early summer of 1999, the dispute goes back six centuries, to the crucial battle of June 28, 1389 at Kosovo Polje in which the forces of the Serbian ruler, Tsar Lazar, were defeated by the Ottoman armies commanded by Murad I.

This led to the creation of a state which was inhabited principally by Muslims, who did not speak the same Slavonic language as their mainly Christian neighbours, and who were seen both by them and by the Serb population they had conquered as invaders and oppressors. When, in 1912, the Serbian army reconquered the province, its soldiers were seen as liberators, and the final disintegration of the Ottoman Empire at the end of the First World War as a piece of historical justice. The battlefield of Kosovo Polje remains a sacred shrine for Serbian nationalists.

In Northern Ireland, the crucial date is July 12, 1691, when the armies of the Protestant William of Orange defeated those of the Catholic James II. The basic problem of a community divided between Catholics and Protestants nevertheless goes back further, at least to the second part of the sixteenth century. Insofar as the problems of Northern Ireland are also those of the whole relationship between Ireland and England, the situation whereby Ireland became a satellite state to its more powerful neighbour first arose in 1170, when the Irish king Dermot Macmurrough invited the Norman Earl of Pembroke, Richard de Clare, over to Ireland, allegedly to help him to win back his wife.

The other provinces of the former Yugoslavia have a comparable background to the one which led to the expulsion of over a million Kosovan Albanians to the neighbouring countries of Montenegro and Albania in April 1999. They are all, like Northern Ireland, parts of the world in which history is the enemy and not the friend of human happiness, and in that respect offer the countries of Western Europe yet another reminder of their good fortune.

France, England, Germany and Italy, like the Scandinavian monarchies and republics, and like Ireland itself, are ethnically homogeneous. Catholics may feel more Irish than Protestants do, but an Ulster Orangeman would not thank you if you told him that he was not Irish. Holland is racially as well as linguistically and culturally a united kingdom, and, however deep the divisions may go in Belgium between the French-speaking Walloons in the south and the Flemish-speaking majority in the north, they are linguistic and cultural in origin. There is no way in which they can be seen as racial.

ETHNIC DIVISIONS

This is not the case in the former Yugoslavia, where Bosnians, Croats, Kosovan Albanians and Serbs see themselves, and are seen by their neighbours, as belonging to different ethnic groups. In Bosnia-Hercegovina, the scene of some of the bitterest fighting between 1991 and 1995, Serbs, Croats and Bosnians live close together. Each group is afraid of its neighbours and has preferred, when it had the power to do so, to strike first in order to avoid becoming a victim. Such divisions may strike the outside observer as absurd. In the classification system used by the immigration authorities in the United States of America, virtually all the inhabitants of the former Yugoslavia would be described as Caucasian. They do not look different from one another in the way that a Negro does from an Arab, or a native of Japan from the average inhabitant of Bombay.

The situation in Northern Ireland is, comparatively speaking, simpler than that in the former Yugoslavia, in that there are only two main groups: the Catholics, who tend to side with the nationalist movement for a united Ireland, and the Protestants, who in their vast majority want to maintain the link with the British crown and the existence which this entails of a state which, at the time of writing, still remains separated from the Irish Republic and independent of it. Neither, in recent years, has there been anything similar to the attempt since 1987 by the Serbian authorities in Kosovo to prevent the Albanian-speaking inhabitants from using their own language. The English stamped out the speaking of Irish as long ago as the eighteenth century.

In Northern Ireland, as in the former Yugoslavia, there are no natural boundaries between the two communities. There are, it is true, towns that are mainly Protestant, such as Coleraine, and cities with a mainly Catholic population, such as Londonderry. But there is less than fifteen miles between the two, and in the principal city of the Province, Belfast, the Catholic area of the Falls Road and the Protestant area round the Shankhill are so close together that an iron barrier had to be put up in order to keep the two communities apart. The intensity of the hatreds in the former Yugoslavia varies with the proximity of the different groups. The closer they are to one another, the more intense the detestation.

In Yugoslavia, the Muslim community has its origins in the Islamic conquest of the eastern Mediterranean and the Ottoman empire of the fifteenth century. The Slovenes, Croats and Bosnians are linked to the Austro-Hungarian empire of the eighteenth and nineteenth century, and thus to the Catholic culture of southern and central Europe. The Serbs, in contrast, see themselves as Slavs and as belonging to the Orthodox tradition of the Eastern Church. Northern Ireland is heir to the warring traditions created by the clash between Irish nationalism and British imperialism, as well as to the conflict between Catholics and Protestants which began with the Reformation and Counter-Reformation of the sixteenth and seventeenth centuries.

A HAPPY ACCIDENT

There is also a more fortunate similarity: neither in Northern Ireland nor in the former Yugoslavia has the violence been in any way connected with the Cold War. The fighting in Yugoslavia did not break out until 1992, two years after the meeting in Paris of the Conference for Security and Co-operation in Europe on November 21, 1990 had officially declared the Cold War to be ended. One shudders to think what would have happened if it had taken place when Mr Khrushchev was in power and on the rampage.

The renewal in Northern Ireland of the violence which had followed its creation as a separate state in 1920 began in 1966, when the elements from the Irish Republican Army began attacks on isolated Protestant communities in order to force them to leave their homes in a process which would now be known as 'ethnic cleansing'. Inter-community violence on a wider scale broke out in 1969, when the Cold War had reached almost exactly the mid-point of its 46-year span. But at no time was it linked on either the Catholic or the Protestant side to the contest between the Soviet Union and the United States of America.

The IRA did receive some arms and training from countries sympathetic to the USSR. But its principal support from outside came from rogue states such as Libya, or from fellow terrorist organisations such as

ETA, the group fighting for Basque independence from both France and Spain. The country with which the IRA wished Northern Ireland to be united – the Irish Republic, or Eire – had from the beginning of the Cold War adopted the same attitude of neutrality which had characterised it between 1939 and 1945. It had, as a state giving a privileged position to the Roman Catholic Church, little sympathy with Marxism or even with the milder forms of socialism developed by the Euro-Communists in countries such as Italy. The Provisional IRA, the body responsible for most of the acts of violence committed in the name of Irish nationalism and aimed at bringing about the unification of Northern Ireland with the Republic, differed from the Official IRA precisely by its lack of interest in Marxism.

In this respect, if in no other, the Northern Ireland problem reflects another essential aspect of the European experience since 1945. As in the former Yugoslavia, socialism has proved as unsuccessful in reducing nationalist hatreds as in solving economic problems. Whatever other explanations there may be for the long European peace which has followed the end of the Second World War, working-class solidarity is not one of them. Nationalism, coupled with religious enthusiasm, remains the most powerful of all forces affecting political behaviour.

THE PROBLEM OF SOVEREIGNTY

The persistence of nationalism in Yugoslavia and Northern Ireland offers a marked contrast to another feature of European political life in the second half of the twentieth century: the gradual reduction in the power of the national state to do what it wishes within its own borders. This reduction has been most visible in the countries of Western Europe, whose membership of what is now known as the European Union is inseparable from a readiness to sacrifice their ability to organise their own economy in the way they think best.

When, in October 1998, Pauline Neville-Jones asked 'What is sovereignty?' and replied that modern political thought would suggest that it is:

> not possessed by governments to do with it as they please, but is held in trust by them for their people[1]

she was not discussing either the European Union or Northern Ireland. She was talking about the former Yugoslavia; and when, in March 1999, NATO aircraft began to bomb Serbia in an attempt to prevent Slobodan Milošević's forces from carrying out their programme of ethnic cleansing in Kosovo, her words took on what already seemed a prophetic significance. They heralded what may turn out to be a major change in

European if not in world politics: the right assumed by some states to interfere by force of arms in the affairs of their neighbours in order to prevent the violation of human rights.

Until the mid-1990s relations between European states had been governed by what is known as the 'Westphalian principle', a term which refers to the treaties, signed in the German province of Westphalia, in 1648 which put an end to the Thirty Years War. The understanding which was then more or less universally adopted, at least as far as the relationships between European powers was concerned, was that each sovereign state had the right to treat its own subjects as it wished. The principle of *cujus regio, eius religio* (the religion is that of the area involved) meant that the ruler of any particular region had the right to require his subjects to accept his version of Christianity.

One of the ideas which had made the Thirty Years War last so long, reducing the population of Germany by almost a third in the process, was that Protestant kings and princes had the right to intervene in Catholic countries to protect their coreligionists, and vice versa. In 1648 this practice was abandoned: a change which led in turn to the idea that, however cruelly a nation state treated its own subjects, that was its own affair. Even if, in the 1930s, Great Britain and France had possessed the will-power and military ability to protect the Jews in Germany and Austria against Hitler's policies of ethnic cleansing, they would not have had the right to do so without previously making a formal declaration of war.

Opponents of the NATO air strikes pointed out that Kosovo had been recognised as part of Serbia since 1912, and that this recognition had been confirmed by the Dayton agreements of 1995 which put a temporary end to the fighting in other parts of the former Yugoslavia. However appallingly Serbian forces behaved, this remained an internal political matter. Military commentators in the United Kingdom also observed that the NATO forces had gone against the second of the three cardinal principles on which British officers are recommended to base their conduct: Don't march on Moscow; Don't get involved in the Balkans; Don't let the RAF transport your kit.

In Northern Ireland, the maintenance of order remained the responsibility of the British government. The treaties of 1920 and 1921 which established the border between what was then known as the Irish Free State and the Six Counties of Antrim, Down, Armagh, Tyrone, Fermanagh and Londonderry were international agreements signed by sovereign states. Apart from a fleeting and rapidly forgotten suggestion from the Irish Republic in 1969 that troops from the United Nations should be deployed in Northern Ireland, the Westphalian principle has been consistently adopted. The British government has been the one seen by the Irish Republic, as well as by everyone else, as the authority responsible for the maintenance of law and order. In the former Yugoslavia, the Westphalian principle has been regarded as less sacrosanct.

The scale on which the horrors of ethnic cleansing took place in Bosnia-Hercegovina or Kosovo offered an obvious justification for this. Thomas Hennessey's detailed and admirably balanced *A History of Northern Ireland, 1920–1996* gives the figure of 2,761 people killed as a result of the violence in Northern Ireland in the twenty years between 1969 and 1989.[2] Terrible though this figure is, it is not on the same scale as the deaths caused by the Yugoslavian civil wars, which by now must be well over a million.

NORTHERN IRELAND

HISTORICAL ANTECEDENTS

Irish history, as the saying goes, is something which all Irishmen should forget, but all Englishmen remember. The event which throws most light on the current situation in Northern Ireland is the confiscation, from the sixteenth century onwards, of almost all the land held by Irish Catholics, and the installation as new owners of this land of Protestant settlers from England and Scotland. In September 1649 the Protestant army of Oliver Cromwell had massacred not only the garrison at Drogheda but also most of the town's civilian population, taking particular care as they did so that not a single Catholic priest should remain alive.

It did so for motives of practical politics as well as religious intolerance. In the course of the sixteenth century, the movement known as the Reformation had transformed England and Scotland into Protestant countries. But it had not crossed the Irish Sea, and the vast majority of the population of the island of Ireland, whether of the original, pure Celtic stock or of more recent Norman or Anglo-Saxon origin, had remained faithful to Roman Catholicism. England's principal enemies in the sixteenth and seventeenth centuries were the Catholic powers of Spain and France. With almost two million inhabitants, as against only nine million in England, Ireland was a formidable potential enemy. Were it to fall under the control of one of the Catholic powers of continental Europe, this could easily mean that England would have to fight a war on two fronts. From the English point of view, the reduction of the power of Irish Catholicism was a political and military necessity.

Between the 1640s and the beginning of the eighteenth century the proportion of land held by Catholics in the whole of Ireland fell from fifty-nine per cent to seven per cent. Catholics could not buy land, hold a long lease, vote, be called to the Bar, or become freemen of a corporation. If the eldest son of a Catholic converted to Protestantism, he automatically inherited all the land. Mixed marriages were illegal, and what were known as 'Charter schools', offering the only form of public education available, were open only to Protestants.[3] From 1800 the Act of Union meant that the Irish could hold seats and be represented only in the Parliament at Westminster.

Between 1841 and 1851, in one of the great demographic catastrophes of Western Europe, a disease broke out which killed the potatoes on which the Irish depended for their survival. The British government, following what was then the received economic orthodoxy, refused to interfere with market forces by supplying emergency food. A million or so Irish people died. A further million and a half emigrated to North America, making Ireland one of the few countries in the world whose population did not increase during the second half of the nineteenth century. In 1850 its population had risen to just over five million; in 1910 it was just over three million.

It is the memory of events such as these which creates the similarity between Northern Ireland and the former Yugoslavia. In both countries history is a divisive force. In the island of Ireland, taken as a whole, there are none of the unifying myths which enable the English or the Dutch to look back on their history with the feeling of pride in a job well done. There are two traditions, two versions of the past. In the one, the Protestant Irish deserve their privileges because of their capacity for hard work and their loyalty to the British Crown. In the other, the Catholic Irish are the victims who deserve compensation for the long oppression from which they have suffered, a compensation which can take the form only of their becoming citizens of the Irish Republic. After centuries of oppression and exploitation, they have managed to win their independence. But they have done so only to find a part of their country kept from them, linked to their former enemy, and inhabited by a people who, if they are racially Irish, tell themselves a totally different story about the past and have an equally different vision of the present as well as the future.

These people are the Ulster Protestants, the descendants of the Scottish Presbyterians who were encouraged to come over in the sixteenth and seventeenth centuries as part of the English policy of trying to ensure that Ireland would not fall into the hands of a continental enemy. They were, from the beginning, different from the richer English emigrants who took the land from the Catholics in the south and built their splendid houses on it. When the rise of Irish nationalism made life difficult for the latter, they could move elsewhere. There were not enough members of what was called the Protestant Ascendancy to put up a serious resistance to the demand for Irish independence, and between 1915 and 1922 there was a 45 per cent decline in the Protestant population of the area around Cork, a 44 per cent decline in Munster, a 36 per cent decline in Connaught and 30 per cent in Athlone.[4] But in the six counties of Northern Ireland, and especially in Down and Antrim, the Scottish settlers were of a different type. As Presbyterians, they were believers in a stricter and more rigorously anti-Catholic doctrine than the Anglicans who tended to live in the south. More importantly, they were poor. They had left their native Scotland permanently behind them, and had nowhere else to go.

They were also more numerous than the Protestants in the south; some 800,000, as against a maximum of 30,000. In 1920, with the passage of the Government of Ireland Act, the British government agreed to the creation of an independent Irish Republic. In June 1937 the Dail, the Irish parliament in Dublin, passed a law creating the new state of Eire, which laid claim to the whole of the island of Ireland. Eire remained neutral during the Second World War and in December 1948 ceased to be part of the British Commonwealth. On April 1948 it officially took the name of the Republic of Ireland, and on January 1, 1973, together with the United Kingdom and Denmark, it became a member of what was then the European Economic Community. It has derived more economic benefits from its membership than any of the fourteen other states which now make up the European Union, largely because of the efficiency of its agriculture. But the fact that Northern Ireland, the region which Unionists like to describe as 'an integral part of the United Kingdom', is also a member of the European Union has not brought a solution to the Northern Ireland problem any closer.

PROTESTANT BELIEFS AND CATHOLIC EXPERIENCE

Although the Orange Order, whose aim is the maintenance of the Protestant religion, was not created until 1795, it sees William of Orange's victory at the Battle of the Boyne on July 1, 1690 as providing the real foundation of Northern Ireland as a state different in virtually every respect from the Republic. Had James won, he would have united Ireland under Catholic rule. There would then have been no struggle between Ireland and England, since under James II England would have become a Catholic country as well, and hence an ally of France. Irish Protestants would then have been persecuted as mercilessly as their French brethren had already begun to be in 1685 when Louis XIV revoked the Edict of Nantes, and as the English who refused to convert to Roman Catholicism would have been by James II.

The more intellectually minded members of the Order even regard William's victory as the decisive turning point in European history. Had William lost, they argue, James would have been restored to the throne of England. He would have maintained his alliance with His Most Catholic Majesty, Louis XIV of France, and enlisted his help in making England a Catholic country again. The Counter-Reformation would then have recovered from the setback which it had suffered in 1648, when the peace of Westphalia had put an end to the Thirty Years War and marked the failure of the House of Austria to unify Europe under Catholic rule. More particularly, by preventing the Glorious Revolution of 1688 from giving birth to the beginnings of parliamentary democracy in England, James's victory would also have meant that Western Europe would never have known the movement of ideas which led to the French Revolution of 1789.

This is a vision of history which expresses the more acceptable side of the Orangeman's dream, and its optimistic view of history is in marked contrast with what actually took place after the Anglo-Irish Treaty of December 6, 1921 divided the island into two parts. In the North, the Six Counties of Antrim, Down, Armagh, Tyrone, Fermanagh and Londonderry remained under the British crown. In the South, the twenty-six others formed an independent state whose Constitution recognised the privileged position of the Catholic Church and based a good deal of its social policy on its teachings. The slogan written on the walls of the Protestant areas of Belfast, 'Six into Twenty-Six won't go', represents a spirit of defiance which suggests a community which is far more united than it actually is. Of the 1.5 million inhabitants of what both sides call the Province, roughly forty per cent are Roman Catholics; of these, ninety per cent support the idea of a united Ireland, and all are conscious of having suffered, ever since the creation of Northern Ireland in 1921, from a systematic policy of discrimination in both jobs and housing. The members of the Protestant majority see matters quite differently: in a united Ireland, it is they who will become the persecuted minority.

The violence which lasted until 1998 had already begun in 1966, in the form of IRA attacks against Protestants living in what were claimed to be mainly Catholic districts. But what some Protestants still see as a justified counter-attack on their part then took on a force of its own. In August 1969 Protestant extremists invaded the Catholic areas of Belfast, burning houses, threatening their inhabitants and carrying out their own process of ethnic cleansing. When the British government sent in the army, the soldiers were initially welcomed by the Catholic inhabitants of Belfast and Londonderry, being seen as more likely to look after them than the Royal Ulster Constabulary. Since its membership was predominantly Protestant, it was seen as unwilling to afford the same protection to the Catholic minority as to fellow Protestants.

There is no evidence that the British army was lured into a trap. The taunt directed at the IRA by its critics in the nationalist community said that these initials meant not Irish Republican Army but 'I Ran Away'. It suggests that, far from having prepared an ambush for the British, the IRA had lost the vigour which it had shown in the fighting of the early 1920s, when it had tried to destroy the 1921 treaty and bring Northern

Ireland into the Republic. The violence which soon began to be directed against the British army came from the group calling itself the Provisional IRA, the Provos. They differed from the Official IRA in being more exclusively nationalist. They were not interested in the Marxism which had inspired a number of the members of the earlier, more traditional movement.

The violence continued, with varying degrees of intensity, until the Good Friday agreement of April 10, 1998 brought what by the time this book is published may well turn out to have been only another in a series of interrupted cease-fires. There is little doubt that any British government, of whatever political persuasion, would be very happy to leave Northern Ireland completely to its own devices. It is equally certain that, if a referendum were held on the British mainland asking whether all ties between the United Kingdom and Northern Ireland should be cut, the question would be answered with an enthusiastic 'Yes'.

In retrospect, it seems an obvious mistake for the British government to have entrusted the government of the Six Counties to a locally elected parliament sitting in the new building of Stormont. However, even without the systematic gerrymandering which effectively disenfranchised large sections of the Catholic community, the Unionists would still have enjoyed a majority which enabled them to practise the discrimination in favour of Protestants – which explains the popularity enjoyed by an organisation otherwise so unattractive as the IRA. Had the direct rule eventually imposed from Westminster in March 1972 existed from the beginning, a London-based administration might have behaved with greater fairness, and the Catholic population might have felt less alienated. But the basic problem would have remained: that the Protestant majority in Northern Ireland did not want to become a Protestant minority in the South.

The strength of the Protestant opposition became visible in May 1974, when a strike organised by the Loyalist Ulster Workers' Council effectively paralysed the whole of the Province and rendered the proposed Northern Ireland Assembly unworkable. The new Council for All Ireland, elected in May 1998, may have better luck. But any proposal for a genuinely united Ireland is bound to come into conflict with the solid Unionist vote, which is especially strong in the Protestant working class. It may well be, as Geoffrey Wheatcroft observed in the June 1998 issue of *Prospect*, that 'partitioned or united, Ireland will become an Islamic republic before it becomes a socialist republic', and there is no doubt of the essentially working-class nature of Unionist opposition to a united Ireland.

In spite of incidents such as Bloody Sunday, when on January 30, 1972 troops fired on a Catholic demonstration in Londonderry and killed 23 civilians, the British government has probably been as successful as any government could have expected to be in the circumstances. In comparison with what happened after 1991 in Yugoslavia, or with the rebellion through which Algeria finally won its independence from France in 1962, the situation in Northern Ireland remains a low-intensity conflict This is even more the case when compared to the 100,000 or so Algerians killed since 1992 in the civil war between the government forces and the *Front Islamique du Salut*. In 1970, there were 19,000 road deaths in West Germany, and some 10,000 people continue to be killed on the roads in France. Even the last of these figures is almost three times the number of lives lost in thirty years of terrorist violence in Northern Ireland.

This statistic is not intended to diminish the gravity and horror of the situation. No words are too strong to condemn what happened on August 15, 1998, when 28 people were killed and 500 were injured by a bomb timed to explode on a Saturday afternoon in the centre of the town of Omagh. But the intensity of the condemnation directed at the dissident nationalist group, the Irish Nationalist Liberation Army, which placed the bomb and left a message directing people towards the point where it had been placed, is also the reflection of the feeling that such things do not happen in the Western Europe of the second half of the twentieth century. This has become a continent which had digested its history. Except in the Balkans, the two great tragedies of 1914–1918 and 1939–1945 have given rise in almost every European country to an unprecedented unity, and to the feeling that the use of violence for political ends has become a thing of the past. Why, then, has this not happened in the former Yugoslavia?

YUGOSLAVIA

RACIAL DIVERSITY AND ETHNIC HOSTILITY

In 1929 the different ethnic and religious groups originally brought together by the formation on December 1, 1919 of the Kingdom of the Serbs, the Croats and the Slovenes took the name of Yugoslavia, or the country of the southern Slavs. It owed its birth to the collapse at the end of the First World War of the Austrian and Ottoman Empires, a process which had been going on for some time. Serbia, the largest and most unified of the territories, had been an autonomous part of the Ottoman Empire since 1830, and an independent state since the Congress of Berlin in 1878. It saw itself as a Slavonic state whose ties of blood made it a natural ally of Russia. In spite of the doctrinal differences between the Russian Orthodox Church and the Orthodox Church in Serbia, the population of both countries shared a common outlook in religious matters. Unlike their neighbours in Bosnia, they were not Muslims, and unlike the Croatians, they were not Roman Catholics.

In 1914 it had been the readiness of the Russian Empire to go to the aid of Serbia after it had been threatened by Austria-Hungary which had helped to set off the First World War. The young Bosnian nationalist Gavrilo Prinzip, who on June 28, 1914 assassinated Prince Franz Ferdinand, the heir to the Austro-Hungarian throne, in Bosnia's capital Sarajevo, was alleged to have been in alliance with a Serb nationalist group calling itself the Black Hand. It was to punish Serbia for its alleged participation in the murder of Franz Ferdinand and his wife that Austria despatched the ultimatum of July 23, 1914, which, in the view of the ruler of Serbia, Peter I, effectively deprived his kingdom of its sovereign powers. Judging the reply to its ultimatum unsatisfactory, Austria-Hungary declared war on Serbia, and Russia mobilised in order to come to the help of its ally. Germany, Austria's principal ally, then declared war on France and Russia, and the First World War had begun.

Croatia, the second largest state, had been under the control of the Austro-Hungarian Empire since 1867. Its links with the Catholic tradition of Austria made it hostile towards the predominantly Orthodox state of Serbia, and religious differences also separated it from Bosnia-Hercegovina, forty per cent of whose inhabitants were Muslims. In 1508 Bosnia-Hercegovina had become part of the Ottoman Empire, but, as this declined, Austrian influence had become stronger, culminating in the Austrian annexation of the state in 1908. From both a racial and a religious point of view, it was the most heterogeneous of the states making up the former Yugoslavia, a fact which helps to explain why it should have been the scene of such bitter fighting. Slovenia, in contrast, had been part of Austria from 1282 to 1918, with over ninety per cent of its population being racially Slovene, and almost all of them Roman Catholic.

THE ACHIEVEMENTS OF MARSHAL TITO

Slovenia achieved its independence as a result of the general break-up of Yugoslavia which followed the death on May 4, 1980 of Josip Broz, who under the name of Marshal Tito had governed Yugoslavia since the Second World War. The roots of his régime were in the resistance movement which had enabled Yugoslavia to drive out the German army in 1944 without any direct military assistance from the Soviet Union. The fact that Yugoslavia was the only country in Eastern Europe to install a socialist régime without the help of the Red Army gave Tito a unique popularity. His increasing opposition to Moscow led in February 1948 to the expulsion of Yugoslavia from the Cominform (Communist Bureau of Information), the grouping of Communist states established on October 10, 1947 to take the place of the Comintern (Communist International), which had been founded in March 1919 but dissolved in 1943 as a sign of the Soviet Union's loyalty to its alliance with the West in the Second World War.

After the 1948 break with Moscow, Tito's Yugoslavia became a force for peace and stability in Europe in general and the Balkans in particular. As one of the leaders of the Non-Aligned movement, whose first meeting was held in Belgrade in September 1961, Yugoslavia was 'Communism with a welcome difference'. It tended, for example, to encourage worker participation rather than a centrally controlled economy. It was also one of the best practical illustrations in the modern world of the advantages of tyranny. None of the republics into which the former Yugoslavia is now divided – Bosnia-Hercegovina, Croatia, Serbia, Montenegro and Macedonia – is any better off now than it was under Tito, and all of them have had to endure a degree of violence unknown in his day. In the former Yugoslavia, as elsewhere in the modern world, warfare remains an occupation of the poor and a calling for the disinherited.

In 1993 Serbia was reported as having an inflation rate of two per cent an hour. On January 24, 1994 it issued a new currency (known, like the previous one, as the dinar) whose value was theoretically pegged to the Deutschmark. But by 1996 inflation in what had been known since 1994 as the Federal Republic of Yugoslavia, and which consisted by then only of Serbia and Montenegro, was back to 120 per cent a year. Its GDP per head of population was listed in 1993 as $US4,950. In Germany, this was $US14,400, in Croatia $US7,110 in Croatia and in Bosnia-Hercegovina, $US3,590.

After the death of Stalin in March 1953 there was a much-publicised ending to the hostility between Yugoslavia and the Soviet Union. In May 1955 Khrushchev and Bulganin visited Belgrade, and in June 1956 the Yugoslav leader Marshal Tito made his first visit to Moscow since 1948. But Yugoslavia gave no support to the Soviet repression of the Hungarian movement for independence in November 1956 or to the intervention by Warsaw Pact troops in August 1968. It was facts such as these which Anthony Parsons, the former British Permanent Representative at the United Nations, had in mind when he later described Yugoslavia as a state which had been:

> more than anything else the leading light of the Non-Aligned Movement, the bridge between the worlds of Western capitalism and Soviet Communism on the one hand, and the Third World of Asia, Africa and the Latin Americans on the other.[5]

This laudable behaviour by Yugoslavia on the international scene was not accompanied by any very generous programme of civil rights. According to its most famous dissident, Milovan Djilas, Tito's régime jailed as many political prisoners, in proportion to its population, as

Stalin's Russia.[6] But from the moment of his break with Moscow in 1948 Tito was able to reinforce national unity by constant evocation of the threat from the Soviet Union, and his broad-minded policy towards the different races contrasted sharply with his refusal to grant his citizens the democratic rights traditional in the West.

Although half-Croat by birth, Tito never openly favoured his own people. He recognised the fact that the Serbians, who numbered almost 10 million, were bound to play a leading role in any Federation. The Serbs formed a united ethnic group, and thus had potential dominance over the 4.5 million Croats, the mixed population of slightly under 4 million in Bosnia-Hercegovina, the 2 million Macedonians and the 2 million Slovenians, as well as over the 650,00 inhabitants of Montenegro, who were all divided in some way one against another. As the British diplomat Frank Roberts observed in 1979, Yugoslavia was a country containing 'six republics, five nationalities, four religions (including Communism), three languages and two scripts'[7]. It was never, therefore, going to enjoy any organic unity, and, although Tito entrusted most of the key roles in the Party and the army to Serbs, he was highly skilful in balancing the different racial groups. Indeed, his 45-year reign was marked by an absence of inter-ethnic conflict which now makes it seem like a golden age.

THE FAILURE OF THE TITO LEGACY

Although Tito failed to make the problems which he had held in check disappear, these did not break out again immediately after his death on May 4, 1980. It was not until May 1987 that the Serb leader Slobodan Milošević told a crowd of Kosovans demonstrating in favour of independence that 'Yugoslavia does not exist without Kosovo' and began to deprive the province of the relative autonomy it had enjoyed under Tito; and it was not until the end of the Cold War in 1991 that the fissiparous tendencies which Tito had kept under control led to the most violent fighting to take place in Europe since 1945.

The first major episode in the disintegration of the Yugoslav Republic took place on June 25, 1991, when Slovenia declared its independence. This was followed by a short civil war in which the former Yugoslav army, composed largely of Serbs, tried to intervene to keep Slovenia under Serbian control. However, since ethnic Serbs constitute only two per cent of the otherwise homogeneous population of Slovenia, the war did not last long, and by July 18, 1991 the Serb leadership effectively recognised Slovenia's independence. Like the Czech Republic, which separated from the largely agricultural country of Slovakia on January 1, 1993, Slovenia is one of the Eastern European countries which seem to have derived most benefit from the collapse of Communism. With a GDP

per head of population of some \$US6,500, its inhabitants enjoy only a rela-
tively modest standard of living, but, in spite of the differences between
the five political parties which share the votes of its two million or so
inhabitants, the country enjoys an enviable political stability.

The real disasters began to take place after Croatia had declared its
independence on October 7, 1991. On December 23, 1991 this independence was recognised by the newly unified Germany, which also used its
influence to persuade the European Community to grant diplomatic
recognition to Croatia and Slovenia on January 1, 1992.

In the light of what had happened during the Second World War, it
was unfortunate that the movement for the recognition of Croatia should
have been led by Germany. During the German and Italian occupation of
Yugoslavia, a Croatian nationalist movement known as the Uštaše had
collaborated enthusiastically with the Germans and Italians. In 1934 this
movement had assassinated Alexander, King of Yugoslavia, and established a puppet government in Croatia. From 1941 onwards, accepting
the frequently expressed claim that Germany and Italy were defending
Christian civilisation, it launched a policy of violent persecution against
the Serbian minority. Orthodox Serbs were compelled, on pain of death,
to convert to Roman Catholicism, and their womenfolk raped. Once the
Second World War ended, the Uštaše régime collapsed, but not without
leaving behind it a memory of the terror which it had exercised, and this
helps to explain why the fighting between Serbs and Croats which broke
out after 1991 should have reached the intensity it did. Ethnic cleansing
took place on both sides, ending in 1995 with a general victory for the
Croats, who had earlier expelled some 300,000 Serbs from the area round
Krajina.

Once Bosnia-Hercegovina declared its independence from Yugoslavia
on March 3, 1992, a similar pattern of conflict began there. Forty per cent
of its population are Muslims, the descendants of the inhabitants who
converted to Islam when the Ottoman Turks conquered the region in the
fifteenth century. Until the 1990s they had lived in relative peace with the
Serbs, who constitute some 32 per cent of the population, and who
belonged to the Orthodox Church. They had also had few conflicts with
the 18 per cent Croat population, who were Roman Catholics. However,
in the spring of 1992 the Serb minority began their version of ethnic
cleansing (a new term at the time) expelling Muslims and Croats from
the areas over which they wished to exercise total control. This led to acts
of great brutality, of mass murder, as well as to the policy of systematic
rape of Muslim and Croat women in pursuit of what the Serbs saw as the
desirable and justifiable aim of producing, within a generation, an ethnically homogeneous population.

Of the two reasons why the Bosnian Serbs embarked on this ethnic
cleansing, the first was probably fear. They were afraid that they might

become a persecuted minority, and decided to strike first. They were successful partly because they had taken the precaution of arming themselves in advance, something which the Croats and Muslims had not done. They also had the advantage of being supported by Serbia itself, the largest state in the former Yugoslav Federation and the one which controlled most of the former Yugoslav army.

The second reason lay in Serbia's ambition to extend its authority as far as possible beyond its official borders. Roughly a quarter of those who think of themselves as Serbs live outside Serbia itself. The Serbian republic consequently sees it as part of its duty to protect its kith and kin wherever they may be. It also sees itself as the true defender of Slav identity, first of all against the followers of Islam, the traditional enemy of the Slavs, and secondly against the Roman Catholic Croats, whose fidelity to Rome is seen as an insult to the Orthodox Church wherever it may be found, in Greece, Russia or in Serbia itself.

In September 1991 the first action of the United Nations Security Council was to decree an embargo on the shipment of all arms to the whole of Yugoslavia. For the supporters of the Croats and the Bosnians this recalled an earlier and even more tragic period in European history, when France and Great Britain refused to send arms to the Spanish Republicans between 1936 and 1939, at a time when Germany and Italy were openly arming Franco's forces in their destruction of Spanish democracy. Anthony Parsons remarks of this decision by the United Nations that it 'must have set the champagne corks popping in Belgrade', since Serbia had, as he points out, been 'systematically impounding' the weapons which should have been divided equally among the other republics. Serbia thus strengthened the advantage it already possessed through controlling the Yugoslavian Federal Army as well as nearly eighty per cent of Yugoslavia's military industry,[8] and enjoyed a military advantage over the other republics which it never lost. Bosnia-Hercegovina, thanks to the United Nations arms embargo, observed with particular strictness by the United Kingdom, could not arm itself to resist Serb aggression. Had it been able to do so, it is argued, the initial fighting might have been fiercer; but it would not have gone on so long.

ATTEMPTS AT MEDIATION

Initially, the main attempts to put an end to the fighting were made by the United Nations and the European Community. The suggestion in 1992 that Islamic states such as Turkey and Iran might intervene to protect the Muslims in Bosnia-Hercegovina came to nothing. This was fortunate, since such an intervention would have served only to widen the conflict. It would also have prevented the temporary alliance in

March 1995 of the Muslims and Croats against the Serbs, which made a contribution to putting an end to the fighting by simplifying the issues and reducing the numerical advantage which the Serbian army had hitherto enjoyed. In 1992, 17,000 troops were deployed under the flag of the United Nations in what was known as UNPROFOR (United Nations Protection Force), and by 1995 the force had grown to 30,000. But the rules of engagement under which it operated meant that it could rarely do much against the more heavily armed Serbian forces whose activities it was supposed to monitor. In 1996 it was reported that in the Bosnian town of Srebrenica, officially a United Nations 'safe area', it was impossible to account for 6,000 people, mostly Muslims, who had totally vanished.

The effort to mediate in the conflict by Lord Owen, representing the European Union, and Cyrus Vance, acting on behalf of the United States, came to nothing; so, too, did the plan carefully drawn up in 1993 by Lord Owen. Only after the United States, acting through the agency of NATO, launched air strikes in May 1995, and again in August and October, against the Serbian forces besieging and bombarding the Bosnian capital of Sarajevo did the way open to the agreement signed at the air force base at Dayton, Ohio, on November 21, 1995. This brought most of the fighting to a temporary end. As in the Middle East, where the Camp David agreement of 1978 marked the first step towards a possible settlement between Israel and its Arab neighbours, it was only when the United States took the initiative that problems even began to look as if they might be solved.

The Dayton agreement provided for a Bosnian state divided between a decentralised Bosnian-Croat Federation and a centralised Serb Republic. Perhaps more significantly, it committed 60,000 NATO troops to replace UNPROFOR. Just as the Cold War showed how incapable Western Europe was of protecting itself militarily against the threat from the East, so the Yugoslav crisis underlined its inability to intervene effectively in a crisis which was taking place, if not exactly at its heart, then close enough to its outer limbs to cause considerable discomfort.

The crisis in Bosnia-Hercegovina also brought out how differently the major states of Western Europe saw their national interests in foreign-policy terms. The French, in spite of François Mitterrand's courageous and much-publicised visit on April 29, 1992 to the Bosnian capital of Sarajevo, then being besieged and shelled by the Serbian army, tended to support the Serbs, their traditional ally since before 1914. The Germans, in contrast, favoured the Croats and the Bosnians, while the British government hoped the problem would go away and waited to see what the Americans would do. The extent of the catastrophe caused by the break-up of Yugoslavia can be seen in the fact that in July 1992 over a million refugees were being looked after by the UNHCR (United Nations

High Commission for Refugees). By the end of 1993 their number had swollen to 3.8 million, and by 1999, with the renewed fighting in Kosovo, the figure was over 5 million.[9]

There remained, at least for a time, one hopeful aspect to the multiple disasters affecting the former Yugoslavia. At least they were taking place in the otherwise relaxed international atmosphere produced by the ending of the Cold War. The Commonwealth of Independent States (CIS), the régime which had replaced the Soviet Union on December 31, 1991, had too many domestic problems on its plate to indulge in an aggressive foreign policy. In spite of the long-standing links between the USSR and Iraq, Russia had made no attempt to resist the American-led alliance that, in the Gulf War of early 1991, successfully expelled the Iraqi forces which had invaded Kuwait in August 1990.

Later on, in February 1994, the President of the Russian Federation, Boris Yeltsin, intervened to persuade the Serbs to accept a NATO ultimatum and withdraw the heavy artillery which had been bombarding the Bosnian capital of Sarajevo. In April 1994 Russia joined the United States, Great Britain and France as a member of the Contact Group who sought to bring about a peaceful settlement in the struggle for dominance between Serbia, Croatia and Bosnia-Hercegovina.

However, when NATO aircraft began to attack Serbia on March 30, 1999, in an attempt to dissuade its President, Slobodan Milošević, from slaughtering or expelling the ethnic Albanians who formed ninety per cent of the population of the province of Kosovo, this show of unity began to disintegrate. Initially, the authorities in the former Soviet Union limited themselves to fairly moderate protests. But on April 4 it was announced that a number of Russian ships were going through the Black Sea straits to monitor the conflict from close by in the Adriatic. On April 9 Yeltsin warned the West that any attempt to send ground troops into Kosovo might well set off a European or even a world war. Mr Seleznyov, the speaker of the Duma, the Russian lower house, accompanied Mr Yeltsin's warning by announcing that Russian missiles had now been retargeted on the NATO countries whose forces might be sent to Kosovo.

Although the Russians later adopted a less aggressive posture, there were continuing signs of divided councils in Moscow, which recalled some of the hesitations and apparent uncertainties that had preceded the crushing of the movement for Hungarian independence in November 1956 and the invasion of Afghanistan in December 1979. The Russian mediator, Victor Chernomyrdin, did most to bring the conflict to what may still be only a temporary end in early June 1999, but the tensions continued. On June 12, 1999 the Russians sent their troops into Kosovo first, and made NATO look extremely foolish by occupying the main airport at Pristina. While their Foreign Minister assured the Western capitals that it had all been a mistake, Boris Yeltsin ostentatiously promoted the General who had taken the initiative.

Such behaviour was fully explicable. Russia had undergone a series of humiliating disasters on the economic front. With a national budget somewhat smaller than the annual turnover of the Sainsbury's super-market group, and an inflation rate of over a hundred per cent, it was visibly being kept alive financially only by hand-outs from the West. While it is unlikely that the former Soviet Union would have done much to protect Tito's Yugoslavia from Western interference, the feeling of racial unity with the Serbs proved a more powerful motive than ideo-logical solidarity. The Serbs cheered when the Russian soldiers arrived, something which they would not have done if they had been carrying the flag of the Soviet Union.

MILITARY INTERVENTION AND EUROPEAN IDENTITY

The NATO air strikes did little to protect the Kosovan Albanians against the Serbs. In under two months, 1.1 million out of total population of 1.8 million had been driven from their homes, and by the middle of March 1999 almost 400,000 refugees had left the country. In that respect, the Western intervention in what critics hostile to it saw as a civil war was not a success. It was certainly inspired by excellent humanitarian motives, though. Such was the impact on public opinion of media reports of Serbian atrocities that it would have been impossible for the Western powers to do nothing. All the same, these powers did not inter-vene to try to end the conflicts going on at the same time in Algeria or Rwanda, and there had certainly never been any question of doing anything to dissuade the Russians from attacking Chechnya when it tried to assert its independence from Moscow in December 1994.

It is true that the Chechnyans proved surprisingly able to look after themselves – so much so that they secured almost complete autonomy – and, as was acknowledged at the time, it would have been unwise to issue a direct military challenge to a Russia described at the time as 'Upper Volta with nuclear weapons', especially when its President was an alcoholic. Geographically speaking, though, Kosovo was much more clearly part of Europe. There was consequently the purely practical consideration that an uncontrolled civil war might spread to neigh-bouring European states such as Greece, or even to Bulgaria or Romania.

The inhabitants of Bosnia and Croatia do not like to be told that they live in the Balkans. In their language, the word simply means 'moun-tains'. They see themselves as culturally European, and both are anxious to join the European Union. In the eyes of the critics of NATO interven-tion in Kosovo, the wars of the Yugoslav secession are nevertheless European only in the sense which the adjective would have carried before 1945, when to be a European was either to be at war with one of your immediate neighbours, to be preparing to go to war, or to be recovering from a defeat. In other, more favourable senses of the term, it is hard to see any part of the Balkans as being European in the sense that France, Germany, Italy or even Great Britain are European. This is a question which recurs in the Prelude to Part 3 of this book, 'The Movement Towards European Unity'.

Part 2 *The rise and fall of the socialist ideal*

Prelude

Marxist analysis and historical practice

MARXIST THEORY

In the opening chapter of *Animal Farm* (1945) George Orwell makes Major, Mr Jones's 'prize Middle White boar', explain the basic idea of Marxism in animal terms. 'Man,' he tells the other animals:

> is the only creature that consumes without producing. He does not give milk, he does not lay eggs, he is too weak to pull the plough, he cannot run fast enough to catch rabbits. Yet he is lord of all the animals. He sets them to work, he gives them back the bare minimum that will prevent them from starving, and the rest he keeps for himself. Our labour tills the soil, our dung fertilizes it, and yet there is not one of us that owns more than his bare skin.

For man, read the capitalist, and for the other animals, read the proletariat. What Orwell omitted was Marx's other idea that this exploitation was bound to destroy the system which had brought it into being. The capitalists, the owners of the means of production, distribution and exchange were in perpetual and ferocious competition with one another in order to produce more and more goods at as low a price as possible. This meant that wages could never be increased beyond the point where they merely kept the worker alive. The price of competition was ruin for those capitalists who could not manage to sell their goods. Individual capitalists who could not keep up with the competition went bankrupt and sank into the mass of the proletariat who had nothing to sell except their ability to work.

The effect of this ruthless and constant exploitation, argued Marx, was thus to make the mass of working people, the proletariat, at one and the same time poorer and poorer and more and more numerous. The capitalists, on the other hand, were destined by the very process of the productive forces which they had brought into being to grow fewer and fewer but richer and richer. Eventually, however, Marx explained in *Das*

Kapital (*Capital*, 1867), the ferocity of the system would make its inner contradictions more and more unbearable, and it would collapse. The expropriators – the capitalists who had robbed the proletariat of the fruits of its toil – would themselves be expropriated, and the system in which one group of men exploited their fellows for their own private benefit would be replaced by one in which private property was abolished; the means of production, distribution and exchange were owned by the whole community; and the injustices of the capitalist system replaced by a new world in which each man worked according to his ability and was rewarded according to his needs.

But all this took time. The workers' state would come into being. There was no doubt about that. That was the way history worked. But history was not to be hurried, and Marx himself did not think that the revolution would take place in Russia. He saw it happening in a modern, industrialised country, where the contradictions of capitalism had reached their peak. In the immediate aftermath of the First World War, it almost did so in Germany, with the headline in the *Daily Express* for November 11, 1918 reading 'Red Flag flies over the ruins of an Empire'. But the forces of reaction in Western Europe were too strong, and until 1945 the attempt to put Marx's theories into practice took place solely in the federal state known as the Union of Soviet Socialist Republics, the USSR, which officially came into being on December 30, 1922.

This was the creation of Lenin, a Marxist revolutionary whose originality was to stand the historical aspect of Marxism on its head. Instead of the workers' state being the product of an economic revolution, it was the forcible creation of this state which would produce the economic revolution that would then make the proletariat into the ruling class. 'Coming, ready or not', was his message.

Lenin took seriously the claim made by Marx in the posthumously published *German Ideology* that force was the midwife of history. When the Revolution of 1917 had lasted one day longer than the Paris Commune of 1871, he danced on the snow of St Petersburg with delight. From his own point of view, he had every reason to rejoice. Without his arrival at the Finland Station in April 1917, the Revolution which overthrew the Tsarist state might never have been transformed in the way it was, and he and his followers would never have been able to create the Soviet Union.

Marx had left no blueprint of how capitalist society should be transformed into a workers' state. But his denunciation of the very principle of private ownership was a fair indication of the first steps to be taken. The radical workers' councils had already been set up before April 1917. They had taken the name of Soviets, the representative institutions first created in the 1905 revolution, and which emphasised local control over factories and workers' councils. It was they which proceeded, against the wishes of the more middle-class politicians in the resurrected Duma, the Russian parliament, to nationalise factories and farms and to throw out their original owners. But it was only the energising genius of Lenin which transformed these changes into an organised system of government.

Once he had achieved power in Russia, Lenin acted exactly as the Germans had intended when they let him travel in a sealed train from Switzerland to St Petersburg. Between February and December 1916 they had failed to win the battle of Verdun. This led them to see that their only hope of victory was to remove Russia, France's ally, from the war in order to be able to concentrate all their forces on the Western front. Since Lenin had made no secret of the fact that he saw the First World War as a capitalist conspiracy, the Germans knew they could count on him to do what they wanted. By allowing him to go to Russia, they showed how completely they gave priority to the national interests of Germany over the needs of the capitalist system as a whole. They were quite prepared to see capitalism destroyed in Russia, so long as Germany won the war.

The Treaty of Brest-Litovsk, signed on March 3, 1918, ceded to Austria-Hungary and Germany the whole of Estonia, Latvia, Lithuania, Belarus, and the Ukraine, as well as the countries of Finland and Poland, over which Russia traditionally exerted a dominating influence. Russia also lost 34 per cent of its population, 54 per cent of its industry and 90 per cent of its coal mines. To historians who support the fight to the finish which the British and French pursued against Germany until November 1918, it was an indication of what might have happened to France and Belgium if the Second Reich had won the First World War. The Treaty of Brest-Litovsk enabled Lenin to devote the whole of his energy to creating a workers' state in Russia.

THE RULE OF THE PARTY AND THE HOSTILITY OF THE WEST

The Soviet Union itself was officially established on December 30, 1922 and based on Lenin's interpretation of how Marxism ought to work in practice. The doctrine known as Marxism-Leninism remained the official ideology of the Soviet Union, and from 1945 onwards, it was the official philosophy of the régimes established in Albania, Bulgaria, Czechoslovakia, Hungary, Poland, Romania and the German Democratic Republic. In the area controlled by the Soviet Union virtually the whole of the economy was controlled and owned by the state, with only a very small part, generally in the agricultural sector, remaining in private hands.

The political system was based on the idea of the Communist Party as the expression of the true nature of the Proletariat, and therefore the only party allowed to exist. It alone understood the historical process whereby the workers' state would be created, and Lenin's principal lieutenant Leon

Trotsky (Lev Davidovitch Bronstein) laid emphasis on its leading role when he said in 1924:

> The Party is always right. We can only win with the Party, for history has provided no other way of being right. If the Party adopts a decision which one or another of us thinks unjust, he will say: 'Just or unjust, it is my party and I shall accept the consequences of the decision to the end'.[1]

In a sense, neither Lenin nor Trotsky had any choice as to the way they governed. Even if Lenin had not developed the idea of the Party as the instrument with which to put into practice what Marx had called the dictatorship of the proletariat, the circumstances in which he came to power meant that he could stay there only by refusing to tolerate either dissent or opposition. A large number of Russians did not agree with Lenin's forcible seizure of power. They were, in particular, horrified by events such as the murder of Tsar Nicholas II at Ekaterinburg on July 16, 1918, as well as by the attempt to abolish Christianity.

This led to a civil war in which France, Great Britain and the United States of America intervened with the declared intention of overthrowing the Bolshevik régime and compelling Russia to stay in the war. Before 1914 Russia had borrowed immense sums of money from the West, especially France, to finance its attempt at modernisation. The Bolshevik government had repudiated all debts, and the Western powers wanted their money back. The official doctrine of Marxism was world revolution. To attempt, as Churchill put it, to 'strangle the Bolshevik revolution in its cradle' was part of a deliberate strategy for defending the capitalist system. Lenin had to use force to defend the state created by the Bolshevik Revolution, because there was no other way of ensuring its survival.

The cold war, in this respect, began by being hot. The hostility towards the West which looked so unprovoked to the Western statesmen in the period immediately following the end of the Second World War in 1945 was, in the view of those who supported the Soviet Union, the direct consequence of the way the West had treated the new régime at its birth. The Soviet Union behaved like a state under siege because it had been placed under siege from the very beginning.

It is this that explains the conspiracy theory of history which argues that the Cold War took place because, from 1917 onwards, the United States and its allies decided not to allow the Soviet Union to exist. In the immediate aftermath of the 1939–1945 war, they tricked it into a confrontation aimed at weakening its already badly damaged economy by forcing it into an arms race which Western strategists knew that they had every chance of winning.

This theory is consistent with the views of American revisionist historians such as Gar Alperovitz and Walter Lafeber, and more recently of the British Marxist, Fred Halliday. It was summarised by another American, D.F. Flemming, when he claimed in 1967 that 'from the first, it was the West which was on the offensive, not the Soviets', a view supported by A.J.P. Taylor when he argued in 1978 that it was impossible to prove that the Soviet Union had any aggressive intentions in the years after 1945. Indeed, he wrote, 'all the evidence points the other way', and he continued:

> In the immediate post-war years Stalin deliberately thwarted the advance of the Communist parties in France and Italy. His concern in the USSR's border states was security, not the advance of Communism. His supposedly aggressive designs, as in Iran or at the Straits, was security and he abandoned them when they were resisted. Throughout those years, the USSR was a frightened power desperately on the defensive. Apart from security, Stalin's other main aim was to gather reparations from Germany, an aim which curiously led him to champion German unity when the Western Allies had already abandoned it.[2]

But if, in this reading of events, the Soviet Union failed because this was what the West wanted to happen, there were other reasons.

RUSSIAN HISTORY AND SOVIET GEOGRAPHY

One of these is that Russia had no tradition either of democratic government or of efficient public administration. Since Lenin did nothing to try to change this situation, it could be argued that the failure of the Soviet Union lay in the inability of any totalitarian régime to win the efficient and enthusiastic support of its citizens.

When the second All-Russian Congress of Soviets met in October 1917, Lenin found himself in a minority. He simply dissolved it, so that, when the Constituent Assembly met in November 1918, the Bolsheviks had a majority. In a few days, between November 10 and December 29, 1918, this enabled Lenin and his followers to take over the whole state. All ranks were abolished, all churches closed down, all factories declared the property of the state, all payment of interest and dividends suspended, most landed estates and large houses confiscated and their owners killed. Lenin made no secret of his desire to rule by terror, and his suppression of the Kronstadt mutiny of February 21, 1921 showed that he had no time for opposition, not even from fellow revolutionaries.

There is little evidence for the view that, had he not died of a stroke on January 21, 1924, Lenin would have pursued a more humane policy than Stalin. Not only did he need to impose the common ownership of property on a country whose inhabitants wanted to keep what they owned. He also had to impose the central authority of the Moscow government on a federation in which the Russians themselves constituted only 53 per cent of the total population.

Thus the USSR (Union of Soviet Socialist Republics) included Azerbaijan and Georgia, originally grouped together as the Transcaucasian Socialist Soviet Republic, but becoming separate states within the Soviet Union in 1936. It contained Belarus, or Belorussia (also known as White Russia), which was one of the founding republics of the USSR in 1922, together with Kazakhstan, originally an integral part of the Russian Socialist Soviet Republic, but which also became what was known as an autonomous member of the USSR in 1936. It included the Ukraine, whose population of almost 50 million inhabitants was over a third of that of Russia itself, which had been one of the founding Soviet Republics in 1922. The only means of holding these disparate peoples together was by a dictatorship, and in August 1940, as a result of the non-aggression pact between Stalin and Hitler of August 23, 1939, the problem of maintaining unity became even more impossible to solve by democratic means.

When the Baltic states of Estonia, Latvia, and Lithuania were incorporated into the Soviet Union, it brought the total number of Soviet Socialist Republics up to fifteen: Armenia, Azerbaijan, Belarus, Estonia, Georgia, Kazakhstan, Kyrgyzstan, Latvia, Lithuania, Moldova, Russia, Tadjikistan, Turkmenistan, Ukraine, and Uzbekistan. According to the 1989 census, there were 147.3 million Russians, 51.7 million Ukrainians, 19.9 million Uzbeks, 16.5 million Belorussians, 7 million Azerbaijanis, 5.4 million Georgians, 5.1 million Tadjiks, 4.4 million Moldovans, 4.3 million Kyrgyz, 3.7 million Lithuanians, 3.5 million Turkmens, and 3.2 million Armenians – in addition to a hundred or so other ethnic and linguistic groups which did not enjoy officially independent status. During the 69-year existence of the Soviet Union the whole of this vast and varied population – many of whose members spoke Russian only reluctantly and purely as an official language, and who identified far more strongly with their local region than they ever did with Moscow – were nevertheless governed by the ideology of Marxism-Leninism, with everything which that implied by way of compulsory economic planning imposed by the state.

It may thus be geography, as much as any flaws which might exist in Marxism, or the diabolical cunning of the West, which explains the failure of the Soviet Union to live up to the hopes expressed for it by its many admirers in the English-speaking world. There was also another factor. This was highlighted by an article entitled 'The Cash Don't Work', published in *The Economist* on December 19, 1998, four months after the Russian government had announced on August 18 that it was to allow the rouble to go into free fall. This argued, as the subtitle put it, that 'A misunderstanding of money is the root of all Russia's evils'.

It began with a quotation from 'The Gambler', a short story by Fyodor Dostoevsky (1821–1881), in which the main character, Alexei, declares:

> the Russian is not only incapable of accumulating capital, he is also a persistent and helpless squanderer.

before continuing:

> Nonetheless, we Russians do have great use for money, and so we are always very happy to come across such things as roulette, which can enable a man to become rich almost effortlessly within two hours.

The article, unsigned as is the custom with *The Economist*, proceeded to argue that the economic system established by the Bolshevik Revolution exactly fitted this aspect of the Russian character. Initially, the Soviet authorities simply printed whatever money they thought they might need. Then, in 1924, they carried out a currency reform which meant that it took 50 billion of the 1921 issue to buy one rouble of the newly minted variety. The dominance of central planning from 1929 onwards meant, as *The Economist* put it, that 'the value of the rouble became both arbitrary and variable'. It became what economists call a 'token currency', one which was valid only within a particular area, as tokens issued by the authorities in a prison have value only within that prison and not in the outside world. Unlike tobacco or drugs, which also exist in the closed environment of a prison, it did not obey the laws of supply and demand. There was no consistency in the system, in that a well-placed bureaucrat might buy a kilo of sugar in the private shop attached to his Ministry, whereas an ordinary person might queue for an hour to pay 50 roubles at a grocer's down the street.

In such circumstances, argued the article in *The Economist*, it was no wonder both that the economy of the Soviet Union broke down and that Russia was still having so much difficulty organising a viable economic system. It is – to use a comparison not made in 'The Cash Don't Work', but one which fits another aspect of the Russian character frequently mentioned in the Western press – as though a man who already had a drink problem had been allowed to live for several years scot-free in a distillery, then suddenly to be told that he had to exist on lemonade.

The idea that the failure of Communism in the Soviet Union is perhaps due less to the inadequacies of Marxism than to the Russian national character can be supported by what happened in both West and East Germany after 1945. In spite of the total destruction of its roads, factories and buildings, the Federal Republic of Germany took less than fifteen years to become the most prosperous country in Western Europe. In East Germany, the system worked less successfully than in the West, where both the economy and society itself recovered with quite remarkable speed from the 'Stunde Null' (year zero) of 1945.

This was not only because the Federal Republic of Germany received money from the Marshall Aid programme which the Soviet Union refused both for itself and on behalf of its satellites. It was also because the Germans had not quite lost the habits of thrift which had always been part of their national culture, and because of a social structure which had miraculously survived both the Nazi revolution of 1933 and the allied bombing campaign. The inhabitants of East Germany had to resort to barter, and what prosperity did exist was created by a barely tolerated private sector. The system was very much one which had been forced upon the Germans by the Soviet authorities, and it had many of the same defects as in the USSR. But – as in Czechoslovakia, especially after 1968 – memories of how a real economy worked remained sufficiently alive for the system to work much better than it had ever done in the Soviet Union, and for people to be ready for the reintroduction of a private-enterprise system as they had never been in pre-revolutionary Russia and were still not in 1990.

EARLY VISIONS OF THE SOVIET ACHIEVEMENT

None of the weaknesses which can now be seen as having brought about the collapse of the Soviet Union was visible in 1945. Thomas Balogh, the Hungarian-born economist who later became an adviser to the British Labour Prime Minister Harold Wilson was announcing that the dynamism of the Soviet economy would, within ten years, give it 'an absolute predominance economically over Western Europe'.[3] Much of the high reputation which it enjoyed was due to the triumphs of the Red Army. Had it not, as Churchill put it, 'torn the guts out of the Wehrmacht', the liberating invasion of Western Europe which began on June 6, 1944 could have never taken place. But there were other reasons, chief among them the prestige which the Soviet Union had always enjoyed in progressive circles in the West, and this helps to explain why its rapid collapse in 1989 and 1990 came as such a surprise.

In November 1935 the English social historians Beatrice and Sidney Webb published one of the most successful and influential books of the 1930s and early 1940s, *Soviet Communism: a new civilisation?* In 1942 the third edition appeared, this time with the question mark removed, and was reissued in 1947, with the re-affirmation of their belief that

A study of the facts suggests that when a revolutionary government is confronted with the task of educating a mass of illiterate and oppressed peoples, of different races and religions, among them primitive tribes, not only to higher levels of health and culture but also in the art of self-government, there is no alternative to the One-Party System with its refusal to permit organised political opposition to the new political and economic order.[4]

It is as good an excuse as any for the dictatorship which Stalin took over from Lenin and intensified. It has the advantage of being free from the cant and illusion of the remark made by the novelist H.G. Wells after his visit to the Soviet Union in 1934, when he said that Stalin 'owed his position to the fact that nobody is afraid of him and everybody trusts him'. It also has parallels with another view of the Soviet Union put forward more recently by a thinker still deeply attached to the Marxist ideal. If the report in the *Times Literary Supplement* is accurate, the Marxist historian Eric Hobsbawm was prepared, even as late as October 28, 1994, to admit to Michael Ignatieff that if 'the radiant tomorrows' had actually been created by the Soviet régime, the twenty million deaths produced by Stalin's terror would have been justified. In 1964, Jean-Paul Sartre had also been sufficiently convinced of the virtues of the Soviet Union to write that:

> whatever its crimes, the USSR has the fearsome privilege over the bourgeois democracies of representing the revolutionary project.[5]

To readers of Arthur Koestler's *Darkness at Noon* (1940), a book discussed in Chapter 5 for the light which it throws on the Moscow State Trials of the late 1930s, there is nothing particularly surprising in these views. Indeed, it is a sign of Koestler's skill as a writer that he should – in the first, and perhaps still the best, novel to be inspired by disillusionment with Communism – present a character, Gletkin, who does make a case for the régime, in terms very similar to those of Beatrice Webb. Gletkin's first question to Rubashov, the Old Guard Bolshevik caught up in Stalin's 1936 and 1937 purges, is an apparently simple one: When were you first given a watch? When Rubashov replies that he must have been about eight or nine, Gletkin tells him that it was not until he himself was sixteen years old that he learned that the hour was divided into minutes. He then proceeds to offer other examples of the backwardness which meant that the Soviet Union could not afford the luxury of democracy when engaged in the construction of socialism. Near his village, he explains, is now 'the largest steel factory in the world'. Until they were shot if they did so, the foremen would lie down to sleep between two emptyings of the blast furnace, thus ruining the whole process and putting the factory itself at risk. 'In other countries', Gletkin adds:

> the peasants had one or two hundred years to develop the habit of industrial precision and of the handling of machines. Here, they had

only ten years. If we didn't sack them and shoot them for every trifle, the whole country would come to a standstill, and the peasants would lie down to sleep in the factory yards until grass grew out of the chimneys and everything became as it was before. Last year a women's delegation came to us from Manchester in England. They were shown everything, and afterwards they wrote indignant articles, saying that the textile workers in Manchester would never stand such treatment. I have read that the cotton industry in Manchester is over two hundred years old. I have also read what the treatment of the workers there was two hundred years ago, when it started.[6]

This had been one of the main themes of *Soviet Communism: a new civilisation*, with its argument that the task of industrialising the Soviet Union had now been successfully carried out. The USSR, in the Webbs' view, had increased productivity by planning every aspect of the national economy down to the minutest detail and transformed the making of private profit into a crime against the state. It had persuaded the trade unions to give up striking for higher wages and instead to co-operate with the Gosplan, the State Planning Commission for industrial development established on February 24, 1921.

More importantly, the Webbs argued, the Soviet Union had done something which no previous movement had ever achieved in the whole of human history. For whereas, in the societies of the West, the religious, political and industrial revolutions necessary to the creation of a modern state were carried out separately, the Communist Party of the Soviet Union had ensured that they were all successfully completed at the same time.[7]

The Webbs thus saw the Soviet Union as a great success, writing of 'the brilliant success of the planned economy', and maintaining that the statistics published by the government must be accurate because the state planning based upon them, was achieving such a high rate of economic growth. Without their realising it, however, the Webbs' remark about the three revolutions being carried out at the same time points to another reason for the contrast between the ultimate failure of the Soviet Union and the ability of Western capitalism, at least for the moment, to have survived and even prospered.[8]

It is no longer fashionable to argue, as Richard Tawney did in *Religion and the Rise of Capitalism* in 1926, that there is a necessary and organic link between the Protestant work ethic and the successful creation of a market economy. The fact remains that capitalism first took off in countries which had experienced the Protestant Reformation. It is equally true that it has achieved its greatest success in societies which, like the United States and the United Kingdom, and like late nineteenth-century France, have succeeded in limiting the role of organised religion to a measure of influence over people's private lives.

All the efforts of the Soviet authorities to destroy the power of the Orthodox Church in Russia failed. As Henry Chadwick pointed out in *The Christian Church in the Cold War*, travelling lecturers on atheism in the Soviet Union found it as difficult to get an audience as travelling preachers do in the West.[9] No European country has yet managed to create a viable market economy on any basis other than that of Protestantism or agnosticism. The achievements of east Asian countries such as Japan, Taiwan, Singapore or South Korea have also taken pace in societies where the role of religion has been limited to that of reinforcing the values of family solidarity, which are, in a sense, even more compatible with free-market economics. By reducing the need for a welfare state, they create a low-taxation régime which makes the pursuit of private profit even easier.

The Protestant work ethic has never existed east of the Elbe. The view that the secular state demonstrates its superiority by the facilities which it provides for the private creation of wealth has also been a characteristic notably absent from Russia, as from the other states formerly constituting the Soviet Union. In that respect, the Webbs were wrong to see that Soviet Union as having successfully combined the religious revolution, which has always been a necessary precondition to the creation of a successful capitalist economy, with the establishment of an industrial state.

The qualities required by such a state are those of initiative and a readiness to pay those taxes which cannot be avoided. (The British philosopher Alan Milne put his finger on this aspect of modern society when he quoted the remark by Mr Justice Holmes, sometime member of the United States Supreme Court, that: 'I pay the tax bill with most readiness, for I get civilisation for it'.[10]) They also include a respect for the rule of law, perhaps the most essential ingredient of any successful form of political or economic organisation, coupled with the ability to create an efficient and politically neutral system of public administration.

These are not qualities which can be created overnight, and in the countries composing the former Soviet Union the attitudes which encourage their development are notable principally by their absence. Another of the Soviet Union's problems, that of establishing an efficient agricultural system, had also been solved in the West, where the Industrial Revolution of the late eighteenth and early nineteenth century had been preceded and made possible by the agricultural revolution of the seventeenth. In 1942 Beatrice Webb wrote in her Introduction to the new edition of *Soviet Communism: a new civilisation* that all the rights now enjoyed in the Soviet Union were:

complemented by obligations on the part of the individual citizen. *Article 12* enacts that 'Work in the USSR is a duty and "a matter of honour" for every able-bodied citizen, on the principle "he who does not work shall not eat"'. Thus 'in the USSR the principle of socialism is realised: "From each according to his ability, to each according to his work"'. Once this principle has been acted on, the human race can progress to the higher level of Communism: 'From each according to his faculty, to each according to his need'.[11]

The selfless devotion to the public good, and a readiness to put the community's interests above one's own, are indeed morally superior to the pursuit of private profit. But even if the qualities praised by the Webbs had existed widely outside the pages of *Soviet Communism: a new civilisation*, there is no way that they could have survived in the atmosphere created by Stalin's atrocities, the millions of citizens sent to the *gulag*, the omnipresence of the secret police and the total absence of any freedom of thought or ability to lead a private life without interference from the state.

Had it been possible for the Soviet Union to live in total isolation from the outside world, the defects in its social and political system might not have proved fatal. But its victory in the Second World War placed it in a situation where it could not help expanding beyond its original borders. These were already vast enough, and the peoples they contained sufficiently various in customs and language for there to be more problems than even the most benevolent and efficient government could have solved. It was thus faced, as several of the countries of Western Europe were faced, with the problem of trying maintain an empire. It was this, the phenomenon which the historian Paul Kennedy has called 'imperial overstretch', which did more than anything else to bring it down.

5 The fruits of victory

THE EXPORTING OF SOVIET POWER

Although there were wide differences between the countries occupied by the Red Army after 1945, they were all treated in very much the same way. This may have been because the Soviet leaders were 'drunk with success' (as Stalin put it in one of his messages to the Soviet people quoted on a number of occasions by the Webbs) and, inspired by missionary zeal, convinced that the system which had worked for them must of necessity work for their neighbours. A more probable explanation is that Stalin wanted a *cordon sanitaire* against the West, and was not interested in the local customs of the countries whose independence was sacrificed in order to provide it.

The differences were nevertheless quite real. In the Balkan states of Albania, Bulgaria and Romania, the Communist revolutions carried out under the auspices of the Soviet Union had what Geoffrey and Nigel Swain call 'more legitimacy'[1] than in the more advanced countries of Czechoslovakia, Hungary, Poland and East Germany. The Balkan states were still semi-feudal, primarily agricultural states where the Soviet experience of wrenching the same kind of country into the twentieth century could have some relevance. According to an article by Vernon A. Aspaturian, Bulgaria was 'probably the only voluntary client state in Eastern Europe' and was typical of the Balkans in that, as Geoffrey and Nigel Swain put it, the Communists 'could have won western style elections in 1945 had they chosen to do so', and had that not been 'alien to the Leninist tradition in which they had been trained'.[2]

The central European countries, in contrast, had already achieved a considerable degree of industrialisation before 1939. (It is significant that the Czech Republic, Hungary and Poland were the first countries to mark their reintegration into the West by becoming members of the North Atlantic Treaty Alliance in March 1999, and are first on the waiting list to join the European Union.) It was in these three countries that the process by which the Communist Party came to power was more blatant in its illegality than in the less developed countries, and it was in these countries that rebellions subsequently took place which showed the whole world how little popular support the régimes enjoyed. Czechoslovakia, for example, had begun in May 1946 by having at least a semblance of democracy, in that the Communists won 114 out of the 300 seats in parliamentary elections and held power in a coalition with the Social Democrats. But, although in 1945 the veteran Comintern leader Georgi Dimitrov had told the Czechoslovak Communists that the time was not ripe for a full take-over of the state, they waited less than three years before bringing this about.

The Marshall Plan, announced on June 5, 1947, was open to all European states, whether in the east or in the west. The Czechs (who had enjoyed a viable system of parliamentary democracy before the Munich agreements of September 30, 1938 had begun the process of dismembering their state and handing it over to Nazi Germany) initially leaped at the offer of aid from the United States. But when their government, under their President, the Communist Klement Gottwald, announced the decision to accept on July 4, 1947, it was immediately summoned to Moscow and told by Stalin to change its mind. On July 10 it obeyed. The Foreign Minister Jan Masaryk – the son of the Tomas Masaryk, the first President of the Czechoslovak state when it was created in November 1918 – later said that he had 'gone to Moscow as the foreign minister of an independent sovereign state', but 'returned as a Soviet slave'.[3]

Stalin's objections to the Marshall Plan were strategic as well as ideological. The message from Moscow sent to Communist Party leaders in Eastern Europe on July 7, 1947 suggested that they should not take part in the conference scheduled to be held in Paris on July 12 and made a particular point of accusing its sponsors of 'planning to set up a Western bloc which includes West Germany',[4] alleging that the plans for a general economic revival of Europe were nothing more than a pretext for this more sinister intention. Since this is what did eventually happen, the Soviet Union may, from its own standpoint, have been justified in refusing either to accept the Marshall Plan itself or to allow its satellites to do so. Its leaders had every reason to be afraid of a revival of German militarism, and they had no way of foreseeing how successfully the Federal Republic of Germany would shake off the legacies both of Hitler and of Wilhelm II.

THE EXPORTING OF THE SOVIET ECONOMIC AND POLITICAL MODEL

Stalin's insistence that Czechoslovakia should reject the Marshall Plan was fully consistent with his remark to the Yugoslav, Milovan Djilas, about the novelty of the modern situation, in which each state is inevitably led to use its military victory to impose its own political system on the country its armies have conquered. The *coup d'état* by which the Communist Party established its rule in Czechoslovakia was nevertheless home-grown, and took place six months after Stalin had made Gottwald's government reject the Marshall Plan. It was facilitated by a miscalculation by the Social Democrats, who decided to resign from the government in order to show their displeasure at the way in which the Communist Minister of the Interior was creating an exclusively Communist police force. This resignation enabled the Communists to accuse the Social Democrats of preparing a coup themselves and provided them with the perfect excuse to act first. On February 21, 1948 they launched a series of demonstrations which enabled them to form a government from which the Social Democrats were excluded. In a temporary alliance with the Socialists, whom they rapidly managed to exclude, they then began to establish the one-party state which remained in existence until 1989.

By the end of 1948 the Communist parties in Hungary and Poland had established their authority by techniques very similar to those used in Czechoslovakia. Whereas Hitler never managed to impose his rule in any country not physically occupied by German troops, Stalin could generally afford the luxury of allowing the Communists in Eastern Europe to take power without direct intervention of the Red Army, and without needing to occupy the country on a permanent basis. His army was always there on the borders, and in February 1948 Stalin offered the Czech Communists military help if they should need it.[5]

Initially, though, the fiction was that the decision to espouse Communism had been taken by peoples of Eastern Europe acting alone. The Red Army nevertheless left East Germany only when the Cold War was over. In Romania the coup which enabled the Communists to take power in February 1945 was made possible by the fact that the Soviet Army had earlier occupied army quarters in Bucharest and disarmed any troops whose loyalty seemed doubtful. However, it was not until 1956 that the Hungarian rebellion led to a direct military invasion of one of what were known as the 'People's Democracies of Eastern Europe' (and gave rise to the phrase 'Oh, he's a "tankin"', currently used in left-wing circles in England to designate a former member of the British Communist Party).[6]

The régimes established in eastern and central Europe followed the same economic policy that, in the Soviet view, had enabled the USSR to modernise its economy after 1917. A centrally planned economic system gave priority to heavy industry over the needs of the consumer, and the needs of the countryside were sacrificed to those of the town. (Marx himself seems to have been interested solely in industry – he spoke scornfully of 'the idiocy of rural life'.) It was the completion of the

collectivisation of agriculture that led to the massive exodus from East
Germany which compelled the authorities to put up the Wall on August 13,
1961. And the protest movements of June 1976 and January 1981 in
Poland, which culminated in the creation of Solidarity, were all set off by
increases in the price of food. Stalin's insistence on the collectivisation of
Soviet agriculture in the 1920s had led to some six million deaths, an
action of which even Beatrice and Sidney Webb disapproved, writing
that 'the sum of human suffering involved is beyond computation'.[7]

The attempt to establish collective farms in eastern and central Europe
did not produce quite the same horrors as it had in the Soviet Union. It
was merely another factor, albeit an important one, leading to the general
failure of what Eric Hobsbawm calls 'really existing socialism'[8]. A more
marked resemblance between the Soviet Union and the satellite states in
eastern and central Europe was the holding of trials in which former
leading members of the Communist Party were executed for treason
after making public confession of their crimes against the state.

THE EXPORTING OF SOVIET LEGAL BEHAVIOUR

The Moscow State trials of 1936–1938 destroyed between a third and a
half of the Soviet officer corps in the years immediately preceding the
outbreak of the Second World War. Altogether, it has been calculated, a
total of ten million Soviet citizens were killed for political reasons,
including a million members of the Party. Out of the 139 members of the
Central Committee elected at the 17th Party Congress of 1934, 98 were
shot on Stalin's orders, and the same happened to 1,108 of the 1,966 delegates to the same Congress.[9]

While many of these murders took place in secret, a significant
number were preceded by a public trial, and what was most extraordinary was the conduct of some of the accused before being taken off to
execution. Men such as Nicholas Bukharin, once described by Stalin as
'the darling of the Party', or G.G. Yagoda, former head of the secret
police, or G.F. Grinko, a former Commissioner of Finance and Director of
the Five-Year Plan, all confessed to sabotage and treason, and pleaded to
be shot so that they could pay for their crimes. None did so in more open
terms than Grinko who stated at his trial in 1938:

> Like some others of the accused, I face the Court as a direct agent
> and spy of fascist powers and their intelligence services, a direct ally
> of fascism in its struggle against the USSR

and all had their behaviour praised by the supporters of the Soviet
Union in the West. Leon Feuchtwanger said of the accused in an earlier
trial:

When I attended the second trial in Moscow, when I saw Pjatakov, Radek and his friends, and heard what they said and how they said it, I was forced to accept the evidence of my senses, and my doubts melted away as naturally as salt melts in water.[10]

Stalin was not the first revolutionary leader to have his former comrades executed. But the Girondins whom Maximilien de Robespierre (1758–1794) had sent to the guillotine on October 31, 1793 died protesting their innocence. So, too, did the radical leader Hébert whom Robespierre and Saint-Just had executed, with twenty-four of his colleagues, on March 24, 1794. Danton was so anxious to proclaim his innocence when Robespierre sent him to the guillotine that a procedural device had to be found to declare that everything he tried to say in the Convention Nationale was out of order.

In Eastern Europe, in contrast, the Communists put on trial by the régimes established after 1945 behaved exactly as the accused had done in the Moscow State Trials of 1937 and 1938. Far from throwing themselves on the mercy of the court and asking for forgiveness, they too confessed themselves guilty of all the charges brought against them and begged, in an orgy of humiliation, to be punished with the utmost rigour.

The best-known of the trials were those of Laszlo Rajk in Hungary, and of Rudolf Slanski in Czechoslovakia. Both, like the victims of the Moscow state trials of the late 1930s, had impeccable records as loyal Communists. In the 1930s Rajk had fought on the Republican side in Spain, before coming back to Budapest and serving as Secretary of the then illegal Communist Party. This led him to be arrested by the Germans and sent to a concentration camp. After the war he became Minister of the Interior and was responsible for organising the terror which accompanied the Sovietisation of Hungary. In May 1949, however, he was put on trial, accused of having worked for the secret police of Admiral Horthy in the 1930s, of seeking to establish an alliance with the dissident Yugoslavian leader Tito, and of plotting to restore capitalism. He made a full confession of his crimes and was executed by hanging on October 15, 1949.

Rudolf Slanski had an equally distinguished record of service to Communism. He spent the Second World War in Moscow, and on his return to Prague in May, 1945 had become Secretary of the Czech Communist Party. He had been instrumental in organising the *coup d'état* of February 1948 which gave the Party absolute power and played a leading role in the Sovietisation of the economic and political life of Czechoslovakia which followed it. But on November 24, 1951, in company with thirteen other senior Czechoslovak Communists, he was arrested and charged with a variety of crimes, including Titoism, Trotskysm, Zionism and preparing the restoration of capitalism. Great publicity was given to his trial, which took place between November 20 and 27, 1952, at the end of which he was sentenced to death and hanged. Like Rajk, he made a full and public confession.

There are few problems in explaining the trials themselves. Just as the USSR had exported its economic system to the countries conquered by the Red Army in the Second World War, obliging them to abolish private property, adopt a planned economy, and give priority to industry over agriculture, so it imposed its own political model on them. Only the Communist Party had the right to put up candidates for election, and indeed to exist as a political organisation. But this party, however fully it might express the true will of the proletariat, always contained potential traitors. If, therefore, it was to fulfil its historic mission and maintain its ideological purity, these had to be rooted out and punished, as much as a warning to others as for the damage they might do. The ultimate victory of Communism was, naturally, guaranteed by the historical process. In the meantime, though, everybody was a potential suspect – a very useful attitude for a régime to adopt if it wanted to exercise absolute power.

This was the explanation for the purges put forward in 1956 by Zbigniew Brzezinski in *The Permanent Purge: politics in the Soviet Union*, in which he argued that their very permanence was 'an effective mechanism of power transmission which does not puncture the monolithic unity of the political system'.[11] It is an explanation which matches George Orwell's analysis of totalitarianism in *Nineteen Eighty-Four*, and makes the long rule which the Communist Party enjoyed in the Soviet Union and elsewhere easier to understand. Nobody dared suggest any changes, in case they found themselves included among the victims of the next purge. Brzezinski's analysis is very convincing, but it nevertheless fails to answer two questions. Why did the purges become gradually less frequent after the death of Stalin in March 1953? And why did the accused behave in so different a way from those brought to trial in earlier periods?

The answer to the first question lies in Stalin's own character, and especially his pathological suspicion of everyone around him. The impact of character traits on the general history of the Soviet Union is inexplicable in Marxist theory, which attributes little importance to the influence which individuals have on historical events. Stalin's behaviour is nevertheless consistent with what historians have told us about other tyrants in the past, and the portrait of him given by Khrushchev is remarkably similar to that of the Roman Emperor Commodus (AD 161–192), for whom Gibbon said:

> Suspicion was equivalent to proof; trial to condemnation. The execution of a considerable senator was attended with the death of all who

might lament or avenge his fate; and when Commodus had tasted human blood, he became incapable of pity or remorse.[12]

It is nevertheless not true that there is nothing new under the sun. Stalin may have behaved in a manner indistinguishable from that of the tyrant Commodus. Nonetheless, his victims either chose, or were required, to perform antics unrecorded even in those pages of *The Decline and Fall of the Roman Empire* that illustrate most vividly Gibbon's contention that history 'is, indeed, little more than the register of the crimes, follies and misfortunes of mankind'.

As befits a set of events which took place in Europe, we must seek an explanation for their behaviour in works of imaginative literature.

LITERATURE AS A KEY TO HISTORICAL UNDERSTANDING

All countries, and all cultures, tell stories. 'Literature,' as G.K. Chesterton remarked 'is a luxury. Fiction a necessity'. The myths which explore psychological truths or express emotional states occur everywhere in the world, often in the same form. But it was only in Europe that the tradition developed of using prose fiction to analyse human emotions in which the author is fully conscious of what she or he is doing. It was only in Europe that the novel became a privileged medium for describing society, diagnosing its failures and, perhaps, occasionally suggesting solutions. It is this which makes Arthur Koestler's *Darkness at Noon*, and George Orwell's *Animal Farm* and *Nineteen Eighty-Four* such typically European books. Not only do the experiences which they describe take place in Europe. The authors analyse these experiences in a way not found in any other culture

The collection of Arabic and Persian tales known as *The Thousand and One Nights* is based on the brilliant idea of holding death at bay by a series of stories so exciting that the Sultan will never kill Scheherazade, because he will always want to know how the story ended and what happened next. But it was not followed, as Boccaccio's *Decameron* (1358) was in European literature, by the development of a tradition which expanded story-telling beyond the exploitation of suspense and in the direction of a realistic depiction of why human beings behave as they do.

THE EXAMPLE OF ARTHUR KOESTLER

The Russian novelist Alexander Solzhenitsyn had a simple explanation for the behaviour of the accused in the Moscow State Trials. In his view, they had been subjected to such horrific tortures that they confessed to save themselves further agony.[13] The same may well have been true of some of those who confessed at the show trials in Eastern Europe – all of whom, like the victims of the Moscow trials, were subsequently rehabilitated. There is, however, one piece of evidence which, coupled with Arthur Koestler's novel *Darkness at Noon*, suggests that torture was not necessarily the only reason for the confessions. It is given on the last page of *The Invisible Writing* (1954), the second volume of Koestler's autobiography.

In *Darkness at Noon*, Koestler presents his explanation for the behaviour of the accused in the Moscow State Trials of the 1930s through the character of Nicholas Salmanovitch Rubashov, a man whom he describes as 'a synthesis of the lives of a number of men who were victims of the so-called Moscow Trials'. Rubashov has been tortured before, by the Gestapo, and remained silent. The explanation put forward by Solzhenitsyn does not therefore apply. What makes Rubashov behave differently is the desire, even at the hour of his inevitable death, to remain useful. If the masses can be persuaded, through his confession, that the failures of the Revolution are due to spies and saboteurs, and not to some inherent defect of Marxism and of the way in which it has been applied in the Soviet Union, there is still some hope for human progress.

It is the Party alone, 'the embodiment of the revolutionary idea in history', which represents the hopes of mankind. For Koestler's Rubashov, as for everyone on the left in the 1930s, capitalism is doomed: it inevitably gives birth to fascism. Only Communism can ensure the future prosperity and happiness of mankind. Hence, all means, including the purges of which he himself is a victim, together with the lies and false confessions which form an integral part of them, are justified if they help to ensure the future triumph of the Revolution.

Koestler called his autobiography 'a typical case history of a central-European member of the educated middle classes, born in the first years of the century'.[14] It was a sentence which evoked a wide range of experiences, some of which, described in the first volume, *Arrow in the Blue*, range from working as a scientific journalist with a German newspaper to writing, under the name of Dr Koster, a splendid encyclopaedia of sexual deviations; and from imprisonment for several months in one of General Franco's gaols, with the daily expectation of being taken out the next morning to be shot, to arriving in England and immediately being interned in Pentonville prison in 1940 as a suspected enemy alien.

In 1954, Koestler summed up his own political evolution by writing on the opening page of *The Invisible Writing*:

> I went to Communism as one goes to a spring of fresh water, and I left Communism as one clambers out of a poisoned river strewn with the wreckage of flooded cities and the corpses of the drowned.[15]

More particularly, he talked about the more typically European experience of having been a Communist and of then having left the Party, and in this respect few books do more than *Darkness at Noon* to show how right was the French biblical scholar Ernest Renan (1823–1892) when he said that anyone wishing to write intelligently about Christianity had to fulfil two conditions: he had to have believed, and he had to have stopped believing.

Koestler's loss of belief when he wrote *Darkness at Noon*, between 1937 and 1939, was absolute. As Rubashov is made to note in his private journal, in a passage which explains the title of the book:

> the people's standard of living is lower than it was before the Revolution; the labour conditions are harder, the discipline is more inhuman … freedom of the Press, of opinion and of movement are as thoroughly exterminated as though the proclamation of the Rights of Man had never been. We have built up the most gigantic police apparatus, with informers made a national institution, and with the most refined scientific system of physical and mental torture.[16]

Twenty years after the triumph of the Bolshevik Revolution of 1917, when all ought to be glorious light, there is nothing but darkness.

It was a darkness which, in Koestler's view, the Soviet Union had now exported, together with the psychology of Communism and the practice of state trials, to its satellite countries in Eastern Europe. In *The Invisible Writing* he was able to produce specific evidence of this. One of the lesser-known Communists to be put on trial alongside Slansky was a friend of Koestler's called Otto Katz, who also went under the alias of André Simon. Unlike Koestler, he had remained a member of the Party and, after spending the war years of 1939–1945 in Mexico, went back to his native Czechoslovakia after the Communist coup of February 1948. There he was appointed editor of the Party magazine and later became head of the Press Department at the Foreign Ministry. But none of this protected him from being swept up in the purges of the early 1950s, and the same court that sentenced Slansky to death also sent him, literally, to the gallows, charged, as Koestler puts it, with being 'a British spy, a saboteur, and – of all things – a Zionist agent'.[17]

Like the other Party members put on trial, Katz made a full confession. But he did so – doubtless with the readers of *Darkness at Noon* in mind, as well, perhaps, as his friend Koestler – by repeating as much as he could remember of the speech which Koestler put into the mouth of the central character of his novel, the Old Bolshevik Nicholas Salmanovitch Rubashov. Trying to use the same words as Rubashov in *Darkness at Noon*, Katz declares:

I belong to the gallows. The only service I can render is to serve as a warning example to all who, by origin or character, are in danger of following the same path to hell.[18]

This paraphrase of Rubashov's confession to the court sums up the central idea in *Darkness at Noon*: that the behaviour of the accused in the Moscow State Trials can be understood only in terms of the particular mentality produced by Communism, one compounded in almost equal proportions of fanaticism, guilt, and the desire to be of service.

In 1950 Koestler summed up what seemed at the time to be a self-evident truth among European intellectuals when he predicted that the next war would be between those who had been members of the Party and those who still belonged to it. Just as no political commentators before 1989 foresaw the collapse of the Soviet Union, there were few philosophers or literary intellectuals in Europe after 1945 who thought that capitalist society would survive long enough to witness this collapse. Koestler himself, like Orwell and Camus, saw the only hope for mankind in a modified form of democratic socialism. It would never have occurred to any of the three writers even to consider the strengths of the liberal capitalism which would eventually defeat the Soviet Union and come to be widely accepted as the best way of organising a modern industrial society.

Rubashov, as *Darkness at Noon* makes clear, is totally innocent of the charges brought against him. At no point has he acted in any other way than as a devoted and faithful servant of the Party. By quoting from Rubashov's final speech, Katz tells his listeners that he has always shown a comparable enthusiasm and fidelity, and is now being sentenced to death on the same totally false charges. Whether he is also saying that his confession is inspired by the same desire to be useful to the last that animated Rubashov is a more open question. This confession could be read, as Koestler seems to read it in *The Invisible Writing*, as a denunciation of Communism and all its works by a man who has given his life to it and been totally betrayed. Alternatively, it could be read as the statement of the same kind of despairing fidelity, the same desire to be useful, which Koestler had presented as the motive for Rubashov's confession.

If this is the case, then the Soviet Union exported more than its economic and political model to the states occupied by its armies after 1945. Through the beliefs inspiring the leaders whom it installed in power, it also exported the faith in the ultimate rightness of its cause. It was a mind-set into which Koestler's membership of the Communist Party between 1931 and 1938 had given him a peculiarly accurate insight.

In the years immediately after the Second World War, Koestler became one of the best-known of the intellectuals disparagingly described as cold-war warriors. In particular, he edited a collection of autobiographical essays entitled *The God That Failed* (1950), in which six authors described how they had once been Communists and explained why they had left the Party. In addition to Koestler himself, they were the German philosopher Louis Fischer, the French novelist André Gide, the Italian novelist and essayist Ignazio Silone, the English poet Stephen Spender, and the American novelist Richard Wright.

The God That Failed was a thoroughly European book (even Richard Wright, the only non-European among the contributors, had recently become a cult figure in the Paris literary world after having translations of his books published in Sartre's *Les Temps Modernes*). It had a preface by the British Labour politician R.C.H. Crossman, who also provided the title. Although he said that he was 'not in the least interested in swelling the flood of anti-Communist propaganda',[19] this was precisely what happened; the book enjoyed numerous reprints and translations. (This was something which may not have delighted Richard Crossman, who at the November 1946 opening of Parliament had moved an amendment to the King's speech repudiating Churchill's remarks, made at Fulton, Missouri, in March that year, about the 'iron curtain' which now divided Europe. Nobody voted for the amendment, whose object was obviously to condemn Churchill as a cold-war warrior, but 130 Labour MPs abstained, nearly all of whom were from the middle class.[20])

Koestler remains a man of whom left-wing sympathisers find it hard to speak favourably. His most recent biographer, David Cesarini, dwelt at some length on how Koestler had raped his friends' wives and compelled one of his many mistresses to have an abortion. Cesarini also made what was clearly intended as a damning remark by describing *The God That Failed* as 'his entrance ticket into McCarthyite America'.[21] In the immediate post-war era *Darkness at Noon* nevertheless became, somewhat paradoxically, one of the books which fulfilled the main condition for good writing set out by Jean-Paul Sartre in his 1947 essay *Qu'est-ce que la littérature?* (What is literature?). What Sartre argued was that books should speak to their readers about the social and political problems of their own day, and nobody could deny that this was something which Koestler's novel did. The only trouble was that, while Sartre presupposed that all good books would automatically serve the cause of socialism, *Darkness at Noon* clearly did not.

This had already become particularly clear in 1945, when the book was translated into French under the title *Le zéro et l'infini*. It immediately became a best-seller, partly because of the ability of the Parti Communiste Français (PCF; French Communist Party) to shoot itself in the foot: it denounced Koestler's novel with such ferocity that everyone dashed out to buy it. At the same time, however, the Party tried to prevent the book from reaching new readers by sending its members out to buy up every available copy, which they then burned. This was not a new experience for Koestler. His pre-war books had all been burned by Hitler's propaganda minister, Joseph Goebbels.

Le zéro et l'infini made such an impression on General de Gaulle that he stayed up all night to read it, and Koestler himself claims that it helped to make a difference in one of the referenda held in France after the liberation of 1945 to decide on a new constitution. A 'Yes' vote in the one held on May 5, 1946 would have led to a system in which one all-powerful popular assembly, with no checks and balances, would have been dominated by the PCF, which would then have effectively called the shots in French internal and external affairs. So strong, however, was the case against the Soviet Marxism, on which the PCF modelled itself, that the proposed single-chamber constitution was rejected.

THE EXAMPLE OF GEORGE ORWELL

There is no means of knowing whether Koestler's novel had the influence which he claimed on the outcome of the referendum of May 5, 1946. Literary men are not averse to seeing their books playing a role in politics, and Koestler was not the most modest of writers. It is an open question, though, whether he would have been pleased if his publisher had remarked of *Darkness at Noon*, as George Orwell's publisher Frederick Warburg remarked of *Nineteen Eighty-Four*, that it was 'worth a million votes to the Conservative Party'. Neither man ever supported anything but a democratic socialist party, and Orwell would have been horrified by the view of the New York newspaper-seller who told Isaac Deutscher, that he ought to read the novel in order to see 'why he ought to go and drop a bomb on the Soviet Union'.[22]

Deutscher, a Polish-born British historian, remained faithful to Marxism despite having been expelled from the Party in 1932 for leading an anti-Stalinist movement. In this respect, as in others, he was a representative figure of the European left in both pre-war and post-war Europe, and his view of *Nineteen Eighty-Four* as guilty of:

> teaching millions to look at the conflict between East and West in terms of black and white, and to see a monster bogy and a monster scapegoat for the ills that claim mankind

was quite widely shared. This, however, was not Orwell's intention, and it is possible that the hysterical note which some readers have found in *Nineteen Eighty-Four* stemmed from his poor health at the time he wrote it (he died of tuberculosis on January 21, 1950 at the age of 46, the year after the book was published).[23] But if he piled on the horrors, it was to make sure that his message got across, and he succeeded. When the

Czech dissident Milan Simecka said that in his interrogation by the secret police he had 'shared Winston's experience in the underground cells of the Ministry of Truth', he confirmed the accuracy of Orwell's grasp of how totalitarian societies work.

The background to *Nineteen Eighty-Four* is also firmly based on how the Soviet Union had conducted its foreign policy between 1917 and the end of the Second World War. Initially, the régime created by the Revolution of 1917 had wanted nothing at all to do with the capitalist world. The conduct of foreign affairs, Lenin remarked, would be entrusted to one of the cooks in the Kremlin. However, once Hitler had come to power in Germany on January 30, 1933, it became clear that the Soviet Union would need friends. From 1935 onwards, it therefore began to denounce the Third Reich as the home of Fascist gangsterism and tyranny, bent on invading the home of the Revolution and destroying the socialist experiment.

This gave rise to the idea of a Popular Front of all democratic peoples against fascism. This policy lasted until August 24, 1939, when, quite suddenly, news arrived of the signature of a non-aggression pact between the Soviet Foreign Minister Molotov and the German Foreign Minister von Ribbentrop. The two countries became, in the twinkling of an eye, the closest of allies, with a strict ban in each of them on any mention of the earlier state of affairs. Then, on June 22, 1941, Hitler attacked the Soviet Union. Immediately, the situation changed again, with an identical but opposite ban on any mention of the earlier alliance

It was these events which inspired the atmosphere of *Nineteen Eighty-Four*. Nobody in Oceania, the political grouping into which England has been placed by the tripartite division of the world, is allowed to criticise the party line. This is nevertheless liable to be changed at a moment's notice, with all trace immediately eliminated of what it had only recently been in the past. Thus when Oceania, having been an ally of Eastasia, suddenly switches sides, it is the job of the main character in the novel, Winston Smith, to rewrite earlier editions of *The Times* in order to show that this has always been the case, and that the alliance with Eastasia never existed. In this respect, it was Lenin himself who provided the starting-point for the Party slogan in Oceania: 'who controls the past controls the future; who controls the present controls the past'. For when Lenin was asked 'Do we need to foresee the future?', he answered: 'Of course. But the essential point is first of all to control the past'.[24]

The publication of *Nineteen Eighty-Four* on May 2, 1949 made an immense impact on public opinion in Great Britain. So, too, did its subsequent appearance in the clandestine publications known as *samidzat* in the People's Democracies to the east of the Elbe. Their inhabitants recognised it as an accurate portrayal of the society in which they found themselves compelled to live. The Party is everywhere, and anyone even suspected of thinking of opposing it is immediately arrested and tortured. While the standard of living for ordinary people is appallingly low, members of the inner Party enjoy access to exactly the same kind of special shops reserved for members of the *nomenklatura* in the Soviet Union. Like the portrait of Stalin at the time Orwell was writing the book, the picture of Big Brother is everywhere, and he is everywhere presented as infallible.

Orwell's essays, as well as the text of *Nineteen Eighty-Four*, show that he was obsessed by the possibility that the technologies of social control developed by totalitarian states would lead to the total disappearance of all objective knowledge of the past. For him, the Cold War was a cultural as well as a political struggle, in which the ideas of free intellectual inquiry, of the rule of law, of the right of individuals to lead a private life free of state interference were under immediate threat from the power-worship which he saw as characteristic of left-wing intellectuals.

It was this worship which he saw as the root cause of the failure of the revolution in his earlier novel *Animal Farm*, finally published, after a great deal of difficulty, on August 17, 1945. The left-wing publisher Victor Gollancz had turned it down flat, and T.S. Eliot, chairman of the less politically committed house of Faber and Faber did the same on July 31, 1944 saying that it was 'not the right point of view from which to criticize the political situation at the present time'.

The revolution by which the animals drive out the old and inefficient Mr Jones, and establish their own society, has become one of the best-known stories of modern times and provided the phrases encapsulating the disillusionment with the Soviet Union which became part of the cultural and political background to the Cold War. The Ten Commandments setting out the ideal of the revolution have to be summarised for the sheep in the slogan 'Two legs bad, four legs good'; then, as the pigs take over and begin to walk on their hind legs, the sheep are taught to bleat 'Four legs good, two legs better'. And the statement 'All animals are equal' becomes, in a phrase now found in every anthology of quotations in the English-speaking world: 'All animals are equal. But some animals are more equal than other animals'.

At first sight, *Animal Farm* throws less light on Orwell's views on the Cold War than *Nineteen Eighty-Four*. It was written before the conflict between capitalism and Communism had taken the form which characterised it after 1945. Indeed, the ending of the book, in which the animals outside the farm house:

> looked from pig to man, and from man to pig, and from pig to man again; but already it was impossible to say which was which

suggests a connivance between free-market economics and state socialism based upon a common desire to keep the lower orders in their place (foreshadowing one of the black jokes of the 1970s: 'Capitalism is the exploitation of man by man; in Communism, it's the other way round'). It is only when Napoleon, 'the prize Middle White Boar' who is an obvious portrait of Stalin, appears on his hind legs carrying a whip in his trotter that *Animal Farm* offers an augury of why *Nineteen Eighty-Four* is so obviously one of the first cultural shots aimed against the Soviet Union in the Cold War.

For Orwell, revolutions are not only betrayed because of human greed. The hopes they represented also fall victim to the lust for power. It is the power to torture Winston Smith and destroy his will to resist that O'Brien finds so attractive, and which inspires the tyranny which the 'Inner Party' exercises throughout the known world. The accuracy of Orwell's description of the inner party was born out by the description, eight years after the publication of *Nineteen Eighty-Four*, of what the Yugoslav dissident Milovan Djilas called 'the new class': the bureaucrats and politicians who had taken control in the socialist countries behind the Iron Curtain and were both more powerful and more corrupt than the old-style capitalists. For the Orwell of *Nineteen Eighty-Four*, this class could not be satisfied with ruling in only one country. It has to extend its rule over the whole world.

Orwell based his description of the 'Inner Party' in *Nineteen Eighty-Four* partly on a book entitled *The Managerial Revolution*, published in 1941 by the American sociologist James Burnham. In 1946 his essay 'James Burnham and the Managerial Revolution' summarised Burnham's thesis that modern industrialised society was marked by what he called 'the divorce between ownership and control'. In the nineteenth century, Burnham had argued, the individual capitalist entrepreneur developed and owned the company he had originally created. He might let his sons into the business, but it remained his property. He took the decisions, he called the shots, and he kept the profits. However, argued Burnham, the increasing complexity of the modern business world meant that this was no longer possible. Instead, a new class of professional managers took over, who did not derive their power from the ownership of shares. They may acquire these in the form of the stock options given to them as part of their salary. But what really matters is their skill at management, their ability to take the decisions which enable the enormous enterprises which they control to survive and prosper.

In the Oceania of *Nineteen Eighty-Four* as in the democratic West the 'Inner Party', the governing class, does not derive its power from ownership. Like the *nomenklatura* in the Soviet Union and its satellites, its members enjoy the privileges described by Milovan Djilas because of their ability to manipulate the system. They maintain their power and privileges by force and fraud – a fact which clearly distinguishes them from the professional managers of the West, who have to remain within the rule of law and give few signs of ever wishing to do otherwise.

In this respect, the Cold War, in the form it took in Europe, could be seen as a contest between two versions of Burnham's managerial revolution: a contest in which the form it took in the democratic West defeated the form it took in the totalitarian East. Neither of the two societies was particularly egalitarian. If the West won, it was because a society in which free speech, free elections, the protection of individual rights and the rule of law are the recognised norm is more efficient than one based on the rule of a single party. However, it was not until thirty-eight years after Stalin's death on March 5, 1953 – which set off the process by which the inadequacies of the model that the Soviet Union exported to its satellites began to be more widely known to the outside world – that the empire which he had constructed finally collapsed.

6 The end of Eastern European socialism

DESTALINISATION AND THE WORKING CLASS

Towards six in the evening on February 25, 1956, as the delegates to the 20th Congress of the Soviet Communist Party were leaving the hall, they were suddenly called back to hear an important speech from the First Secretary, Nikita Khrushchev. It consisted of a long denunciation, lasting some six hours, of the former First Secretary, Joseph Stalin. Among other offences, Khrushchev accused him of crimes against Soviet legality, failure to prepare for the German attack of June 22, 1941, and also what Khrushchev called 'the cult of the personality'. Officially, the Congress was in secret session, but the Reuter journalist Sidney Weiland heard what was happening, flew to Stockholm, and filed his report on March 16. Although the speech then became widely known in the West, it was not until early June that a full version became available within the USSR, Soviet censorship was still functioning with only slightly less rigour than in the days of Stalin.

In 1962 Khrushchev authorised the publication of Solzhenitsyn's *A Day in the Life of Ivan Denisovitch*. Its significance did not lie solely in the strictly factual account of what life was like in the forced labour camps which had housed up to twenty million prisoners, and whose existence had always been officially denied. Equally important was that the central character was not a writer or an intellectual but an ordinary member of the Soviet working class. His very name, the Russian equivalent of John Smith, indicated this, as did the nature of his preoccupations: food, warmth, the avoidance of punishment for some minor offence, the satisfaction of having, in the face of all the difficulties besetting him, actually succeeded in building a wall.

European Communist Parties liked to have artists and intellectuals support them; although there were fewer of them in the West after 1945 (and especially after 1956) than there had been in the 1930s, they were still useful as propaganda. The French Communist Party pointed with great delight at the 'peace dove' which Pablo Picasso painted for their

Peace Campaign of the 1940s and 1950s, while passing over in silence his 1953 cubist-style portrait of Stalin. All the same, intellectuals were suspect: they had joined the Party through free choice, but had kept the awkward habit of thinking for themselves. But to find a working man presented as the victim of the party which was supposed to be his bulwark and defence was the supreme insult – all the more bitter since, long before the publication of *A Day in the Life of Ivan Denisovitch*, it had become obvious from events in East Germany, Poland and Hungary that the movement against Communism in Eastern Europe had widespread working-class support, and in a number of cases working-class leadership.

EAST GERMANY, POLAND AND HUNGARY

The protests in East Germany in June 1953 had been sparked off by a set of contradictory signals which suggested that the Soviet Union did not really know how it should deal with the empire it had acquired in the aftermath of the Second World War. On the one hand, the new Soviet High Commissioner in East Germany announced on his arrival on May 29, 1953 that there was to be a shift away from the emphasis on heavy industry towards the production of consumer goods; that the middle class would no longer be discriminated against in favour of the workers; that taxes were to be levied by consent and not by force; and that permission would be granted to private individuals wishing to open their own businesses. At the same time, the workers were told that the norms they had to satisfy were going to be increased, so that they would now have to work 50 hours a week to receive the salary earlier paid to them for 40.

The threat to increase norms was more credible than the promise to improve living conditions. From June 16 onwards strikes spread throughout the country, culminating in a demonstration in East Berlin so vast that the authorities realised that they could keep order only by calling in the Red Army. Significantly, twenty-four hours elapsed before the Soviet Union agreed to the request: another indication of divided counsels in the Kremlin. When the tanks did appear, on June 17, they showed the complete ruthlessness in firing on civilian demonstrators that was to characterise Soviet intervention in Hungary in November 1956 and Czechoslovakia in August 1968. They killed 23 of the mainly working-class demonstrators and wounded several hundred more.

The West made no attempt to intervene, in spite of the urgent request from some of the demonstrators that it should do so. It already implicitly accepted the 1968 Brezhnev doctrine, that a socialist state had the right to interfere in the affairs of another socialist state in order to defend its system against any change. It was to do the same in Poland in 1956 and again in 1981, following a precedent established in the nineteenth century, when in 1830–1831, 1846 and again in 1863 uprisings in support of Polish independence were ruthlessly suppressed and nobody came to their help. One of the most famous nineteenth-century French cartoons, depicting a mounted Cossack brandishing his sword over the body of a dead Pole, had been captioned 'L'ordre règne à Varsovie' (Order reigns in Poland); between 1945 and 1989, this was frequently reproduced in the Western press – a substitute for the action which the Soviet nuclear arsenal prevented the NATO powers from taking.

On June 28 protests in the industrial city of Poznan against cuts in real wages and food shortages had been put down by the police at the cost of 53 demonstrators killed and over 300 seriously injured. This episode had made the Soviet and the Polish leaderships realise how seriously they were under threat, and an agreement signed in Moscow on November 17, 1956 stated that the Soviet Union agreed that 'the temporary presence of Soviet troops in Poland can in no way affect the sovereignty of the Polish state and cannot lead to their interference in the internal affairs of Poland'.[1] But nobody believed that these troops would ever go away. The leadership of the German Democratic Republic made it the most ideologically reliable of the Soviet satellites, and, by the standards prevailing in Eastern Europe after 1945, it had a modicum of prosperity. Even so, it was still inhabited by Germans, and the Russians were taking no chances. Whatever economic reforms the Poles might be allowed to carry out, Poland had to remain under the control of the Soviet Union because it lay across the supply route leading to the 500,000 Soviet troops permanently stationed in East Germany.

Wladyslaw Gomulka came back to power after the Poznan uprising. (Earlier, he had been excluded from the Party because of his criticism of Stalin, and in July 1951 he had been placed under house arrest.) After successfully negotiating a measure of independence from the Soviet Union in 1956, he implemented a number of reforms, including a reduction in the powers of the secret police and the suspension of the collectivisation of agriculture. He was able to avoid direct Soviet military intervention in Poland because he made no attempt to leave the Warsaw Pact – set up on May 14, 1955 as a reply to the establishment of NATO in April 1949 – of which Poland had been a founder member.

The major tactical mistake made by the Hungarian leadership under Imre Nagy in 1956 was to try to leave the Warsaw Pact. It was this, as much as the abolition of the monopoly of power enjoyed by the Communist Party since the People's Republic of Hungary came into existence on August 20, 1949, which provoked the armed intervention of November 4, 1956 and the crushing of the movement for Hungarian independence by the Red Army. The Soviet authorities drove the point home by requiring forces from other Warsaw Pact members, East Germany and Czechoslovakia, to take part in the repression.

Before then, there had been a period of hope in which it had almost seemed that the Soviet Union was prepared to relax its grip on Eastern Europe. On October 25, 1956 the Hungarian secret police fired on a joint demonstration of students and workers on the streets of Budapest, killing 300 people. A cease-fire was then negotiated, which led to a brief pause in the demonstrations. This was followed by the withdrawal of the Soviet tanks which had earlier made symbolic appearance in support of the secret police, as well as by the formation on October 28 of a new government with Nagy as Prime Minister. Negotiations with the new Hungarian government had been led by the allegedly liberal Anastas Mikoyan, and the day after his return to Moscow on October 30, Tass published a communiqué stating that the Soviet government was 'ready to enter into negotiations with the government of the Hungarian People's Republic and other governments which are party to the Warsaw Pact on the withdrawal of Soviet troops from Hungary'.

Khrushchev was in favour of reform, as his denunciation of Stalin had indicated, but the events in Poland and Hungary had made him acutely aware of how easily matters could get out of hand. He kept his options open by not moving his troops too far from Budapest, and their intervention of November 4, 1956 was given a cover of legality by the action of Nagy's principal rival, Janos Kádár, First Secretary of the Hungarian Communist Party since October 25, who was appalled by the speed with which the old 'bourgeois' political parties were making a reappearance.

Kádár's appeal of November 3 for Soviet intervention may well have been the decisive factor in the debate that must have taken place between the hawks and the doves in the Kremlin as to how best to proceed. Stalin would never have let matters get to the point they had reached by October 31. The Soviet leadership was facing the classic dilemma which inevitably confronts every imperial power: what do you do when those you govern want you to leave? It was a problem which the Athenians had found themselves facing in the fifth century BC, and which Thucydides had analysed in the section of Book III of the *History of the Peloponnesian War* known as the Mytilenian debate. France, Portugal, Holland, Belgium and Great Britain had to deal with the same question from 1945 onwards, and did not always manage notably better than the Soviet Union.

In public-relations terms, the Soviet repression of the Hungarian rebellion was a disaster. It might have stopped Czechoslovakia, Romania and East Germany from taking the road the Hungarians had tried to follow, but it effectively killed off any chance of the Soviet Union retaining the prestige won for it by the heroism of its troops during the Second World War. Even in France, where *Le Parti Communiste Français* maintained its reputation as a party more Stalinist than Stalin himself had sometimes been, more and more members began to leave. Elsewhere in Europe the events of November 1956 marked the beginning of the phenomenon known as Euro-Communism, as the leader of the Italian Communist Party, Palmiro Togliatti began to urge a specifically Italian road to Communism, and had his ideas endorsed by the Party in November 1956.

Even the comrades of the British Communist Party were not all entirely happy with the explanation offered to me at a dinner party in 1966 by the distinguished literary critic Arnold Kettle. In his view, the speed with which antisemitism had reappeared in the Hungary of October 1956 more than justified Soviet intervention. This was not the view of the 200,000 Hungarians who took advantage of the absence of barbed wire barrier along the frontier with Austria to seek refuge in the West.

The repression of the Hungarian revolt clamped the lid down on protest movements until the next attempt to throw off Soviet rule took place in Czechoslovakia in 1968. In Hungary itself there was some improvement in living standards, stemming mainly from the permission granted to peasants, earlier expelled to make way for collective farms, to cultivate small plots of land. Although these amounted to only 3.5 per cent of the area under cultivation, they soon increased to the point where they provided 35 per cent of the food. By 1960 Hungary had become the only country in the Soviet bloc to be self-sufficient in food production.

CZECHOSLOVAKIA

There were no further open disturbances until 1968, when the attempted reforms of Alexander Dubček in Czechoslovakia were suppressed by another invasion of a Communist state by forces from the Warsaw Pact. Like Nagy, Dubček had never been anything but a loyal Communist. Like Nagy, the son of poor peasants who apprenticed him to a locksmith, Dubček was also of impeccably working-class origin: he was the son of a carpenter, and he had been a member of the Czech Communist Party since 1939. His whole political career had been in the Party, and, like Nagy, his membership of the Central Committee had enabled him to hold a variety of government posts.

The main difference between the two men lay in what happened to them after the reform movement which they represented had been suppressed. After the invasion of November 4, 1956 Nagy had sought refuge in the Yugoslav Embassy in Prague. He came out in response to a promise of safe conduct from Kádár – whose appeal to the Soviet leaders had given them the pretext to invade, and who had taken his place as Prime Minister – but was then arrested, placed in chains, put on trial, found guilty, executed, and buried face downwards. He was not, however, required to make the public confession of his crimes expected of earlier Communist leaders. In 1989 he was rehabilitated, as were the vast majority of all the victims of the Stalinist-type state trials in the

Soviet Union and its satellites. Dubček, in contrast, was first sent as Czech Ambassador to Turkey, then brought back and appointed to the forestry commission. He survived long enough to benefit from the collapse of Communism in 1989–1990, and on December 28, 1990 he was elected Parliamentary President. In that respect, if in no other, he benefited from the new mood which Khrushchev had tried to introduce into Soviet politics.

When Khrushchev himself had been ousted by a vote of the Politburo in October 1964, he was not put on trial, made to confess his crimes and then executed, as the losers in the Soviet political game had been in Stalin's day. He was not even, like former Foreign Minister Molotov, who fell from favour in 1957, sent as Soviet Ambassador in Outer Mongolia. He was allowed to retire to write his memoirs. The order, which nobody but he could have given, to have Nagy executed was a reflection of how frightened he and the Soviet leadership had been by the revolutionary potential of the Hungarian revolution in 1956.

In 1968 Brezhnev felt slightly more secure. After all, Dubček had not tried to break ranks by taking Czechoslovakia out of the Warsaw Pact; he had merely tried to introduce what he called 'socialism with a human face'. However, even this was too much for the Communist states bordering Czechoslovakia, as well as for the Soviet leadership. Dubček's suspension of political trials, like his release of political prisoners, his introduction of anonymous voting into elections to committees of the Communist Party, his relaxation of travel restrictions and press censorship had the great drawback, in Soviet eyes, of making his neighbours in Poland and East Germany wonder how long they would be able to hold out against the demand for similar changes which the news of these reforms would inspire in their own citizens. More particularly, the Soviet leadership wondered how long the leaders in their other satellites would be able to hang on to power and prevent the whole system from unravelling. It was a fear those leaders probably shared, and this made them order their forces in Poland and East Germany to join those of the Soviet Union and all the other Warsaw Pact countries except Romania in moving into Prague on August 20, 1968.

The mood throughout Europe, among women and men of the left as well as of those of more conservative disposition, was one of open despair. It did not seem entirely a coincidence that the repression of the 'Prague Spring' should come almost exactly thirty years after the signature of the Munich agreements of September 29, 1938 under which France and Great Britain agreed to hand over the Sudetenland area of Czechoslovakia to Hitler. Six months later, on March 15, 1939, Hitler took over the whole country, which had since lived then without interruption under totalitarian systems, first of the right and then of the left. Among the countries created in Eastern Europe by the Paris Peace Conference of

1919, which wound up the affairs of the defunct Austro-Hungarian Empire, Czechoslovakia had enjoyed the highest level of industrialisation and the most developed form of parliamentary democracy. These qualities were now being lost for a second time, and once again the democratic countries of Western Europe were unable to do anything about it. In 1938, this had been because they lacked the military hardware to oppose Hitler, and in any case geography hindered them from going directly to Czechoslovakia's help, just as it hindered them from doing anything to prevent Poland being overrun in September 1939. In August 1968, though, it was the existence of atomic weapons which prevented the West from doing anything to help Czechoslovakia, just as they had in the case of Hungary in November 1956 and were to do again in Poland in 1981.

In the summer of 1968 there was also another reason for the gloom affecting men and women of a left-wing or liberal persuasion in Western Europe. In May that year a student protest movement in Paris had at one stage seemed to be on the point of overthrowing the Fifth Republic established by de Gaulle ten years earlier. Both François Mitterrand and the much more respected Pierre Mendès-France presented themselves as potential replacements for de Gaulle, and on May 20 the general strike which had begun five days earlier at the state-owned Renault car factories spread to the rest of France. But once the Prime Minister, Georges Pompidou, had offered the trade union leaders wage increases ranging from ten to fifteen per cent, working-class support for the student movement disappeared.

As will be seen in the next chapter, trade union activists in Western Europe could certainly bring down democratically elected governments. But what the example of France in 1968 showed was that organised labour, like the workers it represented, did not want a Workers' State, either of a home-grown variety or of the type developed in Eastern Europe. What they wanted was a larger share of the wealth which capitalism was creating, an ambition which the more enthusiastic middle-class rebels in the student movement seemed unable to understand.

It is possible that, if they had come to power, these rebels might have made France a freer society, though there is little evidence of a serious absence of freedom before 1968. And the claim put forward at the time that capitalism was inherently oppressive has an even shakier basis when applied to the United Kingdom. The only protest movements which changed society were those directed against the régimes officially based on the Marxism which the student rebels of 1968 affected to admire. It was one of the major ironies of European history after 1945 that only when movements were directed against Marxist régimes did they enjoy the undivided support of the working class.

POLAND

The most important of the protest movements was the Polish trade union grouping known as Solidarity. This made its first appearance in August 1980, in protest against a sudden, previously unannounced increase in the price of bread and meat. One beneficial effect of the events of 1956 had been the abandonment of the forced collectivisation of agriculture. Nevertheless, the Party insisted on trying to discourage privately owned farms, which received none of the advantages in the form of guaranteed prices which at the time were making the European Economic Community's main problem the production of surpluses. The priority still given to heavy industry, another inheritance from Stalinism, was not accompanied by the payment to industrial workers of wages high enough to enable them to feed their families.[2]

The originality of the man who emerged as the leader of Solidarity, Lech Wałesa, was to transform these economic grievances into a political movement. This took off in its most spectacular form at the shipyards in Gdansk, better known to older people in the West as Danzig, where Wałesa was working as an electrician. It spread throughout Poland, and eighty per cent of the work force registered themselves as members. By August 30, 1980 Solidarity had become the first trade union movement in Eastern Europe not under the direct control of the Communist Party to be recognised as a negotiating partner by the government of one of the Peoples' Democracies.

It was fed as much by the long memory of the injustices that the Poles had suffered at the hands of their Russian neighbours as by the inefficiency of the Polish economy. It also benefited from the historical accident of the election to the Papacy in October 1978 of Cardinal Karol Wojtyla as Pope John-Paul II, the first non-Italian Pope since 1523, and the first Pole to hold the office. He chose his title in conscious tribute to his predecessor, Albino Luciani, who had been elected in August 1978 and taken the title of John-Paul I, but died 33 days later.

Stalin is reputed to have asked scornfully how many divisions (in the sense of military units) the Pope possessed, but the number of people John-Paul II has addressed and inspired in his innumerable visits throughout the world outnumber the manpower of the Red Army by millions. The doctrines he teaches have little in common with the world view underlying the free-market economics which have replaced the belief in a state-directed economy as the dominant ideology of the modern world. While insisting more than any of his predecessors on the social responsibilities of the Church, John-Paul II has reaffirmed traditional teaching in all matters of faith and doctrine, especially reinforcing the ban on all artificial methods of birth control laid down in the 1967 encyclical *Humanae Vitae*.

The visit of Pope John-Paul II to his native Poland in 1979, and later visits in 1983 and 1987, gave immense encouragement to the movement for national independence which found its expression in Solidarity. By the end of 1981 this had become so popular that Poland was virtually ungovernable. The risk which this posed to Soviet lines of military communication with Eastern Germany, coupled with the danger of the infection spreading to other its other satellites, made some form of inter-vention inevitable. But in 1980 Ronald Reagan had been elected President, taking up office in January 1981. His campaign rhetoric had created the fear that he might be more vigorous than his predecessors in his support for independence movements in Eastern Europe, and might even order military intervention. Perhaps because the Soviet leadership was afraid of this, but also perhaps because it felt that it could not this time rely on the support of the other members of the Warsaw Pact, the USSR decided in December 1981 to intervene by proxy.

On the morning of December 13 the citizens of Poland woke up to find their country under martial law. General Wojciech Jaruzelski, who had been Prime Minister since February 9 and First Secretary of the Polish Communist Party since October 18, had taken over. There is little reason to disbelieve his later claim that he had done so in order to avoid a Soviet invasion. Solidarity was banned and its leaders imprisoned. But if order once again reigned in Warsaw, this time it was not an order which was going to last. Solidarity had gone underground but lost nothing of its appeal, and on March 11, 1985 Mikhail Gorbachev was elected General Secretary of the Soviet Communist Party.

MIKHAIL GORBACHEV AND THE END OF SOVIET COMMUNISM

Without Lenin, the Soviet state would never have come into existence. Without Stalin, it could well have taken a less tyrannical and inefficient form. Without Khrushchev, neither deStalinisation nor the attempt to go back on it in Hungary in 1956 would have followed quite the same pattern that they did. Without Gorbachev, the collapse of Communism would not have begun when it did, and the improvement in relation-ships between the Soviet Union and the West would certainly not have happened with the speed which it did. In 1987 Gorbachev himself was predicting that German unification 'might perhaps come in a hundred years', and the remark made in 1989 by British Foreign Secretary Douglas Hurd, that the division of Europe decided at Yalta in February 1945 had provided a system 'under which we have lived quite happily for forty years', suggests that there was no urgency in the West's desire to see the Soviet Union disappear.[3]

In the years immediately after 1945 the USSR had taken out of Europe roughly the equivalent of what Marshall Aid had put into Europe west of the Elbe. A thousand factories, for example, were taken from Czechoslovakia to the Soviet Union. By the 1980s the German Democratic Republic was being kept alive only by massive financial transfers from West Germany. Between 1963 and 1989 the Federal Republic of Germany paid its eastern neighbour some 3.5 million Deutschmarks in exchange for the release of 250,000 Germans who wished to join their families in the West. In 1983 and 1984 it made what was officially referred to as a loan to the German Democratic Republic of almost two billion marks.[4] On November 24, 1999 it gave Romania a loan of 500 million.

In spite of his earlier position as an apparatchik considered reliable enough to be adopted as a protégé by one of his predecessors, Yuri Andropov, when the latter was head of the KGB, Gorbachev represented a new generation in Soviet politics. In 1985 he had been the top student of his year in the Law Faculty of Moscow University. No previous First Secretary of the Soviet Communist Party had been a graduate (Khrushchev is said not to have learned to read until he was twenty).[5] Admirers of the Soviet Union had always dwelt on the importance which it attached to education. Over and above its failure to gain the support of the working class, there was thus an additional irony, in the fact that the person who did more than anyone else to destroy the Soviet régime should have been a man who had profited from this particular sector.

In a sense, the collapse of this régime was inevitable. The Soviet Ambassador in Bonn, Valentin Falin, may well have been right when he said that the Americans had 'arms-raced the Soviets to death'.[6] However improbable it might seem, the collapse of the Soviet Union could have been the result of a conspiracy by the capitalist West to lure it into a series of cold-war confrontations which would place an unbearable strain upon its economy. But Gorbachev himself pointed out how inherently inefficient the system had become when he said in a speech in April 1986 that it was absurd for the economy to be run by 'trillions of calculations from Moscow.'[7] It might have continued to work, especially if modified, had the Soviet Union continued to live as Stalin had wanted it to live, in isolation from the rest of the world. But once it had expanded beyond its borders, the additional strain of the need to defend the empire which it had acquired after 1945 proved fatal.

It is significant in this respect that the changes which brought about its demise should have begun in Eastern Europe. On January 1, 1988 the Czech government tried to forestall an increase in political protests by launching a programme of limited privatisation. The twentieth anniversary of the repression of the Prague Spring in August 1968 was marked by massive protest demonstrations against the régime. In December 1989 these led to what was known, from the lack of violence with which it was carried out, as the 'Velvet Revolution', led by the playwright Václav

Havel The political career which had followed the success of his plays satirising the Communist régime, such as *A Difficult Understanding* (1968) had begun with the movement known as Charter 77, after the protest document signed by 243 leading members of Czech society and demanding the implementation of Basket III of the Helsinki agreement of July–August 1975, calling upon countries of both East and West to respect human rights.

Since Havel had been one of the instigators and leaders of Charter 77, it was natural for him be chosen as President in the elections of December 29, 1989. He did not prove outstandingly successful in day-to-day politics, largely because his concern for social justice made him unhappy about the speed with which his Prime Minister, Václav Klaus tried to introduce a market economy into Czechoslovakia. Between October 1991 and October 1994 over 1,800 state-owned enterprises were privatised, and six million Czechs became shareholders. This, inevitably, led to the same increase in social inequalities which had accompanied the extensive privatisations carried out by the Thatcher government in Great Britain in the 1980s, and the situation in Czechoslovakia was made more complicated by the disparity between the industrialised and relatively sophisticated Czech part of the country and the less developed rural area of Slovakia. On January 1, 1993 the latter became the independent Slovak Republic, in one of the few examples in post-Communist Europe of the peaceful division of a previously united country into what its inhabitants saw as more natural entities.

It was not, however, a division of which Havel approved, and the persecution of the ten per cent Hungarian minority which has since taken place in the new Slovakia suggests that it is not an ideal state. In 1992 Havel resigned, and on January 26, 1993 he was re-elected to the largely symbolic post of President of the Czech Republic. Together with the leaders of the other protest movements in Eastern Europe, he had begun the process which was to culminate on December 31, 1991 in the disappearance of the Soviet Union and its transformation into what has been known since then as the Commonwealth of Independent States.

The coincidence that these events took place exactly two hundred years after the French Revolution of 1789 created the feeling that Europe was enjoying another 'Springtime of the peoples', this time giving rise to a more permanent summer than had happened when the phrase was first used of the revolutions of 1848. Insofar as there has not so far been a conservative reaction comparable to the one which put an end to the hopes of 1848, the optimism which inspired books such as Timothy Garton Ash's *We The People: The Revolution of '89 Witnessed in Warsaw, Budapest, Berlin and Prague* (1990) or John Simpson's *Despatches From the Barricades: an eye witness account of the revolutions that shook the world 1989–90* remains justified. When the Chinese leader Zhou Enlai was asked whether he thought that the ultimate effects of the French Revolution of 1789 had been beneficial or not, he replied that it was too early to judge. No similar delay has been necessary to give a verdict on the Soviet Revolution of 1917. It failed in every respect.

On June 4, 1989 the pressure on the Polish régime still headed by General Jaruzelski led to the holding of the first free elections in an Eastern-bloc country since 1947, preceding those which had signalled the Velvet Revolution in Czechoslovakia by six months. There were still some restrictions, with opposition candidates able to contest only thirty-five per cent of the seats in Parliament. But the candidates put forward by Solidarity won 160 of the 161 parliamentary seats open to competition, and 90 out of 100 in the Senate. On August 18 Tadeusz Mazowiecki, one of Wałesa's closest advisers, was elected Prime Minister: the first non-Communist to hold such an office since 1945. In November 1989 Wałesa was elected President, and on December 11 Jaruzelski made a public oath of loyalty to the new régime and presented his apologies for the repression which had followed the *coup d'état* of December 13, 1981. On the following day the Headquarters of the Polish Communist Party was transformed into a Stock Exchange.

Up to that point the most dramatic event to signal the end of the Cold War had taken place on November 9, 1989, when the East German authorities suddenly allowed free passage over the Berlin Wall from East to West Berlin. They did not do so willingly. On October 6, 1989 Gorbachev made a formal visit to East Germany to celebrate the fortieth anniversary of the official creation of the German Democratic Republic. He was greeted by wildly enthusiastic crowds, whose expectations of him were somewhat different from those of the East German leadership. Eric Honecker – an old-style Communist who had begun his working life as an apprentice to a roofer and had later been sentenced by the Nazis to ten years in a concentration camp in 1937 – was credited with having taken the initiative in erecting the Berlin Wall on August 13, 1961; he wanted Gorbachev to put an end to all his nonsense about democratic reforms and the abandonment of the leading role of the Party.

Left to himself, Honecker would have had no compunction in using military force; the East German police had already been issued with extra ammunition. But this time, the fact that no leader of any of the People's Democracies had ever been able to take a decision without permission from the Soviet Union worked against the hard-liners. Gorbachev refused to accept Honecker's prescription for dealing with civil unrest and gave the order for Soviet troops to stay in their barracks. Under no circumstances, he told him, would he agree to any shooting.

Honecker's position had already been weakened by the Hungarian authorities' decision on September 10, 1989 to allow East German refugees to go through their country to Austria. Since they could then, if they wished, proceed to West Germany, the Berlin Wall was no longer capable of keeping the citizens of German Democratic Republic from leaving a régime which they so heartily detested. On November 9 the East German government announced that exit visas would automatically be issued to anyone 'wishing to visit the West'. After some initial uncertainty as to what exactly this meant, the border guards suspended the order they had previously received to shoot anyone trying to cross the Wall. Many of them joined the ecstatic crowds which surged over the Wall, and later helped them to demolish it.

Everything was happening so quickly that it evoked the scene which might have taken place in Holland if the little Dutch boy of legend had removed his finger from the hole in the dike and the sea had then come rushing in. On October 3 Germany became a united country again. Neither François Mitterrand nor Margaret Thatcher were very keen on the idea – both sharing the view attributed to the French Catholic novelist François Mauriac that he loved Germany so much that he wanted there to be two of it – and it is a sign of how inseparable the fortunes of the countries of Europe have become that, as will be seen in Chapter 10, one of the effects of German reunification was the undignified exit of the pound sterling from the European Exchange Rate Mechanism on September 16, 1992.

In no Eastern European country did the system the Soviet Union imposed after 1945 survive. In the elections of May 16, 1990 the Hungarian Democratic movement, established on September 27 1987, gained 42.5 per cent of the popular vote. The new Prime Minister, Jozsef Antall began a programme of privatisation which by 1993 was to ensure that almost half the Gross Domestic Product was to come from the private sector. By then, the politicians of Eastern Europe were experiencing some of the drawbacks as well as the advantages of Western-style democracy. In Poland inflation was running in 1990 at 249 per cent a year, and two of the main results of the stringent economies needed to bring it down to 9.5 per cent by 1998 were an increase in unemployment and a reduction in benefits. The problems created by such a massive programme of privatisation gave a boost to the popularity of the former Communist Party, and in the elections of December 1994, under its new name of the Social Democratic Movement, it increased its seats in Parliament from 33 to 209.

In neither Poland nor Hungary, however, did these problems discourage the governments from continuing with their programmes of privatisation, cuts in state expenditure, and a rigid monetary policy. This was the price to be paid if Hungary, like the other countries of the former Soviet bloc, was to qualify for membership of the European Union: a reminder that a market economy does not automatically create wealth for all members of society. Now, a little late, the resultant ability of the former

Communist parties to win votes in Western-style parliamentary elections in other East European countries, such as Poland, raised the intriguing question, of whether some form of Alexander Dubček's 'socialism with a human face' might not in fact have been created in the countries of Eastern Europe, if Stalin had been able to keep his nose out of their business.

In Romania, the change of power was more dramatic. On December 22, 1989 the former Head of State Nicolae Ceauşescu, together with his wife Elena, tried to escape to the West. They were arrested, tried by a military tribunal and shot on Christmas Day. Ceauşescu had never been particularly popular with the Soviet Union. In 1968 he had refused to allow Romanian troops to take part in the invasion of Czechoslovakia alongside their allies in the Warsaw Pact, and he had not endeared himself to the Soviet leadership by his attempts to improve relations not only with the West but also with the People's Republic of China. Like Imelda Marcos, who in 1986 had to flee from the Philippines in company with her husband Ferdinand, Elena Ceauşescu was an advanced foot fetishist. Each woman had a collection of over 2,000 shoes.

THE END OF THE SOVIET UNION AND ITS AFTERMATH

In 1990, on the opening page of *Despatches from the Barricades*, John Simpson quoted a passage from the essay 'Of the Vicissitudes of Things' by Sir Francis Bacon (1561–1626):

> For great empires, while they stand, do enervate and destroy the forces of the natives which they have subdued, resting upon their own protective forces; and then when they fall also, all goes to ruin, and they become a prey. So it was in the decay of the Roman empire; and likewise in the empire of Almaigne, after Charles the Great, every bird taking a feather.

A microcosm of the fundamental weakness which the long experience of socialism had left behind it in the fabric of society was provided by the report that Mr Gorbachev, out of office since 1991, had lost 48,000 roubles when the Moscow bank to which he had entrusted them suddenly collapsed; the report in the *Daily Telegraph* for December 30, 1998 gave the impression that the sum constituted his life savings. And it was one of the sadder ironies of history that *The Economist* should have already reported on July 1, 1998 that the Gdansk shipyards were to go into receivership.

The collapse of the Soviet Empire nevertheless failed to conform to Sir Francis Bacon's generalisation in one important respect. No Western country swept down like a vulture to take either flesh or feather from the fallen foe. On the contrary, both the newly united Germany, the main prize in the Cold War, and the United States of America, the Soviet

Union's principal adversary, competed with one another with loans to help their former adversary readjust its economy and feed its citizens. There was, it is true, a strong element of self-interest in this. Nobody wanted to see Russia fall into the hands of what commentators called a 'Red/Black coalition', an alliance between former Communists and extreme nationalists. No motive other than an understandable desire to ensure the survival of the human race led the United States to spend billions of dollars helping to decommission Russia's nuclear arsenal and pay reliable guards to watch over the airfield and rocket sites where these weapons were stored.[8]

Had the West been inspired by the kind of motives seen as universal by Sir Francis Bacon, it would also have behaved differently in the two crises of August 1991 and November 1993. On August 19, 1991 a conspiracy by Communist hard-liners, all men originally appointed by Gorbachev himself, seized power in Moscow and imprisoned Gorbachev in his holiday dacha in the Crimea. Only François Mitterrand expressed his readiness to recognise the régime which the conspirators were trying to establish. Other Western leaders limited themselves to keeping quiet while the CIA provided covert help for Boris Yeltsin, whose courage and determination defeated the conspirators in two days.

The principal effect of the attempted coup was to put an end both to Gorbachev's career and to the Soviet Union. He proceeded to outlaw the Communist Party and to create the Commonwealth of Independent States, which would replace the Soviet Union on December 31, 1991. Gorbachev had already resigned a week earlier, and when he later stood as a candidate in the Russian Presidential election of 1996 he received only 0.51 per cent of the vote. Here there was a parallel between his career and that of the Polish trade union Solidarity: in the elections of 1993 it failed to win the five per cent of the votes needed to enter the Polish parliament, receiving the support of fewer electors than the Polish Party for the Defence of Beer.

Yeltsin's subsequent dominance of Russian politics stemmed from his action on November 1993, when he ordered the army to storm the Congress of People's Deputies, whose members were becoming increasingly critical of his policies. As in August 1991, the West did nothing which might make the situation worse, and the International Monetary Fund continued to provide generous loans in the hope that Russia, which still had its nuclear arsenal, would develop a viable free-market economy. Russia found great difficulty in doing so, and on August 18, 1998, unable to keep up with the interest payments on the loans from the West, let the rouble go into free fall. Before it was temporarily stabilised by the efforts of Prime Minister Yevgeny Primakov it had lost eighty per cent of its value, and was standing at 25 to the dollar; when Mr Gorbachev came to power in 1985, it had stood at just over 2 to the dollar.

7 Socialism in Western Europe

CONTRASTS, SIMILARITIES AND QUESTIONS

Since 1945, only two countries in Western Europe have made more than one systematic attempt to introduce socialism, France and Great Britain. In France, the Popular Front government which came into office in May 1936 had a brief spell of power of just over one year, ending in June 1937. The left was then in office again in France for a brief period of some eighteen months immediately after 1945. It held power from June 1981 to March 1986, and then again from June 1988 to March 1993. It has been in office since June 1997. In terms of parliamentary arithmetic, and therefore of the ability to decide how the economy of the country is run, the left has governed France for just under twelve years since 1945.

In the United Kingdom, the Labour Party held office twice under Ramsay MacDonald in 1924 and 1929–1931. Immediately after the Second World War, in the General Election of July 1945, it won an overwhelming majority over all parties of 146 and stayed in power until November 1951. It then had to wait thirteen years before being narrowly elected in October 1964, and then re-elected with a larger majority in February 1966. It was defeated in May 1970, and then elected in February 1974, staying in office until May 1979. Altogether, it has thus been in office for just over fifteen years since 1945.

This relatively short period of time underlines an essential contrast between the countries of Western Europe and those of the former Soviet bloc. Its basic cause lies in the new meaning which the word *alternance* took on in French in the 1970s: that of the peaceful transference of power, after elections held according to agreed rules, from the political party which had been in government to the party which had been in opposition. Because this was a new phenomenon in France, a word had to be imported to describe it. Because it had been happening in the United Kingdom since the early eighteenth century, and in the United States of America from 1801, there has been no need to find an English term to designate so familiar a phenomenon. It remains a defining characteristic of democracy that a party should lose power at the hands of the electorate, sometimes just when it thinks it is doing rather well.

It is not so much that a period in power so discredits a left-wing government that it is incapable of retaining office. In the British general election of February 1950 over 13 million people voted for the Labour Party, as against 12.5 million for the Conservatives, and it lost power principally because 2.6 million voted for the Liberals. It is that opinion is so narrowly divided in the countries of Western Europe that only a small change in voting patterns, sometimes no more than two per cent, is enough to bring about a change of government.

There is also another similarity between the fortunes of the democratic left in France and Great Britain. In both countries, not only have the socialist parties in both countries been required, on several occasions, to abandon power after a limited period, they have also undergone a considerable change in their official aims. When the Socialist Party of François Mitterrand took power in 1981 a policy of nationalisation and state control was widely seen as the best way to run an economy. In the France of the late 1990s the party under Lionel Jospin has given up the idea of solving the country's economic problems this way. On June 5, 1999 *The Economist* gave details of the money received by the French state through the privatisation programmes begun in 1986. This showed that since Jospin came to power in June 1997 the sums received were higher than they had been under any former government: 180 billion francs under Jospin; 77 billion between 1986 and 1988, when the Gaullist Jacques Chirac was Prime Minister under Mitterrand's Presidency; and a combined total of 123 billion when the conservative politicians Édouard Balladur and Alain Juppé were in power between 1993 and 1995 and between 1995 and 1997 respectively.

The British Labour Party under the leadership of Tony Blair has also abandoned the idea of public ownership which inspired its election campaigns of 1945, 1964, 1974 and 1979. It has ceased to demand the renationalisation of the industries privatised by the Conservative governments of Margaret Thatcher in the 1980s and of John Major in the 1990s. It is thus a profoundly different party from that of Clement Attlee and Harold Wilson.

How can these similarities be explained? Why have democratic socialist parties proved no more successful in holding on to power than their totalitarian counterparts? And why have they undergone so profound a change?

THE IMPACT OF THE WELFARE STATE

The most immediate explanation is that the economic situation in all the countries of Western Europe is very different from the one which made socialism so attractive in the years immediately before and after the Second World War. This change lies first and foremost in the way in which the societies of Western Europe now treat their members. All of them, whether they have consciously tried to create socialism by the introduction of state ownership or not, have introduced some form of the welfare state. All of them now require everyone to take out insurance against accidents, illness and unemployment, and for the provision of a basic old age pension. All of them also make use of money raised through general taxation to try to improve the general standard of living, especially for their poorer members.

Old age pensions were first introduced in Germany by Bismarck in 1881, and by Lloyd George in the United Kingdom in 1909. In 1911 the first National Insurance Act also introduced into Great Britain the idea of workers making a regular weekly contribution to provide themselves with some form of protection against sickness and unemployment. But the welfare state, in the comprehensive form in which we now know it, did not come into existence in Western Europe until after 1945. True, it was neither an entirely new idea, nor one which the Western Europeans had taken the initiative in bringing to its present form. It became a characteristic feature of New Zealand with the electoral victory of the Labour Party in 1935, and of the Scandinavian countries in the early 1930s. In Great Britain it was created later, and was seen as a well-deserved reward for the contribution made by all members of society to the victory of 1945 (one of the crucial factors in Labour's electoral victory in July of that year was the vote by men and women still in uniform). In France, the establishment of the welfare state also followed the events of the Second World War, and reflected the generally left-wing spirit produced by the triumph over fascism.

This was one of the many contrasts with the situation in 1919. In Britain, in what was known as the 'khaki election' of December 1918, the Labour Party won only 57 seats. The predominantly right-wing parliamentarians elected – whom the Conservative leader Stanley Baldwin himself described as 'hard-faced men who looked as though they had done well out of the war' – made little attempt to implement the promises implied in the slogan about 'homes for heroes to live in' which had been made to the troops between 1914 and 1918. A comparable victory for the right in the December 1919 elections in France produced what was known as 'La Chambre bleu horizon' (the term derived from the colour of French military uniforms). In France, as in Great Britain, it was not until 1924 that a left-wing coalition had the opportunity to try to put some of its ideas into practice, and the generally conservative atmosphere in society at large then prevented any real implementation.

Whatever the tragedies of the Second World War, its effects on the internal politics of both France and England were from this point of view profoundly beneficial. For those members of the working class who were not killed, seriously wounded or taken prisoner by the Japanese, it was far less disastrous an event than the Great Depression of the 1930s. In France, the experience of occupation and resistance also shook up the country in a way which the Popular Front of 1936 had never done. After the German invasion of the Soviet Union on June 22, 1941 had swung the French Communist Party into support for the resistance movement, this took on a predominantly left-wing flavour. The creation of a welfare state became one of its main objectives, one endorsed and put into practice by de Gaulle in the period between the liberation of 1944–1945 and his resignation in January 1946. One of the many obstacles confronting any French government wishing to reform the welfare state remains the objection 'Mais, vous n'allez pas détruire ce que le général de Gaulle a créé!' (But you're not going to destroy what General de Gaulle created!).

The idea of the state looking after all its citizens 'from the cradle to the grave' has led to a very considerable increase in its powers. Until the second half of the nineteenth century the basic function of the state was limited to protecting its citizens from external aggression and internal disorder. Then, in 1871 in the United Kingdom, in 1874 in Germany, in 1881 in France, the state made elementary education compulsory for everyone. Seen in retrospect, this was the first major step in the extension of the powers of the state, as well as in the increase in the money it took from its citizens, in the form of taxes, to finance its activities. Before 1939 the average proportion of the Gross National Product which the state in Western Europe took from its citizens in taxes and other compulsory payments, such as rates, was never more than twenty per cent. In 1999, in the fifteen countries of the European Union, it is on average almost forty per cent.

All political parties deplore this, and all make the same claim that the welfare state is safe in their hands. There is not a single country in Western Europe in which a major party wishes to abolish the provision of a health service financed by regular, compulsory contributions, or which tells the electorate that they will no longer have any form of income if they lose their job. The way the welfare state is organised may differ from one country to another. It is more developed in Scandinavia than in Greece; unemployment and sickness payments are more generous in France and Germany than in the United Kingdom; child allowances are higher in France than anywhere else; and it is still not a good idea to go to a public hospital in the south of Italy. Nonetheless, in spite of these differences, there is an important piece of evidence which illustrates the basic similarity in welfare provision between all the member countries of the European Union, and which marks an important difference between Western Europe and the United States.

This is known as 'Form E111', the document which enables the citizens of any member of the European Union to claim the same benefits in the state of the Union which they happen to be visiting as those to which the citizens of that state are themselves entitled. It is a prosaic example, and in that respect matches the view of one of the founding fathers of the European movement, Jean Monnet, that the best way to build a unified Europe was from the bottom up, preferring concrete realisations to ambitious general ideas.

The establishment and success of the welfare state have given the lie to Marx's claim in *The Communist Manifesto* that 'the executive of the modern state is nothing more than a committee for managing the common affairs of the bourgeoisie'. On the contrary, what has become clear since 1945 is that the organising power of the modern state can be used for the benefit of all its citizens, and can even be used to create more social equality. This equality has not, it is true, grown with the speed which all political parties say they desire. In the United Kingdom, for example, 43 per cent of the national wealth is owned by 10 per cent of the population, and this 10 per cent includes the 1.5 per cent which owns 40 per cent of the land and 48 per cent of the stocks and shares. In 1996, 17 per cent of all households in Great Britain were below the poverty line, the same as in Spain and only a little ahead of Greece and Italy.[1]

In France, where social inequalities are greater than in any other member state of the European Union except Greece, 1 per cent of the population owns 20 per cent of the wealth; these people are included in the 10 per cent who together own 50 per cent. The remaining wealth is shared out among the rest.[2] There is thus, from the standpoint of women and men of the left whose aim has traditionally been a more equal division of wealth, an important unfinished agenda. The fundamental change which has come over the Socialist Party in France and the Labour Party in Great Britain, however, makes it unlikely that the state will be called upon to fulfil the implementation of this agenda.

This is mainly because of a change in attitudes towards taxation. In the 1940s, and in some quarters as late as the 1980s, taxation was not only accepted as a device for raising money to finance the activities which the state organised for all its citizens. It was also seen as a justified instrument for making people financially more equal. The refusal of virtually all political parties to envisage any further increase in taxation has come to mean that this is no longer a fashionable view. In the past, women and men of the left did not see the creation of a welfare state as an end in itself: it was always to be accompanied by the use of taxes as a means of taking money from the rich to give to the poor. Even those parties which are ostensibly of the left have given up this idea. While, in the creation of the welfare state, the European left has fulfilled one of its major objectives, it seems to have abandoned its other principal aim of trying to use the power of the state to create more social equality. At the same time, it has given up the belief that the best way of making people richer is to take as many businesses and services as possible into public ownership.

THE CONCEPT OF CONSUMER CAPITALISM

The faith in the traditional socialist concepts of state planning and public ownership has been confounded by a phenomenon unpredicted by Marx: the ability which capitalism has shown in the second half of the twentieth century to transform itself in such a way as to avoid the collapse predicted in *Das Kapital* (1867; *Capital*). Marx had always entertained a kind of love-hate relationship with capitalism. There is a passage in *The Communist Manifesto* which has something of the horrified fascination of a celibate priest discoursing on the dangers presented to young men by the physical beauty of the female form. 'The bourgeoisie', he wrote in 1848,

> has been the first to show what man's activity can do. It has accomplished wonders far surpassing Egyptian pyramids, Roman aqueducts and Gothic cathedrals; it has conducted expeditions that put into the shade all former Exoduses of nations and crusades.

It is true that the predominant impression of capitalism given by the rest of Marx's work is that of a machine which creates as much, if not more, poverty for the oppressed proletariat as it does wealth for the exploitative and parasitic bourgeoisie. There is no hint of the phenomenon noted at the very beginning of Max-Stephan Schulze's *Western Europe since 1945*, when he notes in his introduction that

> Since the end of the Second World War, western Europe's total output rose fivefold and per capita output increased more than three times. In 1946, European Gross Domestic Product per head was less than half that of the United States. By the mid-seventies, incomes in western Europe had reached about three quarters the US levels and the gap continues to narrow thereafter, albeit at a slower rate. The growth of GDP per head may be a crude proxy for the rise in the 'standard of living', but there is no doubt that the increase in material prosperity has been *the* major characteristic of economic and social development in western Europe since 1945.[3]

The existence of this phenomenon, whose existence is not denied even in as brilliant a diatribe against modern British society as Will Hutton's *The State We're In* (1995), makes it very difficult to believe in Marx's prediction of what he called the progressive pauperisation of the working class. Nobody denies the figure of up to one in five British households living below the poverty threshold. But you only need to go to any supermarket, or to postpone until February the attempt to book a foreign holiday for August of the same year, to see that the other four-fifths of the population is doing quite nicely, thank you very much. Socialism, in the form which it took in the nineteenth century and the first half of the twentieth, was essentially the product of a society in which most people were very poor, of what W.H. Auden called 'that England in which nobody is well'. Now that this poverty is no longer so widespread, it is natural that the enthusiasm for socialist ideas should disappear. When capitalism seems to be delivering the goods for the top two-thirds of the population, a political party setting out to abolish it has little chance of winning an election.

An epigram dating back to the 1950s claimed that Marks and Spencer have done more for social equality than either Marx or Spencer. By making quality goods available at an accessible price to all members of society, the firm which first appeared on a stall in Leeds market in 1884 under the notice 'Don't ask the price – it's a penny' has enabled people to become more equal in the food they eat and the clothes they wear. The generalisation of consumer capitalism which it represents, and to which the epigram referred, has had a deeper and more beneficial effect than the Marxist attempt to create social equality by the abolition of private property. At the same time, the acceptance by Simon Marks, who inherited the 'Penny Bazaars' in 1907, of the idea that the employer has a responsibility both to his work force and to society at large has done more to make society prosperous than the active encouragement of cut-throat competition which Herbert Spencer (1820–1903) derived from his misreading of Charles Darwin.

The idea that capitalism could work for the benefit of all was fundamental to its early prophets such as Bernard Mandeville (1670–1733) and Adam Smith (1723–1790). What Mandeville argued in *The Fable of the Bees* (1723) was that, although bees have no interest except their own satisfaction in seeking the nectar from flowers, they nevertheless perform an essential function for nature by enabling pollination to take place, while at the same time producing the honey which human beings take from the hive. Although Mandeville wrote to some extent with his tongue in his cheek, the idea that there is an innate harmony in society which enables the pursuit of private profit to produce public prosperity is fundamental to the views which Adam Smith developed in his *Inquiry into the Nature and Causes of the Wealth of Nations* in 1776.

What he argued was that, while a man in private business may intend only his own gain, he is, in this and many other cases, led by an invisible hand to promote an end which was no part of it. Nor is it any worse for society that it was no part of it. By pursuing his own interest, he frequently promotes that of the society more effectually than when he really intends to promote it.

'I have', Smith added, 'never known much good done by those who affected to trade for the publick good', and his remark seems an under-statement when applied to the economy of the former Soviet Union and its satellites. The more became known of its deficiencies, the more superior the workings of the invisible hand seemed to those of the omniscient centre, and the more attractive the parties supporting the ideas of Adam Smith became to the electorate of the Western democracies.

In its extreme form, this belief in the quest for personal profit which keeps the free market going finds its expression in the slogan eloquently defended in the 1987 film *Wall Street* by Michael Douglas, in the character of Gordon Gekko, when he proclaims 'Greed is good'. In Great Britain, it is closely associated with the changes introduced by the three successive Conservative governments of Margaret Thatcher (1979–1983, 1983–1987 and 1987–1990). It is therefore vulnerable to the charge of having produced the new phenomenon of young people living in cardboard boxes on the streets of London, and of the change in British society embodied in the fact that, while in 1979 only 4 per cent of households lived below the poverty line, by 1997 this had risen to 21 per cent.[4]

The workings of the free market may not be ultimately beneficial to all its members. Ethically, it would be much better if people were to work selflessly for the common good. But it does not seem to matter, as far as the growth of social inequality is concerned, which party is in power. Will Hutton pointed out in 1995 that social inequality has increased in Great Britain since the victory of the Conservative Party in the May 1979 election. Between 1979 and 1991, he writes, 'the bottom sixth of the population actually saw their real income fall, while income of the top 10 per cent rose by more than half'.[5] But, in spite of all the efforts made by the socialist governments appointed by François Mitterrand over the fourteen years that he was President of France (1981–1995), the value of shares on the Paris Stock Exchange rose by 500 per cent, while the number of those unemployed increased from 1.5 million to almost 3 million.

In both France and England, the fact that fewer and fewer workers have a permanent job is also an indication of the increasing similarity with the United States, where Manpower, which employs people only on temporary contracts, is now America's largest employer.[6] The Canadian-born economist John Kenneth Galbraith commented that the free-market economics recommended by Milton Friedman made a curious presupposition: they justified the reduction of income tax on the grounds that the rich don't work hard enough because they don't have enough money, and the reduction of social security payments on the grounds that the poor don't work hard enough because they have too much. When Ronald Reagan and Margaret Thatcher put these theories into practice, they were widely criticised for making the rich richer and the poor poorer. But neither Bill Clinton nor Tony Blair has so far managed to buck the trend.

Admittedly, as Will Hutton acknowledges, the technological improvements which have taken place since 1945 have made many goods much more accessible to a wider range of people. At the end of the Second World War, the average wage-earner had to work for eleven months to buy a car; now, it takes him only eight months.[7] It is an improvement which has taken place throughout the capitalist world, and is more marked in Germany or the United States than in Great Britain and France. In the countries ruled by Communist parties, it has not taken place at all. If the idea, universally accepted in 1945, that the way to prosperity is by public ownership and state planning seems to have been universally discredited, there is also another reason for this. It is because the attempt to put socialism into practice by democratic means has not been so outstandingly successful as to lead the electorate to vote for it in the numbers needed to keep left-wing parties in power for long enough to let them give permanent form to the idea that the best way to run an economy is by nationalisation and state planning.

THE RECORD OF LEFT-WING GOVERNMENTS IN POWER

THE EXAMPLE OF GREAT BRITAIN

In 1918 the British Labour Party added Clause IV to the Constitution it had adopted in 1900, when it was created as the Labour Representation Committee. This called, in very Marxist terms, for 'the common ownership of the means of production, distribution and exchange', and it remained official policy until 1989, when the Party changed its image. It was an aim which served as the basis for the policies carried out by the Labour government of 1945–1951, and which included the nationalisation of the Bank of England, civil aviation, the coal mines, the steel industry and the railways, together with the electricity and gas industries.

The 1964 and 1966 Labour governments of Harold Wilson were less ambitious. The first contented itself with the 1967 renationalisation of the steel industry, and, when re-elected in 1974, the second undertook virtually no legislation aimed at extending public ownership. One of the reasons for this was that the policy was not seen to be giving the right results in the sectors of the economy which had already been nation-alised. By 1980 the British Steel Corporation was losing £30 a second,[8] and the British economy in general was so unable to compete in the world market that on November 18, 1966 the pound had to be devalued by 14.3 per cent, from $2.80 to $2.40.

This was in the days of fixed parities, and the devaluation had been preceded by a series of denials that it was going to take place. When the Prime Minister appeared on television on November 19 to explain what had been done and why, he made what turned out to be the unfortunate remark that this decision did not mean that 'the pound in your pocket has been devalued'. But this was precisely what did happen, largely because of the events which had made the devaluation necessary in the first place. Chief among these was a constant inability of the British economy either to satisfy home demand or to export enough goods to pay for the imports which consumers demanded. In October 1966 this had led to what was then the unprecedentedly large trade deficit of £162 million, and it was hard to agree with Harold Wilson when he blamed it all on the people he called 'the gnomes of Zurich'. His critics pointed out that the only power which these mysterious malefactors possessed was the ability to follow the law of supply and demand. If the pound was falling, this was because everybody wanted to sell it, and nobody wanted to buy it. Traders on the international money markets had as little ability to determine which way the money flowed as a barometer does to decide the weather.

There are many suggestions as to why the British economy failed in the second half of the twentieth century to maintain the dominant position which it occupied in the nineteenth. Its decline is reflected in the fact that in 1870 Great Britain's economy came top of the league, outstripping those of Austria, Belgium, Denmark, Finland, France, Germany, Italy, the Netherlands, Norway, Sweden and Switzerland in terms of Gross Domestic Product and what are called 'Human Development Indices', but by 1992 it had fallen to twelfth place (and, had the United States and Japan been included in the 1992 analysis, it would have been fifteenth).[9] It is hard to believe that this is because Britain started the Industrial Revolution first and was thus doomed to be overtaken. Neither is it because it spent all its money defending civilisation between 1939–1945. The Germans refer to 1945 as the 'Stunde Null' (year zero) for the good reason that the whole physical structure of their economy had been completely destroyed. Yet by 1959 Germany had become the richest country in Western Europe except Switzerland – a performance soon matched by France, another country apparently ruined by the Second World War.

A more convincing explanation lies in the fact that Great Britain remains a class-ridden society in which a great gulf is still set between those who run the country and those who are expected simply to take orders. There is also the fact that British managers, like the British work-force, are poorly educated by world standards. This might be traced back to the fact that the Industrial Revolution of the late eighteenth and early nineteenth centuries had been carried out largely by artisans and shrewd but not highly educated entrepreneurs. George Stephenson (1781–1848), who made the first steam locomotive, was educated only at night school. James Watt (1736–1819), who first put into practice the idea of using steam as a source of energy, had one year as an apprentice to a maker of mathematical instruments, while Richard Arkwright (1732–1792), whose spinning jenny revolutionised the spinning of cotton, had received no formal education at all.

It is certainly true that the Industrial Revolution in which Great Britain led the world took place with no help from the universities, and with virtually no contribution from the traditional ruling class. Technical education at tertiary level was much slower to develop than in France or Germany, while the Arts faculties in British universities fostered the view that it is not only vulgar and ungentlemanly to go into business but positively immoral. It is nevertheless unlikely that any of these factors has had a more disastrous impact on the British economy since 1945 than the behaviour of the trade unions. It was their behaviour which ruined the Labour governments of the second half of the 1960s, and which cast such a shadow over the performance of the Labour Party when it held office between 1974 and 1979 that it remained unelectable until it changed both its policies and its image.

The document which the Labour Party published on May 4, 1990 under the title *Looking to the Future* abandoned the commitment to dena-tionalise the industries privatised by the Conservative governments of the 1980s, and, perhaps even more important, it made no reference to the earlier promise to repeal Conservative legislation limiting the powers of the trade unions. The party also gave up the idea that the central govern-ment should exercise control over commerce and industry, and ceased to demand that British citizens owning capital overseas should immedi-ately bring it back home. Although it failed to be elected in April 1992, when John Major won a rather surprising victory, it swept back to power with a record majority under Tony Blair on May 1, 1997.

The decisive factor in the failure of the Labour Party to beat the Conservatives in May 1979, June 1983 and June 1987 was the way the trade unions had made it impossible for any government, whether Labour or Conservative, to govern the country. Almost as soon as the Labour Party had been re-elected in March 1966, its majority improved to 98 compared with the narrow margin of 4 by which it had won the General Election of October 1964, it was faced on May 16 with a strike by the National Union of Seamen. This had an immediate and disastrous impact on exports, which was repeated in August as the result of a major dock strike. Then Prime Minister Harold Wilson made what turned out to be a public-relations mistake comparable in scale to his remark about 'the pound in your pocket'. On August 28 he announced that he was taking personal charge of the economy.

The view that he could manage where others had failed was consistent with his reputation as a brilliant economist as well as with the way he had wiped the floor with the then Conservative leader, Alec Douglas-Home in a television debate during the 1966 election campaign. While Home had tried to play the common man by explaining how he used the contents of a box of matches to work out the need for the British economy to balance its books, Wilson had produced a brilliant display of economic analysis which proved beyond doubt that the British economy could not fail to get better under his direction. The devaluation of November 14, 1966 suggested that the country might have been better off with Home's matches.

Much of the time and energy of the Wilson governments of 1964–1970 was taken up with trying to reach an agreement whereby the trade unions would moderate their wage demands. These were seen as ruinous to the British economy because of the increase they provoked in the price of manufactured goods: the root cause of the country's inability to compete in international markets. As became clear when Labour took office again in 1974, none of these efforts succeeded. The contrast was frequently made with the co-operation between management and unions which characterised the German economy, and whose nature is discussed below as both a cause and an effect of the post-war German economic miracle. An improvement on the economic front – brought about partly by the West German government's decision to stave off inflation by revaluing the mark, thus making British exports more competitive – came too late to save Labour from losing the election of May 4, 1979 to the Conservatives.

The swing in voting patterns which then gave the Conservatives a majority of 43 over all other parties had not been expected by the commentators. This, combined with the revelation that the gap between imports and exports which had led to the devaluation of November 1966 had been exaggerated by a series of mistakes made by government statisticians, cast further doubt on the advisability of relying on experts, whether in economics or anything else. The more pragmatic approach traditionally associated with the Conservative Party, and epitomised by Sir Alec Douglas-Home's matches, might therefore have been expected to do better, especially since the election as leader of Edward Heath, a grammar-school boy from Broadstairs, had enabled it to shake off some of its image as the party of landed gentry educated at Eton. But Heath, like Wilson before him and Jim Callaghan in the 1970s, was to fall victim to trade union militancy, rendered more effective by events taking place outside the United Kingdom.

The Labour government of 1945–1950 had not had quite the same problem with the trade unions. Something of the wartime consensus still existed, and the Labour Party was seen as the party which also represented the interests of their members. What blew it off course – after the appalling winter of 1947–1948 had made it seem as though the introduction of state planning could do little to improve the economy – had been the outbreak of the Korean War on June 24, 1950. This made necessary, in the view of the Prime Minister if not of his more left-wing colleagues, a programme of rearmament, and this, in turn, led to the first breach in the Welfare State: the introduction of charges for false teeth and spectacles into the National Health Service, thus abandoning the ideal of dental and medical care 'free at the point of delivery' which was one of its initial basic principles. This exemplifies one of the major features of European history since 1945: the vulnerability of Western Europe to events taking place outside its borders.

Another example was the increase in the price of oil decreed by the OPEC countries in October 1973, which, thanks to the behaviour of the miners, was to have a particularly dramatic effect on the economy of the United Kingdom. Between January 9 and February 27 the Heath government had already been faced by a miners' strike which had forced it to give up any serious attempt to control wage inflation. The publicity given to the threat of an Arab embargo on the sale of oil to Western Europe, and then to the quadrupling of the price of oil, put the National Union of Mineworkers (NUM) into a position of unexpected strength. Since the 1950s coal mining had become a declining industry. Oil was cheaper and more easily accessible. Now the situation was reversed, and the old reliance on coal was back. It is a measure of the change in public mood in Great Britain that no attempt was made to rouse any feelings of patriotism which might lead the miners to postpone their new set of wage demands until the country had had time to adjust to the new price of oil. The predominantly left-wing leadership of the NUM took the quite sensible view that the only role of a trade union in a capitalist system was to do everything possible to improve the position of its members. On November 12, 1973 it began its campaign for higher wages with a ban on overtime, followed by a total stoppage on February 9, 1974.

On January 1, 1974 the combination of the overtime ban, a strike by railway workers and the increase in the price of oil-based fuels had already led to the imposition of the three-day working week – a measure which had the curious effect of bringing about an increase in industrial production. On February 7 the Prime Minister announced that he was calling an election in which the main theme would be 'Who governs the country?' – the government, with a majority in the House of Commons, or the trade unions. In his view, as in that of most right-wing commentators, the leadership of the NUM, and especially the president of the Yorkshire area, Arthur Scargill, were inspired essentially by political motives. Behind their proclaimed desire to ensure that the miners remained at the top of the tree as far as industrial wages were concerned was the desire to turn Great Britain into a workers' state on the model of the Peoples' Republics of Eastern Europe. When the General Election of May 1979 brought a Conservative government to power, Arthur Scargill made a speech comparing it to the Nazi Party, in which he declared:

> A fight against this government's policies will inevitably take place outside rather than inside Parliament. . . . I am not prepared to accept policies proposed by a government elected by a minority of the British electorate. . . . Extra-parliamentary action will be the only course open to the working class and the Labour movement.[10]

In 1974 the nature of the British electoral system prevented the emergence of a clear reply to the question of 'Who governs the country?'. In the General Election of February 28 the Conservative Party received 11,868,906 votes, giving it 297 seats. The Labour Party, with 11,639,243 votes, won 301 seats, while the Liberal Party, receiving a record number of 6,063,470 votes, had 14 seats. Thus, although the Labour Party had a majority of 4 over the Conservatives, it could easily be outvoted in the Commons if the Liberals joined forces with the Conservatives, especially if the 2 Plaid Cymru members and the 7 Scottish Nationalist MPs used their votes. Whoever governed the country, it was certainly not one of the two main political parties, each of which could remain in office only in some kind of coalition, and neither of which had any power over the trade unions.

In so far as the Labour Party had supported the miners' strike, it was seen in Conservative quarters as having broken one of the cardinal rules of British politics: that you do not come to power by allying yourself with sectional interests outside the party political system. In that respect, what the events of 1974–1975 showed most clearly was that it was the trade unions who were calling the shots. The events which followed the General Election of October 10, 1974 seemed at the time to put them in the position of an opposition which could not form a government itself but which could prevent any parliamentary party from governing. After a brief period of minority government, Harold Wilson called another election on October 10, 1974, which the Labour Party proceeded to win quite comfortably. It had a majority of 43 over the Conservatives, and of 30 against a possible alliance between the Conservatives and the Liberals.

The answer to Edward Heath's question now seemed quite clear. The party that governed the country was the one which was prepared to give way to the demands of the powerful trade unions, and especially the NUM, and thus fulfil the promise Harold Wilson had made at the time of the 'three-day week' of January 1974 to 'get the nation back to work'. But the Labour Party's victory in the October 1974 General Election turned out in retrospect to mark the beginning of the end of democratic socialism in the United Kingdom. On March 16, 1976, after only eighteen months back in office, Wilson suddenly resigned. He was just 60, no great age for a political leader in the British system. He let it be known that he was already aware of a loss of memory which betokened incipient Alzheimer's disease, and he did indeed become very ill later on. This explanation remains vulnerable to the alternative proposition that, early on in what was his third period as Prime Minister, he had realised that the economic and social policies traditionally recommended by the Labour Party were not going to work, and wanted somebody else to carry the ultimate can.

This turned out to be Jim Callaghan, who had begun his working life as a tax officer in the Inland Revenue and spent the Second World War as a merchant seaman. He was thus very different from the man who had been the most brilliant student of economics in the Oxford of the 1930s and spent 1939–1945 as a civil servant with the Board of Trade. When Wilson later said that he thought his most important contribution to British society was the creation in 1969 of the Open University, he paid tribute to an admirable institution. A little more might nevertheless have been expected from the man who first came to power in 1964 with the promise of a 'white-hot technological revolution' which would totally transform British society.

All Callaghan's honesty could not prevent the Labour administration which he headed from March 1976 to May 1979 from falling victim to the three forces which could be seen, even at the time, as putting an end to the idea that parliamentary socialism would make Great Britain a more prosperous and equal society. The first of these was the world economic crisis sparked off by President Nixon's decision to float the dollar on August 15, 1971. The second was the oil price rise of 1973. Both of these events were totally beyond the control of any European politician. The third, which any democratically elected government ought to have been able to master, was once again the behaviour of the trade unions.

The pound proved exceptionally vulnerable to the turmoil in the money markets set off by the combination between the dollar's flotation and the oil price rise. In 1975 inflation had risen to 26 per cent, and nobody seriously expected the agreement reached in May 1976 with the Trade Union Congress to limit average pay increases to 4 per cent to be respected by any but the weakest trade unions. In November 1976, the pound was so weak that the British government had to apply for a loan of $3,900 million from the International Monetary Fund. This was granted only on condition that public expenditure would be cut by $2,000 million over the next two years, an obligation which meant that, by force of circumstances, the Labour Party had to behave in very much the same way as a Conservative government might have done through conviction. It refused increases in social benefits and educational spending, and it refused to try to reduce what was then the post-war record of 2.4 million unemployed by adopting the reflationary policies advocated by John Maynard Keynes.

This led to reduced support from the poor and disadvantaged, who had always been Labour's natural allies, and reinforced the view that, if socialism was to work, it had to be in a socialist world, and not a capitalist one. This lesson was to be driven home in France during the socialist experiment of 1981–1984, and, in an international context, is perhaps the reason for the failure of democratic socialism to fulfil the promises in which many believed in 1945. Then, its reputation was reinforced by what were seen as the achievements of the Soviet Union. These were real, in the sense that the Red Army had defeated the Wehrmacht in what the Russians themselves have always called 'The Great Patriotic War', but illusory in the sense that the belief that the USSR had used state planning to create an efficient and prosperous economy was totally unfounded. In 1945, however, the distinction was a difficult one to make, and there was also the view that socialism did not necessarily involve the total loss of personal freedom which characterised the Soviet Union. There was a widespread belief in the United Kingdom that it could be achieved by the natural alliance between the trade unions, which expressed the economic interests of the working class, and the Labour Party, the incarnation of its social and political aspirations.

The main outcome of the Callaghan government of 1976–1979 was to show how illusory the belief in such an alliance had become. In October 1978 the Prime Minister surprised virtually everyone by announcing that there would be no General Election that year. Had he gone to the country then, the Labour Party might well have won, and Margaret Thatcher might now be remembered as the first woman to become leader of the Conservative Party and the first to lead it to defeat at the polls. In February 1975 she had been chosen as successor to Edward Heath, who had offered himself for re-election to the post after thrice losing general elections to Harold Wilson. She had her ideas all ready, but needed to win a General Election to put them into practice. After 1976 the economic situation had begun to improve, thanks largely to the fact that North Sea oil had now begun to be available, and Great Britain was starting to become an oil-exporting nation. If asked in October 1978, the British electorate, divided and tolerant as ever, would almost certainly have kept Callaghan in office. He seemed a good chap, more honest and visibly less cocky than Wilson, whereas Mrs Thatcher was known principally as the Education Minister in Heath's government of 1970–1974 who stopped children having free milk at school: 'Milk-snatcher Thatcher'.

In the event, however, Callaghan's decision not to go to the country proved fatal to the fortunes of the Labour Party, and may well be seen as the most significant tactical mistake made by a British Prime Minister since 1945. But although Callaghan's decision, inspired by better motives than Eden's, led to eighteen years of Conservative government, there is no way in which he can be blamed for it. On January 3, 1979 the lorry drivers went on strike in support of a 25-per-cent pay claim. The tanker drivers followed with a 14-per-cent claim, and on January 22, 1.5 million public service workers began a 24-hour strike. In what was immediately dubbed 'the winter of discontent', the rubbish lay uncollected in the street, the dead were unburied, and the hospitals were manned only by the qualified nursing and medical staff. It was clear that the idea which the government had put forward of a 5-per-cent limit on pay increases was totally unenforceable. After losing by-elections in Clitheroe and Knutsford by swings of 9 and 13 per cent, the Callaghan administration was defeated by one vote in the House of Commons on March 28. It then proceeded to lose the General Election of May 4, 1979, and Margaret Thatcher became Britain's first woman Prime Minister with a majority for the Conservative Party of 43 seats over all other parties.

The changes introduced by Margaret Thatcher in her three successive governments of 1979, 1983 and 1987 changed British society in as funda-mental a way as the Labour administrations of 1945–1950. British Aerospace, the telephone service, gas, electricity and water were all sold to private investors, and there are currently no plans to take them back into public ownership. The same is true of the railways and coal mines, and the independence granted to the Bank of England in 1997 marked the final end of the idea that the state should have control of what Harold Wilson once called 'the commanding heights of the economy'. More particularly, the trade union legislation of 1980 and 1982 created a situation in which it was quite clear who governed the country. It was the legally elected government at Westminster, a fact which became very evident during the miners' strike which began on March 12, 1984 and ended on March 5, 1985.

This was, as the editor of the Sunday Times put it, 'one of the most significant events of post-war history'.[11] The trade union movement had brought down the Heath government of 1970–1974 and had proved equally uncontrollable under Wilson and Callaghan. Weakened by the impact of unemployment and the fear that anyone going on strike might lose his job, as well as by a marked decrease in membership and by the loss of public sympathy created by the 'winter of discontent' of 1978–1979, it made its last stand as a political force and was defeated.

Although the miners went back to work on March 5, 1985 with banners flying and bands playing, there was no doubt that the government had won. The pit closures against which the strike had originally been directed were to go ahead, and there were to be no wage increases.

In March 1984 Arthur Scargill had made a speech in which he declared:

> I made my name with the leadership of 12,000 flying pickets which I brought from Yorkshire to enforce the closure of the Saltley Gate Gasworks in the West Midlands in the 1972 miners' strike

and made it abundantly clear that he was preparing to do the same again. But this technique had been made illegal. The trade union legislation introduced by the first Thatcher government in 1980 and 1982 had given the force of law to the idea that only workers directly involved in a dispute were allowed to picket their own place of work. It also stipulated that, unless a strike had received prior support from a majority of union members voting in a secret ballot, anyone who wanted to continue to work was entitled to do so. Since Arthur Scargill, by now President of the NUM, had not taken the precaution of holding such a ballot, the police had the legal right not only to halt the movement of flying pickets but also to intervene in order to protect miners who wished to work from being prevented from doing so. This led to scenes of unprecedented violence, with heavy police involvement, and a bitterness in the mining villages of Yorkshire, the north-east and south Wales which has still not disappeared.

The ability of the trade unions representing manual workers such as miners, railwaymen or assembly-line workers in a car factory to overthrow or control governments stemmed from their members' possession of skills without which society could not survive. The kind of socialism represented by the British Labour Party before its abandonment of Clause IV expressed the desire of this class to turn its economic muscle into political power. But the economy of Western Europe was changing. It was becoming a service economy in which the old-style industrial workers were no longer in a majority. In the Poland of the late 1970s and early 1980s workers of the same heroic mould as the British miners were to use their power as trade unionists to help bring down Communism in Eastern Europe by going on strike in the shipyards at Gdansk. But, like the coal mines of Yorkshire and the north-east, the shipyards at Gdansk now stand empty. They no longer employ the workers who can overthrow governments.

No British Prime Minister in the twentieth century has been more reviled by progressive-minded thinkers than Mrs Thatcher, who after leaving office in 1990 became Baroness Thatcher of Kesteven. The term 'the Pasionara of privilege' applied to her by Denis Healey is one of the milder epithets.[12] Thanks to her, wrote Eric. J. Evans in 1997, 'Britain has become a more grasping, greedy and meanspirited society. Hers is a legacy to be lived down'.[13] The harshness of these judgements is primarily the result of the electoral defeats she inflicted on the left, and the openness with which she preached the virtues of enterprise and self-reliance. She was not, however, particularly popular with the traditional Conservative Party. Francis Pym (Eton and Cambridge) said of her, 'We've got a corporal at the top, not a cavalry officer'.[14] Alan Clark (Eton and Oxford) describes in his diary how he found her attractive, and shared Julian Amery's view that her attractive ankles indicated that 'There's blood there, you know, no doubt about it, there's blood',[15] but nobody else in the male-dominated English political establishment ever saw her as anything but irretrievably lower-middle-class; her father, after all, was a grocer. To walk from his shop on Grantham High Street to the elegant Anglican Church of Saint Wulfram on the top of the hill, you have to go past the Methodist Chapel where he preached every Sunday. Nobody who has not done that walk will ever understand what gave such an edge to her ambition to alter the balance of power at the top of British society.

What particularly alienated the intellectuals was her decision, in 1981, to make it clear that the universities were to be just as much subject to cutbacks in public expenditure as any other institution funded principally by the taxpayer. It was a decision which led the University of Oxford (where she – the first British Prime Minister to have a scientific education – had obtained her degree in chemistry) to decline to offer her an honorary degree in 1985. It also explains why she is still mentioned in university circles only in the tones which a Jewish mother might use to speak of Herod or of Hitler. Whether she had to deliver the *coup de grâce* to British socialism with quite the jubilation she did, though, is an open question. After all, democratic socialism has died the death in France as well, without a Margaret Thatcher to hasten it on its way.

THE EXAMPLE OF FRANCE

In June 1981 the Socialist Party, created by François Mitterrand ten years earlier, won an election giving it an overall majority and thus secured the opportunity of putting its policy of nationalisation and a state-planned economy into practice. Between June 1981 and March 1983 this led to what may turn out to be the last attempt in Western Europe to implement a consistently left-wing programme.

The government of Pierre Mauroy nationalised 36 major banks. It also took under public control the armaments manufacturer Matra, the glass-making firm of Saint-Gobain, the electronics giant Thompson-Brandt, and confirmed the earlier nationalisation of the steel industry. Another of its basic policies stemmed from its adoption of the Keynesian view that the main cause of unemployment was a lack of demand for the goods produced. It therefore sought to cure unemployment, which in 1981 stood at 1,700,000, by injecting money into the economy.

Because of the role traditionally played in the French economy by the state, this was relatively easy to do on technical grounds; since 1946 France has had a minimum wage centrally decided by the authorities in Paris, and this was increased by ten per cent, as were family allowances and old age pensions. The working week, whose length is also decided by the state, was reduced from 40 to 39 hours. Many workers simply saw this as a means of increasing the amount of overtime they did. And employers were required to give their workers five instead of four weeks paid holiday a year. These decisions illustrated the power wielded by the state being used to try to create a more humane society, doing away with the law of supply and demand which governed economic life in the nineteenth century and putting the interest and well-being of the workers in its place. But neither the increase in the minimum wage nor the reduction of the working week improved productivity. On the contrary, they made French-manufactured goods more expensive, which offers one reason why the experiment in socialism represented by the Mauroy government was abandoned in July 1984.

From 1958 onwards France had derived great advantages from being one of the founder members of the European Economic Community. In particular, the Common Agricultural Policy had enabled it to sell within the protected zone of the EEC its meat, fruit and vegetables, which would have cost far too much on the world market. It had also received large sums of money to modernise its agriculture. But there was a price to pay for this. It took the form of the obligation to keep its frontiers open to the industrial products of the other members of the EEC, and especially Germany. Everywhere else but in France, the early 1980s were a period in which governments were trying to cut down on the money supply and reduce the purchasing power of their citizens. The seller's market produced by adopting the Keynesian policy of increasing the money supply attracted imports into France like a suddenly opened window drawing cold air into an over-heated house.

Since 1979 France had been a member of the European Monetary System (EMS), with the consequent obligation of keeping the value of the franc within a range of ±2.5 per cent of the average of a basket of currencies in which the Deutschmark played the single most important role. In order to enable its citizens to buy the European-made goods for which the reflationary policies of the Mauroy government had created such a demand, the French government had to buy other European currencies. Since it had to do this at a time when French exports were being made more expensive by the creation of the 39-hour week and the increase in the minimum wage, there was no corresponding increase in the demand for francs, and the law of supply and demand led to a fall in the value of the franc on international money markets. On October 4, 1981 the French government had to request what was euphemistically termed a realignment of the franc within the EMS.

What might more honestly be termed a devaluation had to be repeated on June 12, 1982 and again on March 21, 1983. It is an indication of the power given to the President under the Constitution of the Fifth Republic that it was Mitterrand himself who then made the crucial decision to refuse any further devaluation. By choosing to maintain the parity between the franc and the Deutschmark, he ruled out any further devaluation, and thus any further attempt to reflate the economy by increasing the money supply. In other words, he personally suspended the experiment in socialism which had begun in an atmosphere of such optimism in the early summer of 1981. There were no further nationalisations, and no more increases in state-allocated allowances. On July 17, 1984 Mitterrand replaced the traditional-minded socialist Pierre Mauroy with a young technocrat, Laurent Fabius, with instructions to bring in a tight monetary policy in place of the expansionary policy by which it had initially been hoped to cure unemployment. But this continued to rise, reaching 2.5 million by 1986, and proving peculiarly resistant to all changes of economic policy. It currently stands at just under 3 million, or over ten per cent of the work force.

The France of the early 1980s had other economic problems in addition to the effect on the international value of the franc of the imports which the Mauroy government's reflationary policy attracted into the country. France could satisfy only two per cent of its need for oil from resources which it controlled. But the price of oil, then as now, was expressed in dollars, and the Reagan administration's adoption of the monetarist theories popularised by Milton Friedman had led to a sharp increase in the value of the dollar, which at one point reached the value of 9 francs, as compared to 5 under Reagan's predecessor Carter. It was an increase which helps to explain why the French should now be so enthusiastic about the Euro, which they see as a means of reducing their economic dependence on the United States. Perhaps, they hope, the Euro will come to replace the dollar, or at least rival it, as the principal international currency acceptable for the purchase of oil, and France will be freer to pursue the economic policies it prefers outside the orbit of what de Gaulle saw as Anglo-Saxon economic imperialism.

Under the Constitution of the Fifth Republic, legislative elections have to be held every five years. In spite of the fact that the Socialist Party changed the rules governing the election due to be held in March 1986, substituting a system of proportional representation for the single-member, two-ballot system used in June 1981 (*scrutin uninominal à deux tours*), it lost its majority. François Mitterrand, who still had two years to go as President, thus had no choice but to invite Jacques Chirac, the leader of the conservative, Gaullist party, to form a government. Extensive though the powers of the President are under the Fifth Republic, they do not include the right to determine the policy of a political party which has won a majority in the legislative chamber. The conservative government of Jacques Chirac proceeded to privatise most of the enterprises taken into public ownership under Pierre Mauroy, several of which were in very good shape as a result of the cost-cutting policies implemented by Mauroy's successor, Laurent Fabius. Between 1977 and 1985 the British government had raised £97 billion from privatisation. The figures quoted on p. 133 show how very much more successful the French Socialist Party was to be in using privatisation to balance the budget and implement its promise to reduce taxes.

When, in 1988, Mitterrand was re-elected President for a further seven years, he used his constitutional powers to dissolve the National Assembly. This enabled the Socialist Party to win a narrow majority, but the new Prime Minister, Michel Rocard, immediately announced that there would be no further privatisations, and no nationalisations either. In 1993 the Socialist Party again lost the legislative elections, winning only 67 seats as against its former 277, and faced an overwhelmingly powerful right-wing alliance of 428. Further privatisations followed, and the election of Jacques Chirac as President in May 1995 seemed to suggest that the right was firmly in power for the foreseeable future.

As far as economic policy was concerned, this was certainly the case. In May 1997 Chirac dissolved the National Assembly, hoping to secure a more solid majority to see him through what was expected to be the difficult period leading up to the introduction of the Euro on January 1, 1999. To everyone's surprise, the Socialist Party of Lionel Jospin won a comfortable majority. However, it gave no sign of wishing to follow policies which would have been recognised as left-wing in the 1940s and 1950s, or even as late as the 1980s. Indeed, as indicated by the figure of 180 billion francs which it has received as a result of its privatisation, it has done more than the British Tory Party did when the *Punch* cartoon of 1867 accused it of 'catching the Whigs bathing and running away with their clothes' – it has taken the policies of the French right and made them work more successfully than any of its leaders could have imagined.

THE RECORD OF OTHER MEMBER STATES OF THE EUROPEAN UNION

There are several reasons why no attempt was made to introduce socialism into the Federal Republic of Germany. Until May 23, 1949 it did not begin to be an independent state again. It could not therefore have taken fundamental decisions about its economy anyway. Although the British were apparently quite keen on taking the basic industries in their zone into public ownership, the Americans stopped them.[16] The car firm of Volkswagen had always been a state enterprise, established by Hitler in 1938 in Lower Saxony, which was now in the British zone, and in 1946 there was some talk of transferring it to Britain by way of reparations. But British car-makers considered the Volkswagen itself to be too ugly and noisy to be worthwhile, so it stayed where it was. In 1961 the German government sold sixty per cent of it to small investors. In 1988, it sold off the rest.[17]

Once the currency reform of June 28, 1948 had created an economic climate in which the laws of supply and demand could work, the economy of West Germany began to take off. It was helped by the Marshall Plan and by the excellent relations between management and workers which the trade union reform imposed by the Western powers had created. The system known as *Mitbestimmung*, or joint management, creates a system of permanent consultation between the employers and the trade unions brought together in the *Deutscher Gewerkschaftsbund* (DGB), the equivalent of the British Trade Union Congress (TUC). But whereas the TUC groups together some 400 separate unions, the DGB has only 17. What are known as 'demarcation disputes', quarrels about which worker is entitled to do which particular job, are thus virtually unknown in Germany. So, too, is the enormous number of strikes which used to bedevil British industry. In 1985 only 35,000 working days were lost through industrial disputes in Germany, as against 7,070,000 in the United States, 6,402,000 in Great Britain, 3,831,000 in Italy and 727,000 in France.[18]

By the time the Federal Republic of Germany attained full sovereignty, the passion for nationalisation which had characterised other countries in Western Europe immediately after 1945 had begun to fade. Its first Chancellor, Konrad Adenauer, was leader of the CDU, which saw the primary duty of the state as to ensure the rule of law and of fair dealing among the different social and economic groups. Its function was to prevent the formation of monopolies and to redistribute wealth through taxation policy and benefits. It was not to own major enterprises or to run the economy from the centre. In this respect, it has marked parallels with some of the functions now fulfilled by the European Union. This seeks, through the application of Articles 85 and 86 of the Treaty of Rome on open and fair competition, to ensure the existence of a level economic playing field. By the implementation of the Social Chapter, it also creates legislation to protect the interests of all employees.

The fundamentally conservative philosophy of the CDU precluded any attempts at nationalisation while it held power in the 1950s and

1960s. In 1959, at the conference of Bad Godesberg, the more left-wing SPD officially gave up its attachment to Marxism and adopted the idea of the mixed economy. It was the equivalent of the British Labour Party's decision in 1990 to abandon Clause IV, the only difference being that the SPD did it earlier and without being compelled to do so by a series of electoral defeats. Both parties in West Germany were, in any case, far more conscious of the possible dangers of socialism than any left-wing party in France or Great Britain. Next door lay the example of what was known as the *Deutsche Demokratische Republik*.

There are several additional reasons, which have nothing to do with the Cold War, the Marshall Plan or the trade union structure imposed on them by the allies, which explain why, since 1945, Germany has had the most successful economy in Western Europe. The first is the shock of defeat. Unlike the British, who felt after 1945 that the world owed them a living, the Germans were fully aware that they would have to make a determined effort both to rebuild their country and to obtain forgiveness. The best way of fulfilling both aims was to work hard.

There was a particular reason why they were able to reap the rewards of their labours with such relative speed. A major difference between the dictatorship established in Germany in 1933 and the one imposed by Lenin in 1917 is that Hitler's lasted only thirteen years. Communism, in contrast, had eighty years in which to destroy the framework of the Russian state and kill off any chance of creating a viable economy and acceptable system of democratic government. It has been argued that the Soviet Revolution of 1917, like the French Revolution of 1789, resembled a sudden fall of snow on spring blossom. In both countries, a process of gradual reform was already taking place, but was killed off by the brutal imposition of the desire to change society completely.

However, whereas the passion for total reform ran out of steam in France by 1794, and was brought under control by Napoleon I, nothing comparable happened in the former Soviet Union. There, it was not until the arrival of Gorbachev in 1985 that a serious attempt was made to change the system, by which time it was too late. In the Germany of 1945, in spite of all the physical destruction, a number of basic institutions had remained intact. One of these was the excellent apprenticeship system. This ensured an ample supply of skilled craftsmen whose adaptability made possible the *Wirtschaftswunder* (economic miracle) of the 1950s and 1960s. Great Britain has excellent universities but a bad record in technical training. In Germany, it is the other way round. The consequences are visible in the fact that when the Deutschmark was launched in 1949, you got twelve to the pound; now, on a good day, you get just under three.

What was perhaps even more important for the revival of the German economy was the fact that the habit of trust, like the concept of the rule of law, had also escaped total destruction. There still existed the idea of a state which could be neutral in disputes between one group of citizens and another. In spite of all the economic disasters which had laid the seeds of Nazism, people could still believe that, if you left your money in the bank, it would still be there for you next week. In the states of the former Soviet Union, as in the satellites which it dominated in Eastern Europe, this is the exception, not the rule. The revival of Germany, the most important event to have taken place in Western Europe since 1945, bears witness to the fact that the most important structures are those which exist in people's minds.

In recent years, the German economy has not been doing quite so well. Unemployment is at just over 11 per cent, as against 5.3 per cent in the UK, and, although much of this is in the former GDR, it now has a general effect on the whole country. In the past it was a point of pride that welfare benefits were fifty per cent higher than those in Great Britain. This is now seen as imposing too heavy a burden on the economy, although there seems to be no way of bringing them down to the level which those who do not need them see as realistic. All the same, it remains true that an important reason why socialism is no longer as attractive as it used to be in Britain and France is that the most successful economy in Western Europe seems to have managed very well without it.

In 1998 the only two countries in the European Union to be governed by parties of the right were Ireland and Spain. Belgian politics, dominated as they have been since the creation of the state in 1830 by quarrels about the powers of the federal government and the conflict between the speakers of French and speakers of Flemish, are hard to analyse in terms of right and left. The coalition governing Luxembourg was dominated by the moderate Christian Social Party, and there was a comparably centrist alliance in power in Norway. Elsewhere, there was a left–right coalition in Austria, in which the dominant party were the Social Democrats, a term generally associated with the left. In Finland, France, Germany, the Netherlands, Norway, Portugal, Sweden and the United Kingdom the party or parties in power were officially of the left – though this was nevertheless not a left that anyone would have described as such in 1945.

In Portugal, there had been a brief attempt at socialism after the overthrow of the Salazar regime in 1974, when sixty per cent of the economy was nationalised. But this did not last, and in 1996–1997, 22 companies were offered up for privatisation. In Spain, the perpetuation until his death in 1975 of the dictatorship which Franco had established in 1939 meant that there had been no chance of establishing socialism there before the restoration of a democratic system of government. When this came, the socialist Prime Minister Felipe González was too absorbed in giving rights to trade unionists, in promoting autonomy in Catalonia and the Basque country, in reducing the state debt, liberalising the laws on private sexual behaviour and preparing the country for membership of the European Economic Community to think seriously of establishing a socialist-style economy. His narrow defeat by the right-wing José María López Aznar in the 1996 election thus did not lead to any fundamental change of direction in Spanish politics.

In Spain, as elsewhere in Western Europe, the paradox of parliamentary democracy has given a remarkable stability to a country whose past history contained so much violence and hatred. It is a paradox which lies in the fact that parliamentary democracy can exist only where there is sufficient consensus about the basic structure of society to preclude any recourse to violence, but where there are sufficient differences between the parties competing for power to make such a competition meaningful. If this is now the case in all fifteen countries of the European Union, it is perhaps because the idea of creating even a democratic form of socialism has now been abandoned. After all, there was always something slightly odd about trying to combine socialism with parliamentary democracy anyway. A state which became socialist as a result of the total transference to public ownership of all the means of production, distribution and exchange could scarcely envisage the idea of giving up all that power merely because it had lost an election.

Part 3 *The movement towards European unity*

Prelude

European values and the European Union

PARLIAMENTARY DEMOCRACY AND THE RULE OF LAW

Between the signature of the Treaty of Rome on March 25, 1957 and the ending of the Cold War, there was little enthusiasm among men and women of the European left for the European Economic Community (EEC). Not only was it visibly aimed at making the capitalist system more efficient. By using the adjective 'European' to describe solely the countries lying to the west of the iron curtain, it was seen by its left-wing critics as relegating the People's Republics of Eastern Europe to another continent.

Once the Soviet Union began, on November 26, 1981, to talk about 'a Common European Home', the hostility felt towards the EEC by the British Labour Party of the 1980s became more intense. Its electoral manifesto of 1983, described by Denis Healey as 'the longest suicide note in history', recommended not only withdrawal from NATO and the abandonment of Britain's independent nuclear deterrent but also the ending of British membership of the EEC. It was not until the sea change in the politics of Western Europe brought about by the ending of the Cold War that the hostility towards the EEC which also characterised the French Communist Party began to disappear.

Since the countries of Eastern Europe then began to say that they would like to join the EEC, this was a thoroughly understandable change. It was, moreover, a recognition that there had never been any firm basis for the hostility towards what had earlier been presented as misappropriation of the adjective 'European' in the title of what had by then become the European Union. It was the Treaty of Rome which became increasingly recognised as expressing the true nature of Europe in political terms – a nature never recognised by the treaty which established the rival organisation of Comecon (Council for Mutual Economic Assistance), created at the initiative of the Soviet Union in January 1949 in response to the challenge of the Marshall Plan.

The Treaty of Rome itself, concerned as it was with essentially practical matters, such as abolition of customs duties and the prevention of monopolies, does not spell out the political criteria for membership in a detailed form. All it says, in Article 237, is that any European state 'may apply to become a member' of the Community, and it assumes that the leaders of such states will understand what the preamble to the Treaty means when it mentions the wish of the original members to 'strengthen peace and liberty' and calls upon 'the other peoples of Europe who share their ideal to join in their efforts'. What these remarks have always been taken to mean is that a state successfully applying for membership has to be a parliamentary democracy, with everything that implies by way of freedom of speech and assembly. Its government has to accept to leave office if it loses an election, to impose on its citizens only those taxes voted by a freely elected representative assembly, and to respect the rule of law.

'The rule of law' is a phrase which emphasises the main difference which always separated the member countries of the EEC from those of Comecon. In the EEC, as in all the member countries of NATO with the exception of Turkey, it is not only private citizens and public corporations which have to obey the law. It is the government itself. This was never the case either in the Soviet Union itself or in the countries taken into its orbit after 1945. There, the coincidence between the state and the Communist Party meant that neither of them operated under the same rules as other sections of society. The law was what the state and the Party said it was.

The idea of the rule of law in no way implies that the law is unchangeable. It can, after due process, be changed so as better to serve the interests of society as a whole. What this due process implies, in a parliamentary democracy, is the holding of an election in which all parties which have renounced the use of violence may compete, in which none derives a privileged position from the fact of having exercised power, and in which all are allowed total freedom of expression. Once the laws are passed by the parliament issuing from these elections, they are the same for everyone, whatever their religion, their political opinions, the colour of their skin, or whether they are rich or poor.

When the theory is not applied, this is seen as wrong, something which ought not to happen and which should therefore be remedied. This is not a reaction which would have existed in continental Europe before the French Revolution of 1789, or which would occur nowadays in most countries of the Third World. In more practical terms, it means that the people judging you for an alleged offence are not the same as those bringing the charge. You are also, as you would not be in the People's Republic of China, deemed innocent until proved guilty. It is the job of the state to prove your guilt. You do not have to prove your innocence.

The ideas associated with the rule of law are not peculiar to the member states of the European Union. They are found in North America, Australia and New Zealand, and in an increasing number of states in

Central and South America. But they are customs which have their origin in Europe and in Europe alone. No institution modelled on them exists in any Islamic country. If they are found in Japan or the Far East, it is because the Europeans, through the agency of the predominantly European culture of the United States, have taken them there. But, by a curious paradox, they were first developed as a basis for political life in the member country of the European Union where scepticism about its aims and institutions is most widespread and most vocal.

HISTORICAL ORIGINS AND PRESENT PARADOXES

Before the English Civil War of 1642–1645, the idea that the King himself might be subject to the rule of law existed only in the minds of a few eccentric philosophers. It was the defeat of the armies of King Charles I by the parliamentary forces under the command of Oliver Cromwell which produced a state in which the King was compelled to acknowledge that he was not above the law, and that it was not he but parliament which had the right to levy taxes. This did not happen overnight. The most immediate result of Cromwell's victory was the establishment of a military dictatorship which ended only with his death in 1658 and the restoration of the monarchy with Charles II in 1660. It was only after the Bloodless Revolution of 1688 had driven the Catholic James II from the throne and put the Protestant William of Orange in his place that the idea finally came to be accepted that it was parliament which held the purse strings.

It was not democracy in modern terms. The revolution of 1688 was carried out by a group of aristocrats who may well not have had the popular support subsequently claimed. The development of cabinet government owed much to the fact that George I, whose accession in 1714 assured the Protestant succession to the British throne, spoke not a word of English, and had to rely on Robert Walpole for all his communications with parliament. But by 1729 the system was working well enough to enable Voltaire to write enthusiastically in his *Letters concerning the English Nation* that the King was powerful to do good, but had his hands tied if he wished to do evil. Another French visitor, Montesquieu (1689–1755), put forward an ingenious misreading of the situation when he claimed that the way England was governed reflected the idea of the separation of powers, with the King, the executive, being held in check by parliament, the legislative body, and both of them controlled by the third arm of government, an independent judiciary.

It was a misreading in the sense that the Prime Minister, the effective head of the executive, is also an elected member of the legislative body, so that the separation is less absolute than Montesquieu argued. But Montesquieu's view was sufficiently widespread for it to inspire the authors of the constitution of the United States, who in turn influenced the drawing up in 1789 of *La Déclaration des droits de l'homme et du citoyen* which expressed the ideal if not the practice of the first French Revolution.

The ideals now accepted as commonplace in Western Europe, North America and Australia could, theoretically, have arisen anywhere in the world. It may well have been merely a historical accident that they were first given practical expression in the England, which had only recently experienced the Protestant Reformation. The fact remains that the ideals most valued by democratic society originated in countries which had already experienced the Protestant Reformation. In their later development they have enjoyed their warmest welcome in countries which, like France, have also embraced the idea of the secular state.

The reason for the paradox whereby it is the country where modern democracy made its first appearance which entertains the most suspicion of the European Union lies in what is called the 'democratic deficit'. This is a shorthand term for the accusation that the EU, like the EEC before it, has always been a bureaucracy run by unelected civil servants. It is a criticism as frequently heard in Paris as in London, and derives much of its force from the inability of the European Parliament to exercise the same control over the workings of the Commission and the Council of Ministers as the House of Commons, at least in theory, exercises over the British cabinet.

This criticism, discussed in more detail in Chapter 8, is based essentially on the inability of the European Parliament to withhold supply. At Westminster, as on Capitol Hill, the government can carry on only if the House of Commons or Congress votes to approve the budget. It was the claim of Charles I to levy taxes without the consent of parliament which set off the English Civil War, and the crucial consequence of his defeat was the future inability of any executive in a democracy to levy taxes unless it received the approval of the elected legislature. In the European Union, this approval is not necessary. The money distributed by the various bodies in Brussels comes from customs duties over which the European Parliament has no authority, and from contributions from member states which must be made in accordance with the treaties signed at the time of their accession.

The central issue of the democratic deficit is discussed later. Important though it is, it does not overshadow the way in which the ideas implicit in the European Union express other aspects of the European achievement.

APPLIED SCIENCE, INNOVATION AND ECLECTICISM

The vision of a society of human beings enjoying equality before the law and freely choosing how to govern themselves is not the only gift which Western Europe has given the world. In 1919 the French essayist and poet Paul Valéry, published in *The Athenaeum* an article which showed what would nowadays be seen as the height of political incorrectness. What he argued was that it was in Europe that humanity showed itself most truly itself. In his view, what most clearly distinguished human beings from the rest of the animal kingdom, was the combination of the desire for knowledge and ambition to control their environment.

It was this appetite for knowledge and power which first made its appearance in what Valéry described as 'this tiny headland of the continent of Asia', and which the Europeans, as he also pointed out, had exported in its most dynamic form to the New World. In doing so, they had not only created America. They had also given birth to the first genuinely world-wide civilisation, one based on the power of applied science to change the world and the confidence that human beings will be able to master their own inventions.

The idea of Europe as the starting point for this new, world-wide civilisation is inseparable from the fact that it was the ships of the Europeans which sailed to China and Japan; it was not those of Asia which came to Europe. It was the Europeans, for good or ill, who colonised Africa, not the other way round. The continued inventiveness of the Europeans themselves, as well as that of the European culture which they exported to North America, can nowadays be borne out by the statistics of Nobel Prize winners:

- Chemistry: USA 34, UK 22, Germany 14, Japan, 1;
- Physics: USA 40, UK 19, Germany 17, Japan 3;
- Physiology and medicine: USA 42, UK 18, Germany 14;
- Other countries untouched by Europe, 0.[1]

As the English historian T.O. Lloyd pointed out in 1984, it was also as a result of the European voyages of discovery in the fifteenth and the sixteenth centuries that human beings first began to have 'an idea of their geographical relation to one another'.[2]

It was in Europe that the first universities made their appearance, before being exported to North and South America. It was also in the general social and intellectual atmosphere of Europe and North America that science was systematically used to change men's physical and social environment. Just as it was in Europe that Charles Darwin (1809–1882) discovered the laws of natural selection which finally made the traditional belief in God intellectually impossible, so it was in Europe that the Industrial Revolution took place which enables human beings to master nature as well as to understand it. Copernicus, Galileo, Newton, Einstein and Mendel were all Europeans.

As is shown by the example of the Greek historian Thucydides (460–404 BC), it was Europe which gave birth to the modern idea of history in the sense of an enquiry into why men behave as they do. In this respect, Thucydides is not only the founder of the analytical tradition in the writing of history. He is also the first representative in the history of thought of the secular tradition, a style of thinking to which there is no equivalent in any non-European culture. The *History of the Peloponnesian War* makes no attempt to explain what happens by invoking the gods. When they are referred to by the Athenian delegates at Melos, it is only as offering a hypothetical and explanatory parallel as to how human beings behave. If, the Athenians say, the gods exist, as they may perhaps do, they will be very like us, and will be faced by the same dilemma: rule or be ruled. It was Nietzsche (1844–1900), a quintessentially European thinker through his worship of the Greeks and recognition of the drive to power as the animating force in human existence, who said that God was dead. No culture outside that of Europe has faced up to the problem of living in a godless world.

Valéry's unconscious repetition of Tennyson's 'Better fifty years of Europe than a cycle of Cathay' also goes hand in hand with his appreciation of another feature of European culture. Just as no other continent has exported more of its achievements to other parts of the world, no culture has been more eager than that of Europe to absorb and exploit the philosophical ideas, the technical achievements and spiritual insights originally developed elsewhere. We have taken mathematics and distilled liquor from the Arabs; our visual arts have absorbed the ways of depicting the world developed in Africa, China and Japan; our museums give as much place to the sculpture of India as to that of Greece. The skylines of our great cities are enlivened by the domes of Islamic mosques – by 1971, there were 300 of them in Paris alone, and by 1984 over 600 places of Islamic worship.[3]

Our eclecticism in literary matters extends to the cultivation of the Japanese *haiku* and the production of Hindu dramatic sagas or Japanese *nō* plays, our writers celebrate the mystical tradition more fully developed in the East than in the West and which Aldous Huxley called *The Perennial Philosophy*,[4] and our bars echo to the sound of the Japanese karaoke. Immigrants entering Europe undoubtedly bring with them a rich cultural baggage. But they, for their part, also enter a culture which offers them more than wealth. It offers, by the side of the freedom to keep their own life-style if they wish to do so, the opportunity to benefit from what the whole world has to offer by way of cultural achievements.

EUROPE, SELF-CRITICISM AND HAPPINESS ON HUMAN TERMS

European culture also stands out from ways in which human beings have tried to make sense of their own experience in other parts of the world by its ability for self-criticism. This has not always been the case. At the time of the Crusades, it did not characterise the Europe then known as Christendom. It was also absent from the Christian missionaries who presumed to instruct those they called heathens in how best to live. But in the twentieth century, and especially since 1945, it has become an outstanding feature both of Western Europe itself and of its spiritual offshoot in North America. It is in the universities of Cambridge, Paris and Stanford that the term 'Eurocentrism' originated, not in those of Jakarta, Singapore or Tokyo.

There are ample grounds for what can sometimes become a passion for self-denigration. Europeans have not only slaughtered an immeasurable number of their fellow human beings on their own continent. Elsewhere in the world, they have murdered whole peoples and destroyed whole cultures. Between 1914 and 1918, and again between 1939 and 1945, they dragged the whole world into their quarrels. But in so far as the movement towards European unity discussed in this section was inspired by the ambition to do away with Europe's own civil wars, they do at least seem to have learned from their mistakes.

This learning process has also been accompanied, perhaps by accident rather than design, by the most important idea affecting people's daily lives to have arisen anywhere in the world in the twentieth century. Since 1945, Europe has fulfilled the intellectual promise already announced in the eighteenth and nineteenth centuries in the writings of Mary Wollstonecraft (1759–1797), Georges Sand (1804–1876) and George Eliot (1819–1880) by becoming the intellectual birthplace of the women's movement. Its first and still most eloquent apostle was the French philosopher and novelist Simone de Beauvoir, whose book *The Second Sex* (1949) remains the bible of the women's movement. It is impossible to imagine the ideas it expresses arising anywhere but in Europe, or in those parts of the world which, like North America or Scandinavia, have often followed European cultural models. Its other representatives such as Betty Friedan may come from the United States or, in the case of Germaine Greer, from Australia, but many of the ideas they express were first given open expression in Europe.

There is no way in which the women's movement, with everything that it implies about the ability of women to control what happens to their own bodies, could have occurred spontaneously in any Islamic country, in Africa, Asia or east of the Elbe. In the former Soviet Union the absence of sexual education and the difficulty of obtaining contraceptives meant that in 1998 there were seven million abortions a year, thirty-five per cent of them carried out illegally. Even nowadays there are seven abortions to each live birth even in the western part of Russia.[5] Islam is totally opposed both to the idea of equality between men and women and to the practice of scientific birth control. An important contributory factor to the overpopulation of India, as well as to the practice of female infanticide in China, is the belief in Hinduism and Confucianism that the birth of a son is essential.

It is in the context of the failure of organised religion in both Eastern and Western Europe to give support to the movement for equality between the sexes that it is particularly hard to agree with the idea that the cultural unity of Europe should remain inextricably linked to Christianity. This has a long history, and is a claim which runs through one of the most recent studies of Europe, Peter Rietbergen's *Europe: a cultural history* (1988), which argues that ever since the collapse of the Roman Empire in the fourth and fifth centuries, the common fate of Europe has:

> gradually became linked to Christianity, now increasingly seen as the one characteristic and indeed redeeming feature of a geographically well-defined world, which by and large coincided with Western Europe.[6]

This may have been the case in the Middle Ages, when the Catholic Church was the spiritual force which held Christendom together in an age of barbarism. What has become equally important since the sixteenth century is that no culture apart from the one developed in Western Europe has developed the associated concepts of agnosticism and tolerance, or the idea that, if there are any truths to be found, they will be discovered by the patient application of the empirical method in the natural sciences, and of careful and sceptical analysis in what are nowadays referred to as the social sciences.

These methods have, it is true, found their most spectacularly successful application in the United States of America. But from a cultural point of view, as I have argued throughout this book, North America is very much an emanation of Western Europe. It is, in particular, one whose intellectual ideal was expressed in lapidary form by the author of the Declaration of Independence, Thomas Jefferson (1743–1826), when in 1825 he helped found the University of Virginia and had engraved on its portals the words:

> Here, we are not afraid to follow truth wherever it may lead, nor to tolerate any error so long as reason is let free to combat it.

It is not an idea which the founding fathers of the United States could have found anywhere but in the European Enlightenment of the eighteenth century.

8 The establishment of the European Economic Community

INITIAL AIMS

The organisation known since ratification of the Maastricht Treaty on November 1, 1993 as the European Union began life as the European Coal and Steel Community (ECSC). This came into being on April 18, 1951, when Belgium, France, the Federal Republic of Germany, Italy and Luxembourg signed the Treaty of Paris and agreed to accept a common authority to regulate the production of coal and steel. They did so in response to the suggestion, made by the French Foreign Minister in a press conference on May 9, 1950, that French and German coal and steel production should be pooled in order to avoid a fourth war between the two countries. The British government declined the invitation extended to it to join. As Clement Attlee, the British Prime Minister, put it at the time, 'We are not going to join a group of countries in which we have just saved four of them from the other two'.

The avoidance of a fourth war between France and Germany was, certainly, an aim to which no government, and certainly not that of Great Britain, could have any objections. But not in 1870, 1914 nor in 1939 did the British feel that they were responsible for the outbreak of the war. If, in the future, the French and the Germans wanted to give up fighting one another, all well and good. This would mean that the British would not have to come and sort them out. If the Germans wanted to give up trying to dominate Europe, even better. But since the British had never felt deeply involved in their quarrels in the first place, they did not see what role they might play in preventing the conflict between France and Germany from spilling over into bloodshed on some future occasion.

The British government also refused to join the ECSC because it thought it would lead to a loss of national sovereignty. Almost half a century later, this explains the refusal of the United Kingdom to adopt the Euro. If, in its relationship to what is now the European Union, Great Britain has remained what Stephen George calls an awkward partner,[1] after having spent such a long time being a reluctant applicant, it is also because of the difficulty it has had in shaking off its self-image of a country which has never so far been defeated in war. The British government was also busy building socialism, and did not want to be involved in what was immediately seen as an essentially capitalist enterprise.

Winston Churchill, it is true, had made a speech in Zurich on September 19, 1946 declaring that the constant aim of men of good will in modern politics should be to 'build and fortify the strength of the United Nations Organization', and to 'recreate the European family in a regional structure called the United States of Europe'. But the rest of his speech made it clear that this was a task in which the leadership should be provided by France and Germany. As he remarked privately to his doctor in January 1952, 'I love France and Belgium, but we must not allow ourselves to be pulled down to that level'.[2] The rightful place for Great Britain was with the other English-speaking democracies, not with the countries whose record in achieving the kind of mature democracy characteristic of England or America had never been anything but decidedly shaky.

The European Coal and Steel Community nevertheless came into force, as planned, in February 1952, and immediately proved a marked success in economic terms. Its immediate aim was to remove all customs barriers to the sale of coal and steel among the six participating countries, and this proved so effective as a measure of economic liberalisation that by 1958 – the end of the transitional period allowed for in the Treaty of Paris of April 1951 – interstate trading in steel between the six member countries had increased by 151 per cent, that of coal by 21 per cent and that of iron ore by 25 per cent. Thanks perhaps to the creation of NATO, there had been no war in Europe. The time had now come to make the continent richer.

THE CREATION OF PROSPERITY

The initiative to move on from the European Coal and Steel Community to what was known, between 1958 and 1967 as the European Economic Community (EEC), and from 1967 to 1991 as the European Communities (EEC, Euratom and the ECSC) was not taken by France or Germany. In 1950 Konrad Adenauer, the first Chancellor of the Federal Republic of Germany, had replied with great enthusiasm to the Schuman proposal to establish the ECSC. But in 1950, and even five years later in 1955, Germany's past still weighed too heavily on its own public opinion, as well as on that of its neighbours, for it to be able to take an openly political initiative towards the creation of a united Europe. Such a concept had been one of the slogans of the Nazi movement.

In 1955 France was already too embroiled in the Algerian problem to do anything other than try to survive, while Italy was too unstable politically to take any initiative. It was, consequently, Belgium, Holland and Luxembourg who ensured that the path towards European unification remained open in spite of the failure of the attempt to create a European Defence Community, and they were in a good position to do so. In January 1948 they had already signed a treaty providing for the free movement of goods, services, capital and labour between the three countries, and had shown their enthusiasm for further unification by choosing to refer to themselves by the joint name of the Benelux countries. In May 1955 they made a more important contribution to European integration by proposing a motion to the General Assembly of the European Coal and Steel Community which insisted on the need to move forward from the ECSC to the creation of what they called:

> common institutions, the gradual fusion of national economies, the creation of a common market and the progressive harmonisation of social policies.

This was the first statement of what were to become the aims of the EEC, and even more of its successor, the European Union. It led, in June 1955, to a conference at Messina between the Foreign Ministers of Belgium, France, Italy, the Netherlands, Luxembourg and West Germany, chaired by the Belgian Foreign Minister, Paul-Henri Spaak. The British government, now in the hands of the Conservative Party, did not think it worth while to send an elected politician, much less a member of the government. Instead, it despatched a former Oxford economist who had become a career civil servant in the Board of Trade, Russell Bretherton. As the European Foreign Ministers discussed the creation of a further set of supranational bodies to implement economic integration, and proposed the addition to the ECSC not only of an economic community but also of Euratom, a body to co-ordinate the peaceful development of atomic energy, he is reputed to have left with the words:

> Gentlemen, you are trying to negotiate something which you will never be able to negotiate. But if negotiated, it will not be ratified. And if ratified, it will not work.

In the view of the former British Foreign Secretary, Douglas Hurd, it is improbable that the words were actually pronounced. The Foreign Office, in the person of the Permanent Secretary, John Robinson, was quite keen on the idea of an economic community, and Lord Hurd claims that the words attributed to Bretherton were invented afterwards as part of a campaign to criticise successive British governments for their lack of foresight. They nevertheless represent an attitude which was widely shared at the time, and are said to have been based on hand-written instructions which the Prime Minister, the Conservative Anthony Eden, had rushed over to Messina in the diplomatic bag.[3] The quotation was also a kind of negative wish-fulfilment for a failure which never took place.

For the Europeans, having twice asked the British to join them, and having seen their invitation twice refused, proceeded to show that they could do very well without them. One of the main causes of Franco-German dissension had already disappeared when in January 1957, by a large majority, the population of the Saarland, an area rich in coal, voted in a plebiscite to join the Federal Republic of Germany. Since the coal which it produced was now under the control of the European Coal and Steel Community, the French raised no objections, and were happy to rely on the skill of their two main negotiators, Maurice Faure and Robert Marjolin – the former a professional politician and member of the Chambre des Députés, the second a well-known economist who later became a Vice-President of the European Commission – to obtain compensatory advantages in what they rightly saw as the more important area of agriculture.

AGRICULTURAL PRIORITIES

They thus inaugurated what, for its admirers, was to become one of the major success stories of the European Community, while at the same time being the achievement which attracted most criticism both from within the six member states of the EEC and from outside. The Germans, Belgians and Dutch would certainly have preferred the Treaty of Rome to have concentrated more on the creation of a federal state and less on the idea of community preference, which still lies at the heart of the Common Agricultural Policy (CAP). But the French and the Italians had agricultural systems which were outdated and inefficient. The only way in which their agriculture could survive long enough to be modernised was by a policy which protected their products from the foodstuffs which could be bought much more cheaply from North and South America, the Caribbean, and Australasia.

In spite of their rapidly growing prosperity, the Germans were not yet in a position where they could afford to refuse to pay the price demanded by the French for the incorporation of Federal Republic in an economically united Europe. Memories of Belsen and Buchenwald were still strong, and the consciousness of the threat from the Soviet Union made it unwise for them to neglect any possibility of linking their political fortunes to those of the democratic Europe represented by France and the Benelux countries. They therefore agreed to the French insistence that the Treaty of Rome should contain the articles establishing the Common Agricultural Policy, and accepted the basic principles which were to govern the way it worked.

The first of these was the idea of a Common External Tariff. All agricultural and industrial products coming from outside the European Economic Community were to pay the same import duty, irrespective of their country of origin or the country they were entering. The EEC was thus, from the beginning, a customs union rather than a free-trade area, with its six member states defining their economic relationship with the outside world by creating a set of tariffs which were the same whether the agricultural products were imported into France, Germany, Italy, the Netherlands, Belgium or Luxembourg, or exported from Argentina, New Zealand or the West Indies. They also emphasised the nature of this relationship by the use of a term which rapidly took on a particular meaning in Brussels, 'des pays tiers' – 'third states', or Third Countries as they are more commonly referred to in English.

The term did not designate a Third World country, in the sense of one which has not attained the same degree of industrial development and urbanisation as Germany, Japan or the United States. It simply meant a country which was not a member of the EEC. It therefore referred to states as different from one another as Australia and Angola, Brazil and Bulgaria, or Canada and China. All such countries were, from the establishment of the EEC, grouped together in the same category. Whatever they exported to Europe, whether food, industrial products or raw materials, they paid the same tariff to enter the European Economic Community.

The Common External Tariff was never very high. Initially, it was about ten per cent, and successive negotiations carried out under the auspices of the General Agreement on Tariffs and Trade (GATT), known since 1995 as the World Trade Organisation (WTO), have brought it down to round about three per cent.[4] It was nevertheless high enough as far as agricultural products were concerned to enable the Common Agricultural Policy to become a reality and the idea of 'community preference' to be widely accepted. What this term emphasised was the need for Europeans to buy food grown in Europe, not food imported from Third Countries. Agricultural production was also stimulated by the equally important policy under which European farmers were offered a guaranteed price for the food they grew.

Since this was, in many cases, a good deal higher than the price they would have been able to obtain if the European market had been open to competition from Third Countries, it led to a considerable increase in prosperity for certain categories of farmers. The price support system of the CAP is based on the quantity of cereals grown. It therefore favours the large producer. The more crops you grow, the more you get in subsidies. The current British view is that all subsidies based on the amount produced should be phased out and replaced by income support paid directly to individual farmers. This was the idea behind the 'deficiency payments' system on which British agriculture had been based since the nineteenth century. The proposals put forward in the early 1990s by the Commissioner for Agriculture, Ray MacSharry, mark a return to this system.[5]

In Eastern Europe, the Soviet Union required its satellite states to follow its policy of nationalising land and establishing collective farms. This led, as it had in the USSR itself, to chronic shortages.[6] To the west, the maintenance of the basic unit of agricultural production as the family farm led to the main problem of the CAP being the production of surpluses of food for which there was no demand in Western Europe itself. The family farm was, it is true, not operating in a genuinely free market. It was supported by tariff barriers and guaranteed prices, and in this respect the EEC presented the interesting if not uncommon combination of a managed market for agriculture and a free market in manufactured goods and financial services.

Farmers were also encouraged to export their produce by a system of subsidies which enabled them to bring their prices down to the level at which they could sell on the international market. This has proved a fairly expensive undertaking. In 1986, for example, forty per cent of the total EU budget for agriculture was spent on what are known technically as 'export refunds', at a cost of 8,600 million ECUs.[7] Since the ECU, or European Currency Unit, stood at that time at 70 pence, or $US1.17, this meant an expenditure of some £5 billion, or $8 billion.

This system of export restitutions also led to the criticism, especially from the United States of America, that the EEC was indulging in a widespread policy of dumping. The point is also made within the Community itself that the farmers were being given financial support, yet protection was being refused to other sectors of the economy. By 1987, 63 per cent of the Community budget was being spent on agriculture, and although this has now been brought down to 45.7 per cent, critics of the Common Agricultural Policy underline what they see as the injustice as well as the absurdity of a system whereby almost 50 per cent of the budget goes to support 5 per cent of the working population. Why, they argue, should produce of the land receive subsidies not given to the produce of the factory? Why should the producers of butter, wheat and beef be helped by the taxpayer in a way that the makers of cars, television sets or clothes are not?

The answer traditionally offered is that farming is a far more risky occupation than the production of industrial goods or the provision of financial services. The farmer has to cope with the vagaries of the weather, which can sometimes create crops so abundant that they cannot be sold at a price which covers their costs of production, but which in other years gives rise to yields which are so small that they cannot be sold in sufficient quantity to provide an economic return. European farmers also argue that, since farmers in the United States are heavily subsidised by the taxpayer as well, they can compete in the world market only if they receive comparable support.[8] There is also the powerful historical argument that in 1945 Europeans were so short of food that the inhabitants of Holland had to make soup out of the bark stripped from trees in order to survive. No price is too high, it is argued, to ensure that Europe produces enough food to feed itself.

In 1958 twenty per cent of the working population in Europe was engaged in agriculture, and their standard of living was much lower than in other occupations. The reduction of this figure to five per cent, over a period during which there has been an average increase of twenty per cent in the general standard of living, is not only due to increased mechanisation, improvements in yield brought about by the development of better strains of wheat and barley and the wider use of more sophisticated fertilisers. It has been made possible by the use of money distributed by the Community to restructure agriculture, thus making farms larger and more efficient and providing schemes for retraining workers for whom agriculture no longer offers employment.

In 1700 each agricultural worker on the continent of Europe supported 1.4 other people. By 1940 this had risen only to 4.2, and the increase by 1998 to 12 is an indication of how effective the Common Agricultural Policy has been, even though there is some way to go before the figure reaches the level of the United States of America, where one agricultural worker supports 31 people.[9] At the same time, the figure of 1:12 is a reminder of the size of the gap which still separates Europe from the United States of America. Largely because of its climate, which means that it has to import all its consumption of tropical foods, and of the size of its dairy herd, which creates a larger need for animal feed than can be satisfied domestically, the European Union remains the world's largest food importer.[10]

FREE TRADE AND MISTAKEN CHOICES

The Messina conference of June 1955 also established the other main foundation for the European Economic Community by agreeing on the phased removal, over a period of twelve years, of all internal tariff barriers on manufactured goods between the six member states. However, such was the success achieved by this policy that the complete removal of all such barriers was achieved by July 1968, six months ahead of schedule. In the first five years after the Treaty of Rome of March 25, 1957 came into force on January 1, 1958, the Gross National Product of the six member states, taken as a whole, rose by 27 per cent, compared to 18 per cent in the United States of America and 14 per cent in Great Britain. By 1965, trade among the six had increased by 100 per cent.

The failure of the British economy to grow with the same consistently satisfying rhythm as those of France, Germany and the Benelux countries was one of the main factors in bringing about the decision, announced by the Conservative Prime Minister Harold Macmillan in August 1961, to apply for admission to the European Economic Community. The wager which the British government had made in 1950, and repeated in 1957, had not come off. It had been based on what turned out to be the mistaken conviction that Great Britain's principal trading partners would remain the English-speaking countries of North America and Australasia. But the economies of Canada, Australia and New Zealand had not grown with the speed expected of them by the economists and politicians who saw them as the main market for British manufactured goods. The United States proved less anxious than expected to buy many British goods, apart from Scotch whisky and the published works of Winston Churchill.

THE FOUR FREEDOMS

When the six member states of the European Coal and Steel Community created the European Economic Community in 1957, they set out to establish what are known as the 'Four Freedoms'. The first, brought about by the taking down of the protective tariffs which had formerly separated the European Countries from one another, is the free movement of goods. The second is the free movement of capital, the third the free movement of labour, and the fourth the freedom to offer services in all Community countries on the same terms as those applicable to home-based companies.

Each of these freedoms involved the surrender of national sovereignty in a number of areas traditionally under the control of the nation state: that of deciding what duty goods should pay on entering its territory; that of controlling the amount of capital entering and leaving the country; that of deciding who should and who should not have the right to work within its own boundaries; and that of granting or withholding permission to a commercial firm to operate on its territory. None of them is compatible with the doctrine of national sovereignty as understood in the United Kingdom, and it was the way they were spelt out in the 1957 Treaty of Rome which explains why the United Kingdom should have tried, in January 1960, to establish a rival organisation to the EEC in the shape of the European Free Trade Area (EFTA).

In a free-trade area each country abolishes customs duties between itself and its partners, while retaining the right to impose a rate of duty different from that which one of its partners might levy on the same goods entering it from elsewhere. In a customs union, which is a higher stage of economic integration than a free-trade area, countries do not just do away with customs duties among themselves. They also agree – as the six founding members of the European Economic Community did by the signature of the Treaty of Rome, and the creation of the Common External Tariff – to impose the same rate of duty on all goods entering from outside, from whatever source. In this respect a customs union represents, as Dennis Swann puts it, 'a free trade area within a bloc and discrimination against the outside world'.[11]

The British government was not prepared to give up the right to decide which goods should enter its territory and at what rate. Nor was it happy to let capital move freely in and out of the area under its control, or to allow nationals from other countries to work freely within its borders, or to forfeit its right to say which companies should be free to offer services. It showed itself, in this respect as in others, a good deal less flexible than France or Italy, both of whom agreed when setting up the European Economic Community to carry out a fundamental change in their economic policy. Both countries – because of the concept which they had traditionally had of national sovereignty, and because of the relative backwardness of their industry in comparison with that of Germany, the Low Countries or the United Kingdom – had been protectionist states, with high tariff barriers protecting their markets against competition both from their more dynamic European neighbours and from countries outside Europe. By agreeing to the free movement of goods and services within the European Economic Community, France and Italy agreed to become more like Germany and the Benelux countries and adopt policies aimed at the creation of a customs union within Western Europe itself.

For the United Kingdom, in contrast, free trade had to be free trade on a much wider international basis. When, in 1957, Harold Macmillan justified Great Britain's refusal to join the European Economic Community, he described it as 'a high-tariff group in Europe, inward looking and self-sufficient'.[12] It was this attitude, coupled with reservations about the kind of institutions established for its own governance by the EEC, which lay behind the British creation of the European Free Trade Area by the signature on January 4, 1960 of the Stockholm Convention. This grouped together Austria, Denmark, Norway, Portugal, Sweden and Switzerland in partnership with the United Kingdom, a country whose size alone would ensure it a dominant position; in the EEC, by contrast, the UK would have had to compete with Germany and France, and quite possibly with Italy. Each of the seven countries brought together by the Stockholm Convention kept its own ability to agree tariffs with other countries outside the area covered by EFTA, and to do so without having to obtain the approval of its six partners. This was something which France or Germany could not do. They had to accept a Common External Tariff which could be arrived at only by agreement with their partners in the EEC.

ADMINISTRATIVE ARRANGEMENTS

EFTA did not prove a long-term success. All its members except Norway and Switzerland are now members of the European Union. If Western Europe has now ceased to be, as the saying was in the 1960s, 'all at sixes and sevens', this has been through a readiness on the part of all the member states of the EU to accept the administrative framework which had originally constituted another major obstacle to United Kingdom membership.

In British eyes, the primary advantage of EFTA was that it did not include agriculture. But it also had a weak administrative structure, with little loss of national sovereignty, and in that respect was similar to the other international organisations such as the North Atlantic Treaty Organisation, or the United Nations which the United Kingdom had been quite happy to join. In the United Nations each of the five Permanent Members of the Security Council retains the right to block any measure which it does not like by the use of the veto. If a member state does not want to fall in with the policy decided by a majority of the other countries, it simply refuses to join in. Each of the sixteen member states of the North Atlantic Treaty Organisation has a representative on its permanent Council. These representatives must, however, follow the instructions given to them by their governments. There is no way in which NATO can take independent decisions on its own behalf. It must wait for the states which signed the 1949 treaty to act in accordance with what they, in consultation with one another, decide to do. When France decided in 1966 to withdraw its forces from the NATO military command structure, there was no doubt of its right as a fully sovereign state to do so.

The institutions of the European Community, in contrast, were aimed from the beginning at limiting the direct control which a member state has over its own affairs, especially in economic matters. The most important of these institutions is the Commission, a body which exists independently of the individual states, and which alone among all the other bodies of the European Union has the right to take initiatives and introduce legislation on behalf of the Union itself. It is open to an individual member state to propose a new regulation or directive. It can also do so in co-operation with another member or members. But only the Commission can act or bring forward proposals on behalf of the Union itself.

It is this right of the Commission, and of the Commission alone, to take initiatives on behalf of the European Union which is the most original as well as the most controversial aspect of the administrative arrangements governing what has been known since 1993 as the European Union. It helps to explain why the organisation which began life as the

European Economic Community has moved so steadily forward to the stated aim of political as well as economic integration. The Commission is like the engine of a car, carrying it along, whatever reservations some of the passengers may occasionally have about speed or direction, or even about the character of some of those taking the wheel.

Although only the Commission has the right to introduce legislation in the name of the Community, its recommendations have to be approved by the Council of Ministers. From the beginning of the EEC, this has been the main decision-making body of the Community, and has remained so throughout the successive stages of its expansion and transformation into the European Union. Each of the fifteen states now constituting the European Union is represented by a minister from her or his home government, with the identity of the minister attending and voting at any specific meeting of the Council of Ministers depending on the subject under discussion. When an aspect of the Common Agricultural Policy is being debated, the meeting is attended by the Minister for Agriculture; when transport policy, the Minister for Transport. But since the prime responsibility of the Ministers who constitute the Council remains their role in the government of their home country, discussion of matters on a day-to-day basis is carried out by a group of career diplomats – one for each country, and of Ambassadorial status – meeting in Brussels. It is known as the Committee of Permanent Representatives (COREPER) and is in constant touch with the Commission. It is this practice which enables Klaus-Dieter Borchardt to write that if the COREPER:

> reaches full agreement on a proposed piece of legislation, the item is entered on the Council agenda as an A item, meaning that the Council need do no more than formally record its approval without further debate.[13]

When a decision has to be taken by the ministers themselves, it is done by a system of weighted voting. This gives ten votes each to France, Italy, Germany, and the United Kingdom; Spain has eight votes, Belgium, Greece, the Netherlands and Portugal five each, Austria and Sweden four, Finland, Ireland and Denmark three, and Luxembourg two. Unless a state decides to exercise its veto under what is called the 'Luxembourg Compromise', which was introduced after France blocked all progress between June 1965 and January 1, 1966, a proposal from the Commission is approved if it receives what is known as a 'qualified majority' of 62 out of the 87 votes available.

The 'Luxembourg Compromise' stems from the initial refusal of France to accept the Hallstein Plan, named after the first President of the European Economic Community, whereby more and more of the duties levied under the Common External Tariff were used to create an independent

Community budget. The Compromise gave each state the right to veto a proposal which it deemed harmful to its 'vital interests', but has very rarely been used to any practical effect. For example, when the British government tried between March and June 1996 to imitate the French example by refusing to adopt legislation requiring unanimity and blocking progress by simply not turning up for meetings, this ended in ignominious failure.[14]

THE PROBLEM OF DEMOCRATIC ACCOUNTABILITY

The budget of the Community is derived partly from contributions made by member states, and partly from what are known as its 'own resources'. By the Treaty of Luxembourg of April 22, 1970, these consist of the duty paid on agricultural and industrial products entering the countries in the Union, together with 1.4 per cent of the Value Added Tax levied by each individual state. Since the right of initiative which the Commission enjoys in bringing forward legislation also extends to the budget, the legality of their collection does not depend on a vote by the European Parliament. The rate of duty paid by imports into the Union is the result of a long process of joint decision by the Commission and Council, in which the European Parliament plays no role. The minimum rate of Value Added Tax was agreed at 15 per cent by the Council of Ministers on January 1, 1993, and although it is collected by each member state, the European Parliament has no say in how it should be levied or collected, any more than do the parliaments of the fifteen member states.

The European Parliament cannot therefore control what might be thought of as the executive of the European Union – the Commission and Council – in the way that the British parliament, or the United States Congress, can exercise power over the executive by refusing to grant supply. Neither can it act as the British parliament does when it requires an individual Minister to assume responsibility for the actions of the civil servants acting on his behalf. At Westminster, a Minister whose replies fail to satisfy the House often has no choice but to resign, and this concept of ministerial responsibility is seen as essential to the proper control of the executive by the elected chamber. But there is no such provision in the workings of the European Union. The Parliament may, by a two-thirds majority, censure the Commission, and if this happens the Commission is required to offer its joint resignation. But even when the whole European Commission resigned on March 15, 1999 because of the strength of the charges of maladministration hanging over a number of its members, this happened in anticipation of how the European Parliament might behave, not as a result of a vote which it had actually taken. Had the more traditional convention existed, defined by Winston

Churchill in the phrase 'one is enough', the Commission might have been formally dismissed several weeks earlier. However, except for the situation in the United States of America – where a majority of two-thirds in the Senate is required to bring about the conviction of a President impeached for 'high crimes and misdemeanours' – the European parliament is unique in not regarding a simple majority as sufficient.

The Commission is also unusual as an executive body in that, after its collective resignation on March 15, 1999, it was allowed to remain in office on a temporary basis for four months. Normally, in the Westminster model of parliamentary responsibility, a government which loses a vote of confidence in the House may continue on a caretaker basis for a brief period, but rarely for more than six weeks. It is also not the custom for members of a government required to resign under the suspicion not only of maladministration but also of financial dishonesty to receive the generous redundancy payments to which former Commissioners are entitled. The President of the European Commission receives a salary of £220,000, and the other members of the Commission £180,000. The Commissioners who resigned as a body on March 15, 1999 are each due to receive £350,000 in compensation. Because they resigned, and were not dismissed by a two-thirds majority in the European Parliament, they continued to draw their high salaries and generous expenses until they were officially replaced.

It was, in British eyes, quite natural that continental Europeans should voice fewer objections to the apparently unrestricted power which the administrative arrangements adopted by the European Economic Community gave to unelected bureaucrats. After all, the Germans have never enjoyed a particularly vigorous tradition of parliamentary government, any more than have the French. Both under the Third Republic of 1870–1940 and under its successor, which lasted only from 1946 to 1958, the political parties represented in the National Assembly had been so divided among themselves that it was quite natural for the country to be governed by civil servants. While Holland and Belgium were acknowledged to have had a longer and more solid tradition of practical democracy, Italy resembled the France of the Third and Fourth Republics in being a country where the existence of too many warring political parties precluded any serious attempt at parliamentary control of the executive. And since, in the British view, parliamentary democracy stood or fell on the issue of the ability of the elected chamber to keep the civil service in order, there appeared to be more dangers than advantages in linking the country with a group of nations whose political history so clearly failed to satisfy the Westminster standards of executive accountability and ministerial responsibility.

THE BRITISH DECISION TO APPLY AND THE FRENCH VETO

In the course of the 1950s, however, the poor performance of the British economy had already led these reservations to be put aside and replaced by more mundane and less idealistic considerations. Perhaps, the hope was, matters could be improved in Europe by the injection of Anglo-Saxon-style parliamentary democracy, just as the British might succeed in making themselves richer by joining a group of nations which offered a geographically more accessible market than North America or Australasia, and whose growth rate might make them more willing customers. In 1959 former American Secretary of State Dean Acheson, who had helped formulate both the Truman doctrine of 1947 and the Marshall Plan of 1948, had told the British that they had 'lost an empire but not yet found a role'. Perhaps, thought the Conservative government elected in September 1959, it might be an idea to change tack and try to join the EEC. After all, it was clearly not being run by lunatics like Adolf Hitler or buffoons in the style of Benito Mussolini.

The return to power of General de Gaulle in the summer of 1958 had not led to any diminution in the enjoyment by the French of the basic democratic rights of freedom of expression and assembly, any more than the long reign of the German Chancellor Konrad Adenauer had brought about a return to the practices either of the Third Reich (1933–1945) or of the Second Reich (1871–1918). Perhaps, after all, as has indeed turned out to be the case, parliamentary democracy in individual countries can perfectly well coexist with an international authority which is governed by benevolent bureaucrats freed from the tiresome responsibility of answering for their actions to parliament. Thanks, however, to the personality and attitude of Charles de Gaulle, a dozen or so years were to elapse before the British were in a position to find out whether or not this was the case.

When, on January 14, 1963, de Gaulle vetoed the United Kingdom's application to join the European Economic Community, he did not do so purely to avenge himself for the real and imaginary insults which he had received from the British and Americans during the Second World War. He may, indeed, have been inspired by some of the traditional anglo-phobia of the French right, and he may have said, as commentators have alleged, 'L'Angleterre, je la veux dans le marché commun. Mais toute nue' (I want England in the Common Market. But naked and powerless). It is also true that his veto was very closely followed, on January 22, 1963, by the formal signature of a treaty of co-operation between France and the Federal Republic of Germany which laid the foundation for the course which French foreign policy was to take for the rest of the century. De Gaulle is said to have encapsulated his vision of the new Europe by saying 'the EEC is a horse and carriage. Germany is the horse and France is the coachman',[15] and his new Franco-German condominium, reminiscent as it was of the Europe of Charlemagne (747–814), clearly had no place for any offshore islands. De Gaulle's veto also had the effect of preventing Denmark and the Republic of Ireland, which had applied at the same time as the United Kingdom, from joining the EEC until French policy changed.

Perhaps pointedly, De Gaulle abstained at his press conference of January 23, 1963 from using terms such as 'Great Britain' or 'The United Kingdom'. Instead, revealing how much he still thought in terms of long-established nation states, he said that it was 'England' which was, in his view:

> insular and maritime, linked through its trade, markets and food supply to very diverse and often distant countries. Its activities are essentially industrial and commercial and with a relatively unimportant agricultural section. It has retained, in everything it does, highly distinctive customs and traditions. In short, in both its nature and structure, it is profoundly different from the other states on the Continent of Europe.

It was a diagnosis based not only on de Gaulle's reading of English history but also on what had happened in the eighteen months during which negotiations on the British application of membership had taken place. These had revealed a number of problems, of which the most important was certainly that of agriculture.

In the middle of the nineteenth century the British had begun to feed their rapidly increasing population mainly with food imported from abroad, especially from Australia, Canada, New Zealand, the West Indies and the United States, paying for it by exporting the industrial goods in which the United Kingdom then led the world. This food was much cheaper to the consumer than most of the produce which could be grown at home, but British farmers were not driven out of business. What enabled them to survive was not a protective tariff but a system of deficiency payments. This provided farmers with an income which supplemented the otherwise inadequate payment which they received from the sale of their produce. It involved the use of the money which the government obtained from the whole of the tax-paying population, and kept British agriculture sufficiently alive for it to be able to expand as rapidly during the 1939–1945 war as it had between 1914 and 1918, and thus help feed a population threatened with starvation by the German submarines. Its supporters also defended it on the grounds of social justice, arguing that a high-price food policy, such as the one established by the Common Agricultural Policy, is harder on the poor than on the rich. A man earning £40,000 and paying £1 for a loaf of bread has much more money left after this essential purchase than a man earning only £15,000 and paying the same price.

This system was clearly incompatible with the principles on which the Common Agricultural Policy was based. Because this set out to enable the farmer to live on the money paid to him in exchange for the food he grew, it meant that any food brought in from Third Countries would have to be taxed in order to bring its price up to the level demanded for European produce. It was, primarily, the insistence by the British negotiators on the need to maintain imports of butter, cheese and lamb from Australia and New Zealand, as well as wheat from Canada and the United States, that provided de Gaulle with the economic arguments to justify his veto.

The other five member states of the EEC disagreed with him. They wanted Great Britain as a member, partly out of a sense of gratitude for what had happened between 1940 and 1945, partly because they recognised the potential usefulness of having a well-established democracy as one of their number. They also did not share de Gaulle's view of the United Kingdom as a kind of Trojan horse via which the United States of America would make its way into the European Economic Community and transform it into what de Gaulle called 'a colossal Atlantic Community under American leadership'. Unlike de Gaulle, they were grateful to the Americans for continuing to protect them from the Soviet Union, just as they were still prepared to recognise that they had twice saved Western Europe from the Germans, and the Germans from themselves.

On May 15, 1962 de Gaulle had made his general position on Europe very clear in another of the press conferences which he was in the habit of holding in order to announce his views to a sometimes astonished world. What he said then was that the only future for Europe was that of a community of sovereign states, 'l'Europe des Patries'. In spite of the fact that the British would have endorsed this policy, which had in fact remained their ideal, de Gaulle repeated his veto on British entry on November 27, 1967, when the Labour government of Harold Wilson reapplied for membership. His successor, the long-suffering Georges Pompidou, had to wait until he succeeded de Gaulle as President in June 1969 to put his own concept of Europe into practice.

9 The EEC and the oil crises of the 1970s

THE DEPARTURE OF CHARLES DE GAULLE

On July 6, 1967 the European Economic Community decided to change its name, merging the executives of the EEC, the ECSC and Euratom into a single body responsible for the administration of what then became simply the European Communities (EC). But this change in no way strengthened its ability to produce any greater political unity on the question of enlargement than had existed in 1963, and de Gaulle continued to act in a way which seemed deliberately calculated to annoy France's allies in NATO as well as its partners in the EC.

Thus on March 7, 1966 he had suddenly announced that French forces would be withdrawn from the joint military command of the North Atlantic Treaty Organisation, a decision implemented in April 1967, when NATO's headquarters were moved to Brussels and all American bases in France closed down. On January 27, 1966 he had already broken with what was then a guiding principle in American policy on the Far East by establishing diplomatic relations with the Chinese People's Republic, regarded until Richard Nixon's visit in February 1972 and the official exchange of Ambassadors in September of the same year as a pariah state.

This recognition was not out of keeping with the attitude of other Western European powers – Great Britain, for example, had recognised Communist China in January 1950. But on September 1, 1966, in a speech in Phnom Penh, de Gaulle went further when he formally denounced United States policy in Vietnam and called for the withdrawal of the American troops fighting to defend the government of the South from Communist-sponsored guerrillas from the North. Although there was considerable popular opposition to America's Vietnam policy in other countries of Western Europe, as indeed there was in the United States itself, this was further than any Western government would go in criticising the major ally on whom they still depended for their defence against the Soviet Union.

Between July 22 and July 26, 1967 de Gaulle paid a visit to Quebec which followed hard upon the centenary celebrations for the establishment of the Canadian Confederation on July 1, 1867. On July 24 he caused considerable annoyance to the population of English-speaking Canada by giving a speech from the balcony of the town hall in Montreal in which his cry of 'Vive le Québec libre!' gave open support to the Quebec separatist movement. In spite of the withdrawal of its forces from the military command structure of NATO, France had remained a political member of the alliance. It was consequently an ally of Canada, which de Gaulle had chosen to insult on its own territory, encouraging a separatist movement whose terrorist branch was to cause thirty deaths in the early 1970s.

Like the other countries of Western Europe, France continued to benefit from the American nuclear umbrella at a time when the Cold War had still over 23 years to run. No other Western European country followed de Gaulle's example of defying the United States. Similarly, no other responsible Western state was prepared to imitate de Gaulle in any of his eccentricities, and especially not in the implicit support which he was giving to the Palestine Liberation Organisation and its Arab neighbours in their declared aim of totally destroying the state of Israel.

Taken by themselves, these actions did not do de Gaulle much harm in France. As Jean-François Revel commented in 1965, 'Le général de Gaulle a parfaitement raison de penser qu'il incarne la France. Là où il se trompe, c'est de croire que cela soit flatteur pour lui' (General de Gaulle is quite right to think that he is the incarnation of France. Where he is mistaken is in the belief that this is flattering to him)[1]. There were other reasons why his departure was inevitable. He was already 67 when he came back to power in 1958, the same age as Winston Churchill in 1940, and had, by 1963, already performed one of his greatest services to France by enabling it to give Algeria the independence for which its non-European population had been fighting since 1954.

The Constitution of the Fifth Republic was very much his creation, and it seemed to be working better than any previous parliamentary régime in France. Thanks largely to the skill of the Prime Minister, Georges Pompidou, France had survived the student riots of May 1968 without bloodshed. Pompidou had shown himself to be so safe a pair of hands that de Gaulle could no longer convincingly invoke the argument that any vote against him in a referendum would lead to chaos.

When, therefore, de Gaulle decided to ask the French once again whether they still loved him, the answer came back in the form of a 'No' vote in the referendum held on April 27, 1969. Fifty-three per cent of those voting on a somewhat arcane proposal to change the role of the Senate and to reform local government said that they did not agree. In an obvious huff, de Gaulle immediately announced his resignation, in spite of the fact that he had still two years of the Presidency to which he had been elected in December 1965 before him.

On June 15, 1969 George Pompidou was elected as the second President of the Fifth French Republic. At a summit meeting of the EC held at the Hague in December 1969 he made it clear that he was prepared to lift de Gaulle's veto on British entry. Negotiations to bring this about began under the leadership of Geoffrey Rippon, who received strong support from Edward Heath, the leader of the Conservative Party, who had defeated Harold Wilson in the General Election in June 1970. These negotiations reached a successful enough conclusion for the government to recommend to the House of Commons that Great Britain should become a member of the EC on January 1, 1973.

The Labour Party, committing itself to renegotiate the conditions of entry, recommended its members to vote against. Its then leader, Harold Wilson, together with another future Prime Minister, James Callaghan, did so. However, 69 Labour MPs defied the party whip and voted for the government, thus enabling the motion in favour of membership to be carried on October 28, 1971 by a majority of 336 to 224. Denmark and the Republic of Ireland, which had linked their applications to that of Great Britain in 1961, and consequently suffered the same rebuff in January 1963 and November 1967, became members of the EC at the same time.

SOME PROBLEMS OF BRITISH ENTRY

The conditions for British entry represented a compromise in which the United Kingdom made more concessions than the six states which had originally signed the Treaty of Rome. The British had to give up the ambition of torpedoing the EEC, which had been their obvious intention in forming EFTA in January 1960. By accepting the Treaty of Rome in its entirety, including the further arrangements made by its six original members since 1958, the United Kingdom accepted that the movement towards a united Europe would take the form of a customs union and not simply that of a free-trade area. There would, in other words, be an increasing degree of political and economic merging of the member states, not simply an agreement to reduce customs duties between them.

Like the other states applying for membership at the time, Ireland and Denmark, the United Kingdom agreed to accept the Common External Tariff as the basis for its trading relationship with the Third Countries in outside world. All three countries also bound themselves to accept what had become known as the *acquis communautaire*: that is to say all the secondary legislation, the directives, regulations and decisions, agreed by the six original members since the inception of the Community on January 1, 1958. They committed themselves, in other words, to not trying to change the rules of the club to which they had finally managed to secure admittance.

The British also accepted another aspect of the EEC which they had tried to avoid by the creation of EFTA. They agreed to be bound by the decisions reached by the Council of Ministers on recommendations brought forward by the Commission. They also accepted the authority of the European Court in all questions involving the interpretation of the Treaty of Rome, and agreed to send members to the European Parliament at Strasbourg. But although the acceptance of the *acquis communautaire* meant, in particular, that they had to give up any hope of trying to change the Common Agricultural Policy, they were offered a number of concessions which were designed to lessen the impact of this policy on their traditional relationships with Third Countries such as Australia and New Zealand. There could be no question of the six founding members, and especially France, giving up the idea of community preference on which the Common Agricultural Policy was based. Nor would any of them envisage abandoning the system of support prices which kept the cost of food higher within the European Economic Community than in the rest of the industrialised world. But the British were allowed a certain number of transitional arrangements which had the effect of slightly softening the blow.

These included a five-year transitional period during which British food prices would be brought into line with those of the Community. Until 1977 New Zealand was to be allowed to sell eighty per cent of its butter and twenty per cent of its cheese to Great Britain on the same conditions that prevailed before 1973. After that, the situation would be reviewed, with the intention of requiring New Zealand imports to pay the same duty under the Common Agricultural Tariff which applied to products from all Third Countries. At the suggestion of the British, all member countries of the EEC were also allowed a six-mile limit round their coasts in which only their fishermen could bring home catches or sell them abroad; in some areas, such as Cornwall or the west coast of Scotland, this was extended to twelve miles. But the arrangements for fishing were to prove some of the most contentious for the internal relationships of all the member states of the Community.

This was partly due to the fact that the seas of the whole world, and especially those round Europe, were being seriously overfished. In the 1960s the United Kingdom had already been involved in a long-running dispute with Iceland when that country unilaterally extended its fishing zone to two hundred miles round its coast. Defenders of British membership of the European Union still mention this fact when arguing that the restrictions placed by the Common Fisheries Policy on the amount of fish which could be taken from European waters would have become necessary merely to conserve stocks. Eurosceptics, however, vigorously deny this, and maintain that the cunning Europeans tricked the British into accepting an arrangement from which only French and Spanish fishermen derived any benefit, and which consistently discriminated against the British.[2]

It was also urged by supporters of British membership, but hotly contested by Eurosceptics, that another problem, that of the excessively large contribution made by the United Kingdom to the budget of the European Communities did not stem from the basic unfairness of the system devised before British entry. It was, as most of the other member states argued, a result of the British refusal to be either consistent or enthusiastic in their application of the central principle of the Common Agricultural Policy: that of community preference. Under this system, each country's contribution to the budget of the European Union is calculated in the same way: as a percentage of the Value Added Tax collected within the country; together with a proportion of the agricultural levies and duties on industrial goods received for goods entering from Third Countries and thus paying the Common External Tariff. If, it was argued, the United Kingdom were to give up importing a high proportion of its food from Third Countries such as Australia, Canada and New Zealand, the problem would not arise. If no products of these countries were imported into the UK, there would be no duties to pay on them, and no money which the UK was obliged to pay over to Brussels. If the British were to take more apples and wheat from France, and more butter, bacon and cheese from Holland, then Great Britain would not be in the position it was in 1998: that of making the fifth largest contribution to the European budget, while being only the ninth or tenth in the economic league table of the European Union.

There is certainly an element of truth in this. But the fact that the United Kingdom gets noticeably less from the European Community than it puts in also stems from the size and nature of its agricultural sector. This is both smaller and more efficient than that of France or Italy, which until the entry of Greece in 1981 and of Spain and Portugal in 1986 were the principal beneficiaries of the CAP. On the other hand, it could be pointed out that there are advantages to be derived from the relative poverty of the United Kingdom. This has meant that we have benefited almost as much from the allocations available under the European Regional Development Fund (ERDF) as countries such as Italy or Spain, which have in the past been poorer than we are.[3] Great Britain has also managed to secure more exemptions from agreed Community policy than any other member state, ranging from the opt-out for the Social Chapter originally obtained by John Major but later accepted by Tony Blair, to the right to zero-rating of VAT on books, food and children's clothes, to the lower limit of 38 tonnes for lorries (as opposed to 40 for the other countries) and the freedom not to participate in either the

European Exchange Rate Mechanism or its successor, the single currency known as the Euro.

The economic arguments in favour of British membership have always been finely balanced. In 1971, when the question of Britain's application for membership of the Community was being debated in the British press, *The Times* published two letters side by side, each signed by the same number of equally eminent economists. One letter said that it would be in Great Britain's best interests from an economic point of view to join the Community, the other said it would not. This is not a question which can be answered with any certainty. The economist Patrick Minford, writing on June 14, 1999 in the Eurosceptic *Daily Telegraph*, argued that 'our economic relationship with the EU has brought us, under the status quo, no real benefits but no real loss either: even stevens'. This led him to recommend that Great Britain should stay in, though without giving up the pound to join the Euro. A rising tide raises all boats, and it is possible that the improvements which have gone on in the European as well as in the British economy since the end of the Second World War might have taken place anyway, whether the Treaty of Rome had been signed or not.

So too, argue the critics of British membership, might the reduction in tariffs and the consequent advantage which the British economy is said to derive from the fact that membership of the European Union ensures that its goods do not have face a tariff barrier when entering the overseas market nearest to the UK. In 1948 the 23 principal trading nations of the world set up the General Agreement on Trade and Tariffs (GATT), which in 1996 became the World Trade Organisation (WTO). By 1998 the combined effect of the various agreements reached under its auspices had reduced the average tariff to one-tenth of the 1948 figure.[4] The reduction by the European Union of the Common External Tariff from 6.8 per cent in 1990 to 3.6 per cent in 1998 is thus part of a world-wide process. As an article in the *Daily Telegraph* for July 18, 1998 by its proprietor Conrad Black pointed out, the United States did slightly better. During the same period, it brought the average tariff which it charges on imports down from 6.6 per cent to 3.4 per cent.

In 1972, the year before it became a member itself, the United Kingdom conducted one-third of its overseas trade with the six original members of the EEC. By 1995 this had risen to 57 per cent, and Dick Leonard argues that 'horrendous difficulties' would arise if we were to leave.[5] It is an issue on which even professional economists find it hard to defend whatever opinions they may have formed, especially since the figures available can be presented in so many different ways. One particularly Eurosceptic commentator, Martin Holmes, argued on May 24, 1996 in the *Times Literary Supplement* that between 1986 and 1996 the United Kingdom accumulated a deficit of £105 billion with the countries making up the European Union, compared to a trade surplus of £13 billion with the rest of the world, and comparable figures were given by Walter Ablett in a letter to the *Daily Telegraph* on January 5, 1999.

Ablett claimed that, while the UK had a trading surplus with the EEC before 1973, this had now become a total accumulated deficit of £150 billion. In 1996, he continued, the European deficit was £15.75 billion, in contrast to a surplus of £16 billion with the rest of the world. Nonsense, replied Tim McNamara the next day. Using the same source as Ablett, the Office of National Statistics, he showed that we had a deficit in 1996 with non-EU countries of just under £6 billion, and thus no surplus at all. The overall figures for 1995 and 1996, he continued, showed a deficit of £15 billion with all EU countries and a deficit of £14.5 million with the rest of the world. How fortunate, one reflects, that an earlier article, on October 16, 1998, had pointed out that the financial services in the City of London had brought in a record £35 billion in 1997, four times more than North Sea oil.

Emphasis in the British press on statistics unfavourable to British membership of the European Union may be largely a matter of chance. *The Times*, together with its supplements, is owned by the Australian-born publisher Rupert Murdoch. So, too, is the more vociferously Europhobic the *Sun*. The *Daily Telegraph* and its supplements are the property of the Canadian publisher, Conrad Black, who thus has the same power as Rupert Murdoch to put forward his view that the interests of the United Kingdom would be better served by a closer association with the countries of the Commonwealth and the English-speaking world. Scepticism about the economic advantages of EU membership has nevertheless also been encouraged by the fact that the entry of Great Britain into the European Economic Community in January 1973 was closely followed, in October of the same year, by a combination of two economic crises. These seemed, for several years, to have put an end to the continuous improvement in economic well-being which had been so marked a feature of the Western industrialised world since 1945.

AMERICAN CAPITALISM AND THE EUROPEAN ECONOMY

The years which the French economist Jean Fourastié dubbed 'les trente glorieuses', a term best translated for various historical reasons as 'thirty glorious years',[6] had owed their prosperity principally to a combination of the effects of the Marshall Plan and the impact of the Cold War. The former had ensured the rapid economic recovery of Western Europe, and thus provided an additional market for American exports. Whether its leaders liked it or not, the United States had been compelled by the

Cold War to adopt the ideas of John Maynard Keynes and keep recession at bay by a systematic programme of high public spending on armaments.

There were, it is true, other factors in the avoidance of a world-wide recession of the type created by the Wall Street crash of October 24, 1929. The boom which preceded the crash of 1929 had been fuelled by the possibility of buying shares on credit, in the hope of being able to sell them at a profit when they immediately rose in value and thus pay off the debt incurred in their initial purchase. In 1929 you could buy shares on the New York Stock Exchange by putting down as little as one fifth of their face value in advance. In 1934 the law was changed to require investors to put down at least forty per cent of the purchase price of the shares in advance, and in some cases up to seventy per cent. What appears, at first sight, to be purely a change in accountancy procedure had a significant effect in limiting the falls on the stock market created by the financial crises of 1973, 1987 and 1998 and was accompanied by a major, if gradual, change in the personal finances of private individuals.

From the late 1950s onwards more and more members of the professional middle classes, in Western Europe as well as in North America, began to invest money on a regular basis in private pension schemes. This money accumulated, and had to be invested somewhere. Since the early twentieth century the most powerful person on the London Stock Exchange had been the semi-mythological figure of 'the man from the Pru'. With the pension and insurance funds at his disposal, he had more influence than anyone on the price of shares, and the money which he and other institutional investors were required to invest on behalf of their companies had to go somewhere. As more and more private investors on both sides of the Atlantic also proceeded to put their savings into unit trusts and mutual funds, the amount of capital available for investment grew even larger. Since then its existence and availability have provided a kind of cushion which has so far prevented the kind of catastrophic and prolonged fall in share prices which set off the great slump of the 1930s and gave Hitler his chance to rise to power. On occasion – as in the boom in the early months of 1999, which followed the partial collapse in Autumn 1998 and brought the Dow Jones industrial average to over 10,000 – the effect has even been that of a strongly sprung mattress. The Dow is currently at well over 10,000.

Seen in a wider historical perspective, the success of the European Communities in this aspect is only one reason among many for the revival of capitalism which has been so marked a feature of the second half of the twentieth century. This revival, however, has always depended upon the ability and readiness of the United States to combine Keynesian economics with prudent housekeeping. This was possible in the 1940s, 1950s and early 1960s because the military expenditure necessary to contain the Soviet Union was seen as sufficiently acceptable to the American Congress for it to approve the increased taxes necessary to pay for it. However, once the Vietnam war had begun to absorb more and more of the military budget, and to become increasingly unpopular, it came to be funded by the easier but ultimately disastrous technique of printing money. In 1968 the refusal of President Johnson to ask Congress for increased taxes to fund the Vietnam war had led to what was then a record federal budget deficit of $24.2 billion, and the process began whereby one of the major threats to Western Europe seemed to come from the power which had, up to then, done most to protect it.

The increasing unreliability of the dollar as the world's major reserve currency was one of the factors leading to the sudden devaluation of the French franc on August 10, 1969. International money markets became even more unstable when, on August 10, 1971, Johnson's successor, Richard Nixon announced that the dollar would cease to be a convertible currency. Since this was accompanied by a unilateral devaluation of the American currency, the reaction of the Europeans was to try to invent a substitute for the basic medium of economic exchange on which the world had come to rely since 1945. The weakness of the British economy meant that the pound sterling, which had provided the financial stability the indus-trialised world had enjoyed during the nineteenth century, was no longer able to fulfil any international role.

The collapse of the dollar, and the end of the system of fixed exchange rates established by the Bretton Woods Conference of July 1944, led to the first effort to create such a zone of currency stability within the European Community. Initially, this took the form of the system known as 'the snake in the tunnel', established by a meeting of the Heads of Government of the EEC at the meeting of the European Council on April 24, 1972. This was an image which expressed the way that all the curren-cies of the Community would vary together in their relationship with the dollar, rather as a snake might go up and down beneath the ground as it moved along inside a tunnel. This enabled each currency to vary in its relationship to the others, but without ever going outside the skin of the snake. Thus, while all the currencies went up and down together in their relationship to the dollar, none of them varied in its relationship to the other currencies of the EEC by more than ±1.25 per cent. If there was a risk of this happening, the central bank of the country in question would either have to buy its own currency in order to maintain its value, or take other measures in order to bring it up or down.

The system failed partly because the limits were too narrow. But it also collapsed because it was followed, eighteen months later, by another event which occurred outside Europe but whose effect, like the economic fall-out of the Vietnam war represented by the dollar devaluation of August 10, 1971, was something which the states of Western Europe could not avoid. For while it may be true, as Martin Walker claimed in 'Taming the dollar', in the January 1999 issue of *Prospect*, that:

> a European political generation never forgot what they saw as the manipulation of their currencies to ease an American balance of payments problem crisis to pay for a war which few of them supported

there were other factors which encouraged the members of the European Communities to try to create a kind of monetary Fortress Europe. They did so in an international climate dominated less by the financial problems created by the war in Vietnam than by the conflict in the Middle East.

ISRAEL, EUROPE AND ISLAM

The industrial revival of the Western world after 1945 had not been solely the result of the revived dynamism of the economy of the United States. It had also been based on the cheapest and most efficient source of energy available at the time: oil. However, some two-thirds of the most easily available supplies of oil were in the Middle East, an area dominated by one of the major problems of the second half of the twentieth century: the relationship between the state of Israel and its Arab, Muslim neighbours.

In the harm which it did to the economy of Western Europe, the 1971 devaluation of the dollar could be seen as a temporary aberration on the part of the America which was continuing to put its own cities at risk to atomic attack from the Soviet Union in order to protect Western Europe. The balance-of-payments problem which this devaluation reflected could also be seen by Europeans of a conservative disposition as the result of the attempt made by a succession of United States Presidents to protect South Vietnam from a Communist-inspired take-over from the North. If, it was argued, the USA was prepared to go to so much trouble in Vietnam, a country with which it had few cultural ties, then it would obviously continue to ensure the protection of Western Europe.

In the case of the wars between Israel and its Arab neighbours, the political as well as the moral issues were almost as clear-cut as in the defence of West Berlin. At one point they also gave rise to the same danger of setting off a nuclear war. For its enemies as well as for its admirers, the state of Israel was a cultural as well as a political offshoot of Europe, and the United States' determination to support it against its Arab neighbours could thus be seen as the logical extension of the policy which was still protecting Western Europe against the Soviet Union. This was especially the case in 1973, when the centre of the Cold War had moved away from Western Europe and became increasingly situated in the Middle East.

Israel was officially established as an independent state on May 14, 1948. It was immediately awarded diplomatic recognition by the majority of the world's powers, including the Soviet Union, but equally immediately attacked by its Arab neighbours, who saw it as having been set up on land rightfully belonging to them. From their point of view, the decision to make Israel a home for the Jews was yet another example of the aggressive policies which Europe had pursued against Islam and the Arabs ever since Pope Urban II had proclaimed the First Crusade at the Council of Clermont in 1095. Admittedly, it was no longer the Christians who were trying to seize Jerusalem. It was the Jews, long considered as one of the Christians' principal enemies. But, in the eyes of the Arabs, the need to establish a national home for the Jews would never have arisen without the essentially European phenomenon of the persecution of the Jews by Hitler's Germany. What right, they asked, had the Europeans to solve their problems at the Arabs' expense?

Israel could also be regarded as another offshoot of Europe in a more positive and favourable sense than the reminders it provided of the disaster of the Crusades and the even greater horror of Hitler's 'Final Solution'. The 1971 Constitution of Egypt defines it as a democratic socialist republic – there are regular elections and a number of different political parties – but this constitution was not introduced until Anwar Sadat succeeded Colonel Nasser in 1970. Until then Egypt was a military dictatorship, and the most recent elections, on December 6, 1995, had been marked by widespread fraud. Syria is 'a People's Socialist Democracy', but the ruling Ba'ath party does not lose elections. Iraq is a military dictatorship run for the exclusive benefit of the family of Saddam Hussein. Iran is a theocracy. There are few constitutional limits to the powers of the King of Jordan, while in Saudi Arabia the members of the Consultative Assembly introduced in 1993 are appointed by the King and have no powers of decision.

Israel, in contrast, is notorious for the number of its political parties, as well as for the fragility of its coalitions. However badly its government treats the Palestinians on whose land it was originally established, its other political traditions are those of Western Europe and North America. It is true that there is a fundamentalist religious party which would like to impose total conformity to the practices recommended in the Old Testament, but, unlike its mirror image in Iran, it has never taken power. Newspapers are free to print whatever opinions they please, and governments, as in Western Europe and the United States of America, are in the habit of losing elections. This is not a widespread occurrence in Islamic countries.

Consequently, when the Cairo radio announced on May 27, 1967 that

Egypt's basic objective was the destruction of Israel, the feeling in many of the states of Western Europe was that it was they who were being attacked by proxy. President Aref of Iraq made matters even clearer on May 31 when he proclaimed: 'Our objective is clear: to wipe Israel off the map.'[7]

THE ISRAELI WARS AND THE ABSENCE OF A COMMON EUROPEAN FOREIGN POLICY

In May 1948 the Israelis had beaten off the attack by the Arab states which greeted the birth of their country with relative ease. It was, for most observers outside the Middle East, a relatively straightforward affair of self-defence. The same was true of the role played by Israel in 1956, when it felt itself so threatened by Egypt's closure of the Gulf of Aqaba that it had no choice but to strike first to prevent an annihilating attack from its neighbours. Its motives were thus considerably different from those of its two allies, France and Great Britain, whose motives in attacking Egypt are more fully explained in Chapter 15.

In June 1967, faced with what looked like another imminent attack from its Arab neighbours, Israel decided to launch a third Arab–Israeli war by once again striking first. In a series of attacks which began at dawn on June 5 its air force destroyed most of the Egyptian and Syrian planes before they could take off. By the time an armistice was signed on June 10 its forces had captured most of the areas deemed necessary for its security: the Golan heights, the Sinai peninsula, and the east bank of the Suez canal.

It was a victory which both the Soviet Union and General de Gaulle would have liked to avoid. From 1955 onwards, largely through deliveries made via what was then the Communist satellite state of Czechoslovakia, the Soviet Union had become the main supplier of arms to the countries which, like Iraq, Syria and Libya, expressed most hostility to Israel. Since the USSR had in 1948 been one of the first countries to recognise Israel, this offered yet another example of how easily a totalitarian state can change its foreign policy for motives of straightforward *Realpolitik*. Since the United States had become Israel's principal ally, it seemed natural to the Soviet leadership to do everything it could to create problems for the Americans in the Middle East, irrespective of what might be the moral claims or political interests of the Arabs and the Israelis themselves. On June 6, 1967 it broke off diplomatic links with Israel and withdrew its ambassador.

On June 2, 1967 France had also changed tack, and for very similar motives. In 1948, in company with the vast majority of other countries in Europe and elsewhere, it had recognised Israel as a sovereign state and fellow member of the United Nations. But that was in the Fourth

Republic (1946–1958), when foreign-policy decisions were sometimes made on grounds other than those of a mixture of anti-Americanism, antisemitism and de Gaulle's rather curious concept of *Realpolitik*. Such decisions could also be questioned in a parliament where relatively weak governments had to defend and justify their policies.

During de Gaulle's period of office, between 1958 and 1969, governments of the Fifth Republic were not subject to comparable constraints. De Gaulle knew that when he, and he alone, decided not to admit Great Britain into the European Economic Community, he could be sure of support from the Gaullist *Union pour la Nouvelle République*, which had a majority in parliament. He was equally confident that any change of policy on Israel which he decided would, if it did happen to be questioned, meet with comparable approval by the followers who drew their power from his prestige.

When, therefore, he suddenly announced on June 2 that France was imposing an embargo on the shipment of arms to the Middle East, there was no effective protest in France itself. Since France's main client in this area was Israel, which had already paid for a number of *Mirage* jets that had still not been delivered, there were no doubts as to the target of this sudden embargo, and on November 27 de Gaulle made his own position very clear when he held another of his press conferences and denounced the Jews as being 'un peuple d'élite, sûr de lui et dominateur' (an elite, dominating and self-confident people).

In other circumstances, this might simply have been a compliment to the Jews for being so very like the French. However, since what was clearly intended as an unflattering description was coupled with an attack on what de Gaulle, like the Soviet Union, also called Israeli imperialism, there was little doubt as to where his sympathies lay. In neither Russia nor France is antisemitism ever far below the surface, and both countries, albeit for different reasons, were at the time extremely hostile to the United States. Since the Cold War had moved from Berlin and the contest for central Europe to the Middle East and Vietnam, it was no longer necessary for de Gaulle to show the hard-line support for Western policy which had characterised his attitude on Berlin. Instead, he was doing everything he could to show France's independence by systematically opposing America – in Europe, in the Far East and even in North America itself.

On October 6, 1973 – on Yom Kippur, the major Jewish festival of the Day of Atonement, and ten days into Ramadan – Israel's neighbours launched their fourth attack against it and almost succeeded in bringing about its destruction. When it looked as though Israeli forces were about to annihilate the Egyptian Third Army, which they had surrounded in the Sinai desert, the Soviet Union gave every sign of preparing to intervene on the side of the Arabs by airlifting 200,000 troops into the Middle

East. It was dissuaded from doing so by the decision of the United States, on October 12, to order a Stage III nuclear alert: the first since the Cuban missile crisis of October 1962.

As in 1962, the deterrent deterred, Israel avoided annihilation, and the world was saved once again from a third world war. On both occasions it was the prompt and courageous action of the United States of America which avoided the catastrophe, after the behaviour of the Soviet Union had created the danger in the first place. Once again, as in the crises over Berlin in 1948, 1958 and 1961, as at Suez and at the time of the Six-Day War of June 1967, neither the European Economic Community nor any individual European state could take any decisive action.

It was yet another example of how distant a common foreign policy was in Western Europe on any issue other than suspicion of the Soviet Union, and it justified the question which the American Secretary of State Henry Kissinger is said to have asked at the time: 'What is Europe's telephone number?' It was not until 24 years later that an attempt was made to establish even the machinery for giving an answer to his question, when one of the articles of the Amsterdam treaty of June 1997 provided for the appointment of a High Representative who would act as a Secretary General to the Council of Ministers and be able to use a new Policy and Planning Early Warning Unit to try to co-ordinate a common foreign policy.

But in 1973 the European Communities not only lacked a foreign minister, they also had no chance of agreeing on a foreign policy. Great Britain was crippled by the miners' strike and in no position to use its newly acquired membership of the EC to give any kind of lead in foreign-policy matters. Memories of the Holocaust meant that West Germany could do nothing but side with Israel, while France had still not recovered sufficiently from de Gaulle to express any support for the way America saved Israel. But the events which followed the signature of the cease-fire which put an end to the Yom Kippur war on October 24 did more than underline the impotence and divisions of Western Europe. They also pointed to a number of new and important limitations which were then placed on the power of the United States.

THE POLITICS OF OIL

Defeated on the field of battle in 1948, 1956 and 1967, and held to a draw in 1973, the Arab and Muslim states allied against Israel turned to economic warfare. To begin with, they threatened to impose a total boycott on the sale of oil to any state supporting or selling arms to Israel. They were able to make this threat as a result of a new-found unity in the body known as the Organisation of Petroleum Exporting Countries (OPEC). This had been established in 1960 as a belated response to the failure of the attempt made by Iran in 1950 to defy the cartel formed by the Western oil companies and require them to pay a more realistic price for the product on which they depended.

As T.O. Lloyd points out in his history of the British empire, the ability of the powers which dominated the Arabian Gulf, and especially Great Britain, to keep the price of oil down had transferred wealth to the industrialised countries of the West 'on a scale so immense that it dwarfed anything else that could have been called economic imperialism',[8] and one way of looking at the oil crises of the 1970s is as part of an attempt to move power away from Western Europe and North America towards the countries which had earlier been the victims of Western imperialism. OPEC included countries such as Nigeria, Indonesia and Venezuela, which had no direct interest in the conflict in the Middle East but could see themselves as having been exploited by the West. They were therefore, for financial reasons, quite happy to go along with a policy whose supporters in the West presented it as an attempt to distribute the economic advantages of the Industrial Revolution more fairly among the peoples of the earth. This was not one of the conscious aims of the countries originally proposing either the boycott or the price increase. What they wanted to do was weaken Western support for Israel, so that they could more easily destroy it.

The countries of the Third World were already labouring under the immense debts which they had incurred in an attempt to achieve economic take-off. The main consequence of the increase in the price of oil as far as they were concerned was a higher price for a major source of the energy which they needed if they were to improve their economies. Since the main general effect of the oil price rise was to set off a world inflation which particularly affected the dollar, they also found themselves confronted with the need to pay more dollars to keep up the interest on their international debt. In no way did the action of the OPEC states transfer to the Third World countries the financial help which they so desperately needed. The number of Africans and Asians who died of malnutrition and the associated diseases of economic collapse as a result of Arab oil policy must, as Paul Johnson observes, 'be calculated in tens of millions'.[9]

Because the Soviet Union was at the time a major petroleum-exporting power, it was also able to increase the price of the oil which it could sell in the overseas market. This provided it with the money which it needed to finance its attempt to overtake the United States in military hardware, and thus to strengthen its ability to threaten Western Europe. There is, in this respect, a direct link between the increase in the price of oil by the OPEC states in October 1973 and the increasingly aggressive attitude which the Soviet Union adopted towards the West during the 1970s and 1980s. The installation of the SS-20s, the despatch of Cuban troops to fight in Angola in 1975 and the invasion of Afghanistan at Christmas 1979 were all by-products of the increase in the price of oil which the Arab states made for purely political reasons.

The initial threat of a boycott nevertheless proved unrealistic. In whatever part of the globe they were situated, the OPEC countries had to sell their oil to somebody, and their only real clients were the nations of the industrialised West, who alone had the money to buy it. But the fact that the OPEC countries had now formed themselves into a cartel did enable them to increase the price of oil. In September 1973, this had stood at $4 a barrel. By the end of 1973 it was $16 a barrel. The fall of the Shah of Iran in January 1979, and his replacement by a régime dominated by Muslim fundamentalists, led to a further increase in the price of oil, which then rose to $33 a barrel. This was a body blow to the economies of the industrialised countries of the West at whom it was principally aimed, and it seemed for several years to mark the end of the prosperity which Western Europe had enjoyed since 1945.

De Gaulle's hostility to Israel did not enable France to escape the effects of the oil crises of the 1970s. The Dutch government tried to bring home to its citizens the serious nature of the oil crisis by making November 4, 1973 a 'carless day', while even the prosperous West Germany saw the first signs of the unemployment which was to become the major economic problem in Western Europe in the 1980s and 1990s. In December 1973 a summit of European Community leaders was held in Copenhagen in order to try to agree on a common policy towards the OPEC countries. It failed to do so.

The replacement of de Gaulle by the more moderate Pompidou in June 1969 meant that French hostility to Israel remained largely verbal during the 1973 crisis, and in August 1974 his successor Valéry Giscard d'Estaing lifted the embargo on the export of French arms to the Middle East. In March 1980, while recognising that the Palestinians expelled from Israeli territory in 1948 should have the right to self-determination, Giscard d'Estaing also managed to state that Israel had the right to exist. He could not, however, bring himself to pay either a formal or a private visit. This was left to the first socialist President of the Fifth French Republic, François Mitterrand, who in March 1982 became the first French Head of State since the establishment of the Fifth Republic in 1958 to pay a formal visit to Israel.

By then, the state of Israel was no longer under the kind of threat which had faced it in 1967 and 1973. By negotiating the Camp David Accords of September 1978, the United States had shown that it was as essential to the stability of Middle East as it had been since 1945 to the protection of Western Europe. In December 1977 Anwar Sadat, who had succeeded President Nasser as the Egyptian President on the latter's death in September 1970, paid an historic visit to Jerusalem, where he met his Israeli opposite number Menachem Begin. Under the guidance of President Jimmy Carter the two men signed the agreements at the Presidential retreat at Camp David which led to the diplomatic recognition of Israel by Egypt in 1969. Although opposition to his agreement in many Arab states was strong enough to lead to the assassination of President Sadat by Muslim extremists in October 1981, it did mark the beginning of a process which was to culminate in a speech given by Yasser Arafat on March 2, 1989 declaring that the original charter of the Palestine Liberation Organisation, originally founded in 1964 with the avowed aim of destroying the state of Israel, was now out of date.

This speech was given in Paris, the first time that a European capital had provided the setting for a major event in the history of the Middle East since the ending of the British mandate for Palestine in August 1948 and the subsequent creation of the state of Israel. In 1973, at the time of the Yom Kippur war, Yasser Arafat had gone one better than Mr Khrushchev, who when addressing the General Assembly of the United Nations in October 1960 had taken off his shoe to hammer on the rostrum in order to express his hostility to what he called Western Imperialism. In October 1973 Arafat had appeared before the General Assembly with a large revolver sticking out of his belt. But his policy had now become a good deal more moderate, thanks largely to the influence of the United States and the demonstration it had provided by the nuclear alert of October 1973 of the incapacity of the Soviet Union to intervene in any effective manner in the Middle East.

Because of its impotence and divisions, Western Europe had played virtually no role in the bringing of some kind of peace to the Middle East. But it had, by the 1980s, succeeded in being less dependent on the supply of oil. In 1976, thanks to the discovery of large oilfields beneath the North Sea, Great Britain began to find some mitigation for its economic problems by becoming the first country in Western Europe to transform itself into an oil-exporting nation. It did not, it is true, carry its membership of the European Communities to the point of selling oil to its EC partners below the market price fixed by the OPEC cartel. But the power of this cartel over Western Europe gradually diminished, thanks to a more efficient use of energy as well as to more sophisticated techniques of exploration which enabled more oilfields to be discovered. Between 1973 and 1983 the member countries of the European Communities were able to cut their oil imports by half, North Sea production was up to 130 million tons, and the same amount of energy was being provided by nuclear energy.[10] Together with the general fall-off in demand brought about by the various recessions which have continued to affect the world economy since the first oil shock of 1973, these improvements had, by 1999, brought the price down to around $15 a barrel. In real terms, taking account of the fact that inflation has brought down the purchasing power of the US dollar to roughly one-fifth of what it was in 1973, oil is now cheaper than at any time since the Second World War.

10 The enlargement of the EEC and the creation of the Euro

THE CONFIRMATION OF BRITISH MEMBERSHIP

The oil crises of the 1970s did not lead to the break up of the European Communities. On April 1, 1974 Denmark, the United Kingdom and Ireland carried out the first reduction of forty per cent in their customs duties in order to bring their rates into line with those of the Common External Tariffs. Further reductions took place on an annual basis until, on December 30, 1977, the three new member states reached the end of the transitional period allowed to them under the 1973 treaty of accession. They were, in this respect, following the same kind of pattern which had enabled the six original members of the European Economic Community to abolish their customs duties by reducing them on a yearly basis from 1959 onwards, the only difference being that France, Italy, Luxembourg, the Netherlands and West Germany had succeeded in doing so eighteen months ahead of schedule, abolishing customs duties on manufactured goods and introducing the Common External Tariff on July 1, 1967 instead of in December 1968.

In December 1974, at the suggestion of the newly elected French President, Valéry Giscard d'Estaing, the nine Heads of State and of Government formally decided to meet three times a year in what became known as the European Council. Such meetings have continued to take place since 1975, and they supplement but do not replace the basic pattern of decision whereby the Commission sends forward proposals to the Council of Ministers, which then reaches a decision on them by the process of weighted voting. The role of the European Council is to try to solve problems by the more direct and traditional technique of negotiations between individual states. In that respect it is an attempt to combine the Gaullist concept of 'l'Europe des Patries' with the more federalist technique preferred by the Dutch and Germans.

Thus it was at the Council held in Dublin in March 1975 that a settlement was reached on the demand for renegotiation formulated by the British Labour government first elected in February 1974 and re-elected in October of the same year. A referendum held in the United Kingdom on June 5, 1975 gave a majority of 67 per cent in favour of continued British membership of the European Communities on the terms renegotiated at Dublin. Since, however, only 64.5 per cent of the electorate voted, it did not put an end to the arguments about British membership.

These reached one of their many peaks during the premiership of Margaret Thatcher, who held office for longer than any other British Prime Minister in the twentieth century, from May 1979 until November 1990. She claimed that Great Britain was making a disproportionately large contribution to the European budget and insisted on 'getting her money back'. The agreement on an annual rebate of 66 per cent of the net contributions made by the UK was reached at the meeting of the European Council held at Fontainebleau in June 1984, and came about largely through the good offices of François Mitterrand. In 1985, the first full year of its operation, the rebate amounted to about £1 billion.[1]

In 1993 Germany made by far the highest contribution to the European Union budget, some £9,210 million as against £2,433 million from Great Britain and £794 million from France.[2] Great Britain was, at the end of 1998, the only country to receive a rebate. However, this situation is unlikely to last much longer, and an article in *The Economist* for December 19, 1998 underlined other anomalies in the budgetary arrangements for the European Union. Although Ireland and Denmark are among the richest of the EU countries, they are net recipients of the money collected from the other states which provides the EU with its budget. This is made up of the customs duties imposed by the Common External Tariff, as well as a percentage, currently 1.3 per cent, of the VAT receipts of each nation. Seen as a percentage of the GDP of the fifteen nations making up the European Union, this budget is not large: 1.2 per cent of the total GDP, a sum which amounts to about 85 billion ECUs, $US100 billion or £60 billion. However frequently it may be accused of interfering in the internal affairs of its member states, the EU is not a financial Leviathan.

FURTHER MOVES TO MONETARY UNION

French policy throughout the 1980s and 1990s was very much more pro-European than might have been expected from de Gaulle's behaviour in the 1960s. It was France and Germany that continued to make the running in the process of monetary unification which was to lead on January 1 1999 to the introduction of the Euro. Since one of the results of this initiative will be to bring about the complete disappearance of the franc as from July 1, 2002, the approach both of Mitterrand himself and of his Gaullist successor Jacques Chirac marks the final abandonment of the Gaullist concept of 'l'Europe des Patries'. The bipartisan approach to

Europe which now characterises French internal politics has thus come to mark the triumph of the German idea of a federal Europe over the French insistence on national sovereignty.

The 1972 attempt to create a kind of 'Fortress Europe' in monetary terms lasted only until 1976, a victim of the inflation created by the weakness of the dollar and the increase in the price of oil. The idea of using a central pivot as the anchor for a zone of monetary stability nevertheless remained the basic idea when the French President Valéry Giscard d'Estaing and the German Chancellor Helmut Schmidt took the initiative at the European Council of July 1978 to create the European Monetary System (EMS).

The EMS was similar to the 1972 'snake-in-the-tunnel' system, in that it had a mechanism, known as the European Exchange Rate Mechanism (ERM), to which a country taking part had to belong. Membership implied an undertaking by the country in question not to allow its currency to rise or fall in value by more than a certain percentage in relation to a central pivot. The ERM was more flexible than the 1972 arrangement. The margins of fluctuation were wider, and varied according to the country involved. If it was in the narrow band, as Germany and the Benelux countries chose to be, the margin was ±2.5 per cent. If it was in the broader band, as France and Italy were, it was ±5 per cent. A country could also request a change in the exchange value of its currency if it found the going difficult.

As in the 'snake in the tunnel', where the participating countries followed the dollar as it went up and down, the value of the central pivot could vary in relation to other currencies such as the yen, the American or Australian dollar or the Swiss franc. The central pivot was known as the ECU or European Currency Unit, a linguistic compromise which reflected the fact that when Giscard d'Estaing and Schmidt, the two most powerful European statesmen of the 1970s, met each other or spoke on the telephone, they did so in English. The acronym ECU also had the incidental advantage of designating a French coin of the *ancien régime*.

The influence which a national currency had on the value of the ECU was known as its weighting, which depended in turn upon the Gross National Product (GNP) of the country issuing it. The GNP of France is higher than that of Portugal, so the French franc had a higher weighting than the Portuguese escudo, and played a proportionately higher role in determining the value of the ECU in relation to other world currencies. Since the GNP of the Federal Republic of Germany was higher than that of any other individual country in the European Economic Community, the Deutschmark played a larger role than any other currency in determining the international value of the ECU. If the German mark was in demand on the international exchanges, the ECU thus went up more than if the Italian lira, the Greek drachma or the Irish punt did. But since these currencies all had to follow the upward movement of the Deutsch-mark, the system was another aspect of the new Europe which empha-sised the extent to which it was dominated by West Germany.

The system worked relatively well, and had the advantage of avoiding the shocks, secrecy and deceit which had been so marked a feature of the stricter arrangement whereby currencies had a fixed exchange rate. When, for example, the franc was devalued in October 1981, June 1982 and March 1983, it was after prior consultation between France and those of its partners who were in the ERM, and by agreement among them.

THE IMPACT OF GERMAN REUNIFICATION

By 1990 the European Exchange Rate Mechanism was working well enough for the British government to decide to take part in it. Between 1983 and 1989 the Chancellor of the Exchequer, Nigel Lawson, had already experimented with what might happen by arranging for the pound to shadow the Deutschmark. The departure from office in November 1990 of the highly Eurosceptic Margaret Thatcher led under her successor, John Major, to a slightly more favourable attitude towards the process of monetary integration. On October 5, 1990 Great Britain joined the Exchange Rate Mechanism with the pound fixed at what turned out to be the over-optimistic rate of 2.95 Deutschmarks.

The choice of this rate reflected the economic theory of the time, which was that one of the best ways of reducing inflation was to make it more expensive to borrow money. By fixing the value of the pound at a high rate relation to the major currency in the ERM, which has always been the Deutschmark, the government put the Bank of England in a position where it would have to keep interest rates high in order to persuade foreign investors to keep their money in London rather than in Frankfurt or in Paris. Inflation in the United Kingdom was running at 7 per cent, as opposed to an average in the other countries in the ERM of 5.5 per cent. What was then a high exchange rate of 2.95 Deutschmarks to the pound therefore seemed at the time to be a good way of bringing it down.

There were a number of reasons, apart from the inherent weakness of the British economy, why this did not work, and, like the problems created by suspension of the convertibility of the dollar in August 1971 and the oil crises of the 1970s, they offer a reminder of how vulnerable the economies of Western Europe are to events taking place outside its geographical borders. On this occasion, the first and most important of these events was the end of the Cold War, embodied in the first instance by the fall of the Berlin Wall on November 9, 1989, followed by German reunification on October 3, 1990.

This reunification meant that the Federal Republic of Germany, whose dynamic economy had been a major factor in creating the prosperity of

Western Europe, was increasingly preoccupied with trying to bring the economy of the former East Germany up to the level of the West. Because of the runaway inflation of the 1920s, which in 1923 had seen the value of the mark fall to one-million-millionth of its 1913 value, the Germans had retained a vivid awareness of the danger of allowing the money supply to get out of control. After all, it was the inflation of the 1920s, as much as anything else, which had created the circumstances which had enabled Hitler to come to power. The West German government did not wish to try to bring the standard of living of the 13 million inhabitants of the former German Democratic Republic up to that of their fellow citizens in the West simply by pumping more money into the system. They consequently kept interest rates relatively high, thus making the Deutschmark even more attractive to overseas investors than it already was, and greatly strengthening it in its relationship to the pound.

On Wednesday September 16, 1992 this resulted in the United Kingdom having to leave the ERM, in spite of a series of vehement assurances by the British government that this would not happen. It was these denials, rather than the immediate effect of the devaluation, which led to the day on which it took place being referred to as 'Black Wednesday'. Once the pound was allowed to fall to what was then the more realistic level of 2.25 Deutschmarks, British exports enjoyed a spectacular and surprisingly long-lived revival. One result of this was that by 1996 unemployment in the United Kingdom had fallen to 7.6 per cent, as opposed to 12 per cent in France and over 14 per cent in the now united Germany. Italy also had to leave the ERM, and in the summer of 1993 the system underwent a fundamental change, when currencies were then allowed to vary by ±15 per cent in their relationship to the central pivot and still remain officially members.

For Eurosceptics, the events of 1992 and 1993 suggested that the whole idea of using a mechanism such as the European Exchange Rate Mechanism to create monetary stability was ill-founded from the outset. Since, they argued, the value of a currency on the international market was primarily a reflection of the strength or weakness of a country's economy, it was as pointless to try to improve that economy by changing the rate at which its currency could be exchanged as it would be to try to alter the weather by adjusting the barometer. They also pointed out that there was a discrepancy between the way the ERM was supposed to work and what happened in practice.

Thus one of the phrases used to justify the system was that of 'monetary solidarity'. The prime responsibility remained with the country whose currency was going out of line to stop this happening. If its currency was falling by more than a certain percentage in relation to the central pivot, its central bank had to create a demand for this currency by buying it itself, using the stocks of gold and other currencies which it had in its reserves in order to do so. Similarly, if its currency was becoming too valuable, a country was expected either to sell it, or to take other measures – such as an increase in wages for public employees or an expensive programme of public works – which would bring its value down to within the agreed band.

In theory, other Community countries which were members of the ERM were expected to show support by buying the currency of the country in difficulty, an idea expressed in the phrase 'monetary stability'. However, in the period leading up to Black Wednesday, this was something which did not happen. The countries which might have been expected to support the United Kingdom by buying the pound argued that if it had entered the ERM at the artificially high rate of 2.95 Deutschmarks, this was the British government's own fault. They were not going to risk losing their money by buying pounds which would immediately lose twenty per cent of their value when the inevitable devaluation eventually arrived. This refusal to practice 'monetary solidarity' confirmed the British in the Eurosceptic view that no system involving a group of nation states could ever overcome national interests.

FURTHER ENLARGEMENT

After the entry of the United Kingdom, Ireland and Denmark on January 1, 1973, the process of enlargement of the European Communities was continued on January 1, 1981 by the admission of Greece, which had applied to become a member in 1976. Greece had enjoyed an Association Agreement since 1961, but this has been suspended during the military dictatorship of 1967–1974. In the Commission's view, the problems created by the fact that Greece was much poorer than the existing member countries were in any case too great an obstacle to its economic integration. However, the Council of Ministers took a different view. It saw these problems as less important than the political implications of Greece's admission.

In the Council's opinion, it was essential to ensure that democracy remained the mode of government in the country where, in fifth-century Athens, it had made its first and not entirely successful appearance, and membership of the European Communities seemed the best way of doing this.[3] In 1952 Greece had become a member of NATO, only to leave the alliance when the colonels came to power in 1967. It had then rejoined when democracy was restored in 1974. Although there was no direct link between the two organisations, membership of the European Communities seemed a natural accompaniment to membership of NATO, especially since it would also help to maintain stability in the Balkans.

In 1957 the Preamble to the Treaty of Rome had included as one of its objectives the ambition to 'reduce the differences existing between the various regions and the backwardness of the less-favoured regions'. This had led in 1973 to the establishment of what were known as the two 'structural funds', the European Regional Development Fund and the European Social Fund. Until the admission of Greece in 1981, the principal beneficiaries of these funds had been Italy, Spain and the United Kingdom, together with the poorer regions of Ireland, and France. There were, therefore, some reservations about Greek entry, and these were compounded by the fact that Greece, as a country whose economy was based primarily on a Mediterranean-style agriculture, was inevitably going to become a competitor in the fields where the needs of Europe were already fully supplied by Italy, Spain and the south of France.

In addition to the normal five-year transition period for aligning import duties, there was consequently a further two-year period, not ending until January 1, 1988, for peaches and tomatoes, and a similar delay in the implementation of the freedom of Greek nationals to work anywhere in the Community where they could find a potential employer. Greece's population of just over 10 million brought the total number of people in the European Communities up to 190 million, and this rose to 242 million with admission on January 1, 1986 of Spain and Portugal. Here again, there were strong reservations, especially by France, to the entry of two countries where tomatoes and peaches ripened earlier in the year and thus threatened the interests of French farmers in the south. Greece, in its turn, opposed the entry of Spain and Portugal until persuaded to change its mind by the institution in 1985 of the Integrated Mediterranean Programmes which allowed for the spending of 6,600 million ECUs (£5 billion, $US7 billion) over seven years, most of which went to Greece.

However, as in the case of Greece, political considerations were seen as more important than commercial rivalry. Since the final triumph, on April 1, 1939, of the 1936 rebellion by General Franco against the Republican government of the country, Spain had been seen as virtually a pariah nation. In spite of American pressure for earlier admission of a country which was, in spite of its blatantly undemocratic régime, a sufficiently reliable ally against Communism for American military bases to be established there in 1952, it was not admitted to NATO until 1982, seven years after the death of Franco on November 21, 1975. Franco's death led to the surprisingly swift transition to democracy under King Juan Carlos, a transition which meant that Spain then became eligible for membership of the European Communities.

This was also true of Portugal, where on April 25, 1974 a military *coup* by General Antonio de Spínola overthrew the government of Marcello Caetano and led to the final collapse of the reactionary, corporatist state established by António de Oliveira Salazar after he had become Prime

Minister on July 5, 1932. In both Spain and Portugal there was also much more widespread enthusiasm for membership of the European Communities than in Greece. In Spain, the emphasis on the idea that a future Europe might become one of regions rather than of traditional nation states was particularly popular. Movements towards regional autonomy had always existed in Catalonia and the Basque provinces, but had been very firmly repressed by the Franco régime. Portugal had been a member of the European Free Trade Association since its launch in 1960 by the United Kingdom, and could, quite understandably, see no reason for not following its oldest ally, Great Britain, into the larger and more successful grouping established by the Treaty of Rome in March 1957.

What was equally, or perhaps even more, important was that both Spain and Portugal saw the opportunity of putting an end to the quip that Africa began at the Pyrenees. Neither country had been touched either by the Protestant Reformation or by the European Enlightenment. Now, they had a chance to catch up both intellectually and politically with the rest of Europe and adopt the kind of government which existed elsewhere in the civilised world. The revival of the Spanish economy had already begun before the death of Franco in 1975 and was a major factor in facilitating the entry of the Iberian countries into the European Communities. There had been no comparable economic improvement in Greece, where hostility to the European Union, in spite of all the money it has received, is often as strong as it is in Great Britain.

The admission of Greece in 1981, followed by that of Spain and Portugal on January 1, 1986, meant in cultural terms that the European Communities took on a more Mediterranean flavour. With a total population which then rose to 321 million, as against 242 million for the United States of America, it then became the largest trading bloc in the capitalist world. With Bulgaria, Czechoslovakia, Hungary, Poland, Romania and the Soviet Union, Comecon had a European population of 358 million. But, whereas the European Communities accounted for almost forty per cent of world trade, trade among the member states of Comecon never rose above the fifteen-per-cent mark, and its importance as a world trading bloc was negligible. On June 28, 1991, six months before the Soviet Union ceased to exist, Comecon was formally abolished.

On January 1, 1995 the admission of Austria, Finland and Sweden produced a more even balance between the Mediterranean and the countries of central and northern Europe. Since Austria and Sweden were highly prosperous countries, and therefore likely to become net contributors to the European Union budget, there were few problems in admitting them. The collapse of the Soviet Union had begun to threaten the prosperity which Finland had derived from its virtual monopoly as the path through which most of the trade took place between the Soviet Union and the Western capitalist world. It therefore needed to exchange its earlier membership of EFTA for entry into the European Union, and when, by January 1, 1999, its economy had recovered well enough for it to become one of the eleven states to adopt the Euro, its leading newspaper commented 'Better Euroland than Redland'. Throughout the Cold War, the word 'Finlandisation' had been frequently used to evoke the fate threatening Western Europe if the Soviet Union won: that of being unable to conduct an independent foreign policy, and of remaining, even when allowed to retain a capitalist-style economy, something very near a satellite state in the limitations placed upon its freedom of action.

When the Maastricht Treaty of December 11, 1991 agreed to change the name of the European Communities to that of the European Union, it had a population of 370 million. The oil crises of the 1970s had by now become so much a thing of the past that mention was rarely made of them in the press, attention from 1991 onwards being increasingly concentrated on the implementation of the Maastricht Treaty and the proposed introduction of the single currency, the Euro, on January 1, 1999.

MAASTRICHT AND SCHENGEN

The Maastricht treaty of December 1991 defined what it called the 'three pillars' on which European unification would henceforth be based. First of all, there were the European Communities, in the form which they had then reached, especially in the plans for further economic integration and the introduction of a single currency. Secondly, there was the development of a common foreign and security policy. And, thirdly, there was to be increased co-operation on justice and interior affairs. Perhaps understandably, the treaty placed the main responsibility for the second and the third pillars on the Council of Ministers. It is there, more than in the Commission, with its concern for the interests of the Union as a whole, that national attitudes can express themselves, and these have differed even more widely in the area of foreign policy than on security.

Thus the suspicion of American motives which continues to inspire French attitudes to the United States is not shared either by Germany or by the United Kingdom. The Italians were decidedly lukewarm in their attitude towards the British reconquest of the Falkland Islands in 1982, and, had Spain then been a member of the European Communities, it would certainly have supported Argentina. In 1995 a semblance of peace was imposed in Bosnia only by the intervention of the United States. There is no agreement on how to deal with Saddam Hussein, and the lack of consensus about the fighting in Kosovo was underlined by a cartoon in one of the Greek newspapers on April 12, 1999, at the height of the NATO bombing campaign of Serbia. Under a cartoon showing the President of the United States with a funny little black moustache ran the caption 'ADOLF CLINTON'.

January 1, 1993 saw the establishment of the European Economic Area, and the virtual abolition of all customs posts between the fifteen countries of the European Union: Austria, Belgium, Denmark, Finland, France, Germany, Greece, Ireland, Italy, Luxembourg, the Netherlands, Portugal, Spain, Sweden and the United Kingdom. Goods can now travel from Ireland to Germany, from Italy to Denmark or from Portugal to Finland with no more formalities than they do in the United States when they go from Texas to North Dakota, or from California to Massachusetts – that is to say, none at all.

However, this has not been matched by the implementation of the agreement of May 15, 1990 initially signed by France, Germany, Luxembourg and the Netherlands at the small town of Schengen in Luxembourg. When and if this finally comes into effect, another similarity with the United States of America will be produced: all forms of passport control on the borders between the fifteen member states of the European Union will eventually disappear. This would also fulfil the dream expressed in 1945 by the Foreign Secretary in Clement Attlee's Labour government, Ernie Bevin, when he said that the aim of his foreign policy was to enable anyone who wanted to do so to go down to Victoria Station, buy a ticket to wherever they wanted, and go there straight away.

This is not yet possible in every sense as far as citizens of the European Union are concerned. Frontiers are still there, and travellers can still be stopped and have their documents checked. Even though the long waits at the frontier posts separating France from Spain or Italy are now a thing of the past, motorists still do not yet have the possibility of driving from Germany into France with the same total freedom from any check being made on their movements as is enjoyed by travellers entering California from Oregon. The Netherlands has a more liberal attitude to drugs than either France or Belgium, a fact which has led France, on a number of occasions, to invoke the safeguard clause in the Schengen Agreement by maintaining spot checks on all travellers coming into the country, whether citizens of a member state of the European Union or nationals of a Third Country, especially if they are coming in from the north and north-east.

The computer technology enabling information to be sent from one police force to another has not yet reached the stage where information suddenly obtained by the German police can be sent to every port of entry into the European Union fast enough to prevent a suspect individual coming, for example, into Portugal, and thus securing the right theoretically available under the Schengen Agreement to travel right up to Finland without any further check on his identity or motives. It was essentially for security reasons that Denmark and the United Kingdom indicated from the very beginning that they would not implement the

Schengen Agreement, and thus insisted on their right, as sovereign states, to maintain control of who crossed their borders.

Except in wartime, citizens of the United Kingdom have never carried identity cards. Even those issued between 1939 and 1945 did not carry the photograph which is an integral part of the identity cards which citizens of France, Spain, Italy or Germany must be able to produce when asked by a policeman to prove who they are. This is an additional reason why the United Kingdom is reluctant to implement the Schengen Agreement in its entirety. Furthermore, frontier posts are not only very useful in the fight against crime; they can also be used to halt the spread of infectious diseases. A number of countries on the continent of Europe have not succeeded in eliminating rabies. Now that the Channel tunnel has made travel between France and Great Britain so easy, it still seems reasonable to carry out health checks on animals entering the United Kingdom, and on the human beings who might wish to bring them in.

In 1995 France, Germany, Greece, Italy, Spain, Portugal and the Netherlands decided on a common policy on the granting of visas to nationals from Third Countries. What this means is that any traveller entering Europe from any Third Country, whether Australia, Algeria, Brazil, Burma, Canada, Zaïre or South Africa, will have to go through the formalities of immigration only once. Once their credentials have been checked at whatever port or airport at which they enter the European Union – whether in Germany, Finland, France or Portugal – there will be no check on whether they then go to Austria, Spain, Greece or Sweden. Such travellers will not, unless they obtained special permission, be able to benefit from articles 3, 8 and 48 of the Treaty of Rome, establishing the principle of the free movement of workers, but their freedom to move around in Europe is intended to parallel the free movement created for agricultural products or industrial goods which have paid the Common External Tariff and are thus circulating freely within the borders of the European Union.

THE ADVENT OF THE EURO

The Maastricht Treaty of December 1991 set out three criteria for a country wishing to adopt the common currency which it was decided would come into force on January 1, 1999. From that date, the basic rate of interest charged in all countries in the Euro zone would be decided by the European Central Bank. As the Euro moved up and down in relation to the other world currencies, so too would the international value of the currency of any country adopting the Euro. What happened in practice after January 1, 1999 was that the value of the Euro declined in the first six months of its existence from 67 to 62 pence in relation to the pound sterling, and by June 1999 had fallen from its original rate of 1.19 to the US dollar almost to parity.

The basic interest rate for all countries in the Euro zone is fixed by the European Central Bank, on which each of the participating countries has one representative. It was decided that no Euro notes would be issued until January 1, 2002, and during the first six months of 2002 national currencies would circulate side by side with the Euro in the eleven member states which had decided to adopt the common European currency. These were Austria, Belgium, Finland, France, Germany, Ireland, Italy, Luxembourg, the Netherlands, Portugal and Spain. Denmark, in company with Great Britain and Sweden, decided not to join. Greece did not qualify, since it was unable to satisfy the Maastricht criteria for the adoption of a common currency.

Any country wishing to replace its national currency with the Euro has to have an annual deficit of not more than three per cent of its Gross National Product, and an accumulated national debt of under sixty per cent of its GNP. It should also have a low inflation rate, defined as one which was not more than 1.5 per cent higher than that of the average inflation rate of the three countries which had been most successful in maintaining the purchasing power of their national currency. In practice, this meant Germany, Belgium and the Netherlands, each of which had managed to keep its inflation rate at under three per cent. In terms of recent history, this is strict to the point of parsimony. In the 1970s and early 1980s an inflation rate of six per cent was regarded as being fully consistent with an efficiently run national economy, and an accumulated debt of 120 per cent of GDP was by no means unusual.

The responsibility for ensuring that the whole of the Euro zone does not have an inflation rate of more than three per cent a year is entrusted to the European Central Bank. This has fourteen members and will be chaired, at least for the first four years of its existence, by a Dutchman, Wim Duisenberg. In his view, he will continue to chair it until 2008, but this is not quite how the French see it. They maintain that Mr Duisenberg has given his word to step down in 2004 so that he can be replaced by a former governor of the Banque de France, Jean-Claude Trichet. The largely Eurosceptic British press took particular pleasure, in January 1999, in pointing out how well the arrangements for the future Chairmanship of the European Central Bank, whose headquarters are in Frankfurt, illustrated Samuel Goldwyn's remark that a verbal agreement was not worth the paper it was written on.

THE EURO AND ITS PROBLEMS

British hostility to the Euro is partly the result of the long history of suspicion which goes right back to the refusal of the Attlee government in 1950 to involve itself in the European Coal and Steel Community. Another objection, also found among French Eurosceptics such as Charles

Pasqua, is that acceptance of the Euro involves the surrender of what has traditionally been regarded as an essential prerogative of the nation state: the right to issue the coin of the realm, what the French call *le privilège régalien de battre monnaie*. The ferocious punishments inflicted in the past on forgers did not stem solely from the danger that they might be able to buy goods and services with the equivalent of stolen money. – when coins were made of silver or of gold, it might even happen that, in terms of the precious metal from which they were made, the value of counterfeit coins was as great as that of the coins issued by the royal mint – it was because it was the King, whose head was on the coin, who was the only person with the right to issue money, and anyone doing it in his place was usurping a regal function.

In a modern economy, especially in the twentieth century, the equivalent of *le privilège régalien de battre monnaie* is the power to control the money supply. This is not done nowadays solely by printing paper money or making metal coins. It is done mainly by deciding the rate at which banks will be allowed to lend money to their clients. This enables the government, by lowering the rate, to make it easier for people to borrow money. This stimulates the economy, and is seen as means of reducing unemployment, albeit at the risk of causing inflation. By increasing what is known in the United Kingdom as the Bank Rate, and in the United States as the US Prime Rate, a government can also slow down economic growth, and thus, it is hoped, bring down inflation.

A country choosing to replace its national currency by the Euro ceases to be able to do this. Only the European Central Bank (ECB) has the power to raise or lower interest rates, and thus to determine not only the level of economic activity throughout the eleven countries of the Euro zone but also the value of the Euro in relation to those of the other international currencies such as the US dollar or the Japanese yen. By raising interest rates, the ECB can make it more attractive for big international investors to keep their money in Euros. It can also make Euroland a low-inflation zone, with everything which that implies by way of confidence which investors may have of not seeing the value of their money eaten away.

Alternatively, by lowering interest rates, the ECB can make it cheaper for businessmen and others to borrow money, and thus make it more likely that they will invest in new businesses and so reduce unemployment. This creates the danger of inflation, so that any bank has to tread a very fine line between too strict a lending policy, with its attendant dangers of depression and unemployment, and too lax a control of the money supply, with the opposite danger of encouraging inflation.

Between 1919 and 1939, when the value of money remained constant, the great problem was that of unemployment. The view then developed was that governments would be best advised to relax the money supply and adopt what the critics, such as John Maynard Keynes, who recommended this course of action, called a 'tax-and-spend policy'. In what may have been an uncharacteristic moment of frivolity, Keynes said that the best way for a government to reduce unemployment was to put a lot of pound notes in biscuit boxes, bury the boxes in the ground, and pay people to dig them up. In the 1970s, when the major problem was that of inflation, the opposite view became more popular. Under the influence of Milton Friedman and what was known as the Chicago school of economics, the main responsibility of government came to be seen as that of controlling the money supply so as to ensure that no more purchasing power was available than could be satisfied by the productive capacity of the economy.

The philosophy inspiring the Maastricht criteria is that of the 'supply-side' theories of the Chicago school. This is not a philosophy to which British politicians are necessarily hostile. Indeed, it inspired much of the behaviour of Margaret Thatcher, and the Labour government of Tony Blair has given little sign of being tempted by the reflationary and 'easy money' policies associated with Keynes. The criticism most frequently voiced in the United Kingdom concerns the loss of national sovereignty which is seen as inseparable from the adoption of the Euro. For it will no longer be the government of France, Germany, Italy or Spain which decides whether to lower or increase the interest rate charged in their country. It will be the fourteen members of the European Central Bank, meeting behind closed doors in Frankfurt, and forbidden by the statutes of the Bank from receiving advice or instructions from the national government which has appointed them.

In this respect, they will be like the European Commissioners, though with two important differences. Like the Commissioners, they will take account of what they see as the interests of the European Union as a whole and give no consideration to the attitude of any individual state. But, whereas the European Commissioners may only make proposals, which have then to be approved by the Council of Ministers, the members of the ECB take decisions. When they say that interest rates will go up, they go up. When they say they come down, down they come. And, whereas the Commissioners can be required to resign in a body by a vote of censure passed by a two-thirds majority in the European Parliament, there is no mechanism whereby the members of the ECB can be required to give an account of themselves to any elected assembly.

The idea of a bank not subjected to the influence of an elected government is not a new one. The Federal Reserve Bank is not required to follow instructions either from the President or from Congress. From its establishment in 1957 the German Bundesbank has been forbidden by its statutes from receiving advice from the Federal government. Both the Bank of England and the Banque de France are now independent, in the sense that the decisions which they take to lower or increase interest rates are made by a committee on which the government is not represented and whose decisions the government has to accept. But, as the Eurosceptics in both Britain and France rarely fail to point out, the governing bodies of the Bank of England and the Banque de France are able to take account of the particular needs of the British and of the French economies.

This is not a freedom available to the European Central Bank. The decisions which it takes have, in theory, to be equally appropriate to rural Portugal and the industrialised area of the Ruhr, to Finland and to the Mezzogiorno, to Austria and to Spain. In the second half of 1999 the Republic of Ireland was highly prosperous, so much so that it was frequently described as 'overheating'. It could therefore have benefited from an increase in interest rates. The German economy, in contrast, was in a negative cycle, with high unemployment and low productivity. It could therefore have benefited from the stimulus of a cut in interest rates. But with the ECB fixing rates for the whole of the Euro zone, neither measure was possible.

In the period immediately following the end of the Second World War it was seen as axiomatic, especially in France and Great Britain, that the elected government of the country should decide its economic policy. That is why the Bank of England and the Banque de France were nationalised. Control of the economy was rightly vested in the government which the people had chosen. However, in the 1960s and 1970s this theory came to be looked at with a certain suspicion. The government in power was made up of a political party, and one of the principal aims of every political party has always been to get itself re-elected. A good way of doing this is to make sure, as the next general election approaches, that there is a certain 'feel-good' factor in the country. With falling unemployment and more money in their pockets, electors will be urged to vote for the government producing these goodies, not for the opposition, which might ruin everything.

It has nevertheless been noticed that the governments which have succeeded in getting themselves re-elected then encounter problems. The reflationary policies which have created the pre-election boom have to be replaced by deflationary policies which put the finances of the nation back in order but then provoke a post-electoral bust. The need to pay for the brief access of prosperity which everyone has so much enjoyed gives rise to the feeling which parallels the view expressed by Georges Clemenceau (1841–1929), the Prime Minister who had led France to victory in 1918. War, he said, was too important a matter to be entrusted to military men. What the arrangements for the Euro mean is that the running of the economy is too important a matter to be entrusted to politicians. Much better hand the job over to the bankers. It was, after all, the Bundesbank, with its freedom from government interference, which had overseen the great European miracle of the post-war years: the rise of Germany to the position where the prosperity it had achieved could be quoted as a model not only for Europe itself but for the rest of the industrialised world.

The decision to model the European Central Bank on the German Bundesbank underlines one of the major paradoxes of the European Union. Not only is it a rule that no country may join unless it is a democracy. There is also a widely held view that the triumph of democracy in post-war Europe is very much the product of the success of the movement towards European integration which began with the establishment of the ECSC in 1951 and was followed up by that of the European Economic Community in 1958. The countries which are now members of the European Union offer their citizens all the traditional advantages of a democratic society. Citizens may move around as they wish, may go abroad and come back without let or hindrance, and have no fear of a knock on the door at four in the morning betokening the arrival of the secret police. But the decisions which affect their daily lives, and especially their conditions of employment and the possibility of their finding a job, are increasingly taken by unelected bureaucrats.

It was, for example, an unelected official, Jacques Delors, who as President of the European Commission presented on February 7, 1989 a report on economic and monetary union which was to provide an alternative path to the creation of the Euro after the events of 1992 and 1993 led to a loss of confidence in the ERM. It was his report which ensured that the moves towards the creation of a common currency did not run into the sand and which came to be regarded as having an authority which no electorate had ever consciously bestowed upon it.

In the idea of democracy which originated in the English revolutions of the seventeenth century, there was a mechanism whereby citizens could exercise some control over the people who governed them. If they did not like what the government had done, they could use their vote at the next parliamentary election to put it out of office. This applied particularly to a government which had made what came to be seen as a series of mistakes in its economic policy, raising interest rates when it should have lowered them or vice versa, failing to increase taxes to pay for necessary services or omitting to reduce them when the economy needed a boost, making the wrong decisions as to how to spend the money raised in taxes.

With interest rates being decided by the ECB, there is now no means of sanctioning any national government which makes a mistake in the first of these areas. If, as is frequently suggested, taxes are increasingly harmonised throughout the European Union, the ability of the electorate to dismiss a government which makes what is seen as a mistake in fiscal policy will also disappear. Decisions about tax rates will also be taken centrally, perhaps by a committee bringing together representatives of the European Central Bank and the European Commission, but certainly not by one which is responsible to an elected assembly.

It is in this respect that the advent of the Euro is an indication that the political culture of Western Europe has undergone a sea change. It is on the same scale as the gradual triumph, from 1945 onwards, of parliamentary democracy as the universally accepted way of governing an advanced industrial country, but it is of a different, and even contradictory, kind. With a Union consisting of fifteen member states, it is hard to imagine how any mechanism could be devised whereby all the national parliaments might be brought to agree on the same set of measures. Even if they were not required to do so simultaneously, and were allowed quite separate deliberations, the problems would be virtually insurmountable. If the membership of the European Union were to rise to eighteen, as it is planned to do with the admission of Poland, Hungary and the Czech Republic, agreement by normal parliamentary procedure would be quite impossible. If membership were then to rise to twenty-one with the admission of the Baltic states of Latvia, Estonia and Lithuania, national parliaments would find their powers as limited as those of provincial assemblies in traditional nation states. The very enlargement of the European Union, which is one of the most evident signs of its success, virtually condemns it to be a bureaucracy.

The criticisms made of the Euro are thus both practical and theoretical. It is, it is argued, far too clumsy a way of deciding economic policy for so vast and varied an area. In the United States the Federal Reserve Bank has two main areas of responsibility: controlling inflation and helping the job market. The role of the ECB is limited to that of controlling inflation. It has no responsibility for trying to bring down unemployment, which is currently running at an average of over ten per cent in the eleven countries which have elected to replace their national currencies by the Euro.

In the United States there is a system whereby fiscal transfers are made from the richer to the poorer areas of the Union. This enables the taxes levied by prosperous states, such as California or Texas, to fund subsidies to poorer regions, such as Arkansas or West Virginia. Although this is one of the functions of the European Regional Development Fund (ERDF), it does not form part of the responsibility of the ECB. There is also another, even more important difference between the employment situation in the United States of America and the European Union. Because the USA is a single country, where everybody speaks English, it is relatively easy for anyone losing their job because of an economic depression in the area in which they happen to live to move to another area. For obvious reasons, this is much more difficult in the EU. Why, then, have the majority of countries in the European Union taken the decision to replace their national currencies by the Euro?

THE EURO AND ITS ADVANTAGES

The answer most immediately made by Eurosceptics is that the inhabitants of Western Europe were not given any choice in the matter. The bureaucrats decided that it would be a good idea, and the politicians trotted obediently along behind them. A more serious explanation is that the adoption of the Euro is linked to the origins of the movement towards European monetary union. This began because of two events in the outside world which had a devastating effect on the economy of Western Europe: President Nixon's suspension of the convertibility of the dollar in August 1971, and the increases in the price of oil decided by the OPEC countries between 1973 and 1979.

The first argument in favour of the Euro is that it will help the European Union to become more independent in its relationship with the United States. It may even happen – if what is frequently referred to as the bubble of the New York Stock Exchange finally bursts, and the dollar becomes increasingly volatile – that more and more international companies will choose to keep their money in Euros rather than in dollars. This may in the long run, or even the short run, make the Euro the principal international reserve currency, with everything which that implies in the way of power to act on the international economic environment and be protected from currency variations. The situation will no longer arise in which a major and essential economic resource such as oil has to be paid for by Europeans in a currency over which no European country has any control. During the economic crisis which began on August 19, 1998, when Russia defaulted on its international debts and the rouble lost virtually all its real value, the currencies of the countries which were part of the European Exchange Rate Mechanism varied remarkably little in their relationship to one another. The advent of the Euro means that this kind of stability will become a permanent feature of the European economic landscape.

One of the major advantages of a large and stable currency area lies in the greater security which it offers for long-term planning. A businessman can launch a project involving, for example, the ordering of machine tools from abroad a year in advance without having to worry about the possibility that a sudden fall in the value of his national currency will mean that the machines will ultimately cost fifteen per cent more than he expected. From the point of view of the consumer, the disappearance of national currencies will also mean that prices across Europe will become more transparent. When cars are priced in different currencies, it is not immediately obvious to the customer that he is being required to pay ten per cent more for the same vehicle in France than he would do if he were buying it in Germany. When, as will be the case from 2002 onwards, all goods everywhere in the Euro zone will be priced in Euros, price differentials of this kind will be so blatantly obvious that customer pressure to bring them all down to the same level will be very hard to resist.

This particular argument presupposes, of course, that the tax charged on the purchase of motor cars will become uniform throughout the countries taking part in the Euro. This is not currently the case, and it may well be that individual countries will find a way of introducing a form of duty on vehicles which has the same effect as the excise duties on wine do at the moment. If wine is more expensive in the United Kingdom than in France or Italy, this is because the UK has kept the right to levy excise duties on certain products, so long as these duties do not discriminate in favour of British goods.

While it is easy to justify the imposition of such duties in the case of wine, there would be many more problems if a comparable tax were placed upon automobiles; Somerset claret is not a serious competitor to Médoc. The international nature of car manufacturing is underlined by the fact that Vauxhall is owned by General Motors, and Volkswagen by Ford, that Renault is now allied with Nissan, and BMW (Bayerische Motoren Werke), which already owns the Rolls Royce trademark, agreed in March 1999 to keep open the Rover factory at Longbridge only in return for a grant of £350 million from the UK government. However, since all these companies produce cars of roughly similar quality, there would be no justification for making any of them more expensive to buy in England than in France.

Supporters of the Euro also argue that it will have comparable advantages for the European economy as a whole as it will have for the average European citizen. They calculate that the savings it will involve in the abolition of the charges made by banks for changing one currency into another will amount to 0.5 per cent of the Gross Domestic Product of the Euro area. Since the current GDP of all 15 states is 5,905.3 billion ECUs, this would be 29 billion ECUs, a sum equal to almost three-quarters of the GDP of Ireland, which is 40.4 billion ECUs.[4] It would also be a considerable saving for the very large number of citizens of the European Union who go to another member state either for a holiday or on business no longer to have to change currencies when they change countries. The tourist from Japan or the United States would experience comparable benefits, while citizens from a country which belongs to the Euro zone would enjoy the advantage of being able to settle their bills everywhere they went in a Euro unlikely to be affect by the variations which still afflict what are already being referred to as the residual currencies of Europe.

Real though these economic advantages are likely to be, it is the political aspect of the introduction of the Euro which represents the most important change as far as the future of Europe is concerned. The countries which are queuing up to join the European Union – which include Bulgaria, Poland, Hungary and the Czech Republic, the Baltic states of Latvia, Estonia and Lithuania, to say nothing of Turkey, whose first application goes back to April 1987 – have few of the qualms about the loss of national sovereignty which causes so much heart-searching in the United Kingdom.

This, in the view of Eurosceptics, is because such countries have little experience of the link between national sovereignty and parliamentary democracy as understood in Great Britain. They are, therefore, quite prepared to exchange their independence for the mess of pottage offered by the prosperity which the Euro may create. For them, a United States of Europe is so infinitely preferable a prospect to anything that has gone before that they can see only advantages in it. They may well be right. If the aim of the creation of the ECSC in 1950 was the avoidance of war in Europe, as distinct from the Balkans, it has been remarkably successful.

Part 4 *The ending of the European empires*

Prelude

The European empires before 1945

GREED, TECHNOLOGY AND RIVALRIES

In 1945 Belgium, France, Great Britain, Holland and Portugal were still major colonial powers, exercising direct rule over the territory of 55 of the 188 countries which now enjoy membership of the United Nations Organisation as fully sovereign nation states. At least in appearance, the situation which already existed in 1914 had not changed. Seventy per cent of the world's surface was under the control either of the countries of Western Europe itself or of those which, like the United States of America or the countries of Central and South America, were of European origin. What had enabled the inhabitants of this small peninsula on the western extremity of Asia, whose population comprised a mere eighteen per cent of the total number of human beings on the planet, to reach a position where they exercised a political and economic power so disproportionate to the physical size of their homeland?

The main motive which gave the Western Europeans mastery over so much of the globe was greed. The Europeans had always wanted the spices from the East. For the ruling class, which alone could afford them, they were an essential addition to their diet. Satisfied powers rarely develop expansionist ambitions. Those that are dissatisfied are like the boxer who goes into the ring because he is hungry. Like him, they win because they know that they will stay hungry if they don't. Because the Portuguese and Spanish were furthest from the routes which had traditionally brought the silks and spices of the East to Western Europe, they had the greatest incentive to find new sources of supply.

It was also the Spanish and Portuguese who had the means to do something about it. In 1418 the Portuguese prince Henry the Navigator (1394–1460) established the first school for navigation. In 1472 Portuguese ships reached the equator, and by 1488 they had sailed to the Cape of Good Hope. By the end of the fifteenth century Vasco da Gama (1469–1525) had reached Calicut, on the south-west coast of India, and by 1520 he had founded the colony of Mozambique, on the south-east coast of Africa. The Portuguese *barca*, initially used for fishing off the coast of Africa, was transformed into the swifter, ocean-going caravel. It was a highly manoeuvrable ship with the then unprecedented weight of 200 tons. It had three masts and a long, narrow hull and could travel distances earlier thought impossible. When it then gave birth to the carrack and the galleon, the crossing of the Atlantic gradually became a matter of routine, rather than of unpredictable hazards.

The Europeans were also lucky in that the divisions between them inspired a rivalry which constantly drove them to outdo one another. This offers a third reason for their success, and there was also a fourth. Not only were they greedy, technologically advanced and highly jealous of one another. There was nowhere else for them to go. To the east lay the Russian steppes and an increasingly powerful and militant Islam. Christianity had lost its unity and proselytising zeal; with the Reformation, it was about to turn its aggressive instincts inwards against itself. The eight crusades which had absorbed the energy of its warrior class between the eleventh and the thirteenth centuries had ended in failure. Jerusalem was still in the hands of the Turks, and the fall of Constantinople in 1453 had led to a situation in which it was all the Europeans could do to keep the Muslims from penetrating further into the eastern Mediterranean. The north was too cold, and had nothing to offer. Immediately to the south, was the Saharan desert. But to the west and south-west lay the open sea.

The crossing of the Atlantic had originally been based on a mistake, but one which turned out to be immensely fruitful. As Francis Bacon (1561–1626) observed in his *Advancement of Learning* (1605), truth 'emerges more readily from error than confusion' – a remark which has analogies with the comment made centuries later by an English scientist on a theory put forward by a French structuralist: 'That isn't right. It's not even wrong.' The Spanish and Portuguese navigators thought they would reach China and Cathay by sailing west. They did not know that the continent of America stood in their way. But they would not have made this immensely fruitful mistake if they had not developed what David Cardwell calls the 'hypothesis that the world was a finite, spherical body'.[1] They reached America because they had stopped believing that the earth was flat and had ceased to fear that they might fall over the edge.

The magnetic compass had been in existence in India since the twelve century, but its potentialities were not fully exploited until the Western Europeans began to perfect it from 1500 onwards. Once Mercator (1512–1594) had produced maps showing latitude and longitude, the Europeans had the additional advantage of knowing where they were going. By the middle of the eighteenth century, the development of the chronometer, or nautical clock, also enabled them to see how far they had travelled. For the Romans, as Gibbon observes, the sea was a subject of terror, not of curiosity. Theirs, unlike that of the Athenians, was an empire based on the land, sustained by a network of roads and made uniform by a single system of law and administration. They acquired it by systematic conquest, and lost it when they could no longer hold back the pressure of the barbarians on its frontiers. The empires of the Western Europeans, in contrast, were originally based upon sea power, and could thus be extended to the whole globe.

When the Genoese explorer Christopher Columbus (1451–1506) failed to persuade the King of Portugal to finance his project for reaching China and Japan by sailing to the west, he turned to Queen Isabella of Castile (1451–1504). She provided the money for the voyage of 1492 which led to what the Europeans described as the discovery of the New World. It was an event which would not have taken place if Columbus had been confronted with the kind of uniform authority which still governed China, or which characterised the empires of the Middle East. By the fifteenth century the Chinese had the capacity to build ships weighing up to 1,000 tons and which could, if they had wished, have enabled them to travel as far as the Europeans. But the bureaucrats governing the empire were interested in books and in reading, not in exploration and in making money. They argued that, once the canals had been built to bring grain supplies to Beijing, there was no need for a large navy. In any case, their own continent offered every-thing they wanted. The threat from the Mongols was also still great enough for most of the surplus economic capacity of the Empire to be absorbed in building the Great Wall. This, as Arnold Pacey observes, had the disadvan-tage of absorbing vast resources without stimulating much innovation.[2]

When, on May 4, 1493, Pope Alexander VI issued the Bull *Inter cetera divina* dividing up the New World of South America between Spain and Portugal, it was seen by the other European powers as a challenge as well as an injustice. Why, the Protestant English soon asked themselves, should they respect the Treaty of Tordesillas, of June 7, 1494, with its line drawn 370 leagues west of the Cape Verde Islands, giving everything to the east of it to Portugal and everything west of it to Spain – especially when it had been drawn up by a foreign pope to whom England owed no allegiance? The sea belonged to whoever could sail upon it. It was the property of all mankind, not of the self-appointed delegate of God.

There thus are a number of inter-related answers to the question which the French historian Fernand Braudel raised in 1983 when he wrote about 'this vast problem of the domination of the world by the minute continent of Europe'.[3] The European powers took possession of seventy per cent of the world's surface because they were greedy and ambitious, because they had the technology to do so, and because they were so jealous of one another that the refusal of one of them to profit from an opening meant that there was always a rival to leap into the breach.

In the seventeenth and eighteenth centuries the development of rich, commercial towns such as Amsterdam, Bordeaux, Genoa, Lisbon and London provided a more long-term framework for the process of European colonisation, and offered a further answer to another of Braudel's questions. When he asked Joseph Needham, the historian of Chinese science, why the culture which had first made paper and invented gunpowder had not spread its influence beyond the area where Chinese was spoken, Needham replied with one word: capitalism.[4]

What capitalism implies, in this respect, is the organised quest for private profit, if necessary at the expense of other people, but always based on the idea of obtaining the highest return possible on a financial investment. The fifth and final reason why the Europeans colonised three-quarters of the world was that they had the financial organisation to do it, and because this organisation then fed on the wealth which it had initially made possible. The Europeans were also, once again, very lucky. In the long run, the discovery of the gold and silver of the New World was disastrous for the economies of Spain and Portugal; it created confusion between precious metals and real wealth, together with the illusion that you could stay rich without working. But before the arrival of gold and silver from Central and South America also gave rise to a massive inflation which put an end to the feudal system, it solved one of the major problems which the European traders faced as they went on their travels: what could they give for the spices and silks on offer in the Orient? European products, as Arnold Pacey observes, 'were of inferior quality, or irrelevant to Asian needs'.[5] Even the guns which the Europeans had learned to manufacture were inferior to those already available in Islamic countries or in Thailand. But gold and silver were acceptable everywhere, and the Europeans, thanks to the discovery of the New World, has more of them than anyone else.

IDEOLOGY AND ENDINGS

The capitalism which gave the European empires their apparent solidity and permanence also hastened their downfall. Capitalism could not prosper without the exploitation of the peoples whom the Europeans had subjected to their rule. During the second half of the twentieth century, it was the awareness of this exploitation which allied itself with the forces of nationalism to bring about the final collapse of the empires which the Europeans had constructed in Asia and in Africa.

The loss of empire was not an experience to which the Western Europeans were unaccustomed. In 1783 the Treaty of Versailles had recognised the independence of the United States of America, putting an end to the first British Empire. In the nineteenth century the most potent of all the ideologies which Europe has exported to the rest of the world, that of nationalism, had already led to the loss of the empire which Spain had constructed in the sixteenth century in Central and South America. But it was in the second half of the twentieth century that this ideology finally spread to the whole world, making all the European empires equally impossible to maintain.

The concept which it embodied of the nature and rights of nation states had been formally defined a century and a half earlier by the various treaties signed at Westphalia in 1648 which put an end to the Thirty Years War. The principle of 'cujus regio, eius religio' (your religion is that of the region in which you live) marked the abandonment of the medieval idea of Christendom, the communion of all Christian peoples which theoretically united everyone living on the continent of Europe. Each ruler was supreme in the dominions under her or his authority, and the frontiers defining the national territory were deemed to be inviolate. This was not, however, a principle which the Europeans thought they needed to apply when dealing with people outside Europe. These were not seen as having the same rights as the inhabitants of a European state. They were, literally, treated as outlaws, in that their country could be invaded and taken over as though the concept of territorial integrity had never been invented.

Portugal, together with Spain, had been one of the first countries of Western Europe to extend its rule overseas. But in 1823, Portugal had been compelled to recognise the independence of Brazil, while between 1816 and 1839, Spain had been unable to refuse independence to its largest colonies, Argentina and Mexico, before finally abandoning all its remaining possessions in South America in 1898.

In the twentieth century, as Graham Evans and Jeffrey Newman point out in their admirable *Penguin Dictionary of International Relations*, 'the first major revolution that combined nationalism with revolutionary socialism was the Mexican revolution (1910–1917) which was subsequently regarded as the model for the anti-colonial movement'.[6] Just as the British had provided the starting-point for the loss of their first empire in the principle of 'no taxation without representation' which they had taught to the colonial Americans, so the essentially European ideologies of Marxism and nationalism were to bring about the fall of all the other European empires everywhere in the world. It was, as far as Central and South America were concerned, the final proof that the nationalism stimulated throughout Europe by the French Revolution of 1789 and by the Napoleonic wars had now invaded the New World. After 1945 the British, Dutch, French and Portuguese were to prove equally powerless to resist it in Asia and Africa, a further indication of how the continental Europeans had dug their own graves with the ideas which they exported.

This first British empire, begun in Virginia in 1584 but more readily associated with the landing of the Pilgrim Fathers in the *Mayflower* at

Cape Cod in 1620, had also been lost by military defeat, and in a war inspired by the peculiarly European idea that you pay taxes only if your freely elected representative has voted to approve them. In the twentieth century the French were to be driven out of Indochina and Algeria, as the Dutch were out of Indonesia, in the name of the European ideology of nationalism. It is certainly true, as Napoleon I famously remarked, that you can do everything with bayonets except sit on them. The end of the Western European empires, like that of the Soviet empire in 1989–1990, is a classic illustration of his dictum. But there are also cases, especially at the beginning of a political process, where Mao Zedong is right, and power does come out of the barrel of a gun.

It was because the British had defeated the French in the Seven Years War of 1756–1763 that they were able to find consolation for the loss of the American colonies in 1783 in the ability to maintain themselves in Canada. It was through a series of military campaigns which went on for fifty years after Clive's victory at Plassey in 1757 that they succeeded in creating what later became known as the brightest jewel in the imperial crown, the Second British Empire in India. This helped to ensure the subsequent domination of world civilisation by the English language – a process begun with the colonisation of North America by the English-speaking peoples from Scotland, as well as by the English themselves – and reinforced when the British took possession by force of arms of virtually the whole of Australasia. Except when it evokes the independence granted by Great Britain to the West Indies in 1962, the fall of the European empires is the more or less forced departure of the Western Europeans from Asia and Africa. It is not a phrase which applies to the territories won by the Europeans either on the other side of the Atlantic or in Australia and New Zealand.

A phrase such as 'the end of the European empires' does not therefore apply to the United States of America, to French or British Canada, or to Australia or New Zealand. By the end of the nineteenth century the Western Europeans and their descendants had exterminated and enslaved the native population of North America and Australasia with a brutality and ruthlessness unparalleled in history. There had been no mingling of the races, as there had been when Rome established its empire, no policy of live and let live. To speak of Australia, Canada or New Zealand as 'the white dominions' is still to pay unconscious tribute to what was, in practice, a policy of genocide. Like the Spanish *conquistadores* of the sixteenth century, the English-speaking peoples did not use exclusively military means. Ninety per cent of the Native Americans, to the north as well to the south of what is now the Panama canal, died as a result of diseases imported from Europe. But they died because the Europeans had assumed the right to take over their country, and for no other reason.

It could naturally be argued, on a world scale, that the long-term effects of this genocide were ultimately beneficial. This is especially the case when priority is given, as it frequently is in the writing of history, to the interests of the present-day inhabitants of Western Europe. If the territory now occupied by the United States had still been populated by its native tribes, neither the British, the Belgians, the Dutch nor the French would have been saved from the Third Reich. Neither would any of the countries of Western Europe have been protected from the Soviet Union. If, as Isaac Watts remarked in his best-known hymn:

> God moves in a mysterious way
> His wonders to perform

it could even be argued that there is evidence for the Hegelian view of history as the story of human freedom in the fact that in the eighteenth century it was the English-speaking Protestants who won the battle for North America, and not the French-speaking Catholics.

The disadvantage of what Hegel also called 'the cunning of reason in history' is that there is always somebody getting the short end of the stick, generally in the form of the sharp end of the sword. Whether the meaning attributed to history is the transcendental one created by divine providence, or the immanent one produced by the inner logic of the movement of history, there are losers as well as winners. The greatest benefit which the Western Europeans ultimately received from the adventurous spirit which had led them to conquer so much of the world from the fifteenth century onwards was victory in the Cold War. The Apache, the Crow, the Huron, the Navajo and the Sioux had already become the losers. Commentators hostile to the NATO intervention in Kosovo in 1999 remarked on the irony whereby one of the aircraft despatched to the Balkans in order to try to protect the Kosovan Albanians from being ethnically cleansed by the Serbs was the *Apache* helicopter.

Since the native population of the countries still ruled in 1945 by the British, Dutch, French and Portuguese had been too large to be conveniently slaughtered, it was the territories which the inhabitants of Western Europe had acquired between 1600 and 1900 in Africa and Asia which the Europeans found themselves obliged to give up in the years immediately following the ending of the Second World War. They surrendered them, as will be seen, with varying degrees of willingness and good grace, and in some cases only when compelled to do so at gunpoint, and in a way which underlines an important difference between the way the European overseas empires began and the way they ended.

Only a relatively small number of Europeans had been involved in winning the European empires overseas. They were, for the most part, sailors and adventurers, helped when necessary by the small professional armies with which wars were fought by continental Europeans until the

French Revolution of 1789 introduced conscription, and which the British continued to use to fight their wars until 1916. But once it became obvious, as it did in France in the early 1960s and Portugal in the mid-1970s, that the only way that the Europeans could keep their empires was by sending large numbers of their young men to fight and die for them, any imperial enthusiasm which might have existed in the population at large rapidly disappeared.

However differently the countries of Belgium, France, the Kingdom of the Netherlands and the United Kingdom gave up their empires, they all shared one common experience. In no case could they ever argue that the loss of empire made them financially poorer. This might have been the case if they had lost their colonies in the nineteenth century, or even before 1939. But after 1945 it seemed an infallible rule that the faster a European country gave up its empire, the swifter it increased its wealth. The opponents of imperialism, from John Hobson to Lenin, had denounced it as a means whereby the European capitalists increased their wealth by exploiting the workers in the countries they had colonised. Its supporters took a comparable but opposite view, arguing that it was only the possession of an empire which enabled the workers in the colonising countries to live as well as they did.

After 1945 both supporters and opponents of European imperialism were proved wrong. In France, as to a lesser extent in Belgium, Holland and Italy, it was a European thinker less well-known than Marx, Hobson or Kipling who provided a better explanation for what happened. Raymond Cartier, whose contribution to world culture appears at first sight to be the fairly limited one of having founded the illustrated weekly magazine *Paris-Match*, argued throughout the 1950s and 1960s that the only way for Europe to recover any of its past greatness was by giving up its overseas empires and concentrating on the movement towards European unification. It is in this respect that there is a link between the movement towards the creation of an increasingly united Europe and the end of the European empires.

This movement would not have taken place if the countries of Western Europe had still been quarrelling among themselves about who should control the territories which they had been able to seize outside Europe. More particularly, it would not have acquired the impetus it has if the Europeans had not been required to turn their energies and organisational power inwards, and to seek consolation for the loss of their overseas possessions in a greater and more powerful unity at home. If the movement towards European unification has, so far, been less successful in exporting European ideas to the world beyond the seas than the colonising process which began in the fifteenth century, it does have one major compensatory advantage. It is the first major movement in European history not to have caused any bloodshed. Although not originally conceived as a consolation prize for the loss of empire, this is one of the roles which it has tended to fulfil.

The creation of the European Union is nevertheless not the only link between the loss of their overseas empires and the history of the countries of Western Europe since 1945. Another is provided by the light which the way these empires have been lost throws upon the differences of political culture between the various countries of Western Europe which had managed to acquire an overseas empire. In France and Portugal, for example, the process of decolonisation led to a change of political régime. In both countries, the wars which they fought in order to try to retain their empire placed such a strain on their political system that it collapsed. This did not happen in Belgium or in the Netherlands or in Great Britain. Each of these countries managed to decolonise without having to change its constitution. For a variety of reasons, and in a field not marked by strong competition, the British also managed their decolonisation rather better than anyone else.

There is no means of knowing how the Germans or the Italians would have coped with the process of decolonisation which is so dominant a feature of the history of Europe since 1945. The experience both of the acquisition and of the loss of empire had always been limited to the inhabitants of those countries of Western Europe which had a window on the Atlantic or the North Sea, and which had attained national unity early enough in their history to profit from their ability to open it. The empire of the Muscovites, whether under the authority of the Tsars or under that of the Communist Party of the Soviet Union, stretched eastward to the Bering Straits. It never moved nearer to the Atlantic than the River Elbe.

Largely because they did not achieve unity until 1870, but also because they were more interested in extending their power in Europe itself, the Germans were latecomers to the attempt to spread the power of Western Europe overseas. They then lost whatever colonies they had managed to acquire in the nineteenth century in the Versailles settlement of 1919 which put an end to the First World War. Similarly, the Italians were made to lose their empire in Ethiopia immediately after the Second World War. The main empires lost after 1945 were the territories acquired in Asia and Africa between the fifteenth and the late nineteenth centuries by five Western European powers: Belgium, France, Great Britain, the Netherlands and Portugal.

The relative ease with which the British lost their empire may have been, as the account of Indian independence in Chapter 13 suggests, largely a matter of luck. But it may also have been because the ideal which Kipling expressed in his poem 'The White Man's Burden' was not entirely an illusion. The poem was written in 1899 to mark what a modern historian would call the forcible take-over of the Philippines by the United States of America. The American claim was that they had purchased the

Philippines from Spain for the sum of $20 million, and that the islands were in any case due to them as a reward for the help they had provided in the war of 1896–1898 whereby the Philippines won their independence from Spain. The population of the Philippines was not consulted, any more than anyone living between the Sahara and the Cape of Good Hope had been consulted when the European nations meeting at the Congress of Berlin between November 1884 and February 1885 carved up the continent of Africa between them. 'The White Man's Burden' is, in this respect, more than a partial idealisation of what had actually happened. It is also a piece of verse which, as George Orwell put it when talking about a line from the poem 'Recessional' in his 1942 essay on Kipling, 'is always good for a snigger in pansy-left circles'.[7] But, although it can be seen as a remarkable piece of self-deception, it is a poem which stands for an ideal which may help to explain why the British were, by and large, more successful than any other country in giving up their empire.

What dominates Kipling's verses is the idea of the service which the white man has been called upon to provide for:

> Your new-caught, sullen peoples,
> Half devil and half child

over whom he has assumed authority. The fact that it celebrates the Philippines having just passed from the government of Spain to that of the United States makes it clear that Kipling did not see the Spaniards as being white men in quite the same sense as the British or the Americans were. It reflects, in this respect, an attitude towards the inhabitants of the Iberian peninsula which goes from the lines:

> Let us bang those sons of Seville, the children of the Devil
> For I never turn'd my back upon Don or Devil yet

in Tennyson's 1878 'The Revenge: A Ballad of the Fleet' to some of the views expressed in the British popular press about 'the Argies' at the time of the Falklands War of 1982. It is the governments of the English-speaking democracies, and they alone, who are urged by Kipling to 'Send forth the best ye breed', so that they may 'wait in heavy harness' to 'serve their captives' need'.

The injunction to:

> Take up the White Man's burden –
> In patience to abide
> To veil the threat of terror
> And check the show of pride;
> By open speech and simple,

An hundred times made plain,
To seek another's profit,
And work another's gain.

is addressed to the Americans. It is they whom Kipling seeks to encourage in their task of imitating the British in their responsibility to:

Fill full the mouth of Famine
And bid the sickness cease.

At no point in the poem does Kipling suggest that there will be any money in it for them, and in this respect it is a far cry from the motives which originally inspired the Europeans to go out and conquer whichever lands their ships happened to reach. The idea of the British Empire as a vast machine for exploiting non-Europeans, which runs through the whole of the early work of George Orwell, is totally alien to Kipling's idealistic vision. But it may well be, for many of those involved in running the Empire, that Kipling was right, and that this was how the average British colonial administrator saw his task in the nineteenth and early twentieth centuries. If that is the case, it may explain why there was no equivalent in British post-colonial experience to the disasters suffered by the French in Indochina and in Algeria, and by the Portuguese in their African colonies of Angola, Mozambique and Guinea-Bissau.

It may also be, when one compares the enthusiasm of most continental Europeans for the European Union with the indifference or hostility of the British, that there is a link between Kipling's ideas and a major theme in the chapters in Part 3. If the British have shown themselves more reluctant than the Belgians, the Dutch, the Germans or the French to commit themselves to the process of European integration represented by the growth of the European Union, it is because they felt pleased at the relative success with which they disengaged themselves from their colonies in Africa, as well as from India, Burma and Malaysia.

This led them, especially in the twenty or so years immediately after the Second World War, to feel far less need than the French for the acquisition of a new area in which to prove their administrative and political skills. When de Gaulle said in 1962 that the European Community offered France the opportunity of becoming 'what she had ceased to be at Waterloo, the leading country in the world',[8] it was partly because he saw the need for his compatriots to find some compensation for what was widely if mistakenly seen in the France of the late 1950s and early 1960s as the catastrophe of the loss of Algeria. It was also because this loss had followed so hard upon the disaster of the Indochinese War of 1946–1954.

This disaster, like the history of the Algerian war and of the Portuguese experience of decolonisation in Africa, also provides the basis for another generalisation about the relationship between Western Europe and its former colonies. Like the original conquest of three-quarters of the world by the inhabitants of Western Europe, the aftermath of liberation brought remarkably few benefits to the former colonised nations. Except perhaps in India, Malaysia and Hong Kong, the arrival of the Europeans proved total disaster for the original inhabitants of the countries originally classified as the 'Third World'.[9] A number of these countries have now become so poor that they are placed in the new category of the 'Fourth World'. Like virtually all the countries of the 'Third World', they have not only derived no benefit either from the arrival of the Europeans or from their departure, they have seen their situation become very much worse. A detailed account of the disasters to have overtaken Bangladesh, Burundi, the former Belgian Congo, Nigeria, Rwanda and Sierra Leone is beyond the scope of this book. They are relevant to most of the inhabitants of Western Europe primarily as reminders of the good fortune which has been theirs since the ending of the Second World War.

This has not happened to the people of the former European colonies. Almost without exception, they have fallen under tyrannies which have had the almost miraculous effect of making imperial rule seem retrospectively beneficial. It is hard to blame the Europeans for all the disasters which have followed the process of decolonisation. It is certainly not possible to do this in the same sense that it can be argued that Hitler was ultimately responsible for the murder of six million Jews, Stalin for ten million or so deaths brought about by the collectivisation of Soviet agriculture and the Great Purge, Mao Zedong for the thirty million deaths caused by the Great Leap Forward of the late 1960s. It is true that between January 1971 and June 1979 Idi Amin presided over a régime in which a quarter of a million Ugandans were tortured and killed, and he is by no means the only African or Asian tyrant who showed that the Europeans are not unique in their aptitude for slaughter. But there is no means of knowing whether he, or an even more bloodthirsty tyrant, might not have come to power even if no white man had ever set foot in Africa.

All that a historian who is concerned primarily with what happened in Europe can do is to point to cases where a different policy pursued by the Europeans themselves might perhaps have produced slightly less catastrophic results. And, even then, the 20/20 vision traditionally associated with hindsight can do little more than evoke the last lines of W.H. Auden's poem about the Spanish civil war:

The stars are dead. The animals will not look.
We are left alone with our day, and the time is short, and
History to the defeated
May say Alas but cannot help or pardon.

11 France, Indochina and Algeria

HISTORY AND IDEOLOGY

In 1945 the French Empire still officially contained 103 million people. Although 45 million of these lived in Metropolitan France, it remained the second largest after that of Great Britain. With over 600 million inhabitants, of whom only 50 million lived in the United Kingdom of England, Wales and Northern Ireland, the British Empire ruled over one quarter of the world's surface.

What seemed, at the time, to be a highly fortunate situation stemmed from the fact that both these powers had ended the Second World War on the winning side. Both of them, France more obviously than Great Britain, had done so largely through the combined efforts of the United States and the Soviet Union. But there was no question of their being forced to give up their colonies, as the Germans had been in 1919, or as the Russians were to feel compelled to surrender their empire in Eastern Europe as a sign that they had lost the Cold War.

In 1942 and 1943 it was widely held that the sweeping victories of the Japanese which had followed their attack on Pearl Harbor on December 7, 1941 had put an end to any possibility of the Europeans recovering their prestige in the Far East. In 1945 this idea seemed less convincing. By August 2, 1945 the whole of Burma had already been liberated by British forces, and whatever threat there had been of an invasion of British India finally removed. After the atomic bombs on Hiroshima and Nagasaki on August 6 and 9, 1945 the Emperor sued for peace on August 15. The formal surrender of the Japanese to General MacArthur a month later, on September 15, meant that all their forces would rapidly have to go home.

The dismantling of the European empires was the consequence of a different set of historical events from the Japanese victories of 1942 and 1943. It is an illustration of how right Braudel was, though perhaps not quite in the way he had intended, when he wrote in 1983 that the world was 'still largely European and has not yet been freed from this servitude'.[1] For it was ideas, and not the recollection of the temporary triumphs of the Japanese, which inspired the anti-colonialist movements directed against the Europeans in the Far East, and these ideas came from Europe itself.

These were, initially, the two quintessentially European ideologies of nationalism and Marxism-Leninism. Once independence had been won as a result of the inspiration provided by these two ideologies, the newly liberated countries began by adopting the idea of state planning, as used by the Soviet Union. When this proved less successful than expected as a means of creating wealth, they turned to an even more specifically European idea, albeit one which has enjoyed its greatest success in the neo-European culture of the United States of America. They began to adopt the principles and practice of free-market economics. Vietnam, the country whose struggle against France and the United States was seen from 1946 to the 1990s as a model for the justified rebellion of all previously colonised countries is now following the example of the recently liberated countries of Eastern Europe. It has opened a Stock Exchange.

INDOCHINA

On August 14, 1945 the French government appointed Admiral Thierry d'Argenlieu as High Commissioner in French Indochina, part of which was above the sixteenth parallel, and were clearly determined to reassert their authority in what had since the 1880s been a major part of their overseas empire. Forty thousand French administrators, farmers and businessmen ruled a population of some 25 million native inhabitants, exploiting its rich resources of minerals, organising a profitable opium trade and providing a highly protected market for French goods.

In spite of their initial interest in North America and parts of India, the French had not become one of Europe's leading imperial powers. They had never been as interested as the British in building an overseas empire, nor had there ever been enough French people anxious to emigrate to the New World to counterbalance the much larger flow of English-speaking emigrants, and in 1763 the Treaty of Paris led to France giving up the beginnings of its empire in India as well as in Canada. On April 30, 1803, in what is misleadingly described simply as the Louisiana Purchase, Napoleon I confirmed the clauses in the Treaty of Paris by ceding to the new republic of the United States of America the whole of the French claim not only to Louisiana but also to the eleven states of Arkansas, Colorado, Louisiana, Minnesota, Missouri, Montana, North and South Dakota, Nebraska, Oklahoma and Wyoming already surrendered by Louis XV. He received $15 million, roughly four cents an acre.

With no Kipling to tell them to take up the White Man's Burden, the French seem to have felt little sense of responsibility for the inhabitants of the empire in Indochina and north Africa which they had acquired in the nineteenth century. What made them fight for eight years in an attempt to maintain control in Indochina was primarily the need to find some consolation for what had happened between May 1940 and June 1944. Like their British allies, and like the Poles in 1939, the French had been totally defeated by the *Blitzkrieg* tactics which had, by the summer of 1940, given the Germans total mastery of continental Europe from the Pyrenees to the frontiers of the Soviet Union.

On June 17, 1940, faced with casualty figures running at the same rate as those of 1915, the most disastrous year for the French in the whole of the First World War, Marshal Philippe Pétain requested an armistice. After this had been granted, the parliamentarians of the Third Republic (1870–1940), without being asked to do so by the Germans, voted by a majority of 569 to 80 to abolish the Republic and give supreme power to Pétain under a new, authoritarian constitution known as L'état Français.

Again without being asked to do so by the Germans, they had proceeded to introduce a set of violently antisemitic laws. On October 24, 1940 Pétain, the hero who in 1916 had commanded the French army which won the battle of Verdun, requested a meeting with Hitler. He publicly shook hands with him, and called upon the French to 'collaborate'. Although he later claimed that this merely meant working with the Germans in trying to rebuild France after the destruction of 1940, it was nevertheless not long before the word rapidly acquired the more sinister meaning of helping the Germans win the Second World War. About as many French people collaborated in this sense of the word as played an active part in the resistance movement. It is improbable that more than half a million were seriously committed on either side. But the loss of international standing brought about by the reputation of having been the main collaborators of the Nazi régime in Western Europe meant that the French felt more of a need than any other country in Western Europe to reassert themselves as a great power.

Once the Indochinese war got under way, the attitude of the United States towards French colonialism ceased to be as hostile as it had been at the time of President Roosevelt. In 1950 the French showed their support for America by sending a battalion to fight at the side of the United Nations forces against the invasion of South Korea by the army from the Communist North, and by the time the war in Indochina ended in 1954 the Americans were meeting 78 per cent of its military costs. With international politics being dominated from 1947 onwards by the Cold War, the struggle against the Viet Minh forces led by Ho Chi Minh was seen by the American administration as well as by conservatively-minded French politicians as part of the struggle between Western democracy and Communist totalitarianism.

This was probably an illusion. The uprising which began in 1946 was not part of an international Communist conspiracy; it was a war of national liberation. It was only in the 1950s that the Viet Minh began to receive aid from the Soviet Union and the People's Republic of China, and even then this played a relatively modest part by the side of the readiness to fight of the Indochinese peasants. A more skilful approach on the part of the French and the Americans to the movement for Indochinese independence might have transformed Ho Chi Minh into a kind of Asian Tito, with the problems which an independently-minded Vietnam might pose in the Far East paralleling those created from 1947 onwards by Yugoslavia in Eastern Europe.

After the Japanese defeat in August 1945 Ho Chi Minh issued a statement to the effect that the only legitimate government of the country was now the Democratic Republic of Vietnam. This government was never recognised by the French, who in 1949 gave the post of Emperor to the pro-Western Bao Dai. In the 1930s he had co-operated with the French, only to change his mind in 1943 and agree to work with the Japanese. It is thus understandable that, when the French brought him back from Hong Kong in 1949, his authority should never have been widely recognised either in the south or in the north of the country. In this, he incarnated a problem which neither the French nor the Americans were ever able to solve in their relationship with the Vietnamese: that of finding native rulers who at one and the same time enjoyed the confidence of the local population and were prepared to adopt pro-Western policies.

As early as 1946 there had been a campaign of civil disobedience in French Indochina which took the form of a refusal to pay the import duties that the French tried to levy on goods entering and leaving the northern port of Haiphong, on the Gulf of Tonkin. On November 23, 1946, in an attempt to make the Vietnamese pay, the French navy bombarded the native quarter of the town, causing some six thousand civilian casualties, a measure justified in the French press of the time by the fact that several thousand French people had earlier been killed by Indochinese rebels.

Insofar as this first action of the war was linked to the attempt by the French to derive financial benefit from a colonial situation, it fitted the Marxist view that all wars waged by Europeans against Third World countries were inspired by the profit motive which was the driving force of capitalism. But the French then found themselves having to spend so much money fighting the war that any idea of making a profit out of the Indochinese rapidly disappeared. The only exception to this was provided by the soldiers, businessmen and colonial administrators who managed to make a nice little profit for themselves by buying Indochinese *piastres* at 10 francs each in Saigon and reselling them for 17 francs in Paris.

By 1947 France was having to keep some 180,000 troops in Indochina. Had they been conscripts, the unpopularity of the war with the French population at home might have stopped it from lasting so long. But the soldiers on the French side were all professionals whom the French political class was not unhappy to see engaged in a military campaign 6,000 miles from Paris. They included 54,000 French nationals, 20,000 members of the Foreign Legion, 30,000 volunteers from north Africa and a surprisingly large number of Vietnamese, at least 70,000.[2] It was widely claimed by the numerous critics of the war in France that the members of the Foreign Legion included a number of ex-members of the Wehrmacht who were there to avoid being pursued as war criminals. They were nevertheless not treated as such in Indochina, where their military experience was much appreciated.

If made to fight in a formal engagement, the Viet Minh frequently lost. They lacked the fire-power of the French army, as well as the expertise and mobility of the French paratroops. But this was a people's war, exemplified by Mao Zedong's much-quoted remark that the guerrilla fighter lived in the native population like a fish in water. He, and quite frequently she, was difficult to find and even more difficult to kill in any significant numbers. In the countryside, the same man could be firing a rifle or laying a booby trap one minute and peacefully cultivating his rice field the next. In the town, the urban guerrilla was physically indistinguishable from the peaceful passer-by.

It was not entirely a new style of warfare, and not the first time it had been used against the French. It had made its first appearance in 1808, when the population of Spain rebelled against the occupation of their country by the armies of Napoleon I, giving to the vocabulary and reality of warfare what was then the new term of *guerrilla*, little war. After having been used, with a modicum of success, by the European resistance movements of the Second World War against the occupying armies of the Third Reich, it became the standard technique of forcing the Europeans to decolonise, in Africa as well as in Asia.

Most of the fighting in the Indochinese War of 1946–1954 took place in the north, in the Red River Delta. In March 1954, unable to defeat the Viet Minh guerrillas, who were by then also beginning to harass their troops in the south of the country, the French tried to establish an armed camp in the north, at Dien Bien Phu. This, they argued, would enable them to carry the war behind enemy lines and defeat the Viet Minh by using their own tactics against them. The attempt was not successful. The Viet Minh took the French completely by surprise by dragging cannons through the jungle and bombarding the airstrip needed to bring in supplies to the camp at Dien Bien Phu. By April 1954 the situation looked so desperate that French Foreign Minister Georges Bidault went to see the American Secretary of State John Foster Dulles to ask for American help. According to some reports, which he assiduously encouraged, Dulles was dissuaded from agreeing to use American nuclear weapons against the Viet Minh only by the urgent intervention of the British Foreign Secretary, Anthony Eden.[3]

On May 7, 1954 the last of the French garrisons at Dien Bien Phu surrendered. The French had lost 7,184 men in the four months of the siege, as against an estimated loss to the Vietnamese of 20,000. But as in the other colonial wars – as also when Chinese 'volunteers' intervened in the Korean war in December 1950 – the forces opposed to the Europeans seemed able to absorb virtually limitless casualties. For them, at least as seen from a European standpoint, human life was cheap, and there was little to frighten them in the threat which the French Prime Minister, Pierre Mendès-France, made at the Geneva peace conference of July 1954 to reinforce the French army in Indochina with conscripts from metro-politan France. The threat was aimed at his fellow-countrymen. Government, he insisted, was essentially a question of making choices (Gouverner, c'est choisir). France, in other words, must either commit herself completely by sending the whole of its army, with all the risks which that involved, or give up altogether.

The conference was jointly chaired by Great Britain and the Soviet Union, and was thus seen at the time as another sign of the thaw in Soviet attitudes which followed the death of Stalin in March 1953. It was also attended by the United States and the People's Republic of China, as well as by representatives from Indochina, Cambodia and Laos. Indochina itself was divided into North Vietnam, with Ho Chi Minh as President in Hanoi, and Ngo Dinh Diem as President in the South. December 31, 1954 marked the official end of French Indochina, and in April 1956 the last French troops left for home.

Theoretically, the country was then to be reunited by peaceful means, but this never happened. The subsequent disasters of the Vietnam War, the mass exodus of the political refugees known as the boat people, of the 1978–1979 invasion by Vietnamese forces of Kampuchea, and the heavy fighting on the frontier with China in February 1979, are relevant to a history of Europe since 1945 only in one respect. Like the disasters which have followed the process of decolonisation in Algeria, Angola, Bangladesh, Ethiopia, Ghana, Rwanda, Sierra Leone and elsewhere, they are a further reminder, should one be necessary, of how fatal an impact the Western Europeans have had upon almost all the countries and cultures with which they have come into contact. However fortunate the final outcome of the Algerian war of 1954–1962 may have been for France itself, it is hard to believe that the inhabitants of that unhappy country would not now be better off if the Dey of Algiers had never received the French Consul on April 27, 1827 and struck him, as the legend said he did, with his fly-swatter.

ALGERIA

BACKGROUND

That, at least in legend, was the incident which led in 1830 to the French occupation of Algeria, and subsequently to its incorporation, in November 1848, as an integral part of the French Republic. Algeria was said to owe the French a large sum of money for the purchase of grain. The affair had been going on since 1797, with no sign of a settlement, when the French Consul, Pierre Duval, went to pay an official call to demand the payment of the money. When the Dey struck him, it was an insult which the French saw as deserving violent punishment. On March 8, 1829 the town of Algiers was bombarded by a French squadron, and on July 5, 1830 French troops invaded the country.

As might be expected from its situation on the north coast of Africa, immediately facing the south of France, there had already been a number of commercial contacts between the two countries. It was not, however, until the 1840s that Marshal Bugeaud (1784–1849) began the systematic conquest and colonisation of the country, using the technique, as he himself put it, of *ense et aratro*, by the sword and by the plough. The Latin tag was appropriate, in that the colonisation policy followed by France in Algeria during the nineteenth century followed the pattern established two thousand years earlier by the Romans. The best of the land of the conquered race was handed over to the soldiers and citizens of the victorious country, who established themselves there as permanent settlers.

The situation which faced the French when the Algerian rebellion broke out on the night of October 31, 1954 was thus entirely different from anything which the other Western Europeans had to deal with when pressure mounted for them to leave their overseas empire. The two closest parallels are Northern Ireland and Rhodesia, both of which presented a very different situation from that of French Algeria. Rhodesia perhaps offers a closer parallel, and – had it been geographically closer to Great Britain, instead of a providential 6,000 miles away – a problem might have arisen to cast doubt on the view that the English are better at politics than most continental Europeans. But, for reasons discussed in more detail in chapter 13, it never came to that.

There is perhaps at times an echo in the Unionist insistence that Northern Ireland is 'an integral part of the United Kingdom' of the frequency with which the French spoke of 'L'Algérie Française'. But that is where the resemblance ends, and the differences between Northern Ireland and French Algeria are far more striking than any similarities. The descendants of the Protestant settlers who came over from Scotland in the seventeenth century outnumber the Catholic descendants of the native Irish by less than two to one; in Algeria in 1954 there were ten

Arabs for each European. If, in Northern Ireland, the average standard of living of the Protestants is taken as a hundred per cent, that of the Catholics is certainly not below eighty per cent. In Algeria there was a much wider gap between the hundred per cent for the French settlers and the ten per cent, at the most, enjoyed by the Arab majority. In Northern Ireland both Protestants and Catholics are predominantly Celts, and both sides think of themselves as Irish. In Algeria a settler population of Caucasians spoke French, while the native population of Arabs and Berbers spoke Arabic; in Northern Ireland, Catholics and Protestants speak the same distinctively accented brand of English.

From a legal and constitutional point of view, Algeria was not a colony. Since 1848 it had been officially part of France, with the three départements of Algiers, Constantine and Oran being theoretically as French as l'Ardèche, la Corrèze or le Lot. The first reaction of the future socialist leader François Mitterrand, on hearing of the rebellion, was to say that it was a matter with which the police would have to deal, as they would with a disturbance anywhere on the territory of France. He was Minister of the Interior at the time. On November 11, 1954 Pierre Mendès-France, the Président du Conseil at the time, said that Algeria was French, and that there could be no question of compromise when one had to defend 'the integrity of the Republic'. It was not until June 10, 1999 that the Socialist government of Lionel Jospin presented the Chambre des Députés with a motion officially recognising that what had always been described as an operation to maintain order had in fact been 'une guerre', and that the expression 'la guerre d'Algérie' could now be officially used.

The insistence that the fighting which took place between 1954 and 1962 was merely part of an operation to maintain order emphasised only the purely legal aspect of the problem. Officially, the policy followed by the French in Algeria was the same as the one theoretically followed in the territories in Equatorial Africa or the Far East which were classified as part of the Empire. The official ideology of French imperialism was that, since French culture is universal, there was no reason why an inhabitant of Algeria, the Congo or Indochina should not become as totally French as a Parisian or a peasant from the Beauce.

It is hard to think that anybody ever really believed that, especially in the light of the severe restrictions placed on anyone not racially French obtaining French citizenship. In 1919, for example, Algerian Arabs who could prove an ability to read and write French were allowed to apply for naturalisation as French citizens and thus to obtain the right to vote in the same elections which sent European *députés* to the Assemblée Nationale in Paris. But they were allowed to do this only if they gave up their status in Islamic law. In 1947 the Fourth Republic introduced a series of reforms which were intended to give equal powers to both communities, but resistance by the European settlers ensured that they were never put into effect.

The popular name of *pieds noirs* bestowed on the French population of Algerians was not intended to suggest that their feet were dirty. The opposite was more likely to be the case, since the term stemmed from the fact that, unlike the native Arab population, who either went barefoot or wore sandals, the Europeans owned boots or shoes. It was, therefore, a sign of the higher economic status enjoyed by the million or so inhabitants of Algeria who were of European stock. Not all were from France itself. A large number were from Spain, the Balearic isles or Malta. But they kept themselves rigorously apart from the Arabs, of whom there were some nine million, and there was little intermarriage.

The Europeans were practising or lapsed Catholics, the Arabs and the Berbers Muslims. The administrative language was French, which many Arabs did not speak. Twenty French children were at school for every ten Arabs, and the teaching was in French. The medical and dental services which existed were for the French, and the two populations voted in separate electoral colleges. The *députés* whom they sent to the National Assembly in Paris represented the interests of the European community.

The situation was the result of a number of political and economic choices made in Paris during the nineteenth century. Like eighteenth-century Australia, French Algeria had begun as a dumping ground for social undesirables. In June 1848 the government of the Second Republic had put down what it saw as an attempt at a violent uprising in Paris, and the rebels who had not been among the ten thousand or so shot by the police and army were transported to Algeria. In 1870 France had been defeated in the war against Prussia and been compelled to hand over to the newly united Germany the two provinces of Alsace and Lorraine. French families who did not want to stay in what then became part of the Second Reich were told that they could go and live in Algeria.

In 1873 the French introduced a system of land tenure into Algeria which, either by design or accident, enabled them to obtain possession of most of the best agricultural land. Until then, the land held by the Arabs had been in the communal possession of their tribe. The introduction of the European system whereby land was the property of named individuals had the effect of dividing these communal lands into portions which were far too small to be economically viable. This enabled the Europeans to buy them up very cheaply and transform them into large landed estates. Between 1878 and 1907 the area of land used for wine-growing increased tenfold, from 17,000 to 177,000 hectares. This increase was partly due to the fact that it was possible to graft on to the vines grown in Algeria new stock imported from California which was immune to phylloxera, and in this respect the possession of Algeria proved the salvation of the French wine-growing industry. But, since the teaching of

Islam forbade the native Arab population to drink wine, this salvation was of little interest to them, especially since the land used to grow grapes was no longer available to grow cereals. As Jean-Paul Sartre pointed out in an article entitled 'Le colonialisme est un système' (Colonialism is a system) in his review *Les Temps Modernes* in April 1956, the production of cereals in Algeria had declined between 1871 and 1945 from five hundredweight for each inhabitant to two. There had been a similar decline in the number of cattle from nine million in 1914 to four million in 1954 – one of the many statistics used by Sartre to illustrate his thesis that the way France had treated Algeria was a classic illustration of Lenin's theory of imperialism.

According to this, the capitalist creates a captive market for himself abroad in which he can sell the goods which his refusal to share his wealth with his own workers prevents him from selling on the home market. Sartre quotes the principal supporter of nineteenth-century French colonialism, Jules Ferry (1832–1893), as describing how France was 'overflowing with capital' and justifying the colonial expansion which also led Ferry to support the French wars of colonial conquest in Indochina and Madagascar on the very Leninist grounds that France needed markets for its products. As a result of the customs union of 1884, by which the Third Republic forbade other countries to sell their goods to Algeria, France created a captive market for herself, and Sartre concluded his account of French economic policy in Algeria by writing:

> The colonial system is thus installed. The French state gives the Arab lands to the French settlers in order to create the purchasing power which will enable the industries of Metropolitan France to sell them their products. The settlers then sell the fruits of the stolen earth on the French Metropolitan market.

EVENTS

Although the rebellion organised by the *Front de Libération Nationale* (FLN) had very little popular support when it was launched on October 31, 1954, it took only two years to cause the French so much trouble that by the summer of 1956 the government was having to keep 500,000 troops in Algeria. Most of these were national servicemen, who would have been in the army anyway and were receiving only a pittance, but the war was still very expensive to run, and by 1956 was estimated to cost £500,000 a day. The figures quoted by Sartre were certainly accurate as far as the general economic relationship between France and Algeria was concerned, especially before 1954. What they did not reveal was that the vast majority of the French population in Algeria had only a slightly lower standard of living than that of their fellow countrymen in France.

They were certainly rich compared to their Arab neighbours – most of whom had the same standard of living as a peasant or unskilled worker in Egypt, Morocco or even India – but the average *pied noir* still belonged to what Marx called the proletariat. He had, in other words, no source of income other than his ability to work. He was not a bloated colonialist living in luxury on the labour of an over-exploited native population.

This meant that the army, which protected the *pieds noirs* against the FLN, enjoyed a high degree of popularity with the European population. It was also, certainly as far as its officer class and crack parachute regiments were concerned, determined to win the war and convinced that it could do so. This determination stemmed in part from their awareness that the French army had not won a war by itself since the campaigns which had preceded the final defeat of Napoleon I. When, in 1870, it had faced the Prussians alone, it had been soundly beaten. Between 1914 and 1918 it won only with British and American help. Like the British army, it been totally routed by the Germans in 1940. It had seen France freed essentially by the Americans, the British and the Canadians, and had then been totally defeated in Indochina. Now, it faced an enemy which it needed to beat in order to fulfil its role of defending the national territory as well as to maintain its reputation. It had also studied the tactics of this enemy and intended to win by turning them against it.

The FLN, whose military wing called itself the *Armée de Libération Nationale* (ALN) had imitated the Viet Minh in studying and digesting the theories of Mao Zedong. It, too, saw the freedom fighter as living among the civilian population like a fish in water, and it, too, saw the armed struggle as the prelude to the assumption of total political power. The French officers, many of whom had had the experience not only of fighting in Indochina but of being held in Viet Minh prison camps after the fall of Dien Bien Phu, were convinced that these tactics could be defeated in two ways.

First of all, they had enough troops at their disposal to divide the country as a whole, as well as each individual town, into sections. Entry and exit to these were rigorously controlled, and anyone looking even vaguely suspect was arrested and tortured. Then the information collected was used to make further arrests, and more particularly to break up the networks by which money was collected by the FLN, often by force, and then used to buy arms. In Indochina, there had been no means of preventing the Viet Minh from moving freely about in the country, and receiving help from outside. In Algeria, an enormous electrified fence known as the *Ligne Morice*, carrying a charge of 5,000 volts, ran the whole length of the frontier with Tunisia. Like the FLN in the towns, the ALN could not move freely within the country and was deprived of support from outside.

Militarily, these tactics had enabled the French to be in the situation where they had won the Algerian war in military terms by the end of 1957. But they lost it politically for three reasons: they never succeeded in complementing their military campaign by winning over the hearts and minds of the Arab population. Like the Americans at the time of the Vietnam war, they faced increasingly vocal opposition both at home and abroad, and in the early summer of 1958 an alliance between the army and the European settlers made what turned out to be the crucial mistake of enabling Charles de Gaulle to come back to power.

The theories of Mao Zedong had convinced the French army that the enemy they faced was an agent of international Communism. This was not true, and de Gaulle knew it. The FLN received very little support from the French Communist Party, and few arms from Moscow. With the influence which *Le Parti Communiste Français* had in the trade union movement, especially in Marseilles, it could have prevented most of the supplies which the French army needed in Algeria from ever leaving France; it never tried to do so. The FLN drew its support from Arab nationalism, a movement which no European power has yet succeeded in defeating.

At home, the opposition to the war was fuelled by a vigorous press campaign in which left-wing journals such *Témoignage Chrétien*, *Les Temps Modernes*, *L'Express* and *France-Observateur* never ceased to highlight the contradictions in French policy. When the FLN left bombs to explode in crowded markets, and used machine-guns to mow down holidaymakers on the beaches, the soldiers on the ground, especially the paratroops and members of the Foreign Legion, saw torture as a natural and justified weapon against terrorism. But to observers at home, who remembered how the Germans had used torture against the resistance movement, the paratroops were making themselves indistinguishable from the Gestapo and the SS. Horrific though the atrocities committed by the FLN undoubtedly were, there was no way in which the techniques adopted by the French army could be justified as a means of defending the values of Western Europe.

Before de Gaulle's return to power in the early summer of 1958, most French politicians followed the example set in 1954 by Mendès-France and Mitterrand when they insisted on its being an integral part of the Republic. But by the spring of 1958 there were enough rumours in political circles in Paris to make the army and settlers suspect that their government might be preparing a sell-out. They decided not to wait, and on May 13, 1958 set up a Committee of Public Safety devoted to the idea of 'L'Algérie Française'. On May 15, while standing on the balcony of the government building overlooking the Forum, General Salan followed the suggestion whispered to him by a civilian activist called Léon Delbecque, and shouted 'Vive de Gaulle'.

THE IMPACT OF DE GAULLE

Although he had played no part in the preparation of what soon became known as *le coup d'état du 13 mai*, de Gaulle almost certainly knew what was happening. On May 19 he held a press conference in which he uttered the significant words that he was 'ready to assume to powers of the Republic'. What he meant by this was that, while he was prepared to take over the leadership of the country, he was not going to follow the example of the three previous military men who had taken power in France at a moment of national crisis. Unlike Napoleon I, Napoleon III and Philippe Pétain, he was not to going to abolish the Republic. On June 1, by 329 votes against 224, and with 32 abstentions, he was appointed Head Of Government, with power to elaborate a new constitution. On September 28, 1958 this received the support of 80 per cent of those who voted in a referendum, and on December 21 de Gaulle was elected President of the Fifth Republic by 78.5 per cent of a specially constituted electoral college.

For the first time in the history of modern Europe a major European power had changed its government as a result of a crisis in one of its colonies and the impact which this crisis had on its armed forces. General Franco, it is true, had used the Spanish colony of Morocco in order to launch his attempted *coup d'état* of July 18, 1936, which set off the Spanish civil war and created a dictatorship which lasted until his death on November 20, 1975. In March 1914 the announcement by a number of army officers at the Curragh barracks in Dublin that they would 'prefer to accept dismissal' rather than impose Home Rule on Ulster had forced Herbert Asquith to postpone implementing the measure. But this did not bring about the resignation of his government. Asquith stayed in power, arranging in the view of the Irish nationalists to divert attention from their problems by involving Great Britain in the First World War. And it took Franco three years' heavy fighting before he could abolish the Republic and replace it by his own authoritarian régime.

For the left-wing politicians and writers who opposed his return to power, and who included François Mitterrand and Pierre Mendès-France, de Gaulle's character and personality could lead him to behave in only one way. They saw him as a military man, a nationalist, a conservatively-minded Catholic, who would do everything he could to try to keep Algeria French. His supporters among the army and European settlers, as well as on the political right in France itself, saw him in exactly the same light. But what the left feared and rejected, the right hoped for and applauded. They would have quite happily accepted the restrictions on freedom of expression which might have been necessary to keep Algeria French, and which the left saw as the greatest danger accompanying de Gaulle's return to power.

In the event, de Gaulle disappointed his supporters, though without endearing himself to those whose policy he eventually carried out. In June 1958, and again in August 1959, he visited Algeria, the first Head of State ever to do so – and the first well-known French politician since the day when the socialist Prime Minister Guy Mollet had been pelted with rotten tomatoes in the streets of Algiers on February 6, 1956 by European demonstrators afraid he might sell them down the river to the FLN. On his first visit, on June 4, 1958, de Gaulle had expressed himself with what appeared at the time to be admirable clarity when he told an enthusiastic crowd of Arabs and Europeans massed in the Forum of Algiers 'Algériens, je vous ai compris' (Algerians, I have understood you). What he seemed to be saying was that he had understood their desire to remain French, and intended to satisfy it. What he turned out to have meant was that, while he understood them, what they wanted was not going to be possible.

On September 16, 1959 he gave a television address in which he proposed three possible solutions to the Algerian problem: secession, total integration with France, and what he called 'l'association'. In spite of his obvious preference for the third solution, his speech marked the beginning of the end of 'L'Algérie Française'. This finally came about on July 1, 1962, but only after a set of dramatic events which brought France nearer to civil war than at any time since 1945. There had already, in January 1960, been a violent protest in Algiers by European activists who had now become hostile to de Gaulle, and which had caused at least 24 deaths and over 200 wounded. Then, on April 21, 1961, a group of four French Generals, Raoul Salan, Maurice Challe, André Zeller and Edmond Jouhaud, tried to seize power in Algiers and called upon the rest of the army to support them.

This attempt at a new *coup d'état du 13 mai* failed partly because there was no second de Gaulle waiting in the wings. The rebellious generals seemed uncertain of what they really wanted, and they could not rival the authority and prestige of a de Gaulle appearing on the television, in uniform, and calling upon the army to obey him and not the generals. It did so, and within five days the attempted rebellion collapsed. It failed, and not only because the generals had no clear plan of action and little standing outside the army. Their defeat was also the result of a recent technological development in broadcasting. In the old days the officers would have decided when to switch the radio on, and which news bulletins to allow their men to follow. Now, each private soldier had immediate access to his own personal and independent source of information in the form of the newly invented transistor radio.

Since the majority of French soldiers serving in Algeria were young men doing their national service, they all had the same ambition: to return home as soon as possible as undamaged ex-servicemen. The transistors not only enabled them to hear what de Gaulle was saying. They also made it possible for them to follow the reactions to his speech in France itself. It was the support given to de Gaulle by politicians, by trade union leaders and by the press, and which everyone could hear about on their transistors, which encouraged the French national servicemen to disobey the career officers who wanted them to follow the lead of what de Gaulle scornfully referred to as 'un quarteron de généraux en retraite' (a four-some of retired generals). Neither the French national servicemen, nor de Gaulle himself, believed the claim put forward by Salan, Challe, Jouhaud and Zeller that to abandon Algeria would mean handing over the whole of north Africa to the Soviet Union. Paradoxically, the greatest victory which de Gaulle won in the whole of his lifetime was over the French professional army, the body to which he had belonged from 1909 to 1940, and to which he had devoted the whole of the first part of his professional life.

Except for the Algerians themselves, the end of French Algeria turned out to be an unmixed blessing, though one which the French people living in Algeria found fairly heavily disguised at the time. The leaders of the French settlers in Algeria had told their followers that a victory for the FLN would mean that their only choice lay between the coffin and the suitcase. This seemed a fair summary of the situation, and, even before Algeria became an independent Democratic People's Republic on July 3, 1962, a movement had begun which brought some 800,000 Europeans who had never lived anywhere but in Algeria to France. By a stroke of economic providence, there was at the time virtually no unemployment anywhere in Western Europe. It was the beginning of the great economic boom of the 1960s, one of whose results was that the people who were rather oddly referred to as 'des rapatriés' were absorbed without difficulty into a hungry labour market.

Since they tended, like most minorities, to be hard-working and enterprising, their arrival added considerably to the prosperity of France. Insofar as the Algeria which they left behind has become gradually and apparently irreversibly poorer, it is tempting to quote the end of French Algeria as one of the many examples of how disastrous it is for any country to expel one of its minorities. Louis XIV provided one of the first of these examples in 1685 when he revoked the Edict of Nantes and drove out the Huguenots, who then proceeded to take their skills as weavers and merchants to England and Holland. The Tsars and Hitler did the same with the Jews, who then helped to give America the lead in military technology which enabled it to beat both the Third Reich and the Soviet Union. Idi Amin did it in 1972 when he expelled the Asian business community in Uganda, making his country even poorer and providing the United Kingdom with a new group of hard-working and enterprising citizens.

The comparison is not, however, an entirely convincing one. The French-speaking settlers in Algiers constituted a privileged minority devoted to fostering its own interests. Any benefits which their presence produced for the Arab community were very indirect. If they existed at all, they stemmed from the same 'trickle-down' effect by which the wealth of the privileged middle class in Western countries is said to produce long-term benefits for the poor. This is not a theory for which there is much hard evidence, and it was not until the FLN began its rebellion that the French state began to organise a programme of economic help aimed specifically at the Arab community. By the time what was known as the Plan de Constantine was inaugurated in 1960, it was too late.

The ethnologist Germaine Tillion argued that the French had the duty not to leave the Algerians, as she put it, 'au milieu du gué' (halfway across the stream). Having destroyed its original economy and launched Algeria into the modern, industrialised world, they ought to have seen the process through. But this could only have been achieved if the French-speaking minority in Algeria had stayed to help, and there are a number of reasons why this was not possible. They were, to begin with, so unpopular with the Algerians that they would have been lucky, had they stayed, to have avoided the fate of the Jews in Nazi Germany. Another reason lies in one of the main explanations why the inhabitants of Western Europe, like those of North America and Australasia, have come to enjoy the highest standard of living in history. They have learned to control their own fertility.

This may, if present trends continue, have the ultimately disastrous effect of transforming Europe into an underpopulated area in which there are not enough young and middle-aged workers to support a steadily increasing population of old people. For a population to stay at the same level, it must have a fertility rate of 2.1 children per woman. Expressed differently, this means that nine out of ten women must have two children, and one out of ten must have three. At the moment, the average for Western Europe is 1.6, which is clearly not enough. But for the moment, it is fine: there are not too many mouths to feed, and production can more than satisfy demand. The women and men who made birth control technically possible and socially acceptable are among the greatest benefactors of mankind, their achievement far surpassing that of any founder of any religion, of any charitable worker, priest or speculative philosopher. The only disadvantage is that the benefits they have produced have not been spread evenly over the globe.

This has not been because Western Europeans have conspired to keep their former empires in a state of perpetual and inescapable poverty. It is not they who have refused to share with their former overseas subjects the moral and social acceptability of artificial birth control, or who have kept secret the techniques which make it possible. It is their former subjects who have been either unwilling or unable to accept the need to limit population growth. The interdict which Islam places on the use of chemical or mechanical techniques of birth control is as fatal to human happiness and prosperity as the ban imposed by the Roman Catholic Church. It also has the additional disadvantage of being more effectively enforced.

This fact alone makes it unlikely that the population growth in Algeria will ever be brought under control, and here again Western Europe has an immense advantage over most of its former colonies, whether in Africa or Central and South America. This advantage lies in the fact that it has effectively abolished the ability of organised religion to tell people how to order their sexual lives. The growth of the secular state may or may not have led to a higher incidence of extramarital activity. The fading of religious belief may or may not have contributed to the unhappiness produced by the breakdown of the traditional family. What is certain is that the easy availability of efficient contraceptives has had two enormous benefits. It has enabled more people to enjoy sex than at any period in history since the arrival of Christianity. And it has also saved the inhabitants of Europe, as it has saved their descendants in North America and Australasia, from ruining their health, destroying their wealth and endangering the stability of their society by breeding more people than their economy can support or their countries can conveniently contain.

In 1962 the Arab-speaking population of Algeria already numbered almost 10 million. Demographers could predict that nothing short of a series of natural disasters of appallingly unimaginable dimensions could prevent it from rising, as it did, to over 26 million by 1993 and to almost 30 million by 1998. There was no way in which the 60 million inhabitants of France could have been persuaded to make the effort and sacrifices essential if the standard of living of the Algerians was to be brought up to their level. Neither is there any guarantee that they would have succeeded if they had tried. The problem which all decolonised countries face is that there seems to be no means of limiting a country's population growth unless its inhabitants start to become rich, and no way in which they can start to become rich unless population growth is brought under control. In Algeria 300,000 young people come on to the labour market every year, and there is no work for them. Unlike that of France, the former colonising power, the population of Algeria has not grown richer.

One of the arguments put forward in France by supporters of the policy of 'L'Algérie Française' was that the Saharan desert hid vast resources of oil, which France would be foolish to give up. In the 1970s this looked for a time to have been quite a good reason for hanging on to Algeria. The French were made to realise by the OPEC price rises that they had no oil of their own, and had been obliged to console themselves with the slogan that they had lots of ideas. But the gradual decline of the price of oil has meant that Algeria has lost its principal source of hard currency, and the increased poverty which this has entailed has been accompanied by a civil war which seemed, at one point, capable of rivalling the war of national liberation of 1954–1962, at least in brutality if not in the actual number of victims.

The two sides in this civil war are the official government, with its attachment to the idea of Algeria as a secular state, and the Islamic Salvation Front, with its aim of making Algeria into an Islamic country on the model of Iran or Libya. The conflict had existed in practice for some time in the form of murders and kidnappings carried out by both sides, but came into the open in December/January 1992. Constitutionally, Algeria has tried to adopt the form taken by parliamentary democracy in France. There is a President, directly elected by universal suffrage every five years, and a separately elected parliamentary assembly. In each case, there are two ballots, with a run-off to decide the winner if the first round of voting does not produce a fifty-per-cent majority. In January 1992, when it was obvious from the results in the first round of the parliamentary elections that the second ballot was going to produce a majority for the Islamic Salvation Front, the government simply cancelled the second round.

This set off the war which had, by 1997, produced casualties estimated by Amnesty International as at least 80,000 and by the Islamic Salvation Front at over 100,000. Exact figures, at least as far as the Arabic-speaking population of Algeria is concerned, are even harder to obtain for the war of 1954–1962. According to Le Monde for September 1985, at least 300,000 people were killed, but according to figures given by de Gaulle's son, Admiral Philippe de Gaulle in 1993, up to 600,000. A basic difference between Western Europe and its former colonies comes out in the fact that the casualties on the French side of the Algerian war are known with much greater accuracy: 15,583 soldiers killed by the ALN, 2,278 civilians.[4]

POSTSCRIPT

After the dramas of the Indochinese and Algerian wars, any account of the formal departure of the French from the rest of their African colonies is inevitably something of an anti-climax. Between January 30 and February 8, 1944, a conference took place at Brazzaville, the capital of the French Congo, at which de Gaulle outlined the way in which he saw the future development of what was still officially the French Empire. Initially, it was known as L'Union Française, but in 1958 Article XII of the referendum asking the French whether or not they approved the proposed Constitution of the Fifth Republic invited the member states of the Union to say whether or not they wished to become members of what then became known as *La Communauté Française*.

All said yes except Guinea, which then immediately became independent, with French economic aid being withdrawn overnight. However, by 1960 the Community had ceased to exist in any real sense. Most of its members, such as Chad, Congo, and Gabon, which had earlier formed part of French Equatorial Africa, are now independent states. Others, like Guadeloupe, Martinique or L'Île de la Réunion, became what are known as *Départements d'Outre-Mer*. This entitles them to direct representation in the French National Assembly, and their inhabitants have the right to full French citizenship. Others, such as the Polynesian island of New Caledonia in the Pacific and the North American islands of Saint-Pierre-et-Miquelon off the coast of Newfoundland, are *Territoires d'Outre-Mer*, with more autonomy but without automatic French citizenship. In no case, however, have any of these changes of statute had an impact upon French internal politics, and the links between these countries and France are primarily commercial and cultural.

Culturally, France's former colonies form part of the movement known as La Francophonie, a movement whose main preoccupation is to ensure that as many people as possible speak French, an ambition not necessary to the maintenance of the spontaneously Anglophone Commonwealth. The inclusion of Belgium, Bulgaria, Luxembourg, Romania and Switzerland among the 44 members of La Francophonie also gives it a European air absent from the Commonwealth, while at the same time suggesting that the linguistic criteria for membership are not excessively rigorous. The fact that Burundi, the Congo, Haiti and Rwanda also belong to La Francophonie shows that no rigidly democratic criteria have to be satisfied by countries applying for membership.

12 Portugal, the Netherlands and Belgium

PORTUGAL

The Portuguese were the first European country to extend their authority outside western Europe, and did so to begin with in Africa. It was in 1446 that the navigator Nuno Tristão arrived in what is now Guinea-Bissau on the west African coast, and in 1482 that Portuguese sailors first reached Angola. In 1484 they declared the coastal region a Portuguese colony, and in 1574 gave the whole region the name of Angola, a Europeanised version of the term for a king in that part of Africa, *N'Gola*. Portugal acquired Mozambique after Vasco da Gama had landed in 1498 when seeking to reach India by rounding the Cape, and in 1508 established a colony there. In 1607, faced with opposition from the local emperor, the Portuguese then sent a punitive expedition, and obtained a monopoly for the mining of gold, lead, iron and tin.

After a series of struggles with the Dutch in the eighteenth century, and some verbal disputes with the British in the nineteenth, Portugal achieved international recognition of its African possessions at the Congress of Berlin of November 1884–February 1885. Just as Pope Alexander VI had divided the New World between Spain and Portugal by the Treaty of Tordesillas of June 7, 1494, so the fifteen European nations invited by Bismarck to Berlin in 1884 agreed on how Africa should be split up between them. Portugal was confirmed in its possession of Angola and was to maintain its rule over its 8–9 million inhabitants for the next eighty years.

Portugal's neutrality during both World Wars enabled it to avoid the spread of many of the ideas which had provided the starting point for the Algerian rebellion of 1954, and until the rebellions broke out in Guinea-Bissau, Angola and Mozambique in the late 1950s and early 1960s its colonies were the only section of the Portuguese economy which regularly made a profit. On January 16, 1950 it decided that Angola, together with Macao, Mozambique and São Tomé would become overseas provinces, and the official doctrine was that, since the long term aim was the assimilation of the Africans into what was presented to them as the higher civilisation of Western Europe, there was no racial discrimination.

This was nowhere truer than it was in the French colonies in Africa and Asia. By 1961 only about one per cent of the Africans in Angola, Guinea-Bissau and Mozambique had attained the status of *assimilados*, which gave them legal equality with the citizens of Portugal. For all its imperfections, the British experience of decolonisation suggests that a policy based upon an open recognition of differences has more chance of succeeding than one based on the abstract belief that all human beings are basically the same. Although the West Indians were initially allowed to take part in cricket matches only as fielders, the game eventually became even more popular with them than with the English, whom they regularly beat. So, too, do the Australians, the Indians, the Pakistanis and the South Africans. No other imperial power has left the inhabitants of its former colonies playing its national game. No other country has acquired so wide an experience as England of ending up on the losing side when taking part at an international level in the games which it invented.

The fighting which finally compelled the Portuguese to abandon their African colonies began in Guinea-Bissau in August 1959, in Angola on February 4, 1961, and in Mozambique on September 25, 1964. In each country it took the Portuguese by surprise, perhaps an indication that they had made the fatal mistake of believing their own propaganda. Since they had fewer than 3,000 troops in Angola, and none in Guinea-Bissau, the initial reaction of the Portuguese in February 1961 was to launch a series of air strikes, which are said to have killed some 30,000 Africans between August and September 1961.[1] By 1970 the Portuguese found themselves required to keep over 150,000 men in Africa, and by the time the war ended in August 1974, 11,000 Portuguese soldiers had been killed and 30,000 wounded or disabled. Figures for the rest of the fighting suggest a total of over half a million Africans killed before Portugal officially gave its former colonies their independence on November 10, 1974.

As in the case of the Algerian war of 1954–1962, there was thus an immense discrepancy between the number of Europeans who lost their lives and the number of what it was still acceptable, in the 1960s, to refer to as natives. But Portugal, at the time, had a population of less than nine million, so that its losses expressed as a proportion of its total population were much higher than those of France in Algeria or the United States in Vietnam. In the Algerian war, 15,583 French soldiers were killed at a time when the total population of metropolitan France was just over 55 million. The United States, with a population of 180 million, had 57,978 soldiers killed in Vietnam. Because of the relatively modest rank which it occupies in the world of the late twentieth century, it is easy to forget how large an empire Portugal once possessed. Because the wars which it fought in an attempt to retain this empire took place so far from Europe, and at a time when the world's attention was so taken up with the Cold War, it is equally easy to forget how long these wars lasted and how costly they were for the countries involved.

Just as by 1957 the French had succeeded in winning the Algerian war in purely military terms, so the Portuguese army by the early 1970s had produced what Ian Beckett calls 'stalemate' in Angola, and 'low-intensity stalemate' in Guinea-Bissau. There were more problems in Mozambique, where 60,000 of the 150,000 Portuguese soldiers stationed were fighting, but where the rebellion could probably have been defeated if there had been the political will to do so. But the bulk of the Portuguese army, like the majority of the French soldiers in Algeria, were conscripts, a fact which increased the unpopularity of the war at home. And although it was, in Portugal, as in France, an action carried out by the army which finally had the effect of bringing its last colonial war to an end, the initial aims of the soldiers were totally different in Portugal from what they had been in France.

On May 13, 1958 in Algiers the ambition of the French officers who supported the French-speaking settlers was to keep Algeria French. They made the mistake, as has been seen, of lending their support to the return to power of Charles de Gaulle, who proceeded to disappoint them in every respect. In Portugal the rebellion of the armed forces set out to achieve the totally opposite objective of putting an end not only to the fighting in Africa but to the history of Portugal as a colonial power. This revolt took place on April 25, 1974, after General Antonio de Spínola, a former military governor of the Portuguese colony of Guinea-Bissau, had published a book under the title *Portugal and its Future* in which he argued that there was no way of putting an end by military force to the wars which had been going on for over fifteen years in the three colonies of Angola, Guinea-Bissau and Mozambique.

The government refused to accept his view that the only solution was a negotiated settlement, and dismissed him. His fellow officers rallied to his support, seeking, as they put it, to 'save the nation from the government'. In three dramatic months what was known as 'the carnation revolution' put an end at one at the same time to the right-wing régime which dated back to the assumption of power on July 7, 1932 of António de Oliveira Salazar and to the Portuguese empire. The carnations which the people in the street handed to the soldiers in order to express their gratitude, and which gave their name to what turned out to be one of the most peaceful revolutions in the history of Western Europe, also celebrated the end of the longest record of any European county as a colonialist power. By 1975 the Portuguese had been in Africa for 320 years.

The régime inaugurated by Salazar in 1932 was officially known as the *Estado Nuevo*. In the 1930s it had succeeded in its ambition of keeping Portugal as an authoritarian, corporatist state, and thus provided a model for Franco's Spain. As in Spain, the régime had been successful in keeping the country out of the Second World War, and Salazar's government had enjoyed the additional advantage of not being preceded by the kind of civil war set off by Franco's unsuccessful attempt at a *coup d'état* on July 18, 1936. When Salazar retired in 1968, after the longest period in power of any politician in twentieth-century Europe, he was succeeded by a trusted subordinate, Marcello Caetano, who gave little sign of wanting to make the régime more liberal. It was the trauma created by its attempt to hold on to its African colonies by force, coupled with the rebellion of the officer corps inspired by Spínola's protest against the wars in Mozambique, Guinea-Bissau and Angola, which brought the régime down.

As in France, it was a close-run thing. Without de Gaulle, the *coup d'état du 13 mai* could well have set off a civil war between supporters and opponents of 'L'Algérie Française'. In Portugal the 'carnation revolution' of 1974 came near to being hijacked by an alliance between the extreme left and the Communist Party. It was only an agreement between the newly elected President, General da Costa Gomes and the socialist leader, Mario Soares which prevented the Communist Party from carrying out a *coup d'état* on November 25, 1975. But there were few casualties in the long series of demonstrations and counter-demonstrations which preceded and accompanied the first free elections to take place in Portugal for fifty years. These were held on April 25, 1976 and initially produced a series of left-wing governments which tried to solve the country's problems by a programme of large-scale nationalisations.

However, neither these measures nor the confiscation of 600,000 hectares of land as the first step in the establishment of a nationally controlled agricultural system proved either effective or popular. In August 1976 this land was handed back to its original owners, and a further step away from what was then the ideology of large sections of the European left was taken on February 25, 1977 when Portugal put in its first application to join the European Communities. Because the Socialist Party, led by Mario Soares, received only thirty-five per cent of the vote in the April 1976 elections, it could form only a minority government. This did not last, and there followed a long series of political crises which led to the holding of new elections in December 1979 and again in October 1980. Although there was, by that time, sufficient unanimity for Portugal to become a member of the European Communities, alongside Spain, on January 1, 1986, it was only in July 1987 that the Social Democrats, headed by Aníbal Cavaco Silva, were able to form a government with an absolute majority.

They proceeded to follow what by then had become the widely accepted policy of privatisation. What had seemed, between 1974 and 1976, to be the strong possibility of Portugal becoming a left-wing republic disappeared to the point that, when the new Constitution was finally approved on August 8, 1988, it was simply referred to as a Republic, with no mention of the word 'socialist'. Although the Socialist Party headed by António Guterres came to power as a result of the elections of October 1995, it showed no more sign of being interested in widespread nationalisation than the French Socialist Party headed by Lionel Jospin, or the Labour Party of Tony Blair. It was happy to carry out the 'bankers' agenda' needed for Portugal to become one of the eleven member states of the European Union to adopt the European single currency on January 1, 1999, and thus to fix the value of the escudo irrevocably against that of the Euro.

The fact that Portugal currently has one of the most successful economies in the European Union is another sign of how lasting the advantages have been of its abandonment in 1974 of its African empire. Although the Economic Intelligence Unit has scaled down the government's estimated growth rate from 3.8 per cent to 2.99 per cent, it remains one of the highest in Western Europe. Inflation is down to 2.7 per cent, and only 5 per cent of the working population is unemployed. This compares very favourably with that of France, the other European country to have had trouble decolonising, which has 11.7 per cent of its workforce unemployed, as well as with Germany, which currently has 11.1 per cent.

The advantage which Portugal acquired from its long history as a colonial power has thus been an exemplary as well as a paradoxical one. It has become, through the loss of its empire, a stable parliamentary democracy whose economic performance is steadily improving. So, too, has France, which acquired with the return to power of Charles de Gaulle in May 1958 the most stable parliamentary régime in its history. During the three centuries in which it exercised effective control over Angola, Mozambique and Guinea-Bissau, Portugal had access to considerable resources in copper, bauxite, diamonds, iron ore, minerals and uranium. It nevertheless remained one of the poorest countries in Western Europe, though with less disastrous long-term consequences than those which have afflicted its former colonies.

These have taken what is now the depressingly familiar form of a series of civil wars, made more destructive than the one currently raging in the former French Algeria by the intervention of outside powers. Mozambique, described in the 1999 edition of *Quid* as the poorest country in the world, lost 2,057 soldiers, killed in the ten years' fighting which began in September 1964 and led to its independence on June 25, 1975. But the civil war which followed, in which the Marxist *Frente de*

Libertação de Moçambique (Mozambique National Liberation Front, FRELIMO) was opposed by the *Resistência Nacional Moçambicana* (Mozambique National Resistance, RENAMO) is said to have caused at least half a million deaths. RENAMO was a right-wing movement, financed and armed by an alliance between Ian Smith's government in Rhodesia and what was then the *apartheid* régime in South Africa. The ferocity of its attacks on the FRELIMO régime, inspired by the fear that its ideas and example might spread to the white-dominated countries of Rhodesia and South Africa, is a reminder of how relatively moderate and inefficient the Portuguese attempt to hang on to that part of its African empire had been. Had outside intervention taken place earlier, the situation might have become as catastrophic before 1975 as it has done in Angola since that country attained formal independence.

Angola has an annual inflation rate of a hundred per cent. Its heavy dependence on oil, a commodity whose price is steadily falling, suggests that matters are unlikely to improve. In Angola and Mozambique the experience both of empire itself and of its aftermath reinforced the view that it would – for the rest of the world, if not for themselves – have been better if the Europeans had never left home. Although the former Portuguese colony of Guinea-Bissau won its independence on September 10, 1974 with what was, compared to events elsewhere, remarkably little bloodshed. This does not, however, invalidate the general rule whereby the advantages of decolonisation, like those of the colonisation which preceded it, have gone exclusively to the Western European coloniser.

THE NETHERLANDS

Indonesia, a country with a population of now almost two hundred million spread out over 13,000 islands, began to be colonised by the Dutch in 1602. In 1667 they took possession of Surinam, which then became Dutch Guyana, the scene of one of the most telling incidents in Voltaire's *Candide* (1769). This takes place when the hero and his companion Cacambo come across a negro who has lost his right hand and left leg. He explains to them that his hand had been cut off, in accordance with established custom, when it caught in the millstone grinding the sugar cane. When he had then tried to escape, and was caught, his leg was cut off in accordance with a similar custom. The whole early history of Europe's relationship with the Third World is summed up in his comment 'C'est à ce prix-là que vous mangez du sucre en Europe' ('That's the price to be paid for you to eat sugar in Europe).

It is an incident which could well have taken place in the eighteenth century almost anywhere on the continent of South America, where the early cultivation of coffee in Brazil was carried on almost exclusively by slaves taken there from one of the Portuguese colonies in Africa. In

Indonesia, which in 1823 became an official part of the Kingdom of the Netherlands, the treatment of the native population was less inhumane, principally because of the reasons for its being colonised. As in the earliest days of European expansion, the interest of the Dutch was in the spice trade, an activity which did not involve either the attempt to settle Europeans in lands overseas or the use of forced labour.

Decolonisation, when it came, was thus relatively easy, and the Dutch took less time than any other country in Western Europe to free themselves from what, in 1900, had been the third-largest colonial empire in the world, after those of Great Britain and France, but containing more people than those under the rule of Portugal. In 1945 these were mostly concentrated in what was still known as the Dutch East Indies, which then had a population of 65 million. Dutch Guyana, still referred to in some books as Surinam, was also still part of the Empire, but gradually evolved to the point where, in 1975, it received full independence.

This had been preceded, in 1949, by the establishment of universal suffrage, and in 1954 the territory had been made an autonomous part of the Kingdom of the Netherlands. The granting of independence on November 25, 1975 had been accompanied by a contribution towards its future economic development of $1.5 million from the Netherlands, but the fact that over 100,000 people out of a total population of under half a million chose to take advantage of the Dutch citizenship which they still enjoyed as subjects of Queen Juliana of the Netherlands led to the unusual phenomenon in a former European colony of an acute shortage of labour.

There are a number of reasons for the fact that the Dutch had fewer problems than the Portuguese or the French in decolonising after the Second World War. The Netherlands had, since the seventeenth century, been a byword for intellectual, political and religious toleration. The size of its country had precluded it from pursuing the kind of foreign policy associated with the Germany of Wilhelm II and Adolf Hitler, and it had none of the acute divisions which, in Belgium, continue to set the French-speaking Walloons against the native speakers of Flemish. It had also avoided the kind of quarrels which used to set Catholics against Republicans in what the French call *les guerres franco-françaises* (the wars of the French against the French), which they sometimes take an almost perverse delight in presenting as an integral part of their history.

There had, it is true, been a home-grown Nazi Party in the Netherlands in the 1930s, which between 1940 and 1944 had helped the Germans to send Jews to the gas chambers. But the Dutch government itself had not collaborated. Although Queen Wilhemina had been forced to seek refuge in Great Britain, she had steadfastly supported the resistance movement, which had organised a number of successful strikes against the German occupying forces. There had been no equivalent to the Vichy régime, whose readiness to collaborate with the Germans had led to the situation where the conflict between the official French state and the resistance movement had been one of the worst of *les guerres franco-françaises*. In 1948, with great dignity, Queen Wilhelmina had abdicated in favour of her daughter Juliana, who in her turn vacated the throne in favour of her eldest daughter Beatrix in 1980.

Initially, it is true, there had been one or two vigorously mounted 'police actions' against the rebels in Indonesia. But these had been so universally condemned by public opinion in the world at large, and more especially by Australia and India, that the Dutch government agreed in August 1949 to hold a conference at The Hague to discuss the future of Indonesia. It still remains significant that the Dutch yielded to international pressure without too much reluctance, something which the French steadfastly refused to do in Algeria, and the Portuguese in Angola and Mozambique.

Only the five countries of Belgium, France, Great Britain, Portugal and the Netherlands were involved in the process of Western European decolonisation. It is therefore difficult on purely statistical grounds to say that monarchies have tended to do better than republics. In spite of the problems which culminated in Belgium in the abdication in July 1951 of Leopold III, it might be argued that the countries which have remained monarchies have done so because they have already solved their main political problems. Although no Scandinavian country has been faced with the trauma of decolonisation, further evidence of the advantages of monarchism might be found in the history of Norway, Sweden, and Denmark. It is also perhaps significant that twentieth-century Spain has never been so much at ease with itself politically as since Juan Carlos succeeded to the throne on the death in 1975 of Franco.

The Dutch also replied swiftly to the invitation to take part in the process of European unification which began with the signature of the Treaty of Paris of April 18, 1951 establishing the European Coal and Steel Community. Their long and successful history as a trading nation had made them aware of the benefits of free trade, and they had already established, on January 1, 1948, the Benelux Customs Union with Belgium and Luxembourg. The loss of empire had been less traumatic for them than it was to prove for the French, and they did not need to seek consolation in the subsequent establishment of the European Economic Community for political failure in their relationship with countries outside Western Europe. The history of the Netherlands, like that of other Western European countries which have given up their overseas empire, has served to underline the lesson that the sooner you get out the better – for you if not necessarily for the people you leave behind.

Politically, the history of Indonesia since independence has not been a happy one. The reign of its first President, Achmed Sukarno, was marked by the introduction of what was known as 'Guided Democracy', the increasing influence of the army, and a policy of confrontation with Malaysia over the possession of the territory of Sabah and Sarawak, in north Borneo. In the absence of any effective machinery for a party wishing to pursue an alternative policy, Sukarno was overthrown in a military *coup* by Raden Suharto, and he ruled until overthrown by a largely student-led protest movement in May 1998.

It was a movement set off by the dramatic effects on Indonesia of the apparent collapse of what had been known until then as the 'tiger economies' of south-east Asia, a collapse which seemed at the time to call into question the validity of one of the most frequently made comparisons between the formerly colonised countries of Asia and those in Africa. Because, it was claimed, countries such as Malaysia, or island states such as Hong Kong, Singapore and Taiwan, had a long history of a highly sophisticated civilisation behind them, they possessed a degree of intellectual and social awareness which enabled them to adjust rapidly to the modern commercial and industrialised world. In Africa, in contrast, where the Europeans had found much less developed cultures on their arrival, a comparable adaptation had not taken place for that very reason. Africans had also, it was argued, a much less developed trading tradition than the countries of the Far East, where the Chinese diaspora had already created a well-developed network of communities linked together by a common language as well as by the idea of making a profit. The impact of Europe was thus in a way beneficial to certain Asian countries, hastening a process which needed only a stimulus from outside to set off a whole process of modernisation.

The speed with which the tiger economies began to recover from the crash of 1998 suggests that they possess a dynamism which will enable at least part of this generalisation to remain true. It may, as in South Korea, be a dynamism which owes a good deal to the impact of America and Japan, and thus have relatively little to do with the direct impact of Western Europe. But elsewhere in Asia, as in the whole of Africa, it is hard to see how either the arrival or the departure of the Europeans have brought any real benefits to the native population. Only in India does a democratic process which would be recognised as such at Westminster or on Capitol Hill seem to work in the way intended. Only in India has the army stayed out of politics, and only in India has the British legacy of a neutral and incorruptible civil service survived after independence. But India remains desperately poor. Although now in possession of its own nuclear weapons, it is barely able to feed its population of 970 million; Pakistan, still ruled by the army, has long been in a similar plight.

When the financial crisis of 1998 led to the overthrow in May of

President Suharto, he left as his principal legacy to Indonesia an almost complete political vacuum.

BELGIUM

Belgium was one of the states which received most territory when the fifteen major European powers answered Bismarck's invitation to meet in Berlin between November 1884 and February 1885 in order to prevent what was known as 'the scramble for Africa' from degenerating into war between them. An area eighty times the size of Belgium itself was declared to be the personal possession of King Leopold II (1835–1909), who therefore had sole right to its vast resources of ivory, minerals and rubber.

In spite of his earlier initiative in establishing in 1876 the *Association Internationale Africaine*, with the proclaimed aim of 'opening Africa to civilisation and abolishing slavery', Leopold proved a totally selfish and irresponsible ruler. The treatment of the forty million or so African natives by the Belgian authorities was, if anything, worse than in the days of slavery. The details made public in 1904 by Sir Roger Casement (1864–1916), the British consular official shot in 1916 for alleged high treason, resulted in a campaign being launched against Leopold II in Great Britain and the United States of America.

This culminated, in 1908, in his being required to hand over his possessions in Africa to the Belgian state. But it turned out that its officials had not read 'The White Man's Burden' either, and the change did not lead to any great improvement in the treatment of the Africans. It was not until 1956 that a small number of Africans – referred to, as they were in French colonial territories, as 'des évolués' – were given the vote, and no attempt had been made to train either military officers or civilian administrators to take over the country when the Belgians suddenly left on June 30, 1960. When the country was then declared independent, it rapidly subsided into chaos and civil war. The existence of some three hundred different tribes meant that there was no basis for any kind of ethnic unity, and the political departure of the Belgians did not mean that they had given up their economic interests in the region. On July 11, 1960 the mineral-rich province of Katanga seceded, theoretically under the leadership of Moïse Tshombe but in fact at the instigation of white mercenaries in the pay of the Belgian-controlled mining company *Union Minière*.

The intervention of the United Nations may have been successful in 1960 in preventing the former Belgian Congo from becoming one of the battlefields outside Europe where, as in Indochina, the Cold War turned hot. Although Katanga's secession officially ended on January 14, 1963, the Congo itself continued to slide into the situation where it became one of the most tragic illustrations of the problems which the European colonisers left behind them. In 1971 it changed its name to Zaïre, and undertook a programme of extensive nationalisation. In 1976 this was abandoned, and sixty per cent of the companies originally nationalised were given back to their original owners. This did not bring about any improvement in the economic situation, and a currency reform in 1992 introduced a new zaïre whose value corresponded to that of three million former zaïres. Civil war is endemic, and there seems to be no way of ending it.

Belgium, in the meantime, has continued to be one of the most economically successful countries in Western Europe. Since 1966 its capital, Brussels, has housed the Headquarters of the North Atlantic Treaty Organisation, and it was chosen from the beginning as the administrative centre for the European Economic Community. Had Belgium tried to hold on to its African empire, it might not have enjoyed these advantages, which do a great deal to compensate for the virulence of the divisions between the Walloon and Flemish sections of the population. It might or might not, had it made more of an effort to prepare the Congolese for independence, have avoided the disasters which followed its departure in 1960. There is little support for such an idea in the history of the other countries in Africa where the colonial power did show a greater sense of responsibility.

Thus the British left no firmer legacy of parliamentary government in Africa than did the Portuguese, the Belgians or the French. The civil wars now raging in Uganda or Sierra Leone, territories once under British control, are just as disastrous as the fighting going on in the former Portuguese colonies of Angola or Mozambique, the former Belgian Congo or the countries which once made up French Equatorial Africa. The only difference is that, while the British extricated themselves from Africa without very much bloodshed and with no impact on the domestic politics of the United Kingdom, the French and Portuguese managed to do so only by changing their political systems. This does not, however, add much support to the view that this happened because the English are good at politics and had constructed a set of political conventions in the British Isles which enabled them to take the strain of losing their empire without too much difficulty. After all, the Belgians gave up their empire without any problems – as far as their domestic politics were concerned anyway.

the orders came from a Conservative government. There was never the same kind of popular opposition among the British population at large to the fighting in Malaysia as there was to be in France and Portugal to the savage wars of peace in Indochina, Algeria, Angola, Mozambique and Guinea-Bissau that helped to bring about the end of the French and Portuguese empires. It was not until the Suez expedition of 1956 that the national unity which had been both the result and a cause of the victory of 1945 broke down in the United Kingdom.

SUEZ

Between 1859 and 1869 French engineers under the direction of the ingenious and polyphiloprogenitive Ferdinand de Lesseps (1805–1869)[2] constructed the Suez canal, linking the Mediterranean to the Red Sea and thus to the Indian Ocean. The project ran into financial difficulties, and in November 1875 the British Prime Minister Benjamin Disraeli (1804–1881) purchased forty per cent of the shares in the Suez Canal Company, whose headquarters remained in Paris. It was Disraeli's contention that, while everybody liked flattery, when dealing with royalty you should lay it on with a trowel, and one of his motives in thus obtaining a controlling interest in the Canal became clear in 1876 when he persuaded the House of Commons to bestow upon Queen Victoria the title of Empress of India. The 'jewel in the crown' was now far more accessible to ships sailing from England than it had been in the days when they had to make the long voyage round the Cape.

It is, from this point of view, ironic that the one unsuccessful military campaign fought by the British armed forces after 1945 should have been aimed at maintaining control over a waterway whose principal economic and military interest for the United Kingdom had disappeared when India became independent on August 15, 1947. It is this fact, among others, which makes the fiasco of the Suez expedition of October 1956 so much a watershed in the political as well as the military history of the United Kingdom.

After it, Great Britain could no longer be taken seriously in its claim to be a Great Power. It was, as its request to join the European Community five years later was to show, at best a medium-sized power whose political future lay in the hands of others. In internal politics, the failure of Great Britain to impose its will on Egypt also marked the beginning of a fundamental change in the Conservative Party. Except perhaps at the time of the Falklands War of 1982, it was to base its appeal to the electorate on prosperity at home. Imperial greatness abroad was no longer on the agenda.

Neither France nor Israel, Britain's allies in the attack on Egypt, was affected in the same way. The Suez expedition was seen by the French as a logical extension of the war against the FLN and of the attempt to defend 'l'Algérie Française'. Israel's attack on Egypt on October 29, 1956 marked the beginning of the second of the four wars in which it successfully defended itself against Arab attempts to destroy it. There again, it was justified as a defensive war against an enemy which already existed.

In neither France nor Israel was there the same intense opposition to the Suez expedition as showed itself in Great Britain. The few politicians who were openly against the policy of 'L'Algérie Française' merely needed to extend their existing opposition to what France was trying to do against Egypt. Most, however, supported the undertaking, and it is significant that the clandestine meeting to finalise arrangements should have been held at the Château de Sèvres, near Paris, between October 22 and October 24, 1956.

Only in the United Kingdom did the Suez expedition raise the question of the kind of society its citizens wanted to live in, and how they wanted it to behave. It did so, moreover, in a way which remains as disturbing in retrospect as it was at the time. The self-confidence which had helped the British give independence to India had disappeared, to be replaced by the racialist jingoism that inspired the young miner who commented after it was all over 'We should have gone right on in there. But this country isn't capable of it any more. Not even against the bloody wogs.'[3]

Rumblings of what might be going to happen had already been heard two years earlier in the protests from the right wing of the Conservative Party against the Anglo-Egyptian Treaty of October 19, 1954 agreeing to withdraw within two years the last units of the troops who had been guarding the Canal since 1882. Because of the importance of the Suez Canal as the route through which most of its oil came to Great Britain, Egypt had been the scene of some of the fiercest fighting in the Second World War. It was there that the British Eighth Army finally defeated Rommel at El Alamein between October 23 and November 28, 1943. Memories of what Churchill called 'the end of the beginning' were still sufficiently alive to create the feeling that a victory against a much more formidable foe could easily be repeated against obviously inferior, non-European opposition.

A number of Conservative members of parliament, known as the Suez Rebels, had gone so far as to vote against the government when it had been agreed to withdraw British troops from the Canal Zone in October 1954. It was their attitude which came to the fore when on 27 July, 1956, six weeks after the last British troops left Egypt on June 13, President Nasser nationalised the Suez Canal. Technically, he was in the wrong, since the concession which had originally enabled the Canal to be built was not due to expire until 1968. But he had just undergone what he saw, perhaps rightly, as the deliberate humiliation of seeing the loan he had obtained from the International Monetary Fund to construct the Aswan Dam cancelled as a result of joint pressure by the British and American governments. He therefore needed the money paid in fees by ships passing through the Canal. Since the Soviet Union had already come up with an offer to build the dam for him, he was able to show that the Egypt which he ruled could stand up to Western imperialism in a way it had not done in the past.

Nasser had come to power in October 1954, two years after a successful military revolt had overthrown the corrupt and ineffectively anti-Western government of King Farouk, and perhaps more than any other leader, he represented what was seen as the new and revolutionary force of Arab nationalism. The main instrument whereby it was propagated was Cairo radio, which enabled Nasser to be seen as its principal and most dynamic representative. Arab nationalism had been exacerbated by the creation of the State of Israel and the defeat of the Arab armies by the Israelis in May 1948. This had been a crucial factor in the overthrow of King Farouk and had underlined the need for this nationalism to assert itself – and the obvious way was to reject the influence of the European powers which had been humiliating Egypt since the Napoleonic invasion of 1798. Nasser succeeded through what turned out to be a providential readiness by the United States not to offer its support to Britain and France. Had this support been forthcoming, it is quite possible, given the attitude of the Soviet Union, that the Suez crisis of October 1956 might have made the Cold War turn disastrously hot.

There would, if this had happened, have been no historians alive to underline the irony of the situation that the politician most responsible for the immediate crisis was the man seen up to 1956 not only as one of the greatest experts in foreign affairs in British history but one of the most experienced statesmen in the Western world. On February 20, 1937 Anthony Eden had resigned as Foreign Secretary in protest against the Appeasement policy adopted by Neville Chamberlain towards Nazi Germany. From 1940 to 1945 he had served with distinction as Churchill's Foreign Secretary, and in 1954 had been the key figure in the Geneva negotiations leading to the end of the Indochinese war. After the rejection of the European Defence Community by the French parliament in August 1954, it was his initiative which led to the compromise whereby West Germany could become a member of NATO in May 1955. At the London conference of October 1954 he had agreed to keep four British divisions and a tactical air force on European soil in peacetime. By thus breaking with the long tradition that British troops moved on to the continent of Europe only after fighting had begun, he helped to ensure that Western Europe would remain militarily united against any threats from the Soviet Union.

It may well be, as Martin Walker suggests, that 'all this success went

to Britain's head', and 'fed Eden's legendary vanity'.[4] It is certainly difficult to find a rational explanation for Eden's behaviour in 1956. It is open
only to psychological or perhaps psychiatric analysis, and serves as an
illustration of the verdict formulated by the Roman historian Tacitus
(55–120) when he wrote of the Emperor Servius Galba (3 BC–AD 69)
'Maior privato visus dum privatus fuit, et omnium consensu capax
imperii nisi imperasset' (When he was a commoner, he seemed too big
for his station, and, had he never become emperor, nobody would have
doubted his ability to reign). Everybody, in other words, thought that
Eden would make a marvellous Prime Minister until he actually took up
office. It was only when he had to do the job that he was a disaster. He
had done very well as Churchill's deputy when the Conservative Party
had been in opposition between 1945 and 1950, and again in Churchill's
last administration from October 5, 1951 to his retirement on April 6,
1955. The claim made both for his rival in the Conservative Party, R.A.
Butler, and for his principal opponent, the leader of the Labour Party
Hugh Gaitskell, was that of having been 'the best Prime Minister we
never had'. If Eden had never taken office, it might well have been
applied to him.

It was, perhaps, not entirely Eden's fault. By hanging on until he was
eighty, Churchill prevented Eden from assuming the premiership until
he was sixty-one. He may have done so deliberately, suspecting that his
brilliant lieutenant would never become a competent captain. It is only
the very best actors who can give a good performance after so long a
wait in the wings, and a botched operation on his gall bladder had also
left Eden in poor health. He had shown so uncertain a grasp of economic
matters in his first months as Prime Minister that the *Daily Telegraph* in
one of its most celebrated editorials, had called for 'the smack of firm
government' to show the country who was really in charge.

Therefore, when Colonel Nasser nationalised the Suez Canal on July
27, 1956, it seemed at first sight an opportunity for Eden to show that he
did, after all, have the ability to be a leader of Churchillian style. But his
long fidelity to Churchill had made him incapable of thinking in
anything but the terms on which Churchill's own reputation was based,
and especially of Churchill's denunciation in the 1930s of the policy of
Appeasement. This led Eden to see Nasser as the modern equivalent of
Hitler, a dictator bent on profiting from the weakness of the democracies
in order to impose his will on an increasingly large portion of the globe.
In his view, Nasser had broken international law by nationalising the
Suez Canal in the same way that Hitler had broken it by sending his
troops into the demilitarised Rhineland on March 7, 1936, or in breaking
another article of the Versailles Treaty of 1919 by carrying out the
Anschluss of March 15, 1938 and merging Germany with Austria.

Churchill had argued, both at the time and after the outbreak of the

Second World War, that if the democracies had then threatened Hitler with force and made him withdraw, the conflict of 1939–1945 could have been avoided. Eden saw the challenge posed by the nationalisation of the Suez Canal as a repetition of March 7, 1936 and March 15, 1938, and any failure to respond as indistinguishable from the Munich agreements of September 30, 1938 whereby Chamberlain gave way to Hitler's demands on Czechoslovakia.

Militarily, the plan prepared at the Château de Sèvres on October 22 and 24, 1956 was a success. This had been that the Israelis should attack Egypt, and the British and French should intervene, ostensibly to separate the combatants but in fact to reoccupy the Canal Zone and topple Nasser from power. On October 29 the Israelis launched their attack, and won a series of fairly easy victories. Two days later, after issuing an ultimatum to both sides to cease fighting, the British and French governments sent their aircraft to bomb Egyptian military installations. By November 3 British and French paratroops were in sight of the Canal, and encountering little serious resistance.

Initially, the United States had greeted the nationalisation of the Suez Canal with considerable disapproval. Nasser, after all, had only done it because the United States had put pressure on the IMF and the World Bank not to provide the funds for the Aswan Dam, and he was receiving arms from the Soviet Union via Czechoslovakia. In July 1956 the American Secretary of State John Foster Dulles had commented that 'a way has to be found to make Nasser disgorge what he has attempted to swallow', and hinted that military force might be necessary.[5] He had then given a different set of signals when he tried to defuse the situation by proposing the formation of a 'Canal Users' Association', and on October 2 he warned Britain and France that the United States would not 'identify itself 100 per cent with the so-called colonial powers'.[6] American hostility to European colonialism was not all rhetoric, and the United States also had to think of its own interests in the area from which it obtained much of its oil, as well as of the danger of allowing the Soviet Union to portray itself as the main ally of the Arabs in the Middle East.

President Eisenhower, deeply involved in the re-election campaign which was to win him a second term at the White House, was reportedly furious when he learned of the attack on Egypt, and reacted in a way which he knew would hit Britain hardest. He ordered the United States Treasury to sell sterling. The Chancellor of the Exchequer, Harold Macmillan, had been one of Eden's keenest supporters. Overnight, faced with the prospect of having either to devalue the pound or to sell all Britain's gold and dollar reserves in an attempt to support it, he began to argue in favour of accepting the cease-fire called for by the United Nations. On November 7 this was accepted, but not before an even more worrying prospect had emerged as a result of a speech delivered in

Moscow by the then Prime Minister of the Soviet Union, Marshal Bulganin. On the evening of October 31 he publicly warned Britain and France that the USSR had at its disposal nuclear-armed rockets capable of hitting London and Paris, and was prepared to use them, as he rather oddly put it, 'to defend the cause of peace'.

It is from this point of view that it is so providential that the United States should have been as keen as the Soviet Union to see Britain and France give up their attempt to retake the Suez Canal and overthrow Colonel Nasser. Had President Eisenhower supported the Suez expedition, he would have had no choice but to up the ante and tell the Soviet Union to stop threatening America's allies. Bluff and counter-bluff, threat and counter-threat, could well then have set the two superpowers on the path to a nuclear confrontation whose outcome might have been to make the question of who did or did not own the Suez Canal a matter of total indifference. It could of course be argued that the Soviet Union would not have made its threat if it had not known that the United States was as opposed as it was to the British and French attack on Egypt. It is, however, equally tempting to argue that Mr Khrushchev, without whose support Marshal Bulganin would not have made his speech on October 31, drew a different conclusion from what happened. For him, the speed with which Great Britain and France accepted the cease-fire once the Soviet threat had been made was a sign that they might prove equally wobbly over Berlin.

The Suez expedition produced none of the advantages which the two European powers that instigated it hoped to obtain. While it helped Israel to live to fight another day and introduced United Nations observers into the Middle East to monitor the cease-fire, it did nothing in the long term to help to keep Algeria French. Although he was not in power at the time, it almost certainly increased de Gaulle's suspicion of the British. It was one of the events which helped to inspire the veto on the first British application to join the European Community that he pronounced on January 14, 1963 and the *rapprochement* with West Germany symbolised by the signature on January 22 of the formal Franco-German alliance.

The only positive effect of the Suez expedition on the United Kingdom was to remove a Prime Minister whose incompetence had already become so evident that the survival skills of the Conservative Party would soon have got rid of him anyway. Since the Egyptians sank so many ships in the Suez Canal that it remained closed to all shipping for over a year, the argument that the expedition had been inspired by the ambition to ensure free passage from the Mediterranean to the Red Sea fell peculiarly flat. What was even more serious was that it diverted away from the Soviet Union much of the obloquy which it so richly deserved for its repression of the Hungarian revolt on November 4, 1956, and diverted it on to the more incompetent attempt of Britain and France to put into practice their less efficiently exercised concept of *Realpolitik*.

In spite of the divisions provoked at the time by the Suez expedition, the dust settled so quickly in England after the Suez expedition that both sides were able to express a degree of satisfaction. Left-wing intellectuals said that, whereas their fathers had lost their struggle when they failed to persuade the government of the 1930s to intervene on the side of the Republican government in the Spanish civil war, they had succeeded in stopping Eden from trying to bully the Egyptians. Right-wing politicians argued that British intervention had, after all, 'stopped the bush fire' before it became a general conflagration, and that Colonel Nasser would step more carefully in future. Perhaps more significantly, no new political party emerged to defend one interpretation over another at the hustings, and the Conservative Party soon showed its traditional ability to close ranks and repel boarders.

THE COMMONWEALTH AND AFRICA

GHANA, SIERRA LEONE AND KENYA

It was able to do so both as a result of the remarkable personality of Harold Macmillan and also because a source of consolation lay conveniently to hand in the form of the British Commonwealth. The gradual change from the term 'British Empire', first to 'British Commonwealth', and in 1947 simply to 'Commonwealth', began in 1867 when Canada received Dominion status, followed in 1900 by Australia and in 1907 by New Zealand. It was clearly felt that the ethos governing what are still occasionally referred to in conservatively-minded circles as 'the white Dominions' was different from the one characterising the relationship between Great Britain and the countries inhabited principally by people of non-European origin.

At the Imperial Conference of 1918 this situation began to change. The idea then developed that all the countries which had formerly been part of the Empire should enjoy equal status, and the Statute of Westminster of 1931, under which India was given dominion status, reinforced this concept when the term 'British Empire' was replaced by 'British Commonwealth of Nations'. The accession of India and Pakistan to independence in 1947 led to the dropping of the word 'British', and with 53 members the Commonwealth has survived rather better than *La Communauté Française*. Although the Queen is officially its head, not all of these are monarchies, and the only real criteria for membership are a willingness to join and an apparent readiness to respect certain human rights.

It was this which led to the expulsion of Nigeria from the Commonwealth in 1995, and to the voluntary absence of South Africa between

1961 and 1994, as well as of Pakistan between 1972 and 1989. The fact that Ghana and Uganda are listed as members also suggests that a genuine respect for human rights is no more necessary as a qualification for membership than it is of *La Francophonie*.

In this respect, as in others, it is the contrasts between the countries of Africa and Asia formerly subjected to the rule of the Western Europeans which are often more noticeable than their similarities. Some, like India, achieve democracy, but not prosperity. Others, like Singapore, which left the Malaysian Federation on September 8, 1965, achieve remarkable rates of economic growth, but do not give the appearance of being particularly interested either in the formal trappings of parliamentary democracy or in the implementation of its more humane conventions. There is nevertheless a noticeable difference between what happened to the former European colonies in Asia and what happened to those in Africa.

The immediate historical reason for this is that, while the Europeans went to Asia for spices, they went to Africa for slaves. Slavery was not an institution which they brought with them, and the slaves taken from west Africa to work the sugar and cotton plantations of the West Indies and the southern states of North America were sold by other Africans who had captured them in tribal raids. But relations between Europe and Africa have never recovered from the revival of a practice endemic in Greece and Rome but whose disappearance from Europe itself was one of the undoubted social triumphs produced by Christianity.

Once they had ceased to be seen as a source of cheap human labour, the territories of west Africa were absorbed into the European empires for the sake of what they could offer by way of raw materials. In 1945 Great Britain still ruled what was significantly, if misleadingly, known at the time as the British Colony of the Gold Coast. The gold which could be mined there was less profitable than the cocoa bean, and chocolate became increasingly popular as something which could be eaten as well as used as a basis for a drink. In this respect the products of Africa began to bring about in the nineteenth century rather more of the same improvement in the diet of the Europeans that spices had played in the fifteenth and sixteenth. Cocoa had also, in the eyes of its most fervent admirers, the advantages of being non-alcoholic. It thus provided an admirable basis for the one form of religious belief which has done more good than harm. The Cadburys, the Frys, the Rowntrees and the Terrys were all Quakers.

The British Colony of the Gold Coast became officially independent on March 6, 1957 under the name of Ghana. On the west coast of Africa, the British also held Sierra Leone, whose capital city of Freetown still bears witness to the fact that it was originally established in 1788 as a refuge for escaped slaves from America. In 1808 it had become the first British Crown Colony in Africa, and it was granted independence on

April 27, 1961. Nigeria, the most populous country in Africa, which then had some sixty million inhabitants – rather more than that of the United Kingdom which had administered it, together with part of the Cameroons, as a colony and protectorate since 1914 – became independent on October 1, 1960.

In none of these countries, however, have the traditions of parliamentary democracy and the rule of law which the British had tried to leave behind them lasted very long. Ghana soon became a socialist dictatorship under Kwame Nkrumah, until he was overthrown in 1966 by a military *coup d'état*. Although it has so far avoided the civil war currently raging in Sierra Leone, its history has been a series of unstable civilian governments followed by military dictatorships. Like other Third World countries, it has had to be rescued from bankruptcy by the International Monetary Fund, an organisation regarded by Marxist critics as an instrument of neo-colonialism and by its admirers as a benign carrier of the White Man's Burden. Nigeria has ample resources of oil, but in 1995, its annual income per head was $300. It is able to avoid civil war only by what is clearly a reluctant acceptance of the military dictatorship of General Abdulsalam Abubakar. British citizens considering the possibility of a visit there are advised that kidnappings are frequent, and that they should under no circumstances go out after 6 p.m.

In Kenya, a British protectorate since 1895 and a Crown Colony since 1920, all the best land had been taken from the tribes which originally owned it and given to what are still officially referred to as 'White farmers'. Between 1952 and 1959 the resentment which this provoked led to the violent insurrection known as the Mau Mau rebellion, and the British took the view that they could not grant independence until this had been defeated. This was not unreasonable, and when independence came on December 1963, it was followed by a period of relative peace under Jomo Kenyatta. But, as in other newly liberated countries, the economy was highly vulnerable to changes in the price of its main products (coffee and tea), and by 1995 the economic depression had produced a state of near civil war with what Amnesty International estimated as 2,000 deaths and 250,000 refugees.

RHODESIA

With the best will in the world, the countries of Western Europe could do nothing to help their former colonies except try to ensure that the transfer of power, when it came, was as smooth as possible. Macmillan saw this as the only course of action, and the speech which he gave to the South African parliament on February 3, 1960 insisted on the acceptance by the European settlers of what he called 'the wind of change blowing through this country'. The response of the South African Prime Minister

Hendrik Verwoerd was unenthusiastic. He continued to insist on the destiny of South Africa as 'a true White state in Africa'. He thus offered a reminder of how fortunate Great Britain had been to have concluded the Boer war of October 1899–May 1902 by signing the Treaty of Vereeniging and granting the Transvaal and Orange Free State the self-government which they eventually took in 1907. The British had, as it was, enough trouble with the only one of their African colonies to contain a large settler population when Rhodesia made its Unilateral Declaration of Independence (UDI) on November 11, 1965.

This confronted the British government, then a Labour administration headed by Harold Wilson, with the most serious problem of decolonisation since Suez. Historically, it was the first time since July 4, 1776 that a stretch of territory ruled by the British had officially declared itself independent without first obtaining permission from the government at Westminster. There was nevertheless an essential difference. The wording of the formal document issued by Ian Smith's government was modelled on that of *The Unanimous Declaration of the Thirteen United States of America*. But it consciously omitted the truth which the Continental Congress had found self-evident, that 'all men are created equal'. The whole point of the UDI was to ensure that Rhodesia became as much like South Africa as possible. There, the victory of the Nationalist Party of Daniel François Malan in the general election of May 1948 had resulted in the strict application of the principle of *apartheid*, or 'separate development'. What this meant in South Africa was that the 2.4 million whites who made up twenty per cent of the population should exercise permanent rule over some 7.43 million blacks, 930,000 people of mixed race known as 'Cape Coloureds', and 29,000 Asiatics. What UDI was intended to produce was a comparable situation, in which the 270,000 white settlers in Rhodesia, who already owned most of the best land, continued to rule over nine million blacks.

If world circumstances in general had not been against Ian Smith, it is quite possible that the Rhodesian Republic whose existence was proclaimed on March 2, 1970 would have survived at least until the formal abandonment of *apartheid* in South Africa in June 1991. There was nothing that any country in Western Europe could do about it. Even if Great Britain had possessed the military capability to send a force three thousand miles to fight a well-organised army made up of men described by the Conservative politician Lord Salisbury as their own 'kith and kin', there would have been little support for such an action either in Parliament or from the general public. If the British had learned one thing from Suez, it was that they could do nothing without active support from the United States. It was clear from the outset that this was not likely to take the form of military assistance.

In spite of attempts made by the Commonwealth to impose sanctions on Rhodesia, the real economic pressure on Ian Smith's government came when President Carter persuaded Congress in January 1977 to ban the import of Rhodesian chrome. This pressure had been preceded by the Portuguese government's acknowledgment in 1974 that it could no longer continue the fight against the independence movements in Angola and Mozambique. This deprived the South African government of the *cordon sanitaire* to the north which its then Prime Minister, Balthazar Johannes Vorster 'hoped would insulate South Africa from external threat'.[7] It was, in other words, the acceptance of military and political defeat by Portugal, the first European power to obtain an overseas empire, which put an end to the last attempt by European settlers to impose their authority in Africa.

The Lancaster House Conference of December 1979, which brought UDI formally to an end, gave Ian Smith a better deal than he might have obtained if he had not gone for UDI. Although the civil war which UDI had provoked had caused some 30,000 deaths, the two races managed to settle down in reasonable harmony, with the white settlers keeping possession of most of the better land and achieving a per capita income six times greater than the farms run by the Africans. Although they constituted only 1.2 per cent of the population, the new Constitution guaranteed them a ten-year period in which they had 20 per cent of the seats in the new parliament, and the threat by the first President of Zimbabwe, Robert Mugabe to create a one-party state has not yet materialised.

THE FALKLANDS AND HONG KONG

It is an open question whether the Falklands War of April–June 1982 was an example of British colonialism. But, however supportive their governments proved at the time, this is how many Europeans see it. It was a salutary if disturbing experience for English tourists in France in the summer of 1982 to discover how completely the high standing which Great Britain had enjoyed immediately after 1945 had now disappeared.

In Parliament there was virtually unanimous support in favour of military action to recover the islands after the Argentine invasion of April 2, 1982. In the debate on May 20 only 33 Labour members of parliament could be persuaded to vote against the Conservative government of Margaret Thatcher. Only among left-wing intellectuals was there serious opposition to the retaking of the Falklands by force. Since the final outcome of the Falklands War was to be the replacement in Argentina itself of a military dictatorship by a democratic government run by civilian politicians, this proved rather an odd attitude for anyone to have taken.

The important difference between the Falklands campaign and the other wars fought by European powers after 1945 in order to maintain their situation abroad was that the 1,800 inhabitants of the Falkland Islands did not want the British to leave. They were, in this respect, very different from the Greek-speaking inhabitants of Cyprus, whose desire for *enosis*, or unification with Greece, was so strongly resisted by Great Britain that it inspired a rebellion which began in April 1955 and eventually led in 1974 to a division of the island into a Greek-speaking section and a Turkish-speaking section.

It was argued by critics of the Conservative government that the Argentinians would never have launched the invasion of April 1982 if the British had not given the wrong signals. By announcing in the Defence White Paper of July 1981 that the ice-patrol ship *Endurance* would be withdrawn from the south Atlantic, they are alleged to have given the Argentine government of General Galtieri a nod and a wink to let him know that the long-standing Argentinian claim to the islands would not now be resisted, and there are other cases where it is argued that the issuing of a clear warning might have avoided a conflict.

If, for example, Great Britain had made it clear to Germany in 1914 that any invasion of Belgium would be treated as a *casus belli*, there might never have been a First World War. It is also sometimes alleged that the Korean War would never have taken place if the American Secretary of State Dean Acheson had not given a speech at the National Press Club in Washington on January 12, 1950 in which he did not include South Korea behind the defensive line which the United States was prepared to defend against Communist intrusion in the Far East. However, as also in the case of the Iraqi invasion of Kuwait in August 1990, when the American Ambassador apparently failed to issue a specific warning to Saddam Hussein about American interests in the Middle East, it is very odd to say that the power which allegedly gave out the wrong signals is therefore responsible for the conflict which followed. A householder who accidentally leaves a window open does not thereby invite burglars to come in and steal his property.

But why, the critics of Mrs Thatcher's Falklands policy asked, was it right for Great Britain to sacrifice the lives of 225 British soldiers, to kill three times as many Argentinians, and to spend as much money as it costs to belong to the Common Market, only to hand the colony of Hong Kong over to an even worse tyranny than that of General Galtieri only fifteen years later?

HONG KONG

There were three principal reasons for the event which finally marked the end of the British empire. The first was the fact that Great Britain knew that it would not receive any support from the United States. The second was that there was no chance of anyone mounting a successful military defence of a densely inhabited island containing almost seven million people. The third was that Hong Kong was totally dependent for its water supply on the People's Republic of China.

In the quarrel about the Falkland Islands the United States went through an initial period of hesitation in which the Reagan administration tried to reconcile the claims of its most reliable European ally with those of the second most populated country in South America. When the Galtieri government refused to give serious consideration to any of the various compromises proposed, the United States had no choice but to come down on the side of the United Kingdom. This was very fortunate for Britain. Without the communications support from the US, it might well have lost the war. But in the case of Hong Kong, there was no chance of American support for the defence of what was officially described as a British colony, and for whose continued status there were no grounds in international law. Whatever happened, the lease whereby the British held the island was due to expire in 1997, the year that the British left.

The inhabitants of Hong Kong, like those of the Falkland Islands, would undoubtedly have preferred Great Britain to stay. This is another reason for insisting on the difference between what happened there from what might be called the classic process of decolonisation. Nobody in India seriously wanted the British to stay, any more than anybody in Africa or Asia wanted the Belgians, the Dutch, the French or the Portuguese to stay. Ian Smith's supporters in Rhodesia would have welcomed a continued British presence only if it had involved the provision of military assistance against the nationalist Patriotic Front. In Hong Kong, the situation was also different in another way from that of traditional colonialism. Hong Kong was undoubtedly a pleasant place for members of the Hong Kong Civil Service to live and work. But it was the Hong Kong Chinese who derived the greatest overall benefit from the process of European colonisation which had begun in 1841 when the British occupied the island and declared it a Crown Colony.

They had not done so for altruistic reasons. Like the other European powers which went a-colonising in the happy days when the world was seen as Europe's oyster, they did it for the money. The East India Company was at the time one of the world's largest producers of opium, but was denied access to the Chinese market. When the Chinese government seized and destroyed a large quantity of the drug which had been smuggled into Canton, the British Navy bombarded the town until the Chinese paid compensation and opened their ports. The British also compelled the Chinese to yield occupation of Hong Kong, and in 1898 to grant a 99-year lease of the 'New Territories', the 300 square miles on the mainland behind Kowloon, and on which Hong Kong depended for its water supply. Even before the lease was due to run out in 1999 the Chinese could have put an end to the colony at any time they pleased, simply by turning off the taps.

After the Second World War, and the end of the Japanese occupation which had begun in December 1941, the colony attained a remarkable degree of prosperity. This was especially marked after 1949, when the triumph on October 1 of Mao Zedong and the proclamation of the People's Republic of China led to an unprecedented inflow of cheap labour in the form of a million or so political refugees. Growth rates of ten per cent a year became the norm, and it was claimed by the colony's admirers that it combined the best of two cultures. An efficient and incorruptible British civil service provided a stable legal and administrative framework for the diligent and enterprising Cantonese, whose readiness to rely on extended-family support systems meant that there was no need for high taxes in order to provide welfare benefits.

On July 1, 1997, however, the 99-year lease was due to expire. In August 1984 an agreement was reached whereby both the New Territories and the colony itself would revert to China, though under the formula known as 'one country, two systems'. What this meant was that Hong Kong would keep its capitalist economy until 2049, but come under the authority of the Beijing government as a Special Administrative Area. The problem remains that of retaining the political and intellectual freedoms traditionally associated with free-market economics in an area governed by a totalitarian state which still proclaims its allegiance to Marxism-Leninism.

As was expected, the pro-democratic 'United Democrats-Meeting Point' alliance easily won the local and territorial elections of September 18, 1994 and March 5, 1995 which preceded the formal handing over of power on July 1, 1997. It then repeated its victory in the directly elected constituencies in May 1998, but found itself up against a problem. The Basic Law under which the Beijing government exercises its authority provides for an automatic two-thirds majority for the parties which it dominates. Economically, the island seems to have weathered the currency crisis of August 1998, though perhaps without ever recovering the prosperity which, for some free-market economists, made it a model for the rest of the world. Politically, however, the outlook is less promising, and there was a note of sadness about the formal ceremonies which accompanied the lowering of the Union Jack on July 1, 1997 and the final parade of the Black Watch.

These marked, in a real as well as a symbolic sense, the end of the British Empire. The obvious reluctance of the vast majority of the Chinese population to see the British leave offered an unconscious echo to what Arthur Koestler had written in the closing pages of his autobiography in 1954:

The fall of each of the great Empires of the past was an ugly and catastrophic event. For the first time in history, we see an Empire gradually dissolving with dignity and grace. The rise of this Empire was not an edifying story; its decline is.[8]

14 The aftermath of empire

CLAIMS, DEFINITIONS AND STATISTICS

In 1994 the American scholar Patrick Ireland claimed that 'European politics is in many respects becoming the politics of ethnicity'.[1] The arrival of a large number of immigrants from outside Europe is certainly a new phenomenon in European history. Traditionally, Europe exported people as well as revolutionary ideas and new technologies. From the beginning of the European diaspora in the early sixteenth century up to 1915, some 52 million Europeans emigrated, about 34 million of them to the United States.[2]

The fact that immigrants from outside Europe may nowadays make up as much as five per cent of the total population of the fifteen countries of the European Union is thus a considerable novelty, the largest addition to the gene pool of Western Europe since the barbarian invasions of the fifth century. Insofar as it is part of the aftermath of empire, it is primarily the result of the attraction which the higher standard of living enjoyed by Europeans has for the inhabitants of the countries which they formerly conquered and occupied. And to the extent that this higher standard of living is partly the outcome of the way the Europeans exploited their former colonies, there is perhaps a certain historical justice in the problems said to be created by the immigrants' presence in Western Europe. The objection to this argument is that the price is not being paid by the section of society which most benefited from the European colonisation of Africa and Asia, the upper and upper middle classes. It is being paid by the poorest members of the urban proletariat.

So long as it remained relatively easy to gain admittance to Australia, Canada or New Zealand, the British still went there. In the late 1940s and early 1950s overseas emigration still accounted for a net loss of between two and three million people from the UK.[3] Since then, however, opportunities for emigration have become much more limited. It is no longer as easy as it was to obtain permission to settle in Australia or Canada, and only the very gifted have been able to take advantage of the brain drain and go and work in the United States. From the mid 1950s onwards a general increase in prosperity has also enabled Western Europeans to make themselves more comfortable at home than at any other period in their history. Instead of being a continent which sent people out because they could make a better life elsewhere, Western Europe has become what North America has always been: a place where other people from all over the world want to come and live because they hope to enjoy a higher standard of living than they would at home.

Since migrants have always gone, wherever possible, to areas of high prosperity, there are few non-European immigrants arriving in the countries of the former Soviet bloc. Ethnic Germans or emigrants from Hungary may be a source of difficulties when they move to the countries of the more affluent West. One of the major problems in Germany after its reunification on October 3, 1990 was the tension between the inhabitants of the former German Democratic Republic and their richer neighbours in the FRG. But what Patrick Ireland calls 'the politics of ethnicity' are first and foremost the problems stemming from the fact that a number of people from the Third World now living in Western Europe have black or brown faces. It is a question of colour, an issue with which the inhabitants of the United States have been familiar for some time. Of the 270 million or so people living in the USA, at least 35 million, or some thirteen per cent, are visibly not what demographers call Caucasians.

The problem of how the largely white population of Western Europe should deal with the presence of a coloured minority is made more difficult by the fact that most members of this minority, like the Blacks and Hispanics in the United States, are poorer than the majority of their white neighbours. In both Europe and America, it is thus a social and economic problem as much as a racial one. There are, however, two similarities between the United States and Western Europe which only those who possess the advantage of a white skin tend to mention.

The first of these is that nowhere in the world do people with a black or brown skin have a higher general standard of living than in the United States. The second is that, although the ancestors of the American negroes were for the most part taken there as slaves, and the discrimination from which they have always suffered has still not disappeared, they also live in a society which, on an official level, continues to make considerable efforts to improve their lot. The same two factors apply to the immigrants who have arrived in Western Europe since 1945. Whether they came from Algeria, India, Pakistan, Turkey or the West Indies, they have done so through their own free choice, as people in search of a better life. This, in general, is something they have obtained. In spite of the racism of which they are often the target, they are almost always better off in Europe than they would be at home. They also, like the coloured population of the United States, live in a society which, on an official level as well as through the privately organised efforts of a considerable number of its members, is seeking to give them the opportunity of obtaining a better life-style.

Politicians who try to use the issue of racism as a means of getting themselves elected make great play with the possibility that the officially published statistics about immigration hide the exact extent of the phenomenon. There are, they say, so many non-Europeans who have come in illegally that the danger of a cultural take-over is much greater than officially recognised. They dismiss with contumely the normally suggested figure of 3 million illegal immigrants in Western Europe and allege that it is at least twice that number. And since, in their view, it is immigrants from the Third World who create the problems, they depict Europe as confronted by a danger which is all the more insidious for being impossible to evaluate.

It is indeed hard to know exactly how many non-European immigrants there are in Western Europe. In 1950, according to an article by the demographer Dudley Baines, there were about 5 million non-Europeans living officially inside Europe. By 1992 this had risen to over 18 million. However, Sarah Collinson quotes the figure given by Eurostat of between 13 and 14 million foreigners living in 1993 in what were then the twelve states of European Communities, which at that time had a total population of 329 million: under five per cent. According to Patrick Ireland, up to 30 million people have entered Western Europe since 1945 either as workers or workers' dependants.[4]

By international standards, these figures are relatively modest. Sarah Collinson points out that in 1993 there were some 80 million people, as she puts it, 'resident outside their country of citizenship', and 100 million 'international migrants world-wide'. The three countries in continental Europe to have received most immigrants from non-European countries are France, Germany and Switzerland. Patrick Ireland puts their number in France at 3.5 million, the British scholar Cathie Lloyd quotes the French *Haut Conseil à l'Intégration* as giving the figure of just over four million for immigrants from all countries, pointing out that they represent 'roughly the same proportion of the population (between 6 and 8 percent) as they did in 1931'.[5]

Patrick Ireland gives the same number for Germany as he does for France, 3.5 million, and 1.2 million in Switzerland. John Ardagh says at one point in *Germany and the Germans* that there are well over four million in Germany; at another, that there are 6.8 million. Dudley Baines says that one and a half million of these are from Turkey. John Ardagh says 1.6 million. *The Statesman's Year Book* for 1998 gives the precise figure of 7,314,000 resident foreigners in Germany out of a total population of eighty-two million, of whom 2,049,100 are Turks.

Although the French government refrains from keeping the same kinds of records of the ethnic origins of migrant workers as the British Office of National Statistics, it is known that the largest individual group comes from Portugal, the second largest from Algeria.[6] In 1985, according to Dudley Baines, there were 621,000 Algerian immigrants France, 585,000 from Morocco. In Great Britain, *The Statesman's Year Book* quotes the 1991 census as giving a total of 3,015,023 people of non-European origin, as against 51,873,794 whites. An increasing number have been born in the UK. The largest group, 840,225, had its racial origins in India. The second largest, 499,964, classified themselves as Black Caribbean. The third largest, 476,558, either came from Pakistan or were descended from ancestors who did. In all, it is just over five per cent of the UK population.

It is unusual for ethnic Europeans who go from one country to another inside Europe to be seen as presenting a difficulty. They are merely fulfilling one of the aims of the movement towards European unification which began with the signature of the Treaty of Paris on April 18, 1951. What Patrick Ireland calls 'the politics of ethnicity' are a reflection of what is now seen as the undesirable presence of people whose faces are a different colour. They were useful in the years immediately after the war. They filled the many gaps in the labour market and did the more unpleasant jobs that the Europeans did not want to do. Now that one of the main problems in Western Europe is that of unemployment – with some ten per cent of those living in the fifteen states of the European Union being unable to find a job – their presence has not only looked increasingly unnecessary, it has come to be seen in some quarters as a threat to the economic prosperity of Western Europe as well as to its political stability and its cultural identity.

The official figures for immigration from outside Europe do not suggest a continent about to lose its identity under the impact of an uncontrolled invasion, and Richard Bessel puts it rather strongly when he claims that what was happening at the end of the twentieth century was that it was 'the former colonisers who were being colonised'.[7] In this and other respects the situation is totally different from what happened after the Europeans began arriving in North America from the seventeenth century onwards or in Australia after 1788. There are areas of France, Germany or the British Isles where the 'politics of ethnicity' have the urgency which unemployment had in the 1930s. One-third of the pupils in the northern French town of Roubaix are from parents born outside France.[8] But, although the situation is very similar in Bradford, there are many other towns where this is not at all the case. In the Cumbrian town of Penrith, for example, you rarely see a black or brown face, any more than you do in Lincoln or Evesham. The same is true of the average French village or small German town.

Race relations is not an issue which dominates national elections either in smaller European countries, such as Belgium, Denmark or Ireland, or in larger countries such as Germany or Great Britain. The presence of non-European migrants is also too new a phenomenon in Mediterranean countries such as Italy, Portugal or Spain, which have traditionally sent migrants abroad, rather than receiving them from elsewhere, to be a major factor in either local or national politics. Only in France has an openly racialist party won seats in a national legislative assembly.

THE POLITICS OF RACISM

It is true that this party, *Le Front National*, increased its share of the vote in European elections from under one per cent in 1979 to fifteen per cent in 1984, and now regularly polls about the same figure. Elections held, as elections to the European Parliament are, on a proportional representational system do give a more accurate picture of public opinion than the British 'first-past-the-post' system or the French *scrutin uninominal à deux tours*. In March 1986, because it knew it would lose under the two-ballot, single-constituency system, the French Socialist Party introduced a system of proportional representation. This enabled *Le Front National* to obtain what remains its maximum score of 35 out of the 574 seats in the *Chambre des Députés*. But no French political party is likely to make the mistake of reintroducing proportional representation. This allows supporters of *Le Front National* to argue that all the mainstream parties are conspiring against it, and that it would win more parliamentary votes in a fairer system. But it has never received more than fifteen per cent in the first round of a Presidential election, which is probably a better test of public opinion than elections to the European Parliament.

There are also a large number of issues dominating European politics and which have nothing to do with race relations. Between 1993 and 1999 ethnic hatreds led to more deaths in the former Yugoslavia than were suffered during the Second World War in the whole of the Balkans. They play virtually no part in the politics of any country in mainland Europe except France. Elsewhere politicians, voters and party activists are all far more interested in issues such as education, the social services, taxation levels and the future of the European Union. Some of these, like education, may have implications for race relations. Children who underachieve at school are frequently of non-European origin. But this is because they tend to live in inner cities, where the educational achievements of almost all children, irrespective of their racial origin, tend to be low anyway. What are presented as the problems of a minority ethnic group are often the economic and cultural problems shared by a particular social class, and have nothing to do with the colour of their skin.

This is not to say that some sections of European society do not feel threatened by the influx of immigrants from non-European countries which has taken place since 1945. A joke sometimes told by comedians whose ancestors lived in the Indian sub-continent describes an incident which allegedly took place in 1947 when the British were preparing to give up the Raj. 'We're going home now', says one of the members of the Indian Civil Service, ironically dubbed 'the heaven-born', to his flock. 'And we hope you will be very happy in what is now your own country'. 'No, no,' comes the chorus from the crowd. 'No, no. We're not staying here. We're coming with you'. It is a story which is funnier for the inhabitants of the leafy, middle-class suburbs of Leeds or London, where you see as few black or brown faces as you do in the Cotswold village of Broadway, than it is for those who live in working-class areas such as Brick Lane in Bethnal Green, or in towns in the north or midlands such as Bradford, Leicester or Smethwick.

In the last of these the Conservative candidate in the 1964 General Election is alleged to have beaten the general swing towards Labour by conducting so viciously racialist a campaign against immigrants that the Labour leader, Harold Wilson, recommended that he should be treated as 'a parliamentary leper'.[9] But he got elected. And, although Jacques Chirac did not owe his election as President of the Republic on May 7, 1995 to his remark on June 21, 1991, when he spoke publicly of the 'noise and the smells' to which native-born French working-class families were subjected by the immigrants from the former French colonies in north Africa who are now their close neighbours, his comments are unlikely to have done him much harm.

What is nevertheless striking about these incidents is their comparative rarity. The vast majority of politicians in Western Europe have consistently abstained from playing the racialist card. It is only people like Jean-Marie le Pen, who is clearly not quite right in the head, or the Austrian neo-Nazi Gottfried Helder, who have tried systematically to use the presence of non-European immigrants in order to try to get themselves elected. What is most significant about the speech made by the British politician Enoch Powell on April 28, 1968 about the inflow of coloured immigrants into Britain is that it marked the effective end of his career in British mainstream politics. By evoking, like an ancient Roman, 'the river Tiber flowing with much blood', he had ceased to be a good chap, and had put himself beyond the pale. No other British politician has made the same mistake. Even Mrs Thatcher limited herself in her 1979 election campaign to saying that many people feared being 'swamped' by immigrants. She did not make it a main feature of her campaign, any more than Chirac did in 1995. Once elected, as Alan Sked and Chris Cook put it, she realized that immigration controls apart, her best policy with regard to Britain's blacks must be a mixture of retaining previous legislation on racial discrimination, encouraging consultation between black community leaders and the police, and most of all ensuring that blacks benefit at least as much as whites from youth opportunity programmes and can thus hope to be in a position to benefit from any economic recovery that may arrive.[10]

There was certainly an element of hypocrisy about the way in which Enoch Powell was immediately cold-shouldered by his own party. One of Le Pen's claims is that he says out loud what most other people really think but dare not say. After his 'rivers of blood' speech, Enoch Powell received 100,000 letters of support, and the London dockers organised a march to express their approval. But there are occasions when hypocrisy is very useful. It helps to win support for those who are trying to improve matters, and it does not need much knowledge of history to see how the Europeans have improved in the matter of race relations. In 1492 all the Sephardic Jews were expelled from Spain. Between 1492 and 1715 over a million Europeans were forced to leave their homes in order to avoid religious persecution. Although only the Germans carried racialism in the twentieth century to the point of genocide, the British Fascist leader Oswald Mosley never had any difficulty in holding rallies which filled the Albert Hall. In France the right-wing journalist Charles Maurras said of the French Socialist leader Léon Blum, 'C'est un homme à fusiller. Mais dans le dos' (He's a man to be shot. But in the back).

It is not only because Maurras then received a prison sentence for incitement to murder that people don't say things like that any more. It was characteristic of Jean-Marie Le Pen to dismiss the holocaust as 'a detail' in the Second World War. If this remark was, as his critics allege, a coded invitation to his followers to repeat the operation on the north African immigrants, nobody spelt this out; its principal result was a growth in the popularity of the many anti-racist movements in France.[11]

CULTURAL VALUES AND OFFICIAL ATTITUDES

Just as organised warfare has disappeared from mainland Europe, so has racism as part of official government policy or as the main plank in the programme of any major party. It is certainly still there as part of the conscious or unconscious make-up of many of the inhabitants of Western Europe. It may even, as some of its most vigorous opponents allege, take the form of a refusal to tolerate the expression of certain kinds of cultural behaviour. This may, as is often argued, have been the case in France in the early 1990s, when a number of Muslim girls were excluded from their local school for insisting on wearing a headscarf in class. But there is another way of looking at this particular problem, and one which emphasises the values which are peculiar to European culture. Since 1945 Western Europe has done more than enable its citizens to grow richer in a climate undisturbed by war. It has also developed a desirable as well as a defensible set of intellectual and social values which might, alongside the opportunities which it offers of greater wealth, constitute yet another reason for people to want to come to live there.

Since 1881 state education in France has been organised on strictly secular principles, with a total ban not only on the teaching of religion but also on any attempt by either teachers or pupils to make other people come round to their way of thinking on religious or political matters. By wearing the *chador*, it was argued, these girls were trying to spread the message of Islam, just as a Christian does by wearing a crucifix. Indeed, supporters of *la laïcité* quoted cases where girls and boys in the state-run *lycées* had been asked not to wear their crucifix in class, and, although nobody could give an example of a Jewish boy being told to remove his *yarmulka*, or skullcap, there could be no intellectual objection if this were to happen. The affair, which began in October 1989, still rumbles on, and provides an interesting insight into comparative attitudes being offered by what happened in England: there, the headmistress of a school in the West Midlands said that there would be no objection to the girls expressing their allegiance to Islam by what they wore on their head, so long as the scarf or top-knot was in the school colours.

While critics of the exclusion of the Muslim girls from their school in France said that it was a form of disguised racism, supporters of the action taken by certain head teachers took a different view. They pointed to the fact that the wearing of the *chador* was often accompanied by a refusal to attend classes in biology or other natural sciences. This led them to emphasise the traditional role of 'l'école de la République' of enabling all citizens to develop their minds in an atmosphere of intellectual freedom. Islamic fundamentalism is as opposed to the Darwinian theory of evolution as the Catholic Church used to be, and you cannot teach biology without acknowledging the strong possibility that it may be true. It was argued in this context that, since part of the Republic's mission had also become that of enabling women to become equal citizens with men, any move to allow them to miss out on certain subjects was to condemn them to permanent intellectual as well as social and professional inferiority.[12] It was this which was at stake in the argument over the Islamic headscarf, just as much as the demand on the part of Muslims not to keep to the same rules as the Christians.

The arguments over the Muslim head are not peculiar to the countries of the European Union. Turkey, which has been a candidate for membership since 1982, has long insisted that the secular state created by Kemal Ataturk involves a ban on the wearing of the Islamic-style headscarf in public schools. The problems encountered in France nevertheless offer a good example of the problems facing the whole of Western Europe when it seeks to identify itself in cultural terms. The predominant lifestyle which it has developed since 1945, and which has brought it an unparalleled period of peace and prosperity, has been one of hedonistic, secular humanism. This is based on the achievements of applied science and technology, but also upon a generally sceptical attitude towards religion and a tolerant approach to all forms of belief and social behaviour which do not threaten to disturb the peace.

Like the women's movement, it is a peculiarly desirable manifestation of one of the most valuable aspects of European culture. It represents the characteristically European drive to free people from all forms of oppression, and especially those encouraged by religion. There is certainly a case for saying that European society ought to tolerate forms of religious expression. But it is hard to maintain, in the specific instance of Islamic fundamentalism, that it should go along with practices such as the refusal to give girls the same kind of education as boys, which thus prevent some of its members from attaining what it sees as the desirable aim of the full and free development of all their human potentialities.

In the view of Gayatri Chakravorty Spivak, Professor of English and Cultural Studies at Pittsburg University, no Western culture has the right to expect people of non-European origin to conform to its values. 'Tolerance', she writes:

> is a loaded virtue, because you have to have a base of power to practice it. You cannot ask certain people to 'tolerate' a culture that has historically ignored them, at the same time that their children are being indoctrinated into it.[13]

In Paris and in Pittsburg, in Berlin as in Berkeley, differences of opinion among the intellectual élite follow the same lines of argument, and use the same formulae. The fact that the views of one of the most radical American feminist critics can be quoted in the context of the arguments raised by the exclusion of three Muslims girls from a school in the small town of Noyon, to the north of Paris, is an indication of how many similarities sometimes exist between European culture and that of the United States. There are nevertheless important differences in attitude.

As in the case of the word 'welfare', these differences reflect a set of different historical experiences which recur in the different associations of certain words. In Europe, 'welfare' has positive connotations, evoking the readiness of the community in general to accept responsibility for its less fortunate members. It has a more negative image in the United States, where it suggests laziness and desire to live off the efforts of others. The former US Ambassador to Britain, Raymond Seitz, underlined how uncomfortably the United Kingdom was poised between the two worlds of Europe and the United States in this respect, when he commented that:

> Historically, Britain has admired the compassion of Europe's welfare system and the dynamism of America's market system, but European welfare is too pampering for the British to accept economically and the American market is too cruel for the British to accept socially.[14]

The concept of immigration is different on the two sides of the Atlantic, with some of America's characteristic attitudes recurring in the UK. America, a nation of immigrants, does not see them as a problem. Traditionally, they have brought wealth, and have been expected to be absorbed into the melting-pot of American culture. Europe, in contrast, does not quite know what to think, a fact which comes out in the different way in which immigrants are treated.

Thus in the United Kingdom, the immigrants who came from countries such as India, Pakistan or the West Indies before the Commonwealth Immigration Act of July 1962 were broadly welcomed. They enjoy the same rights as citizens born here. Like citizens of the Irish Republic living in Great Britain, they vote in parliamentary as well as local elections, have the same rights to social security and other benefits, and hold British passports. In France and Germany, immigrants who have not taken out French or German nationality are seen as having retained rights of citizenship in their country of origin. They may be eligible for social security payments but, if they wish to vote, they must do so in their home country of Portugal, Algeria or Turkey. If they are Turks, or the children of Turks, living in Germany and want a passport, they must obtain it from the Turkish authorities.

There is little enthusiasm in German society at large for the proposed abandonment of the traditional German attachment to the *jus sanguinis*, the principle which says that you have the same nationality as your parents. This contrasts with the British or French acceptance of the *jus soli*, which gives you the automatic right at the age of eighteen to choose between the nationality of your parents and that of the country in which you are born. It may seem odd that someone who has German parents, but who has lived for the whole of his life in Hungary or Turkey and speaks not a word of German, should have the immediate right to German nationality, while someone born to Turkish parents in Hamburg, who has spoken German all his life and never set foot in Turkey, has great difficulty in becoming a German citizen. But that is the law, and there is some doubt whether the attempt to change it will be successful.

In France, in contrast, there was a different outcome when a campaign was mounted in the early 1990s to require the children of north African immigrants to pass a certain number of tests before exercising their right to choose at the age of eighteen between full French citizenship and the retention of the Algerian or Moroccan nationality which they inherited from their parents. They should, according to the supporters of the campaign, be obliged to prove their Frenchness by being able to write coherently in French and to answer a number of questions on French history.

It was a project which underlined the difference between the Jacobin, assimilationist model which the French had tried to adopt in their colonies and what they disparagingly refer to as the 'Anglo-Saxon ethnic pluralism' found in English-speaking culture. This is fully accepted in Switzerland, where citizenship is conferred very grudgingly, and then only to those who can show a satisfactory knowledge of Swiss civics.[15] But, as the opponents of the French project pointed out, no comparable requirement was going to be placed on the sons and daughters of ethnically French parents to prove that they could use the imperfect of the subjunctive correctly, or knew that Louis XIV's mistress, Madame de Maintenon (1635–1719), was the grand-daughter of the sixteenth-century Protestant writer Agrippa d'Aubigné (1552–1630). The idea was therefore turned down on the grounds that it was a thinly disguised form of racism.

The considerable support expressed for the project in the more popular and populist press in France offers one of several indications of a general split in contemporary European society, one which separates the enlightened and generally progressive views of the mainly middle-class people who take decisions on contentious matters of social policy from the more neanderthal approach likely to be found in the general public. It is not a split which is limited to questions of race and citizenship. If, in England, a referendum were to be held on the restoration of capital punishment, the rope would be back in action within a week. If the Houses of Parliament were to agree to the proposal made by Field Marshal Montgomery in 1967 that the age of consent for sexual acts between consenting adults should be set at eighty, and not as it had been at eighteen, there would be celebratory double gin and tonics in the nineteenth hole at every golf club in the land.

SOME CONTRASTS WITH NON-EUROPEAN CULTURES

It is fortunate in this respect that Edmund Burke's view of the role of a member of parliament remains an integral part of European democracy. Burke saw him as the representative of the people who elected him, not the delegate whom they send to implement specific measures. It is partly because most members of parliament throughout Europe are more broad-minded than the people who elected them that the situation of immigrants in late twentieth-century Europe is far better than it is in the countries of the Middle East or in Asia.

Just as they have come to Europe in search of a higher standard of living, migrants have gone to the Gulf States in order to work. But when, in 1979, the increase in the price of oil set off by the revolution in Iran led to an economic downturn, Saudi Arabia simply expelled 80,000 illegal immigrants whom it no longer needed. In the recession of 1990–1991, over two million workers were thrown out of Saudi Arabia, Iraq and Kuwait.[16] The Indians, Pakistanis and Bangladeshis currently working in Dubai do so in conditions of virtual slavery. Their passports are taken from them when they arrive; they live in labour camps which they are forbidden to leave; and they are lucky if they work only a twelve-hour day, with no breaks from the sun. Whatever the origins of racism, it is no more a peculiarity of Western capitalism, or even a characteristic expression of it, than is the exploitation of the weak and vulnerable in the quest of profit elsewhere in the world.

In Europe, as distinct from virtually every country except the United States of America, attempts are made to deal with the problem formulated by the Swiss writer Max Frisch when he said 'We asked for labourers, and human beings came'.[17] When, in the early 1980s Nigeria expelled two million Ghanaians whose labour was no longer needed, no protests were allowed, and no exceptions made. In 1981 the French government rounded up 101 illegal immigrants from Mali and sent them home on a charter flight. Although there was nothing that anybody could do about it, there were widespread protests, and it is not an action that has been repeated.

One of the great differences between Europe and the rest of the world, and one which again emphasises the similarity between European culture and that of the United States, is the existence of organised pressure groups. One of the most powerful in the United Kingdom is what its opponents call 'the anti-racialist lobby'. It undoubtedly makes some daft proposals, as in the suggestion in March 1999, in the report on the murder of the black teenager Stephen Lawrence, that the police should be encouraged to bring prosecutions on a charge of racialism on the basis of remarks uttered in private.

It would be idle to pretend that in almost every European country somebody with a white face is not at a considerable advantage over someone with a black or brown face when looking for a job or somewhere to live. The contrast is illustrated by the fact that, while forty-five per cent of the population of greater London has a black or brown face, only four per cent of police officers belong to an ethnic minority.[18] In Germany, hostility to Turkish immigrant workers takes the form of setting fire to the hostels provided for them. In June 1993 five Turks were killed in an arson attack near Cologne. But neo-Nazi groups are officially banned, and the police do what they can to offer protection to immigrants. It is not as it was at the time of Hitler, when the police supported, and sometimes led, racist attacks. In the United Kingdom the Race Relations Act of 1968 banned discrimination in housing, employment, insurance and other services, and made it illegal to put up advertisements of the 'No Poles, Jews, Blacks or Irish' variety, which used to be so marked a feature of private rental arrangements in London and the larger cities. It is as illegal to make racial remarks in public as it is to recommend violence.

Some European countries, it is true, are better at giving immigrants a fair deal than others. Perhaps because the British do not pursue an active policy of integration, and accept what the French socialist politician Michel Rocard calls 'Anglo-Saxon ethnic pluralism', they pass more laws than the French or the Germans to try to help migrant communities to live their own lives without interference. In France and Germany, the ideal is one whereby immigrants become as much like Frenchmen or Germans as possible. In January 1991 a new Foreigners Act was passed in Germany, stating that:

> a process of adaptation to German conditions requires some participation of the aliens who have to accustom themselves above all to the values, norms and ways of living prevailing here. Respect for our culture, abandonment of excessive national-religious behaviour and integration into school and professional life are the prerequisites that have to be fulfilled.[19]

It is a harsh requirement to impose on people devoutly attached to their way of life. But it represents an attitude which is not inconsistent with the idea of the rule of law common to all citizens, which is one of the key ideas in European political culture. If, the Germans say, non-Europeans come to live and work in Europe, they must behave as a polite guest would do in somebody else's house, and not try to change the domestic arrangements to suit his convenience.

This is a very different attitude to Jean-Marie Le Pen's remark that, if he asked a plumber to come and mend a leak in the bathroom, he would not expect him to stay to dinner, and even less to marry his daughter. It is far more of an invitation to make themselves at home, something which a large number of the Asians who have come to live in Great Britain have done with remarkable success. There are 1.5 million of them, the equivalent of the total population of Northern Ireland, and they contribute an annual £5 billion to the British economy.[20]

Notes

PART 1: PEACE AT THE CENTRE AND WAR AT THE EDGES

PRELUDE: PEACE IN EUROPE

1   Eric Newby, *The Big Red Train Ride*, Penguin, London, 1980, p. 88. I am indebted to my friend Brian Innes, creator of the group The Temperance Seven, for this reference.
2   Quoted in Raymond Seitz, *Over Here*, Phoenix, London, 1998, p. 118. Ambassador Seitz also quotes (p. 55) the reply which Jim Baker of Texas made before he became Secretary of State to the question of whether he had ever visited a Communist country: 'No, but I've been to Massachusetts.' However, as President Reagan's behaviour showed in the 1980s, the undoubted differences between East Coast liberals and politicians from California do not prevent the latter from defending the more outspokenly European values of the former. See Chapter 3, pp. 63–65, below.
3   Winston S. Churchill, *The Second World War*, Cassell, London, 1954, vol. VI, p. 561. Quoted by Timothy Garton Ash in *In Europe's Name*, Vintage, London, 1994, p. 406.
4   J.M. Roberts, *The Penguin History of Europe*, Penguin, London, 1996, p. 606.
5   Paul Valéry, *Regards sur le monde actuel* (1919), Pléiade, Paris, 1962, p. 930.
6   Its original version, formulated by Lord Ismay (Martin Walker, *The Cold War and the Making of the Modern World*, Vintage, London, 1994, p. 98) contained no reference to the French. Their inclusion is my addition, justified by the behaviour of General de Gaulle once he had solved the Algerian problem (see Chapters 10 and 11).
7   See John Ardagh, *Germany and the Germans*, Penguin, London, 3rd ed., 1995, p. 499.
8   *Ibid.*, p. 510.
9   John Keegan, *War and Our World*, Hutchinson, London, 1998, pp. 69–70.
10 See John Killick, *The Impact of the Marshall Plan*, Edinburgh University Press, Edinburgh, 1997.

11 Graham Evans and Jeffrey Newnham, *Penguin Dictionary of International Relations*, Penguin, London, 1998, p. 566. For the effect of the 'Concert System', see p. 90.

1 THE CONTEST FOR WESTERN EUROPE(1): THE BERLIN CRISES OF 1948–1949 AND 1958–1962

1 Quoted on the last page of John Mander, *Berlin: hostage for the West*, Penguin, London, 1952.
2 Caroline Kennedy-Pipes, *Stalin's Cold War*, Manchester University Press, Manchester, 1995, p. 4.
3 Martin Walker, *The Cold War and the Making of the Modern World*, London, 1993, Vintage, 1994, p. 1.
4 See Jeremy Isaacs and Taylor Downing, *Cold War: for 45 years the world held its breath*, Bantam Press, London and New York, 1998, pp. 58–9.
5 Milovan Djilas, *Conversations with Stalin*, Penguin, 1962, pp. 90, 119.
6 Quoted from Robert Murphy, *Diplomat Among the Warriors* (Collins, London, 1964) in John and Ann Tusa, *The Berlin Airlift*, Hodder & Stoughton, London, 1988; reissued by Spellmount, Staplehurst, Kent, 1998, p. 20.
7 See Tusa and Tusa, *op. cit.*, p. 140.
8 Bertel Heurlin, *Germany in Europe in the Nineties*, Macmillan, Basingstoke, 1996, p. 1.
9 This superiority may have been an illusion, and the strength of Soviet armed forces deliberately exaggerated by the Central Intelligence Agency in order to increase its own importance and to provide the excuse for its allies in what President Eisenhower called the 'military-industrial complex' to increase the amount of taxpayers' money spent on both nuclear and conventional arms. This view has been defended by Tom Gerassi in *The Myth of Soviet Supremacy*, Harper & Row, New York, 1986, and also formed the starting point for John Le Carré's novel *The Russia House*.
10 See Gwynneth Dyer, *War*, Crown, New York, 1985, p. 200, who gives the proportions of 6,000:800, and argues on p. 226 that neither side ever considered the possibility of a limited nuclear war.

Marc Trachtenberg, in his article 'The Influence of Nuclear Weapons in the Cuban Missile Crisis', *International Security*, Summer 1985, pp. 137–203, discounts the direct influence of American nuclear superiority and quotes President Kennedy himself as saying: 'What difference does it make? They've got enough to blow us up anyway.' This article points out that, whereas American forces were placed on full alert from the moment the crisis broke on October 22, the Russians made no detectable preparations either for a limited or a full-scale war. The explanation for the fact that, as General Burchinall put it, 'we had a gun at Khrushchev's head, and he didn't move a muscle' was that the Russians realised that their bluff had been called and that they had no option but to withdraw.

The discussions in the National Security Council were taped during most of the sessions held while the crisis lasted, and show the American planners speculating a great deal about the possibility that the Russians wanted to see American missiles removed from Turkey. The idea of the installation of rockets in Cuba being linked to a future move on Berlin, however tempting as an explanation in retrospect, does not seem to have attracted much attention at the time.

2 THE BERLIN CRISES AND THE CONTEST FOR WESTERN EUROPE: EXPLANATIONS ANCIENT AND MODERN

1 See Ernest R. May (ed.), *American Cold War Strategy: interpreting NSC 68*, Bedford Books, New York, 1993, pp. 35 and 25
2 Norman Davies, 'Visions of Europe', in *Time*, January 1999, p. 31. Professor Davies is, of course, well known for his very successful *Europe: a history*, Oxford University Press, Oxford, 1996. Although a highly stimulating read, it is a book which has a fault more frequently illustrated by newspaper articles or television programmes. For it is a common experience to find that every time they deal with a subject which one knows reasonably well oneself, they get the details wrong. See my review in *European Studies*, xxvii (1997), pp. 92–9.
3 Ardagh, *op. cit.*, p. 378.
4 Thucydides, *History of the Peloponnesian War*, book V, para. 105. The most readable translation is Rex Warner's of 1954, with introduction and notes by M.I. Finley added in 1972 (Penguin, Harmondsworth, 1972).

Not all historians agree with Thucydides' presentation of the Athenian attack on Melos as an act of aggression against an inoffensive neutral. A.H.M. Jones writes on p. 71 of his *Athenian Democracy* (Blackwell, Oxford, 1957) that 'in point of fact, Melos had been a non-belligerent ally of Sparta since the beginning of the war, subscribing to the war fund and sheltering her fleet in 427, and Athens had, not unnaturally, been at war with the Melians since 426'. Mr Khrushchev might have taken a very similar view of West Berlin. Although it existed financially only as a result of a heavy subsidy from the government of the FGR, it was the headquarters for a number of radio and television services which served to destabilise the East German régime by enabling its citizens to see how much more prosperous life was in the West.
5 Isaac Deutscher, *The Great Contest: Russia and the West*, Oxford University Press, Oxford, 1960, pp. 53–4
6 G.E.M. de St. Croix, *The Origins of the Peloponnesian War*, Duckworth, London, 1972, pp. 18, 23.
7 Walter Lafeber, *America, Russia and the Cold War*, Knopf, New York, 1985, p. 58.
8 Fred Halliday, *The Making of the Second Cold War*, Verso, London and New York, 1983, p. 3; D.F. Flemming, in Thomas T. Hammond (ed.)

Witnesses to the Origins of the Cold War, Seattle, WA and London, University of Washington Press, 1982 p. 16.

9   Stephen J. Whitfield, *The Culture of the Cold War*, Johns Hopkins University Press, Baltimore, MD, 1991, p. 210; May (ed.), *op. cit.*, p. 117.

3   THE CONTEST FOR WESTERN EUROPE(2): DÉTENTE AND THE MISSILES OF THE 1980s

1   Jim Petras and Morris Morley, 'The New Cold War: Reagan's policy towards Europe and the Third World', *ENDpapers*, 4, p. 110.

2   Isaacs and Downing, *op. cit.*, p. 326.

3   Figures taken from Walker, *op.cit*, p. 250.

4   Quoted by Alex R. Alexiev in his 1985 article 'The Soviet Campaign against INF (Intermediate Nuclear Force): strategy, tactics and means', *Orbis*, vol. 29, no 2, pp. 319–50. The fact that Dr Alexiev is a Senior Analyst of Soviet Affairs with the Rand Corporation remains enough to discredit him with most of my former colleagues.

5   E.P. Thompson (ed.), *Protest and Survive*, Penguin, London, 1980. Thompson is best known among historians for his authoritative *The Making of the English Working Class* (Gollancz, London, 1963), an account in Marxist terms of the suffering and exploitation which characterised the Industrial Revolution of the late eighteenth and early nineteenth centuries.

6   Whitfield, *op.cit.* p. 220. It will be recalled that one of the first orders that General J. Ripper gives when sending his wing of the Strategic Air Command off to attack the USSR is that all private transistor radios must be immediately impounded. Had the French Generals who tried to organise the *coup d'état* against General de Gaulle in April 1961 taken the same precautions, they might have got away with it. See Chapter 12.

7   Anthony Kenny, *The Logic of Deterrence*, Firethorn Press, London, 1985, p. x.

8   This figure varies from one authority to another. On p. 1097 of *Europe: a history*, *op.cit*, Norman Davies gives 30 per cent. Arnold Beichman, in *The Long Pretence: Soviet treaty diplomacy from Lenin to Gorbatchev*, Transition Publishers, New Brunswick, 1991, p. 45, gives between 13 per cent and 19 per cent. *Quid 1999*, Robert Laffont, Paris, 1999, p. 1177, gives 25 per cent. It bases this on the discrepancy between the claim made by the Soviet Union that its total annual GDP was 50 per cent of that of the USA and the more realistic figure of 14 per cent, and maintains that the USSR spent 200 billion roubles on defence, and not the official figure of 70.

4 WAR AT THE EDGES: NORTHERN IRELAND AND YUGOSLAVIA

1 Pauline Neville-Jones, review of Richard Holbrooke, *To End a War* (Random House, New York, 1998) in *Prospect*, London, October 1998, p. 60.
2 Thomas Hennessey, *A History of Northern Ireland, 1920–1996*, Macmillan, Basingstoke, p. 250, where the statement appears that 'the Provisional IRA and other republicans were responsible for the murder of about 70 per cent of the 2,859 victims of violence'.
3 See Keith Feiling, *A History of England*, Macmillan, Basingstoke, 1996, p. 751. For population figures, see Feiling, pp. 386, 752; for land held by Catholics, Robert Kee, *Ireland: a history*, Weidenfeld & Nicolson, London, 1981, p. 11.
4 Hennessey, *op. cit.*, pp. 11–12.
5 Anthony Parsons, *From Cold War to Hot Peace: UN interventions, 1947–1995*, Penguin, London, 1995, p. 221.
6 Milovan Djilas, interview in *New York Times*, February 2, 1971, quoted in Teresa Rakoswska-Harmstone and Andrew Gyorgy, *Communism in Eastern Europe*, Indiana University Press, Bloomington IN and London, 1979, p. 302. Djilas was a former colleague of Tito's who was jailed for criticising the régime. His best-known book, *The New Class* (1966) is discussed in Chapter 6.
7 Frank Roberts, *Dealing with Dictators: the destruction and revival of Europe. 1930–1979*, Weidenfeld & Nicolson, London, 1979, p. 176. The six republics were Bosnia-Hercegovina, Croatia, Macedonia, Montenegro, Serbia, and Slovenia; the five nationalities presumably – though, one would have to ask them – Bosnians, Croatians, Montenegrins, Serbians and Slovenians; the four religions Communism, Roman Catholicism, Orthodox Christianity and Islam; the three languages Serbo-Croat, Montenegrin, and Slovenian; and the two scripts Cyrillic and Roman.
8 Parsons, *op. cit.*, p. 224.
9 See the 1992 edition of *The Annual Register*, Longmans, London, 1992, a publication first compiled by Edmund Burke in 1758 for the fee of £100. It has been in continuous existence since, and offers the best and most reliable way of checking facts on world events. On p. 116 of the 1996 edition, it gives the figure of 441,938 for the refugees in Bosnia in 1994, and reports 600,678 Bosnians as having fled to other countries.

PART 2: THE RISE AND FALL OF THE SOCIALIST IDEAL

PRELUDE: MARXIST ANALYSIS AND HISTORICAL PRACTICE

1 Trotsky, quoted in Robert Conquest, *Stalin: breaker of nations*, Weidenfeld & Nicolson, London, 1991, p. 119.

2 For D.F. Flemming, see *The Cold War and its Origins*, 2 vols, Doubleday, Garden City NY, l960, vol. I, p. 31.

For Lafeber, see *America, Russia and the Cold War*, Knopf, New York, 1985 (originally published by Wiley, New York, 1967).

For Gar Alperovitz, see *Atomic Diplomacy: Hiroshima and Potsdam*, Penguin, London, 1985.

For a discussion of the 'Revisionist' historians, see Joseph M. Siracusa, *New Left Diplomatic Histories and Historians*, National University Publications, Kennikat Press, Port Washington, 1973.

For A.J.P. Taylor, see his review of Daniel Yergin's *The Shattered Peace: the origins of the Cold War and the national security state* (Houghton Mifflin, New York, 1978) in *From the Boer War to the Cold War*, Penguin, London, 1996, p. 403. The review first appeared in *The New Statesman* on January 13, 1978.

3 Thomas Balogh, quoted by Noel Annan in *Our Age*, Fontana, London, 1991, p. 299.

4 Beatrice and Sidney Webb, *Soviet Communism: a new civilisation*, 3rd ed., reissued, Longmans, Green, London, 1947, p. xxii.

5 Jean-Paul Sartre, 'Merleau-Ponty vivant', *Situations* IV, Gallimard, Paris, 1964, p. 227.

6 Arthur Koestler, *Darkness at Noon*, Penguin, London, 1940, pp. 119–20.

7 Webb and Webb, *op. cit.*, p. 490.

8 *Ibid.*, pp. 511, 533. The alert reader will have noticed, through my *caveats* about the survival of Western capitalism, my awareness of the reader over my shoulder mentioned in note 7 to the Prelude to Part 4.

9 Henry Chadwick, *The Christian Church in the Cold War*, Penguin, London, 1992, p. 24.

10 Alan Milne, *Ethical Frontiers of the State*, Macmillan, Basingstoke, 1998, p. 150. Milne was once informed by his accountant of a perfectly legal scheme whereby he might reduce his tax liabilities. 'Thank you very much,' he said. 'But if I do that, and everybody else does the same, who is going to pay for the fire service?'

11 Webb and Webb, *op. cit.*, p. xxxvii.

5 THE FRUITS OF VICTORY

1 Geoffrey and Nigel Swain, *Eastern Europe Since 1945*, Macmillan, Basingstoke, 1993, p. 7.

2 Vernon A. Aspaturian in Rakoswska-Harmstone and Gyorgy (ed.), *op. cit.*, p. 21; Swain and Swain, *op. cit.*, p. 32.

3 Isaacs and Downing, *op. cit.*, p. 52.

4 *Ibid.*, p. 51.

5 Swain and Swain, *op. cit.*, p. 61.

6 'Oh, you know, Philip', as my friend and former colleague Max Silverman explained to me, 'tanks into East Germany, tanks into Hungary, tanks into Czechoslovakia, tanks into Poland.'

7 Webb and Webb, *op. cit.*, p. 468. In Russian, the term *kulak* means 'tight-fisted', and the Webbs reduce the effects of their earlier condemnation

by describing the typical *kulak* as 'a terrible oppressor of his poorer neighbours'. They also write of the *kulak*s as being 'universally hated', and regard their elimination as essential to the creation of large-scale agriculture in the Soviet Union. They also mitigate their criticism of this aspect of Soviet behaviour, by making two points which recur quite frequently in the books written by other fellow travellers.

Thus there is the 'we have behaved just as badly in the West' argument, as when they write on p. 471 that 'We have no wish to minimise, still less to justify, this ruthless expropriation of the occupiers and kulaks, any more than we do the equally ruthless expulsion, little over a century ago, of the crofters from so much of the Scottish highlands, or the economic ruin of so many small-holders that accompanied the statutory enclosure of the English commons.' This is accompanied by the anxiety to see the Soviet Union avoid the mistakes made by the French Revolution, as when they write on p. 466 that 'the Communist Party was determined that the USSR should not follow the example of France in permanently establishing a class of peasant proprietors'.

8   The phrase occurs in Hobsbawm's *Age of Extremes: the short twentieth century, 1914–1991*, Michael Joseph, London, 1994. Centuries do vary in length and from country to country. The sixteenth century in England begins with the accession of Henry VII in 1485 and ends with the death of Elizabeth I in 1603. In France, in contrast, it starts with the accession of Francis I in 1515 and ends with the end of the wars of religion and the Edict of Nantes in 1598. The eighteenth century in England goes from the Glorious Revolution of 1688 to the end of the Napoleonic Wars in 1815; in France it is again much shorter, going from the death of Louis XIV in 1715 to the outbreak of the Revolution in 1789.

9   Ronald Hingley, *Joseph Stalin: the man and his legend*, Hutchinson, London, 1974, p. 436.

10 Leon Feuchtwanger, *Moscow 1937: my visit described for my friends* Gollancz, London, 1937, p. 135.

11 Zbigniew Brzezinski, *The Permanent Purge: politics in the Soviet Union*, Harvard University Press, 1956, p. 74. As his name suggests, Brzezinski was of Polish origin, a fact which explains his critical view of the Soviet Union. His hawkish attitude made him a surprising choice as the dove-like President Carter's special adviser on national security.

12 Edward Gibbon,*The Decline and Fall of the Roman Empire*, Chapter 4.

13 Alexander Solzhenitsyn, *The Gulag Archipelago*, Collins, London, 1974, p. 133.

14 Arthur Koestler, *The Invisible Writing*, Hamish Hamilton, London, 1954, p. 423.

15 *Ibid.*, p. 15.

16 Arthur Koestler, *Darkness at Noon* (1940), Penguin, London, 1946, p. 144.

17 Koestler, *The Invisible Writing, op. cit.*, p. 405.

18 *Ibid.*, p. 405. Although the textual similarity with p. 216 of the Penguin edition of the English translation of *Darkness at Noon* is not strong, the ideas are identical. Katz was presumably speaking in Czech, and *Darkness at Noon* was originally written in German.

This was something of which F.R. Leavis, the best-known and most influential literary critic writing in twentieth-century England, seemed to be unaware when he described it in 1955, in *The Great Tradition*, as a 'very distinguished novel', which showed that Koestler, like Joseph Conrad, another author 'not born to the language' could nevertheless write admirable English. The compliment, albeit sincere, was based on a misunderstanding. Koestler wrote *Darkness at Noon* in German and had it translated into English by his mistress, Daphne Hardy.

19 See Arthur and Cynthia Koestler, *Stranger on the Square*, Hutchinson, London, 1984, p. 50. Cynthia, *née* Jeffreys, was Koestler's third wife, whom he married in 1965. On March 3, 1983 her body was found in the same room as Koestler's in their apartment in Montpelier Square. They had both taken a massive dose of barbiturates, Koestler because he was suffering from Parkinson's disease and did not wish to inflict his physical decay either on himself or his friends, Cynthia, who was 22 years his junior, for reasons which remain hidden.

20 Noel Annan, *Changing Enemies: the defeat and regeneration of Germany.* HarperCollins, London, 1995, p. 219.

21 David Cesarini, *Arthur Koestler: the homeless mind*, Heinemann, London, 1998, p. 343. It will be recalled that Senator Joseph McCarthy was a ferocious anti-Communist whose mendacity launched the witch-hunts for alleged Communists and former Communists in the United States which inspired Arthur Miller's 1956 play *The Crucible*. He was eventually censured by his fellow Senators, and sank into alcoholism and obscurity.

22 From Isaac Deutscher's essay *Heretics and Renegades*, Hamish Hamilton, London, 1955, reprinted in Raymond Williams (ed.), *George Orwell: a collection of critical essays*, Prentice Hall, Englewood Cliffs, NJ, 1974, p. 132.

23 In his 1954 introduction to the American edition of Orwell's early novel *Keep the Aspidistra Flying* (1936), Anthony West argued that the horrors characterising the Oceania of *Nineteen Eighty-Four* could be traced back to the unpleasantness of Eric Blair's early schooldays, described in the essay 'Such, Such Were The Joys'. The question is well analysed on p. 390 *passim* of Bernard Crick's biography, *George Orwell: a life*, Secker & Warburg, London, 1980.

24 *Nineteen Eighty-Four*, Penguin, London, 1949, p. 199. For Lenin, see Eric Laurent, *La Corde pour les pendre*, Fayard, Paris, 1985, p. 109.

6 THE END OF EASTERN EUROPEAN SOCIALISM

1 Quoted in Swain and Swain, *op. cit.*, pp. 95–6.

2 A good account of the problems of the Polish economy, as indeed of the all the events which took in the Soviet satellites between 1946 and 1993, can be found in Ben Fowkes, *The Rise and Fall of Communism in Eastern Europe*, Macmillan, Basingstoke, 1993.
3 Ash, *op. cit.*, Vintage, 1994, p. 356 and p. 2.
4 *Ibid.*, pp. 9. 146, 155.
5 *Quid 1999, op. cit.*, p. 1173.
6 Ash, *op. cit.*, p. 119.
7 R.W. Davies, *The Soviet Union*, 2nd ed., London, Unwin Hyman, 1989, p. 97.
8 *The Economist*, December 12, 1998.

7 SOCIALISM IN WESTERN EUROPE

1 Information provided by Dr Ray Davison, of the East Devon Labour Party. See also David Childs, *Britain Since 1945*, Routledge, 1997, p. 298.
2 Malcolm Cook and Grace Davie, *Modern France: a society in transition*, Routledge, 1999, p. 22. Also *Quid 1999, op. cit.*, p. 1858.
3 Max-Stephan Schulze, *Western Europe: economic and social change since 1945*, Longman, 1999, p. 1.
4 Information supplied by Ray Davison.
5 Will Hutton, *The State We're In*, Vintage, 1995, p. 172.
6 *The Economist*, June 12, 1999, p. 102.
7 Hutton, *op. cit.*, p. 195.
8 Peter Pugh, *Thatcher for Beginners*, Icon Books 1997, p. 118.
9 Schulze, *op. cit.*. p. 384. An article in *The Times* for June 8, 1999 suggested that some improvement in Britain's relative position might now be taking place. If the annual GDP of the UK were taken as 100, that of France was 85 in 1960; 115 in 1970; 123 in 1980 and 1990; 131 in 1984 but only 105 in 1998. That of Germany was 113 in 1960; 167 in 1970; 169 in 1980; 201 in 1994; and 157 in 1998. Italy had gone from 56 in 1960 to 86 in 1970, 84 in 1980, 112 in 1990, 100 (exactly equal to that of the UK) in 1994, but was now only 86. Britain had, in other words, slightly improved its position in relation to the three largest European economies, being now only slightly behind France, slightly ahead of Italy, and not quite so far behind Germany as it was in 1994.
10 Quoted in Pugh, *op cit.*, p. 86.
11 Quoted by Alan Sked and Chris Cook on p. 444 of *Post-War Britain*, 4th ed., Penguin, London, 1994, which gives an excellent account of these events.
12 The word means 'passion flower', and refers to Dolores Ibarruri Gómez, who helped found the Spanish Communist Party in 1920, and whose songs inspired the fighters on the Republican side during the Spanish civil war of 1936–1939. She is credited with the invention of the slogan 'It is better to die on your feet than live on your knees'.
13 Eric. J. Evans, *Thatcher and Thatcherism*, Routledge, 1997, p. 124.

14 *Ibid.*, p, 43. Pym did win the Military Cross, a decoration awarded only for courage on the field of battle, so some tolerance should be extended to his judgment on military matters.
15 Alan Clark, *Diaries*, Phoenix, 1994, p. 69. Blood in the sense of breeding, aristocratic lineage.
16 Childs, *op. cit.*, p. 40.
17 Ardagh, *op. cit.*, p. 114.
18 *Ibid.*, p. 128.

PART 3: THE MOVEMENT TOWARDS EUROPEAN UNITY

PRELUDE: EUROPEAN VALUES AND THE EUROPEAN UNION

1 See *The Pocket World in Figures, The Economist* in collaboration with Profile Books, London, 1998, p. 86.
2 T.O. Lloyd, *The British Empire, 1558–1983*, Oxford University Press, Oxford, 1984, p. 2.
3 Patrick Ireland, *The Policy Challenge of Ethnic Diversity: immigrant politics in France and Switzerland*, Cambridge, MA and London, Harvard University Press, 1994, p. 71.
4 Published in 1947, at the height not only of Huxley's own mystical period, but at a time when Christopher Isherwood was publishing his translations of the Bhaghavad-Gita and other Hindu classics, and Somerset Maugham's *The Razor's Edge* (1945) had also helped to inspire George Orwell's comment, in his essay 'Lear, Tolstoy and the Fool' about 'this Yoga ridden age'.
5 *Quid 1999, op. cit.*, p. 1170.
6 Peter Rietbergen, *Europe: a cultural history*, Routledge, London and New York, 1998, p. 87.

8 THE ESTABLISHMENT OF THE EUROPEAN ECONOMIC COMMUNITY

1 See Stephen George, *An Awkward Partner: Britain in the European Community*, Oxford University Press, Oxford, 1990.
2 Quoted by Alfred Grosser, *The Western Alliance: European–American relations since 1945*, Macmillan, Basingstoke, 1980, p. 121.
3 See Hugo Young, *This Blessed Plot: Britain and Europe from Churchill to Blair*, Macmillan, Basingstoke, 1998, pp. 97–104. For Lord Hurd's review, see *Daily Telegraph*, November 11, 1998. Hugo Young also points out that Russell Bretherton had been the tutor of the young Harold Wilson when the latter had been the most brilliant student of economics in his year at Oxford.
4 Dick Leonard, *Guide to the European Union, The Economist* in association with Profile Books, 6th ed., London, 1998, p. 95.

5 *Ibid.*, p. 143.
6 For a fuller discussion of the issue, see Rosemary Fennell, *The Common Agricultural Policy of the European Communities*, BSP Basic Books, Oxford, 1987.
7 Leonard, *op. cit.*, p 141.
8 Perhaps significantly, the French one-volume encyclopaedia *Quid* gives a very full account of the American price-support system, pointing out on p. 1670 of the 1999 edition that the Federal government provided $52 billion in direct support for agriculture between 1985 and 1990, and that the USA has a surplus of $17 billion in its agricultural trade with the rest of the world. Since it also, according to *Quid*, exports twice as much to the EEC as it imports from Europe, there is little justification for the remark which President Bush made on January 13, 1992 about 'the protectionist iron curtain of the CAP'.
9 Figures from *Quid 1995*, Robert Laffont, Paris, 1995, p. 1555.
10 Leonard, *op.cit.*, pp. 136, 190 and p. 101.
11 Dennis Swann, *The Economics of the Common Market*, Penguin, London, 1990, p. 98.
12 Quoted in George, *op.cit.*, p. 26.
13 Klaus-Dieter Borchardt, *The ABC of Community Law*, 4th ed., Office for Official Publications of the European Communities, Luxembourg, 1994, p. 24.
14 The tactic was used in an attempt to counteract the refusal of the Commission to allow the export of British beef, widely seen as dangerous on health grounds because of the danger of human beings contracting the human equivalent of 'mad cow' disease (bovine spongiform encephalitis), Creutzfeldt-Jacob's disease, CJD. The boycott lasted eight weeks, and had no effect. The ban on the export of British beef was not lifted until late in 1998, and its existence offers an illustration, especially to Eurosceptics, of the dangers of the loss of national sovereignty implied in the Treaty of Rome. Not only does this treaty restrict the right of member states to decide on the customs duties to impose on its imports, it also forbids them to export what they wish, a fact greeted with astonishment and indignation by the British press. It is nevertheless improbable, after the world-wide publicity given to the existence of CJD, that many Third Countries would have allowed British beef to be imported on to their territory anyway.
15 Quoted by Bernard Connolly, *The Rotten Heart of Europe*, Faber, London, 1995, p. 7

9 THE EEC AND THE OIL CRISES OF THE 1970s

1 Jean-François Revel, *En France*, Julliard, Paris, 1965, p. 42.
2 The matter is more fully discussed on pp. 66–9 of my *An Historical Introduction to the European Union*, Routledge, 1987.
3 See Leonard, *op. cit.*, p. 154, which lists the UK as the third-largest recipient, with a lower limit of 14.48 per cent and an upper limit of

19.31 per cent of European Regional Development Fund (ERDF) allocations, compared with 17.95 and 23.93 for Spain and 21.59 and 28.79 for Italy. In 1997 the money available to the ERDF was about thirty per cent of that for agriculture.

4   *The Economist*, May 16, 1998.
5   Leonard, *op. cit.*, p. 262.
6   Fourastié's book, *Les Trente Glorieuses*, was published in Paris in 1979. Its title evoked the 'trois glorieuses', the 'journées révolutionnaires' of July 29, 30, 31, which overthrew the Restoration monarchy in 1830, and which are commemorated in the column in the Place de la Bastille. The term 'sixty glorious years' evokes the triumphs celebrated in 1897 by the Diamond Jubilee of Queen Victoria.
7   Quoted by Paul Johnson, *A History of the Modern World*, Weidenfeld & Nicolson, London, 1978, p. 666.
8   Lloyd, *op. cit.*, p. 370.
9   Johnson, *op. cit.*, p. 669
10 Leonard, *op. cit.*, pp. 175–6.

10 THE ENLARGEMENT OF THE EEC AND THE CREATION OF THE EURO

1   Timothy Bainbridge and Anthony Teasdale, *The Penguin Companion to the European Union*, Penguin, London, 1997, p. 23
2   *Ibid.*, p. 83. The smallness of France's contribution stems from the fact that she imports very little food from Third Countries.
3   Athenian democracy lasted, roughly, from 508 to 398 BC and differed markedly from its modern form. It was based on a meeting of all the citizens, excluding women and slaves, which took political decisions on immediate issues. There were no political parties, no regular elections, and no civil service either to ensure continuity of policy, to advise ministers, or to make sure that the decisions of the assembly were put into effect. It can nevertheless be seen as a forerunner of what Karl Popper called 'the open society' in that it allowed freedom of speech and respected the right of individuals to lead their private life without state interference.
4   See Leonard, *op. cit.*, p. 270.

PART 4: THE ENDING OF THE EUROPEAN EMPIRES

PRELUDE: THE EUROPEAN EMPIRES BEFORE 1945

1   See D.S.L. Cardwell and Donald Stephen Lowell, *The Fontana History of Technology*, Fontana, London, 1994, p. 74.
2   Arnold Pacey, *Technology in World Civilization*, MIT Press, Cambridge, MA, 1991, p. 55.

3 Fernand Braudel, *Europe*, Arts et métiers graphiques, Paris, 1983, p. 123.
4 *Ibid.*, p. 132.
5 Pacey, *op. cit.*, p. 68.
6 Evans and Newman, *op. cit.*, p. 348.
7 Sonia Orwell and Ian Angus, *The Collected Essays, Journalism and Letters of George Orwell*, Secker and Warburg, 1968, vol. II, p. 184.

The line in question from 'Recessional' is 'Lesser breeds without the Law', and is generally interpreted as expressing the disparaging attitude of British imperialists towards the nations they had taken it upon themselves to govern. Orwell points out that this was not Kipling's intention. The line almost certainly refers, as he says, 'to the Germans, and especially the pan-German writers, who are "without the Law" in the sense of being lawless, though not in the sense of being powerless'.

I am, in quoting without disapproval one of Orwell's more homophobic remarks, and in making favourable reference to Kipling, acutely aware of the person whom Virginia Woolf calls 'the reader over my shoulder'. It is someone for whom it is axiomatic that no Western politician exercising power has ever done anything right. This reader is younger than I am, and has imbibed from her or his upbringing in the 1960s and 1970s an opposite set of presuppositions to those which I acquired in the 1940s and 1950s and of which I have been acutely conscious when writing this book.

8 See Alain Peyrefitte, *C'était de Gaulle*, Fayard, Paris, 1997, p. 159.
9 The 'First World' is that of the industrialised countries inhabited by the inhabitants of Western Europe or by their descendants in North America and Australasia. Since the 1950s it has become applicable to Japan, and since the 1970s to the 'Tiger economies' of South East Asia. The 'Second World', a political rather than an economic or geographical concept, used to be applied to those countries, especially the Soviet Union and the People's Republic of China, whose rulers had decided to modernise by the application of Marxism-Leninism. It has now largely disappeared. The 'Third World', a term now increasingly replaced by 'the developing' or 'the newly developed world', was made up of countries which had not yet reached what Western commentators call 'economic take-off'; in other words, which had not yet begun to industrialise themselves.

11 FRANCE, INDOCHINA AND ALGERIA

1 Braudel, *op. cit.*, p. 126.
2 Sir Robert Thompson and John Keegan (eds), *War in Peace: an analysis of warfare from 1945 to the present day*, Orbis, London, 1981, p. 67.
3 According to Louis J. Halle, *The Cold War as History*, Chatto & Windus, London 1967, p. 297, two American aircraft carriers, bearing nuclear weapons, were on their way to Indochina, and alarm in the United Kingdom was such as to compel Winston Churchill to state

categorically in the House of Commons on April 27, 1954 that the British government had committed itself to no military action of any form in Indochina.

4   *Quid 1999, op. cit.*, p. 915.

12 PORTUGAL, THE NETHERLANDS AND BELGIUM

1   Thompson and Keegan, *op. cit.*, p. 156.

13 THE RECORD OF GREAT BRITAIN

1   Thompson and Keegan, *op. cit.*, p. 89.
2   He had ten children, and it is alleged that his unsuccessful attempt to construct the Panama Canal in 1869 was inspired by the need to provide for them all.
3   Quoted by Dilwyn Porter, in Nick Tiratsoo (ed.), *From Blitz to Blair: a new history of Britain since 1939*, Phoenix, London, 1998, p. 115.
4   Walker, *op. cit.*, p. 97.
5   Alan Sked and Chris Cook, *Post-War Britain: a political history*, 4th ed., Penguin, London, 1993, p. 130.
6   Walker, *op. cit.*, p. 99.
7   Quoted in Sked and Cook, *op. cit.*, p. 365.
8   Koestler, *The Invisible Writing, op. cit.*, p. 457.

14 THE AFTERMATH OF EMPIRE

1   Ireland, *op. cit.*, p. 1.
2   Sarah Collinson, *Europe and International Migration*, Pinter, London and New York, 1993, pp. 3, 34.
3   *Ibid.*, p. 156.
4   Ireland, *op. cit.*, pp. 2, 84. Collinson, *op. cit.*, p. 84. Dudley Baines, 'European Immigration Since 1945', in Max-Stephan Schulze (ed.), *op. cit.*, pp. 177–189.
5   Cathie Lloyd in Malcolm Cook and Grace Davie (eds), *Modern France: society in transition*, Routledge, 1999, p. 40.
6   Ireland, *op. cit.*, p. 11; Ardagh, *op. cit.*, p. 274 and p. 14; Lloyd in Cook and Davie (eds), *op. cit.*, p. 40.
7   Richard Bessel in T.C.W. Blanning, *The Oxford Illustrated History of Modern Europe*, Oxford University Press, Oxford, 1996, p. 235.
8   Ireland, *op. cit.*, p. 137
9   Sked and Cook, *op. cit.*, p. 269.
10 *Ibid.*, p. 358–9.
11 For a good if pessimistic account of these, see Peter Fysh, 'The Failure of Anti-Racist Movements in France, 1981–1995', in Mairi Maclean (ed.), *The Mitterrand Years: legacy and evaluation*, Macmillan, Basingstoke, 1998, pp. 198–213.
12 There is a good account of the matter, together with some useful dates, on pp. 207–210 of Grace Davie's 'Religion and *laïcité*' in Cook

and Davie, *op. cit.* I discuss some of the social and philosophical issues in the entry 'veil' in part V of *Don't Do It: a dictionary of the forbidden*, Athlone, London, 1998. My friend and former colleague Max Silverman, classifies the phenomenon on pp. 58–9 of his *Facing Modernity: contemporary French thought on culture and society*, Routledge, 1999, as an example of what he calls 'new racism'.

13 Gayatri Chakravorty Spivak, 'Who Needs the Great Works?', *Harper's Bazaar*, September 1989, p. 46.

14 Seitz, *op. cit.*, p. 303.

15 Ireland, *op. cit.*, p. 20.

16 Collinson, *op. cit.*, p. 16.

17 Quoted by Ireland, *op. cit.*, p. 154. Patrick Ireland does not make Switzerland sound a very welcoming place for migrant workers, or indeed for any kind of foreigner. On p. 148 he writes that Swiss governments and institutions have since 1945, 'worked even more earnestly than their French counterparts to keep foreigners out of host-society politics, and divided along ethnic lines'. Before naturalisation is granted, they demand a complete break with the migrant's home culture and a large sum of money in legal fees and expenses. They also insist even more rigidly than the Germans on the *jus sanguinis*.

18 *Daily Telegraph*, February 26, 1999.

19 Quoted in Collinson, *op. cit.*, p. 96.

20 Review of Ram Gidoomal, *The UK Maharajas* (Nicholas Brearly, 1997) in *Journal of the Royal Society of Arts*, April 1998, p. 128.

Guide to further reading

PART I PEACE AT THE CENTRE AND WAR AT THE EDGES

Ardagh, J. (1995) *Germany and the Germans*, 3rd edn, Harmondsworth: Penguin.

Childs, D. (1997) *Great Britain since 1945: a political history*, London: Routledge.

Djilas, A. (1996) *The Contested Country: Yugoslav unity and Communist revolution, 1919–1953*, London: Harvard University Press.

Ellwood, D. W., Nicholls, A.J. and Alexander, M. S. (1992) *Rebuilding Europe: Western Europe, America and postwar reconstruction*, Harlow: Addison-Wesley Longman.

Ermarth, M. (ed.) (1993) *America and the Shaping of German Society 1945–1955*, Oxford: Berg Publishers.

Evans, G. and Newnham, J. (1998) *Dictionary of International Relations*, Harmondsworth: Penguin.

Fraser, T.G. (1999) *Ireland in Conflict*, London: Routledge.

Garton Ash, T. (1994) *In Europe's Name*, London: Vintage.

Lydon, J. (1998) *The Making of Ireland from Ancient Times to the Present*, London: Routledge.

Oberdorfer, D. (1998) *From the Cold War to a New Era – the US and the Soviet Union*, New York: Johns Hopkins University Press.

Painter, D.S. (1999) *The Cold War in International History*, London and New York: Routledge.

Roberts, J.M. (ed.) (1996) *The Penguin History of Europe*, Harmondsworth: Penguin.

Walker, M. (1994) *The Cold War and the Making of the Modern World*, London: Vintage.

PART 2 THE RISE AND FALL OF THE SOCIALIST IDEAL

Brunt, B. (1997) *Western Europe: a social and economic geography*, London: Gill and Macmillan.

Cook, M. and Davie, G. (1997) *Britain Since 1945*, London: Routledge.

Fowkes, B. (1993) *The Rise and Fall of Communism in Eastern Europe*, London: Macmillan.

Hobsbawm, E. (1994) *The Short Twentieth Century 1914–1991*, London: Michael Joseph.

Keep, J. (1996) *Last of the Empires: a history of the Soviet Union 1945–1991*, Oxford: Oxford University Press.

Lester, J. (1995) *Modern Tsars and Princes: the struggle for hegemony in Russia*, London: Verso.

Lewis, P. G. (1994) *Central Europe Since 1945*, Harlow: Addison-Wesley Longman.

Pond, E. (1993) *Beyond the Wall: Germany's road to unification*, Washington DC: The Brookings Institution.

Rothschild, J. (1994) *Return to Diversity: a political history of East Central Europe since World War II*, New York: Oxford University Press.

Sked, A. and Cook, C. (1994) *Post-War Britain*, 4th edn, Harmondsworth: Penguin.

Swain, G. and Swain, N. (1998) *Eastern Europe Since 1945*, London: Macmillan.

Unwin D.W. (1997) *A Political History of Western Europe Since 1945*, Harlow: Addison-Wesley Longman.

PART 3   THE MOVEMENT TOWARDS EUROPEAN UNITY

Armstrong, D., Lloyd, L. and Redmond, J. (1996) *From Versailles to Maastricht: international organisations in the twentieth century*, London: Macmillan.

Bambridge, T. and Teasdale, A. (1997) *The Penguin Companion to the European Union*, Harmondsworth: Penguin.

Dinan, D. (1999) *Ever Closer Union*, London: Macmillan.

George, S. (1998) *An Awkward Partner – Britain in the European Community*, Oxford: Oxford University Press.

Greenwood, S. (1992) *Britain and European Cooperation Since 1945*, Oxford: Blackwell.

Harryvan, A.G. and van de Harst, J. (1997) *Documents on European Union*, London: Macmillan.

Leonard, D. (1998) *A Guide to the European Union*, London: The Economist in association with Profile Books.

Rietbergen, P. (1998) *Europe: a cultural history*, London: Routledge.

Swann, D. (1995) *The Economics of the Common Market*, Harmondsworth: Penguin.

Thody, P. (1997) *An Historical Introduction to the European Union*, London: Routledge.

Unwin D. W. (1991) *The Community of Europe: a history of european integration since 1945*, Harlow: Addison-Wesley Longman.

PART 4 THE ENDING OF THE EUROPEAN EMPIRES

Aldrich, R. (1996) *Greater France: a history of French overseas expansion*, New York: St. Martin's Press.

Ansprenger, F. (1989) *The Dissolution of Colonial Empires*, London: Routledge.

Berend, I.T. (1996) *Central and Eastern Europe, 1994–1993: detour from the periphery to the periphery*, Cambridge: Cambridge University Press.

Betts, R.F. (1998) *Decolonization*, London: Routledge.

Chamberlain, M.E. (1999) *Decolonization: the fall of European empires*, 2nd edn, Oxford: Blackwells.

Cook, C. and Paxton, J. (1998) *European Political Facts 1900–1996*, London: Macmillan.

Crafts, N. (ed.) (1996) *Economic Growth in Europe Since 1945*, Cambridge: Cambridge University Press.

Darwin, J. (1991) *The End of the Empire: the historical debate*, London: Basil Blackwell.

Fox, E.W. (1991) *The Emergence of the Modern European World*, London: Blackwell.

Gildea, R. (1997) *France Since 1945*, Oxford: Oxford University Press.

Graham, B. (1998) *Modern Europe*, London: Arnold.

Holland, R.F. (1985) *European Decolonization 1918–1981: an introductory survey*, London: Macmillan.

Hollifield, J. F. and Ross, G. (eds) (1991) *Searching for the New France*, London: Routledge.

Larsen, S.U. (ed.) (1998) *Modern Europe after Fascism*, New York: University Presses of California, Columbia and Princeton European monographs imprint.

Mendras, H. and Cole, A. (1991) *Social Change in the Fifth Republic: towards a cultural anthropology of modern France*, Cambridge: Cambridge University Press.

Remond, R. (1999) *Religion and Society in Modern Europe*, London: Blackwell.

Shipway, M. (1999) *Decolonization and its Impact: a comparative perspective*, Oxford: Blackwell publishers.

Sinfield, A. (1997) *Literature, Politics and Culture in Postwar Britain*, London: Athlone Press.

Sutcliffe, A. (1996) *An Economic and Social History of Western Europe Since 1945*, Harlow: Addison-Wesley Longman.

Index